THE QUEST FOR ENVIRONMENTAL JUSTICE

The Quest for Environmental Justice

Human Rights and
the Politics of Pollution

EDITED BY

ROBERT D. BULLARD

Sierra Club Books
SAN FRANCISCO

Copyright © 2005 by the individual authors as credited.

Chapter 8, by Al Gedicks, was originally published in *Resource Rebels: Native Challenges to Mining and Oil Corporations* (Boston: South End Press, 2001); chapter 12, by Oronto Douglas, Dimieari Von Kemedi, Ike Okonta, and Michael J. Watts, was originally published in *Foreign Policy In Focus (FPIF)*, a joint project of the Interhemispheric Resource Center (IRC, online at www.irc-online .org) and the Institute for Policy Studies (IPS, online at www.ips-dc.org) (July 2003).

First Edition

Published by Sierra Club Books
85 Second Street, San Francisco, CA 94105
www.sierraclub.org/books

Produced and distributed by
University of California Press
Berkeley and Los Angeles, California
University of California Press, Ltd.
London, England
www.ucpress.edu

SIERRA CLUB, SIERRA CLUB BOOKS, and the Sierra Club design logos are registered trademarks of the Sierra Club.

Library of Congress Cataloging-in-Publication Data

The quest for environmental justice : human rights and the politics of pollution / edited by Robert D. Bullard.— 1st ed.
     p.   cm.
    Includes bibliographical references and index.
    ISBN 1-57805-120-7 (acid-free paper)
    1. Environmental justice.   2. Environmental justice—Political aspects.
    3. Human rights.   I. Bullard, Robert D. (Robert Doyle), 1946–

GE220.Q47 2005
363.7—dc22   2004065349

Printed in the United States of America on New Leaf Ecobook 50 acid-free paper, which contains a minimum of 50 percent postconsumer waste, processed chlorine free. Of the balance, 25 percent is Forest Stewardship Council certified to contain no old-growth trees and to be pulped totally chlorine free.

09   08   07   06   05
10   9   8   7   6   5   4   3   2   1

In memory of women of color environmental justice activists who are no longer with us physically (although they will always be with us in spirit) —

Dana Alston *of Washington, D.C.*
Nellie Jean Sindab *of New York*
Patsy Ruth Oliver *of Texarkana, Texas*
Jeanne Gauna *of Albuquerque, New Mexico*
Nilak Butler *of Oakland, California*
Janice O'Neal *of Flint, Michigan*
Bonnie Sanders *of Camden, New Jersey*
Juanita Tate *of Los Angeles*
Genevieve Eason *of West Harlem, New York*
Nan Freeland *of Raleigh, North Carolina*
Janice Stevens *of Sac and Fox Nation and Stroud, Oklahoma*
Delores Simmons *of Convent, Louisiana*

— and to the current and future generations of environmental justice warriors worldwide

Contents

Foreword

In *The Quest for Environmental Justice,* Robert D. Bullard has once again provided community activists, researchers, health and environmental protection advocates, policy makers, and civil rights proponents with a refreshing and timely overview of contemporary environmental justice struggles and the fight against environmental racism around the nation and, indeed, the world.

I am familiar with the important quest for clean air, water, land, schools, recreation areas, and communities, in large part because I represent in Congress the residents of the city I now call home—Los Angeles. Despite measures in place in California to substantially curb air pollution, this city—a place where many Latinos, African Americans, Asians, and whites reside together—still has some of the dirtiest air in the country. Nationwide studies have shown that air pollution levels are higher in poorer areas, such as those where African Americans and Latinos live, and that higher percentages of African Americans and Latinos than whites live in areas with poor air quality.

This is certainly the case in Los Angeles. As a result, groups such as the Concerned Citizens of South Central Los Angeles and Mothers of East Los Angeles have—with the support of regional and national environmental groups—organized important local campaigns to protect the health of their families and neighborhoods. These groups have stopped proposed incinerators, which threatened to further endanger air quality and the health of those living in nearby neighborhoods and attending nearby schools.

In fact, throughout my home state of California, and throughout the nation, scores of organizations representing African Americans, Native Americans, Asians, Latinos, and poor and working-class whites have organized and often joined together with like-minded groups to fight back and protect their neighborhoods and families from life-threatening environmental hazards. These efforts are responses to racism, poverty, economic and social inequality, and unequal protection policies sponsored by government bodies such as the U.S. Environmental Protection Agency.

In his earlier edited work, *Unequal Protection,* Professor Bullard documented and analyzed patterns of environmental racism. He found that communities made up of poor people and people of color are disproportionately exposed to a variety of environmental threats. Racially discriminatory local and state policies governing the siting and licensing of industrial facilities allow polluting facilities of all kinds to be built closer to these communities.

Communities of color and impoverished neighborhoods throughout the country have become the primary dumping grounds for our nation's waste disposal and incineration facilities, and home to agricultural and manufacturing industries that pollute. Moreover, a disproportionate number of people of color are employed at low wages in unsafe and hazardous work environments, where their employers, and regulatory agencies such as the Occupational Health and Safety Administration, fail to provide them with adequate protection.

In recent years I and other members of Congress have often had to intervene on behalf of communities who appealed to us for help when they believed environmental threats violated their civil and human rights, and when their local elected officials and government agencies had failed to act on their behalf. We have written letters to the Environmental Protection Agency, for example, expressing our concern, and that of members of the Congressional Black Caucus and other supportive lawmakers, about the agency's failure to effectively enforce Title VI of the Civil Rights Act of 1964. If this provision were to be enforced in a manner consistent with historical civil rights jurisprudence and practice, it could help communities of color receive equal protection and justice under the law, as promised by our Constitution. In a 2003 report, the U.S. Commission on Civil Rights cited the fact that numerous communities have filed Title VI administrative complaints with the EPA's Office of Civil Rights, only to have their complaints languish for years in an administrative time warp—receiving no response or action from the very agency charged with protecting our health and environment in a nondiscriminatory manner.

Communities are organizing to take back their health and their environment. In April 2001, I was invited by Damu Smith of the National Black Environmental Justice Network—who at the time worked for Greenpeace USA—to participate in an environmental justice "Celebrity Tour" sponsored by Greenpeace. Among those who joined us on the tour were author Alice Walker, actor Mike Farrell, activist poet and author Haki Mahtibuti, and several other noted civil rights and environmental justice activists, including Dr. Bullard and Dr. Beverly Wright, director of the Deep South Center for Environmental Justice at Xavier University, located in New Orleans, which helped host the event. Our group toured mostly black, semirural, small-town communities located along the Mississippi River between Baton Rouge and New Orleans. This infamous area is known as "Cancer Alley" because of the numerous cases of cancer among the people who reside there. Near the towns, scores of petrochemical and other polluting industries dot the riverside landscape.

On the tour, we spent a long day traveling to communities severely affected by the suffocating toxic emissions from these huge facilities. We saw firsthand a landscape that constitutes one of the worst environmental nightmares in the nation and, in fact, the world. At one town hall meeting, we heard riveting, emotional testimony—mostly from black children, women, and men—about the deadly and debilitating effects of some of the most dangerous chemicals known to science, which rained down on them almost daily from the sprawling, nearby oil refineries, plastics-manufacturing plants, and other industries. Residents told us of chronic asthma and other respiratory illnesses, skin rashes, heart ailments, cancer, and other serious illnesses, which they believed were the result of their exposure to a "toxic soup" of chemicals that emanated from these plants.

We visited Convent and Norco, Louisiana, where residents were, at the time, in the midst of now-famous battles. Residents of Convent were fighting with government officials about the Shintech Corporation's proposed polyvinyl chloride production facility, and Norco residents were battling the Shell Oil Company. In one of the most important civil rights/environmental justice battles ever fought, the residents of Convent successfully defeated a proposal to build the world's largest polyvinyl chloride production facility, which was to be located in the most impoverished section of the mostly black town, near an all-black elementary school. Norco residents were fighting to get Shell to cover the costs of relocating residents of four streets as far as possible out of town and away from the Shell plant, which for years had tormented the community with its toxic emissions and frequent accidental chemical releases.

When I visited Norco that day, I promised the leader of Concerned Citizens of Norco, Margie Richard, as well as all the other individuals I met with on a playground next to the Shell facility, that I would call and write Shell's chief executive officer, Steven Miller, and ask him to meet the demands of the community to relocate everyone on the four streets under consideration who wished to relocate. After several exchanges of letters and phone calls with Miller's office—during which he retreated from his initial promises to me—and after continued pressure by Norco residents and their supporters from around the nation, Shell finally agreed to buy out those residing on the four streets so they could relocate out of harm's way.

My next visit to Norco in July 2002 was a joyous occasion. My husband and I and other family members attended a community event in which the residents of Norco celebrated this victory for the environmental justice movement. The community presented me with an award for my efforts, but I told them that they and their allies were the true heroes and sheroes. Together they had persisted. They had stood up to Shell and said they wanted justice, dignity, and respect for their community. These economically poor and politically disenfranchised men, women, and children had taken on one of the richest and most powerful multinational corporations in the world and won. Nothing that anyone else did would have mattered had they not stood up, organized, and spoken for themselves.

The stories of Norco and Convent, and of the communities within Los Angeles who fought back, are part of a larger heroic story about countless efforts waged by scores of marginalized communities throughout the United States and other powerful industrialized nations, as well as in the less industrialized nations of Africa, Asia, Latin America, the Caribbean, and the Pacific islands. This larger heroic story is about standing up for environmental justice, which is part of the global struggle for human rights and racial, social, and economic justice.

I would be remiss if I did not specifically mention the pivotal role of black women and all women of color in the fight for environmental justice. From California to Louisiana, from New York to Washington State, and elsewhere around the world, women of color especially have taken their rightful place in these battles as leaders, organizers, and defenders of their communities on behalf of their children and other family members. And black women have been at the forefront of this female leadership. Around the world, they have taken up the mantle to protect communities under toxic siege.

I congratulate Margie Richard for winning the 2004 Goldman Environmental Prize (the first black woman to receive the honor) for her leadership and sacrifices on behalf of Norco's residents; Peggy Shepard of New York's West Harlem Environmental Action for receiving the 2003 Heinz Award; and Florence Robinson of Alsen, Louisiana, for winning the 1998 Heinz Award. Other black women—such as Charlotte Keyes of Jesus People against Pollution of Columbia, Mississippi; Donele Wilkens of Detroiters Working for Environmental Justice; and Monique Harden of the New Orleans–based Advocates for Environmental Human Rights—have also received notable awards and recognition for their efforts.

At the Second National People of Color Environmental Leadership Summit held in Washington, D.C., in October 2002, Dr. Beverly Wright—a woman warrior who has immeasurably helped numerous communities in Louisiana—led the effort to honor women of color in the environmental justice movement, which was a highlight of the conference. From Africa to America, and all around the world, women of color have risked their lives to defend their communities.

In this book you will find the stories of many of these women, the organizing strategies used by communities who have waged important environmental justice battles, descriptions of the conditions under which many people of color are forced to live, and details about effective strategies for achieving environmental justice. Take the time to read and learn.

Preface

On October 9, 2004, I scanned the front page of the *New York Times* and discovered with pride that Wangari Maathai had won the 2004 Nobel Peace Prize for her pioneering work in launching Kenya's Green Belt Movement, in promoting sustainable development, and in seeding ecodevelopment projects for women in rural Kenya. Six months earlier, Margie Eugene Richard of Norco, Louisiana, had won the prestigious Goldman Environmental Prize for her victorious campaign to protect her community from toxic emissions from the Shell Oil Company's plant near her home. And four months before that, I had won the tenth annual Heinz Award for the Environment as a, according to the award's wording, "passionate crusader for protecting the environmental health of urban inner cities."

Yet not long ago I was amazed, but not surprised, to find that a magazine article titled "The Best of 2004," which featured a section on environmentalists, included no people of color. In the span of eleven months, three of the world's largest individual achievement prizes for 2003–2004 went to black women working for environmental justice, who had acted as agents for change in their rural, urban, and global communities. This oversight testifies to the continued invisibility of people of color. It also underscores the fact that work remains to be done in order to overcome classism, racism, sexism, and paternalism.

The Quest for Environmental Justice pays a long overdue tribute to the women of color who are the grassroots warriors fueling our movement, who bring to it their vision, love, and intensity yet get little recognition. Though many of them have passed from this earthly struggle, their legacy is uplifting, endearing, and ultimately, strengthening. Those of us working within the movement have the privilege of building on their accomplishments. They form a solid foundation that we can step up on in order to move forward.

This book recalls to mind the First National People of Color Environmental Leadership Summit, which transformed the dominant paradigm of environmentalism and defined the environment holistically as being where we live, work, play, pray, and learn. Those of us in the movement see our concerns as interrelated: disinvestment, transportation, poverty, racism, pollution, deteriorating housing, land use and zoning, health disparities, environmental health, and sustainable development.

Environmental justice has broadened its focus beyond pollution and environmental hazards to focus on benefits and amenities. For example, the themes of open space and waterfront access, environmental benefits that historically have been withheld from communities of color, have emerged as major issues in grassroots communities around the country through proactive community planning. West Harlem will see the construction of its first waterfront park, on the Hudson River, which has been designated an American Heritage River and yet is, ironically, the largest Superfund site in the nation.

The politics of pollution that govern the siting of industrial facilities pose a special threat to our parks and open space, as well as to the neighborhoods in which we live. My eyes smart at the notion of a "neighborhood zoned for garbage," because I can still taste the moment in 1986 when I realized that this label characterized the neighborhood in which I lived. But I smile when I remember the phone call in 2004 telling me that the mayor had heard the message of our Northern Manhattan Environmental Justice Coalition's eighteen-month campaign, Fair Share, Not Lion's Share. The campaign had persuaded the mayor not to reopen and expand a marine transfer station (a facility where household garbage is offloaded from trucks to river barges) in a community disproportionately exposed to environmental hazards.

Our local struggles over waste and toxic chemicals are linked to global environmental struggles. *The Quest for Environmental Justice* connects the struggles of people of color in the United States with the emerging international environmental justice movement that seeks to address threats resulting from globalization, corporate greed, poverty, the waste trade, military toxics, and human rights violations. The environmental and economic conditions in Louisiana's petrochemical corridor and in the Southwest, for example, are linked to some of the same transnational corporations that have waged resource wars against native and indigenous peoples around the world, exploited the people and spoiled the land in the oil-rich Niger Delta, and created environmental wastelands in South Africa.

This type of environmental devastation is not limited to the Third World. Rolling along Louisiana's Plantation Road in 1998, I saw for the first time the Mississippi River, a plantation, and a levee—things previously known to me only through literature, songs, and film. Seeing tiny communities there, and meeting residents living sandwiched between industrial monoliths, while I was on the "toxic tour" of Louisiana's petrochemicals corridor reminded me of the warm, stoic, and pragmatic seniors I had worked with in Harlem, like Genevieve Eason and Edythe Beltz. They had been catalysts for my getting involved in the fight against environmental racism. They did not know this phrase in 1985, but a fight was something they recognized all too well. Getting to know the dynamic residents of Convent and Norco, and learning how they've struggled over the years, has been as transformative for me as my experiences in Harlem.

The "toxic tours" that I went on in Durban and Johannesburg showed me that the communities in which residents must share a fence line with toxic facilities look much like the ones here at home. However, life there is made even worse by the harsher circumstances of human rights abuses, as well as by poor sanitation infrastructure, the lack of solid waste disposal, the lack of electricity, and the lack of other basic services usually provided by government. I remember the anticipation I felt on my first trip to Africa—to Nigeria, where I traveled with Connie Tucker of the Southern Organizing Committee to Abuja, Lagos, Kaduna, Owerri. I was paired with consultants from a Nigerian nongovernmental organization, helping to deliver organizational-development workshops to Nigerians involved in leading or starting nongovernmental organizations and community-based organizations. Though we were not permitted to enter the controversial Niger Delta area, we were allowed to travel as close by as Owerri, where, on the second day of the environmental law workshop that we presented, Nigerian military police entered the complex with drawn guns to disrupt the workshop and disperse its participants. This last point shows the connection between environmental degradation and the military dictatorship, a point discussed in depth in chapter 12 of this volume.

With the reelection of President George W. Bush in 2004, there have been calls for reassessing mainstream environmentalism, a movement that pioneered environmental regulation in the 1970s, but that finds itself sorely challenged to provide transformational leadership in the twenty-first century. The effectiveness and moral authority of the environmental justice movement have infused a gritty new spirit into a new model of environmentalism. This model redefines the environmental protection and conservation paradigm, transforming it into one that is accountable to its grassroots base, replicable, multiethnic, multiracial, and multidisciplinary. The activist-scholars of this movement lift up the voices and show the perspectives of the grassroots, who rarely have the time or resources to document their own work.

To build robust communities that speak for themselves, we must first teach people to exercise their power and make use of democracy. Building democratic institutions that have power will aid the struggle for peace development and environmental justice. Dr. Maathai said in the lecture she delivered at the Oslo City Hall in December 2004, when she accepted her Nobel Prize, "The Norwegian Nobel Committee has challenged the world to broaden the understanding of peace: there can be no peace without equitable development; and there can be no development without sustainable management of the environment in a democratic and peaceful space. This shift is an idea whose time has come."

Acknowledgments

This book represents the hard work of many dedicated leaders in the environmental justice movement. I thank the thousands of grassroots and community-based organizations for the hard work that makes this and other environmental justice books possible. I am especially grateful to the book's contributors, who took time out of their extremely busy schedules to write the chapters and who endured the constant nagging about deadlines. A special effort was made to include diverse voices, perspectives, experiences, and writers from a wide array of backgrounds, including grassroots activists, educators, urban planners, lawyers, sociologists, anthropologists, geographers, epidemiologists, and environmental scientists.

Documenting the history, milestones, and contributions of the environmental justice movement is important if we want to understand how far the movement has progressed. Such documentation is also important in building a movement for future generations. This takes resources. Our thanks go to the Ford Foundation, Public Welfare Foundation, Turner Foundation, Surdna Foundation, and Nathan Cummings Foundation, all of which supported this book project and the work of the Environmental Justice Resource Center.

Finally, I owe special gratitude to my colleagues, Glenn S. Johnson and Angel O. Torres, at the Environmental Justice Resource Center, who were able to juggle their regular work schedules, supervise three major book projects, including this one, and follow up with the book's contributors and keep us on track. Lastly, I thank two other center staff, Lisa Sutton and Michelle Dawkins, who also assisted us in tracking the mountains of paperwork associated with an edited volume.

Robert D. Bullard

ROBERT D. BULLARD

Introduction

It has been just over a decade since my book *Unequal Protection: Environmental Justice and Communities of Color* was first published, in 1994. Over the past two decades, the terms "environmental justice," "environmental racism," and "environmental equity" have become household words. This was not always the case. Out of small and seemingly isolated environmental struggles emerged a potent grassroots movement. The 1990s saw the environmental justice movement become a unifying theme across race, class, gender, age, and geographic lines.[1]

In just two decades, the grassroots environmental movement has spread across the globe. The call for environmental justice can be heard from Chicago's South Side to Johannesburg's Soweto. The environmental justice movement is largely a response to environmental injustice. All around the world, groups are challenging the transboundary waste trade, "blood for oil" deals, environmental racism, nonsustainable development, and globalization. Environmental racism is a link in the chain of acts of unsustainable development. It involves the denial of human rights, environmental protection, and economic opportunities to the communities where people of color live and work.[2]

Today, millions of Americans, ranging from constitutional scholars to lay grassroots activists, recognize that environmental discrimination is

1

unfair, unethical, and immoral. They also recognize that environmental justice is a legitimate area of inquiry inside and outside the academy. Moreover, environmental justice is a civil rights and a human rights issue. How decisions are made and who makes them can have important health implications. Two decades or so ago, few academicians, government bureaucrats, environmentalists, or civil rights or human rights leaders understood the racial dynamics involved in environmental decision making.

Health is the main focus of the environmental justice movement in the United States. Here, "environment" is generally defined as being where we live, work, play, worship, and go to school, as well as the physical and natural world. The World Health Organization defines health as "a state of complete physical, mental, and social well-being, not just the absence of disease or infirmity."[3] These definitions of environment and health capture the essence of the struggles for environmental justice being fought by communities made up of people of color and low-income groups.[4]

Why do some communities get dumped on while others don't? Why are environmental regulations vigorously enforced in some communities and not in other communities? Why are some workers protected from environmental and health threats while other workers (such as migrant farmworkers) suffer poisoning? How can environmental justice be incorporated into environmental protection? What institutional changes are needed in the United States to achieve a just and sustainable society? What community-organizing strategies are effective against environmental racism? These are some of the many questions addressed in this book.

RACE MATTERS

Many people of color assume they "don't have the complexion for protection." However, a growing number of groups made up of people of color, whose communities are threatened by nearby polluting industries, have organized themselves into potent networks and coalitions to confront large corporations and government agencies who would turn their neighborhoods into toxic wastelands. For communities located on the front lines of the environmental assault, environmental protection is a life-and-death issue. These communities define environmental protection as a basic right. This thinking is captured in the preamble to the Principles of Environmental Justice (see appendix A), adopted October 27,

1991, in Washington, D.C., at the First National People of Color Environmental Leadership Summit:

> We the People of Color, gathered together at this multinational People of Color Environmental Leadership Summit, to begin to build a national and international movement of all peoples of color to fight the destruction and taking of our lands and communities, do hereby re-establish our spiritual interdependence to the sacredness of our Mother Earth; to respect and celebrate each of our cultures, languages and beliefs about the natural world and our roles in healing ourselves; to insure environmental justice; to promote economic alternatives which would contribute to the development of environmentally safe livelihoods; and, to secure our political, economic and cultural liberation that has been denied for over 500 years of colonization and oppression, resulting in the poisoning of our communities and land and the genocide of our peoples, do affirm and adopt these Principles of Environmental Justice.[5]

Recognizing that the environmental protection apparatus was broken in many communities in which people of color and low-income groups live, and after much prodding from environmental justice leaders, the U.S. Environmental Protection Agency (EPA) acknowledged its mandate to protect all Americans. In 1992, during the George H. W. Bush administration, the EPA administrator William Reilly established the Office of Environmental Equity (under the Clinton administration it was renamed the Office of Environmental Justice) and produced *Environmental Equity: Reducing Risks for All Communities,* one of the first comprehensive government reports to examine environmental hazards and social equity.[6]

On February 11, 1994, environmental justice reached the White House when President Bill Clinton signed Executive Order 12898, *Federal Actions to Address Environmental Justice in Minority Populations and Low-Income Populations.* The order mandated federal agencies to incorporate environmental justice into all their works and programs. The Presidential Memorandum accompanying the order offered a clear path for using existing laws to meet environmental justice objectives:

> Environmental and civil rights statutes provide many opportunities to address environmental hazards in minority communities and low-income communities. Application of these existing statutory provisions is an important part of this Administration's effort to prevent those minority communities and low-income communities from being subject to disproportionately high and adverse environmental effects.[7]

The EPA defines environmental justice as "the fair treatment and meaningful involvement of all people regardless of race, color, national origin, or income with respect to the development, implementation, and enforcement of environmental laws, regulations, and policies. Fair treatment means that no group of people, including racial, ethnic, or socioeconomic groups, should bear a disproportionate share of the negative environmental consequences resulting from industrial, municipal, and commercial operations or the execution of federal, state, local, and tribal programs and policies."[8] Poverty and pollution are intricately linked.[9]

Numerous studies have documented the fact that, in the United States, people of color are disproportionately affected by environmental hazards in their homes, neighborhoods, and workplaces.[10] In 1999, the Institute of Medicine of the National Academies, a nongovernmental organization that provides guidance on matters of science and medicine, issued *Toward Environmental Justice: Research, Education, and Health Policy Needs*. This report concluded that communities populated by low-income groups and people of color are exposed to higher levels of pollution than the rest of the nation, and that these same populations experience certain diseases in greater numbers than more affluent white communities.[11]

A 2000 study by the *Dallas Morning News* and the University of Texas at Dallas found that 870,000 of the 1.9 million (46 percent) housing units for the poor, mostly minorities, sit within about a mile of factories that reported toxic emissions to the EPA.[12] Homeowners have been the most effective groups to use NIMBY (Not in My Back Yard) tactics to keep polluting industries out of their communities. However, discrimination also keeps millions of African Americans from having backyards—from enjoying the advantages of home ownership. In 1999, only 46 percent of blacks owned their own homes, compared with 73 percent of whites.[13]

Even schools are not safe from environmental assault. A 2001 study by the Center for Health, Environment, and Justice, *Poisoned Schools: Invisible Threats, Visible Action*, reported on more than six hundred thousand students at nearly twelve hundred public schools located within a half mile of federal Superfund or state-identified contaminated sites in Massachusetts, New York, New Jersey, Michigan, and California. Most of the students attending these schools were low income or people of color.[14] No state except California has a law requiring school officials to investigate potentially contaminated property, and no federal or state agency keeps records of public or private schools that operate on or near toxic waste or industrial sites.[15]

The idea of assault by toxic chemicals is not new to the many Americans forced to live adjacent to, and often on the fence line of, chemical industries that spew poison into the air, water, and ground. Even before the terrorist threat of September 11, 2001, these residents experienced a form of toxic terror twenty-four hours a day, seven days a week.[16] When (not if) chemical accidents occur at the plants, government and industry officials often instruct the fence-line community residents to "shelter in place"—that is, to lock their doors, close their windows, and stay inside. In reality, locked doors and closed windows do not block the chemical assault, nor do they remove the cause of residents' anxiety or their fear of the unknown health problems related to the chemical assault, which may not show up for decades.

The "shelter in place" emergency response—if you can call it a response, given that it is more a hope for divine intervention than a real emergency plan—allows poor people and people of color to be disproportionately exposed to health risks from pollution hot spots such as Louisiana's petrochemical corridor, commonly referred to as Cancer Alley; Texas' Gulf Coast communities; North Richmond, California; and Los Angeles' South Bay communities.

The environmental justice framework attempts to turn the dominant environmental protection paradigm on its head: it seeks to prevent environmental threats before they occur.[17] The framework incorporates other social movements and principles (for example, the Precautionary Principle) that seek to prevent and eliminate harmful practices in land use, industrial planning, health care, waste disposal, and sanitation services.

In 1979, *Bean v. Southwestern Waste Management Corp.* became the first lawsuit to challenge environmental racism using civil rights law. Now, after more than two and a half decades of intense study, targeted research, public hearings, grassroots organizing, network building, and leadership summits, the struggle for environmental justice has taken center stage. Environmental racism is out of the closet. All communities are *not* created equal. Some neighborhoods, communities, and regions have become the dumping grounds for household garbage, hazardous wastes, and other sources of toxins. From West Dallas to West Harlem, and from the South Side of Chicago to South Central Los Angeles, people of color are demanding, and in some cases winning, solutions to their environmental dilemmas.

The decade of the 1990s and the first half of the current decade are different from the late 1970s and the 1980s. Some progress had been made in mainstreaming environmental protection as a civil rights and social justice issue. Environmental justice is also now framed as a human rights issue. When I started in 1978, few environmentalists, civil and human rights advocates, or policy makers understood or were willing to challenge the regressive and uneven impact of this country's environmental and industrial policies—policies that dispersed benefits while localizing burdens. In the end, communities made up of low-income groups and people of color paid a heavy price: diminished health, lowered property values, and reduced quality of life.

The United Nations' Universal Declaration of Human Rights, passed in 1948, recognizes that people everywhere have an intrinsic right to life, health, and a healthy environment.[18] Nevertheless, many nations, including the United States, "have relinquished the power to protect such rights when doing so would interfere with corporate profits."[19] Clearly, if all the politically disenfranchised and vulnerable members of society—impoverished people, indigenous peoples, ethnic minorities, women, children—had access to environmental information and could exercise their right to free speech, then potential polluters and profligate consumers would no longer be able to treat them as expendable and would have to seek alternatives to polluting activities and overconsumption.[20]

Grassroots human rights activists have shown environmentalists that confronting the *polluters* with the *polluted* is a strategic path for protecting the right of the next generation to inherit a planet worth inhabiting. For billions of people across the globe, human rights and the environment are life-and-death matters.[21] A bureaucratic toleration of environmental degradation almost always assumes human inequality and lowers the quality of life. Throughout the world, poor people and people of color, who have the least political power and who are the most marginalized, are selectively victimized by environmental crises.[22]

Today, many well-established groups have teamed up to address environmental justice and health issues that differentially affect poor people and people of color. These groups include the NAACP, NAACP Legal Defense and Education Fund, Earthjustice Legal Defense Fund, Lawyers Committee for Civil Rights under the Law, International Human Rights Law Group, Center for Constitutional Rights, National Lawyers Guild's Sugar Law Center, American Civil Liberties Union, Legal Aid Society, and others. Environmental racism and environmental justice panels have become hot topics at conferences sponsored by law schools, bar associations, public health groups, scientific societies, social science meetings, and even government workshops. Environmental justice leaders have had a profound influence on public policy, industry practices, national conferences, private foundation funding, and academic research. Environmental justice courses and curricula can be found at nearly every university in the country.

A half dozen environmental justice centers and legal clinics have sprung up across the nation—four of these centers are located at historically black colleges and universities, or HBCUs: the Environmental Justice Resource Center (Clark Atlanta University, in Atlanta, Georgia), Deep South Center for Environmental Justice (Xavier University of Louisiana, in New Orleans), Thurgood Marshall Environmental Justice Legal Clinic (Texas Southern University, in Houston), and Environmental Justice and Equity Institute (Florida A & M University, in Tallahassee).

Environmental justice groups are beginning to sway administrative decisions their way. Environmental justice trickled up to the federal government and the White House when environmental justice activists and academicians convinced the EPA to create the Office of Environmental Equity. The Reverend Benjamin Chavis (who at the time was executive director of the United Church of Christ Commission for Racial Justice) and I were selected to work on President Bill Clinton's Transition Team in the Natural Resources Cluster (the EPA and the Departments of Energy, the Interior, and Agriculture).

Environmental justice leaders quickly persuaded the Clinton administration to establish the National Environmental Justice Advisory Council to advise the EPA. In 1994, President Clinton signed Executive Order 12898. This order is not itself a law but is built around two important laws: the Civil Rights Act of 1964 (which prohibits government funds from being used to support discrimination based on race, color, and national origin) and the 1969 National Environmental Policy Act (which requires that environmental impacts be assessed before major development projects can go forward). Although these two laws have been on the books for decades, the United States is a long way from achieving a fair and just society in the environmental and other arenas.

LEVELING THE PLAYING FIELD

Progress has been hard and slow, but environmental justice networks and grassroots community groups are making their voices heard. In 1996, after five years of organizing, Citizens against Toxic Exposure convinced the EPA to relocate 358 Pensacola, Florida, families from a dioxin dump, tagged "Mount Dioxin," marking the first time a black community was relocated under the federal government's giant Super-fund program.

Executive Order 12898 was also put to the test in rural northwestern Louisiana in 1997. Beginning in 1989, the U.S. Nuclear Regulatory Commission, an agency governed by the executive order, had under review a proposal from the Louisiana Energy Services (LES) to build the nation's first privately owned uranium enrichment plant. A national search was undertaken by LES to find the "best" site for a plant that would produce 17 percent of the nation's enriched uranium.[23] LES sup-posedly used an objective scientific method in designing its site selection process.

The southern United States, Louisiana, and, in particular, Claiborne Parish ended up being the unwilling "winners" of the site selection process. Residents from Homer and the nearby communities of Forest Grove and Center Springs—the two communities closest to the proposed site—rejected the site selection process and its outcome. They organized a group called Citizens against Nuclear Trash (CANT) and charged LES and the Nuclear Regulatory Commission staff with practicing environ-mental racism. CANT hired the Sierra Club Legal Defense Fund (later renamed the Earthjustice Legal Defense Fund) and sued LES.

The lawsuit dragged on for more than eight years. On May 1, 1997, a three-judge panel of the U.S. Nuclear Regulatory Commission Atomic Safety and Licensing Board issued their final initial decision on the case, stating that racial bias played a role in the selection process.[24] A headline in the *London Sunday Times* proclaimed a victory for environmental justice: "Louisiana Blacks Win Nuclear War."[25] LES spent more than $33 million in a failed attempt to acquire a permit. The precedent-setting federal court ruling came two years after President Clinton signed Exec-utive Order 12898. In their thirty-eight-page written decision, the judges chastised the Nuclear Regulatory Commission staff for not addressing the executive order's provisions. The court decision was upheld on appeal on April 4, 1998.[26]

A clear racial pattern emerged during the so-called national search and multistage screening and selection process.[27] For example, African Americans constitute about 13 percent of the U.S. population, 20 percent of the southern states' population, 31 percent of Louisiana's population, 35 percent of Louisiana's northern parishes (parishes are equivalent to counties), and 46 percent of Claiborne Parish. This progressive trend, involving the narrowing of the site selection process to areas of increas-ingly high poverty and African American representation, is also evident in an evaluation of the actual sites considered in the intermediate and fine screening stages of the site selection process. The aggregate average percentage of blacks in the population within a one-mile radius of the seventy-eight sites examined (in sixteen parishes) is 28.35 percent. When LES completed its initial site cuts and reduced the list to thirty-seven sites within nine parishes, the aggregate percentage of blacks in the population rose to 36.78 percent. When LES then further limited its focus to six sites in Claiborne Parish, the aggregate average percentage of blacks in the population rose again, to 64.74 percent. The final site selected, the LeSage site, has a 97.10 percentage of blacks in the population within a one-mile radius.

The plant's proposed site was located on Parish Road 39 between two African American communities—just one-quarter mile from Center Springs (founded in 1910) and one and one-quarter miles from Forest Grove (founded in 1865, just after slavery ended). The Nuclear Regulatory Commission's draft environmental impact statement described the vicinity of the proposed site as rural and largely uninhabited. These two black communities had been around since 1865 and 1910, yet they were not mentioned. The proposed site lies within a Louisiana parish that has per capita earnings of only $5,800 per year, or just 45 percent of the national average, which is almost $12,800. The earnings of over 58 percent of the African American population in these two communities fall below the poverty line. The two African American communities were rendered invisible, since they were not even mentioned in the draft environmental impact statement.

Only after intense public comment did the Nuclear Regulatory Commission staff attempt to address environmental justice and the disproportionate-impact implications as required by the National Environmental Policy Act and Executive Order 12898. For example, the National Environmental Policy Act required the government to consider the environmental impacts and weigh the costs and benefits of the proposed action. These include the risk of accidental but foreseeable adverse health and environmental effects and the socioeconomic effects.

The Nuclear Regulatory Commission staff devoted less than a page to addressing environmental justice concerns in its final environmental impact statement for the proposed uranium enrichment plant. Overall, the final environmental impact statement and environmental report were inadequate in the following respects: (1) they inaccurately assessed the costs and benefits of the proposed plant, (2) they failed to consider the inequitable distribution of costs and benefits of the proposed plant to white and African American populations, and (3) they failed to consider the fact that siting the plant in a community of color followed a national pattern in which institutional decision making led to siting hazardous facilities in communities of color and resulted in the inequitable distribution of costs to those communities.

Among the distributive costs not analyzed in relationship to Forest Grove and Center Springs were the disproportionate burdens of health and safety, property devaluation, fire and accidents, noise, traffic, radioactive dust in the air and water, and dislocation resulting from the closure of a road that connected the two communities. Ultimately, the CANT legal victory points to the utility of an approach that both draws on environmental and civil rights laws and stresses the requirement that governmental agencies must consider Executive Order 12898 in their assessments.

In addition to its remarkable victory over LES, a company that had the backing of powerful U.S. and European nuclear energy companies, CANT members and their allies won much more. They empowered themselves and embarked on a path of further political empowerment and self-determination. During the long battle, CANT member Roy Madris was elected to the Claiborne Parish Police Jury (that is, the county commission), and CANT member Almeter Willis was elected to the Claiborne Parish School Board. In 1998 the town of Homer, the incorporated town nearest to Forest Grove and Center Springs, elected twenty-four-year-old David Jeroune Aubrey as its first African American mayor. And as of 2005, the Homer Town Council has two African American members. In the fall of 1998, LES sold the land on which the proposed uranium enrichment plant would have been built. The land was put back into timber production, as it was before LES bought it.

Another Louisiana environmental justice struggle was waged 290 miles south of Homer. In September 1998, after more than eighteen months of intense grassroots organizing and legal maneuvering, the community organization St. James Citizens for Jobs and the Environment forced the Japanese-owned Shintech Corporation to scrap its plan to build a giant polyvinyl chloride plant in Convent, Louisiana, a community that is more than 80 percent black. The Shintech plant would have added six hundred thousand pounds of pollutants to the air annually.

Polluting industries are not the only targets of environmental justice groups. Some government policies and practices have been the focus of environmental justice claims. In January 1999, the U.S. Department of Agriculture signed a consent decree that effectively settled a long and bitter class action discrimination lawsuit brought by black farmers. The lawsuit awarded over $300 million in damages to thousands of African American farmers who had been wronged by racist government practices. In 2004, the National Black Farmers Association, along with the Black Farmers and Agriculturalists Association, Federation of Southern Cooperatives, and Arkansas Land Development Fund, among others, filed a new class action lawsuit against the Department of Agriculture. The new coalition, representing as many as a hundred thousand black farmers, contended that a large majority of the ninety-six thousand black farmers who sought restitution under the 1999 settlement were unfairly rejected.[28]

The environmental justice movement has continued to make its mark in the twenty-first century. In April 2001, a group of fifteen hundred plaintiffs from the Sweet Valley and Cobb Town neighborhoods of Anniston, Alabama, reached a $42.8 million out-of-court settlement with the Monsanto Company. The group had filed a class action lawsuit against Monsanto for contaminating the black community with polychlorinated biphenyls. Monsanto manufactured this chemical from 1927 through 1972 for use as insulation in electrical equipment. The EPA banned its production in the late 1970s amid questions concerning health risks. Two years later, in August 2003, Monsanto, Solutia, and Pharmacia agreed to pay $700 million to settle state and federal lawsuits brought against them by some twenty-thousand Anniston plaintiffs alleging damage from polychlorinated biphenyl contamination.[29]

In June 2002, victory finally came to Norco, Louisiana. Residents of the town's Old Diamond neighborhood were sandwiched between the Shell Oil Company's chemical plant and its refinery. The citizens group Concerned Citizens of Norco and their allies forced Shell to agree to a buyout that allowed residents to relocate. The residents also secured a $5-million community development fund and full relocation costs for residents of all four affected streets in the Old Diamond neighborhood. As of April 2004, Shell had bought about 200 of the 225 lots at a minimum price of eighty thousand dollars per lot.[30]

These and similar victories have laid the foundation for a strong and resilient environmental justice movement. They also show the world that this is not a "here today, gone tomorrow" movement. Although still young when compared to, for example, the conservation and preservation movements, the environmental justice movement is maturing, learning, and growing.

But much has changed since 1994. Environmental justice has faltered under the George W. Bush administration. A decade after Executive Order 12898 was signed, environmental justice has become all but invisible at the EPA. In March 2004, the EPA's own Office of the Inspector General, in a report titled *EPA Needs to Consistently Implement the Intent of the Executive Order on Environmental Justice*, blasted the agency for not implementing the order.[31]

In March 2005, lawyers with Advocates for Environmental Human Rights, on behalf of African American residents in Mossville, Louisiana—after the latter organized as Mossville Environmental Action Now—filed a petition with the Organization of American States' Inter-American Commission on Human Rights in Washington, D.C. Advocates for Environmental Human Rights alleges that the unhealthy and hazardous conditions that result from the U.S. government's authorization of toxic industrial operations in close proximity to communities like Mossville violate fundamental human rights to life, health, and racial equality.

The Mossville community is surrounded by fourteen industrial facilities that together emit millions of pounds of toxic chemicals into the air, water, and soil each year. The U.S. environmental regulatory system actually sanctions the dumping of these industrial pollutants, which have severely damaged the environment and are associated with the pervasive and serious health problems suffered by Mossville residents. These health problems include cancers, respiratory ailments, reproductive disorders, and other diseases associated with industrial pollutants.

The Mossville human rights petition filed with the Inter-American Commission on Human Rights seeks medical care for Mossville residents, relocation of residents to healthier environs, and health-based reforms to the environmental regulatory system. The Inter-American Commission defends human rights laws and standards that are binding on the United States and has the authority to investigate complaints of human rights abuses in the United States and other membership countries. In previous cases, the commission has found that a country's failure to adequately protect the environment can constitute a human rights violation.

Despite government inaction, many environmental justice struggles and challenges continue in the early years of the twenty-first century, as this book makes clear. The book is divided into four parts and fourteen chapters. Part 1 chronicles the early environmental justice struggles and lays out the general thesis and framework of the book. The purpose of this book is to continue where *Unequal Protection: Environmental*

Justice and Communities of Color left off. It uses the same environmental justice lens, but it incorporates changes and developments that have taken place since 1994.

In chapter 1, I provide a historical overview and critique of the environmental justice movement and its milestones, accomplishments, pitfalls, and challenges. The chapter illuminates the complexities of building a multiethnic movement whose leaders often have divergent worldviews and sometimes competing interests. It traces the environmental justice movement from the early days in the late 1970s to the Second National People of Color Environmental Leadership Summit, held in Washington, D.C., in October 2002.

In chapter 2, I review my groundbreaking study of waste facility siting in Houston, Texas, the only major U.S. city without zoning. From the 1920s through the late 1970s, Houston city leaders used NIMBY policies to situate garbage dumps and incinerators in the city's black communities—a pattern referred to as "PIBBY" (Place in Blacks' Back Yards). In 1979, black residents of Houston filed *Bean v. Southwestern Waste Management Corp.*, the nation's first lawsuit to make use of civil rights law to challenge environmental racism.

In chapter 3, Damu Smith and I, both members of the National Black Environmental Justice Network, examine the work of women on the front lines of the environmental justice movement, who provide the grassroots movement's backbone. The chapter includes a selection of the voices of women of color as they tell their stories of struggle and triumph. These and thousands of other women of color are the unsung "sheroes" of the environmental justice movement.

Part 2 examines the lives of residents of "sacrifice zones," the toxic hot spots or corridors where high concentrations of polluting industries are found. Written by sociologist Beverly Wright, chapter 4 outlines the many community struggles that have taken place along the eighty-five-mile stretch of the Mississippi River between Baton Rouge and New Orleans commonly known as Louisiana's Cancer Alley. The author examines small fence-line communities that are bombarded with some of the nation's worse pollution, which emanates from the more than 135 plants lining this stretch of the river.

In chapter 5, economist Manuel Pastor Jr., environmental scientist James L. Sadd, and epidemiologist Rachel Morello-Frosch use geographic information systems mapping to examine the geographic distribution of industrial pollution in the Los Angeles area in relation to residents' ethnicity and income. They show that people of color and low-income groups are on the front lines of environmental assaults in Los Angeles.

Chapter 6, by the environmental attorney Olga Pomar, examines a community's struggle to keep Canada's St. Lawrence Cement Company from locating a plant in the already heavily polluted Camden, New Jersey, waterfront neighborhood. Residents sued the company, winning a major victory in a U.S. district court in 2001. Several months later, however, they lost their case after the U.S. Supreme Court ruled, in *Alexander v. Sandoval,* that plaintiffs must prove "intentional" discrimination, rather than "disparate impact," to show effect.

Part 3 examines land use, land rights, sovereignty, resource extraction, and sustainable development conflicts. Chapter 7, by attorneys Robert García and Erica S. Flores, looks at the grassroots struggle by poor people and people of color to gain access to urban parks and green space. The authors analyze land use inequities in communities inhabited by people of color in sprawling Los Angeles. They also describe how the urban parks movement is greening Los Angeles, building a sense of community among neighbors, empowering ordinary citizens, and diversifying democracy from the ground up.

In chapter 8, sociologist Al Gedicks illustrates the effects of transnational corporations and the extraction industry on native and indigenous peoples and their lands. He also details the numerous "resource wars" and grassroots campaigns waged by indigenous peoples around the world to preserve their cultures and ways of life.

Chapter 9, by anthropologist Devon G. Peña, looks at the Chicano land movement and environmental justice struggles in the southwestern United States. He also details the plights of migrant farmworkers, acequia farmers, and industrial workers of the maquiladoras along the U.S.-Mexico border, workers in land grant communities, and the environmental and health conditions of the urban barrios and rural *colonias.*

Part 4 examines human rights and global justice issues. In chapter 10, law professor Robin Morris Collin and urban planner Robert Collin offer an analysis of environmental racism as a violation of human rights. They propose a form of reparations for redressing the wrongs incurred by toxic dumping near, and contamination of, communities in the United States inhabited by people of color.

In chapter 11, sociologist Déborah Berman Santana describes the effects of the U.S. Navy's six decades of bombing and war games on the small island of Vieques, Puerto Rico. Santana also examines the history of the land, its people, and their long legacy of exploitation and resistance. The sixty-year struggle to evict the navy from the island has made headlines worldwide and attracted the interest of peace, environmental justice, and human rights activists.

Chapter 12, by attorney Oronto Douglas, environmental activist Dimieari Von Kemedi, journalist Ike Okonta, and political economist Michael J. Watts, provides a historical analysis of the violence and unrest in the Niger Delta. Their critique points to the oppressive Nigerian government, corrupt oil production, long-standing poverty, and a low standard of living as major contributors to the growing militancy and violence in this oil-rich region.

Chapter 13, written by political scientist David A. McDonald, examines the environmental destruction caused by the brutal apartheid system and outlines the challenges faced by the current government. It also looks at the rise of the environmental justice movement in South Africa and its strategies for addressing the legacy of toxic dumping and the systematic denial of basic health care, water, sanitation, electricity, housing, transportation, and other goods and services to residents of black communities.

In chapter 14, sociologist Glenn S. Johnson, urban planner Angel O. Torres, and I examine globalization trends in relation to poverty, environmental quality, public health, and human rights. The antiglobalization movement is anchored in the age-old quest for social justice, human rights, and democracy. The need for clean air and water and clean, affordable energy are major global issues of the twenty-first century. The chapter also examines the infusion of environmental justice into global summits and international forums such as the 2001 World Conference against Racism, 2002 World Summit on Sustainable Development, 2005 World Social Forum, and others.

PART ONE

A LEGACY OF INJUSTICE

THE FIRST PART OF THIS VOLUME chronicles the early environmental justice struggles and lays out the general thesis and theoretical framework of the book. Clearly, the world today is different from what it was in the late 1970s and early 1980s, when the concept of environmental justice began to take root in politically disenfranchised communities across the United States. After more than a decade of isolated local grassroots struggles, environmental and economic justice has emerged as a unified movement.

This section captures the voices of front-line grassroots warriors who are battling environmental racism. These warriors do not get their stories from a library. They live them twenty-four hours a day, seven days a week. In Warren County, North Carolina, in Houston, Texas, and in other sites of early struggles against environmental injustice, these warriors learned key lessons. From Native Americans' reservations to the urban barrios, from Texas to California, grassroots community leaders are saying no to toxic poisoning.

The environmental justice movement has matured, diversified its tactics, and adopted an international worldview. Activists understand that what happens to disenfranchised people in the United States and elsewhere in the developed North also affects people of color, indigenous peoples, and poor people in the developing South. Mobilization of grass-roots groups has spawned new leadership, new definitions, new members, and new energy that has benefited both the environmental and civil rights movements. People of color have filled the leadership vacuum in many grassroots environmental struggles from New York to Alaska. Women activists are assuming key leadership roles. Environmental racism is now a household word. Yet the struggle against racism and sexism continues.

1

Environmental Justice in the Twenty-first Century

Hardly a day passes without the media discovering some community or neighborhood fighting an attempt to build near it a landfill, incinerator, chemical plant, or other polluting facility, or fighting to bring attention to the harmful effects that people are suffering as a result of such an entity already located nearby. This was not always the case. Just three decades ago, the concept of environmental justice had not yet registered on the radar screens of environmental, civil rights, and social justice groups.[1] Dr. Martin Luther King Jr., however, went to Memphis in 1968 on an early environmental and economic justice mission for striking black garbage workers. These strikers had demanded equal pay and better working conditions. Of course, Dr. King was assassinated before he could complete his mission.

Another landmark garbage dispute took place a decade later in Houston, when African American homeowners in 1979 began a bitter fight to keep a sanitary landfill out of their suburban middle-income neighborhood.[2] Residents formed the Northeast Community Action Group. The group and their attorney, Linda McKeever Bullard (my wife), filed a class action lawsuit to block construction of the facility. The 1979 lawsuit, *Bean v. Southwestern Waste Management Corp.*, was the first to use civil rights law to challenge the siting of a waste facility.

Three years later, a similar case catapulted the environmental justice movement into the limelight. The movement has come a long way since its humble beginnings in Warren County, North Carolina, a rural and mostly African American community, where a proposed landfill for disposing of polychlorinated biphenyls (PCBs) ignited protests that resulted in more than five hundred arrests. These protests prompted a study by the U.S. General Accounting Office, *Siting of Hazardous Waste Landfills and Their Correlation with Racial and Economic Status of Surrounding Communities*.[3] This study revealed that three of the four off-site, commercial hazardous waste landfills in the U.S. Environmental Protection Agency's Region 4 (composed of eight southern states) happen to be located in predominantly African American communities, although African Americans made up only 20 percent of the region's population. The protesters of Warren County put the term "environmental racism" on the map.

The protests also led the United Church of Christ Commission for Racial Justice in 1987 to produce *Toxic Wastes and Race in the United States*, the first national study to correlate waste facility sites and demographic characteristics.[4] The study found that race was the most potent variable in predicting where such facilities would be located—more powerful than poverty, land values, and home ownership. In 1990, my book *Dumping in Dixie: Race, Class, and Environmental Quality* chronicled the convergence of two social movements—the social justice and environmental movements—into one, the environmental justice movement. This book highlighted African Americans' environmental activism in the South, the same region that gave birth to the modern civil rights movement. What started out as local and often isolated community-based struggles against the siting of toxic waste and industrial facilities blossomed into a multi-issue, multiethnic, and multiregional movement.[5]

The 1991 First National People of Color Environmental Leadership Summit was probably the single most important event in the environmental justice movement's history. The summit broadened the movement beyond its early focus against toxics to include issues of public health, worker safety, land use, transportation, housing, resource allocation, and community empowerment. The meeting also demonstrated that it is possible to build a multiracial grassroots movement around environmental and economic justice.[6]

Held in Washington, D.C., the four-day summit was attended by more than 650 grassroots and national leaders from around the world. Delegates came from all fifty states, Puerto Rico, Chile, and Mexico, and from as far away as the Marshall Islands. People attended the summit to share their action strategies, redefine the environmental movement, and develop common plans for addressing environmental problems affecting people of color in the United States and around the world.

On September 27, 1991, summit delegates adopted seventeen "Principles of Environmental Justice." These principles were developed as a guide for organizing, networking, and relating to governmental and nongovernmental organizations. In June 1992, Spanish and Portuguese translations of the principles were used and circulated by nongovernmental organizations and environmental justice groups at the Earth Summit in Rio de Janeiro.

In response to growing public concern and mounting scientific evidence, President Bill Clinton on February 11, 1994 (the second day of the "Health Research Needs to Ensure Environmental Justice Symposium," organized by the National Institute for Environmental Health Sciences and held in Washington, D.C.) issued Executive Order 12898, *Federal Actions to Address Environmental Justice in Minority Populations and Low-Income Populations*. This order attempts to address environmental injustice within existing federal laws and regulations.

Executive Order 12898 reinforces Title VI of the four-decades-old Civil Rights Act of 1964, which prohibits discriminatory practices in programs receiving federal funds. It also focuses the spotlight back on the National Environmental Policy Act, a law that set policy goals for the protection, maintenance, and enhancement of the environment. The act's goal is to ensure for all Americans a safe, healthful, productive, and aesthetically and culturally pleasing environment. To that end, it requires federal agencies to prepare a detailed statement on the anticipated environmental effects of proposed federal actions that will significantly affect the quality of human health and the environment.

The executive order calls for improved methodologies for assessing and mitigating impacts of proposed projects, for determining the anticipated health effects that will result from multiple and cumulative exposure to these impacts, for the collection of data on low-income and minority populations who may be disproportionately at risk to exposure, and for determining the effects of exposure on subsistence fishers and wildlife consumers. The executive order specifically focuses on subsistence fishers and wildlife consumers because not everyone buys his or her fish at the supermarket. Many individuals augment their diets by fishing from rivers, streams, and lakes that may be polluted. These subpopulations may be underprotected when basic assumptions about environmental safety are made using the dominant risk paradigm. The order also encourages participation by the affected populations in the various phases of assessing impacts, including scoping, data gathering, discovery of alternatives, analysis, mitigation, and monitoring.

Many grassroots activists are convinced that waiting for the government to act has endangered the health and welfare of their communities. Unlike the U.S. Environmental Protection Agency (EPA), communities of color discovered environmental inequities long before 1990. That year the EPA took action on environmental justice concerns, but only after extensive prodding from grassroots environmental justice activists, educators, and academics.[7] Making government respond to the needs of communities composed of the poor, working-class, and people of color has not been easy.[8] Environmental justice advocates continue to challenge the current environmental protection apparatus and offer their own framework for addressing environmental racism, unequal protection, health disparities, and nonsustainable development in the United States and around the world.[9]

THE 2002 PEOPLE OF COLOR SUMMIT

In October 2002, environmental justice leaders convened the Second National People of Color Environmental Leadership Summit (Summit II) in Washington, D.C. Organizers planned the four-day meeting for five hundred participants. However, over fourteen thousand individuals—representing grassroots and community-based organizations, faith-based groups, organized labor, civil rights groups, youth groups, and academic institutions—made their way to the nation's capital to participate in the historic gathering.

The vast majority—over 75 percent—of attendees came from community-based organizations. Summit II brought three generations (elders, seasoned leaders, and youth activists) of the environmental justice movement together. The "new" faces—persons not present at the First National People of Color Environmental Leadership Summit, held in 1991—outnumbered the veteran environmental justice leaders two to one. Summit II attendees came from nearly every state, including Alaska and Hawaii, and from Puerto Rico. Other delegates came from elsewhere in North America, the Caribbean, South and Central America, Asia, Africa, and Europe. The nations represented were Mexico, Canada, Jamaica, Trinidad, Panama, Columbia, Dominican Republic, Granada, South Africa, Nigeria, the Philippines, India, Peru, Ecuador, Guatemala, the Marshall Islands, and the United Kingdom.

The environmental justice movement continues to expand and mature. For example, the 1992 *People of Color Environmental Groups Directory* listed only three hundred environmental justice groups in the United States. By 2000, the list had grown to include over one thousand organizations and consisted of groups in the United States and Puerto Rico (see Figure 1.1) as well as in Canada and Mexico.

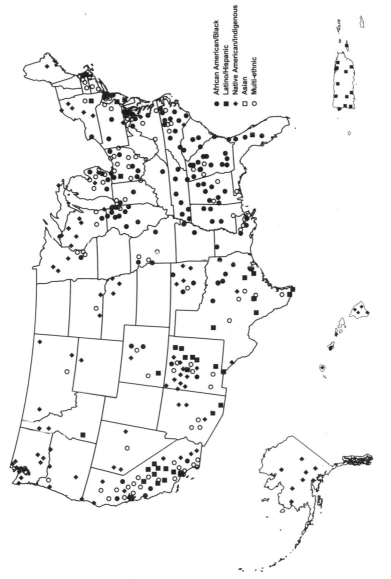

Figure 1.1. Environmental justice groups in the United States anc Puerto Rico that have been coordinated by people of color, for the year 2000.

African American/Black
Latino/Hispanic
Native American/Indigenous
Asian
Multi-ethnic

Women led, moderated, or presented in more than half of the eighty-six workshops and plenaries. Summit II leaders honored twelve outstanding "sheroes," the women warriors of the movement, in the Crowning Women Awards Dinner. The awards event was dedicated to the late Dana Alston and Jean Sindab, two giants in the environmental justice movement, and other women of color who were deceased and who had dedicated their lives to environmental justice. One of the twelve sheroes, Hazel Johnson of People for Community Recovery—a Chicago-based grassroots environmental justice organization—was also presented with the Dana Alston Award.

Students and young people have fueled every social movement in the United States, including the civil rights, environmental, antiwar, and women's movements. Several hundred youth and student leaders attended the conference and made their voices heard by means of a well-timed protest demonstration and long hours of hard work. The young people were able to incorporate many of their issues and priorities into the program.

In an effort to have substantive materials for use at Summit II, conference organizers put out a nationwide call for resource policy papers. The end result was two dozen resource papers on subjects including childhood asthma, energy, transportation, "dirty" power plants, climate justice, military toxics, clean production, brownfields redevelopment, sustainable agriculture, human rights, occupational health and safety, and farmworkers. The resource papers provided background materials for hands-on training sessions in the workshops.

The environmental justice movement has made tremendous strides over the past decade. When the First National People of Color Environmental Leadership Summit convened in 1991, there was no environmental justice network or university-based environmental justice centers or environmental justice legal clinics. Today, there are a dozen environmental justice networks, four environmental justice centers, and a growing number of university-based legal clinics that emphasize environmental justice. The University of Michigan offers master's and doctoral degrees in environmental justice; it is the only such program in the country.[10]

In 1991, there was only one book—*Dumping in Dixie*—published on environmental justice. Today, there are dozens of books in print on the subject. Six leading environmental justice authors were brought to Summit II to discuss their writings and research. These authors' work helped lay the foundation for environmental justice theory, policy, community-university partnerships, and legal practice.

Several general themes emerged from the four-day meeting. There was a consensus among participants that environmental justice had to be a top priority in the twenty-first century. Despite improvements in how the government addressed environmental protection, gaps persisted. Communities were faced with the steady chipping away of civil liberties, basic civil and human rights, and environmental and health protection.

Summit delegates called for students and other youths to be integrated into the leadership of the environmental justice movement. "Growing new leaders must be a top priority of the movement," said Angelo Pinto, a youth delegate and student at Clark Atlanta University. "Leadership by example and mentoring will go a long way in training young people to take up the torch of environmental justice."[11]

Summit II delegates reaffirmed the Principles of Environmental Justice and the Call to Action adopted at the 1991 summit. Delegates adopted three principles—Principles of Working Together, Youth Principles, and Principles Opposing the War against Iraq—and presented fifteen resolutions.

AN ENVIRONMENTAL JUSTICE FRAMEWORK

The question of environmental justice is not anchored in a debate about whether decision makers should tinker with risk management. The framework seeks instead to prevent environmental threats.[12] Moreover, it incorporates the aims of other social movements that seek to eliminate harmful practices in housing (discrimination harms the victim), land use, industrial planning, health care, and sanitation services. The effects of racial redlining (an illegal practice in which mortgage lenders figuratively draw a red line around minority neighborhoods and refuse to make loans available to those who live inside the redlined area), economic disinvestment, infrastructure decline, deteriorating housing, lead poisoning, industrial pollution, poverty, and unemployment are not unrelated problems if one lives in an urban ghetto or barrio, in a rural hamlet, or on a reservation.

The environmental justice framework attempts to uncover the underlying assumptions that may contribute to and produce unequal protection. This framework brings to the surface the ethical and political questions of "who gets what, why, and how much." General characteristics of the framework include the following:

The framework incorporates the principle that all individuals have a right to be protected from environmental degradation. The precedents for this point of the framework are the Civil Rights Act of 1964, Fair Housing Act of 1968 and its amended 1988 version, and Voting Rights Act of 1965.

The framework adopts the public health model of prevention as the preferred strategy: it focuses on eliminating a threat before harm occurs. Affected communities should not have to wait until causation or conclusive proof is established before preventive action is taken. For example, the framework offers a solution to the problem of lead poisoning in children by shifting the primary focus from treatment (after children have been poisoned) to prevention (elimination of the threat by removing lead from houses).

Overwhelming scientific evidence exists concerning the ill effects of lead on the human body. In fact, Louis Sullivan, while serving as secretary of the U.S. Department of Health and Human Services, identified lead as the "number one environmental health threat to children."[13] However, actions by state and federal governments to eliminate this source of preventable childhood illness have been inadequate. It took a lawsuit, *Matthews v. Coye,* by a parent and a community organization to get some 557,000 poor children tested for lead under the federally mandated Medicaid program.[14] In 1991, an Oakland parent and the organization People United for a Better Oakland, with the help of the Natural Resources Defense Council, NAACP Legal Defense and Educational Fund, American Civil Liberties Union, and Legal Aid Society of Alameda County, won an out-of-court settlement from the state of California worth $15–20 million for an ongoing blood-lead testing program in California. As a result, in 1991 the California Department of Health Services, via its Child Health and Disability Prevention Program, issued a directive to physicians to screen all children under the age of six when they undergo health assessments. This historic settlement triggered similar actions in other states that failed to live up to federally mandated screening.[15]

Lead screening is an important element in this problem, but screening is not the solution. Prevention is the solution. Surely, if termite inspections can be mandated to protect individuals' investments in homes, then lead-free housing can be mandated to protect public health. Ultimately, the lead abatement debate, which concerns public health (who is affected) vs. property rights (who pays for cleanup), is a value conflict that will not be resolved by the scientific community. Lead poisoning is a classic example of an environmental health problem that disproportionately affects low-income children and children of color.[16] Over the past four decades, the U.S. Centers for Disease Control and Prevention lowered the threshold for lead levels considered dangerous in children by 88 percent, from 60 to 10 micrograms per deciliter. Even 10 micrograms per deciliter is not safe. Some medical and health professionals advocate lowering the threshold to 2.5 micrograms per deciliter.[17]

On January 31, 2003, the Centers for Disease Control and Prevention released its *Second National Report on Human Exposure to Environmental Chemicals*. This report includes exposure information on the concentration of 116 chemicals measured in blood and urine specimens in a sample of the population for the years 1999 and 2000.[18] Progress has been made in reducing human exposure to dangerous chemicals and heavy metals, but concerns remain. According to the new report, in 1999–2000, among children aged one to five years, 2.2 percent had elevated blood-lead levels (levels greater than or equal to 10 micrograms per deciliter). This percentage decreased from 4.4 percent for the period 1991–1994.

The Environmental Justice and Health Union conducted a racial analysis of the findings published by the Centers for Disease Control and Prevention. This racial analysis, published in "Environmental Exposure and Racial Disparities," revealed the following: Non-Hispanic blacks are much more likely to be exposed to dioxins and PCBs and to be exposed at higher levels. Mexican Americans are much more likely to be exposed to pesticides, herbicides, and pest repellants and to be exposed at higher levels. Non-Hispanic whites are much more likely to be exposed to polycyclic aromatic hydrocarbons and phytoestrogens and are more likely to be exposed to phthalates at higher levels. Non-Hispanic blacks and Mexican Americans are much more likely to have higher levels of less common chemicals. Non-Hispanic blacks are exposed to the greatest number of chemicals in the study.[19] Although the federal government banned lead paint in 1978, it still poses a threat in millions of older homes.

There have been numerous attempts in recent years to target lead paint in class action suits. None has been successful.[20] In the meanwhile, children continue to be poisoned. It would cost between $50 billion and $100 billion to eradicate lead poisoning in the United States. It also costs to do nothing. Significant health costs, education costs related to lead-caused learning disabilities, and other social costs have resulted from the presence of lead-based paint in public and private buildings, including housing.[21]

Inspired in part by the recent tobacco industry settlement, states, counties, municipalities, school districts, and housing authorities have joined in the lawsuits against the lead industry for medical and other costs associated with lead poisoning that has resulted from exposure to deteriorated lead paint in homes. The legal assault on big tobacco yielded a $240-billion settlement by cigarette makers after states took on the industry in a series of lawsuits.[22] The lead lawsuits seek unspecified money damages from eight manufacturers and a trade association. Even though no previous lawsuit against the lead industry has succeeded, there is hope that one will succeed in the future. Lawsuits filed over the decades against the tobacco industry failed too, until the Tobacco Settlement Agreement, finalized on November 23, 1998, between the tobacco industry and forty-six states, five commonwealths and territories, and the District of Columbia.

The environmental justice framework rests on the Precautionary Principle for protecting workers, communities, and ecosystems. The Precautionary Principle evolved out of the German sociolegal tradition and centers on the concept of good household management. It asks "How little harm is possible?" rather than "How much harm is allowable?" This principle demands that decision makers set goals for safe environments and examine all available alternatives for achieving the goals, and it places the burden of proof of safety on those who propose to use inherently dangerous and risky technologies.[23]

Essentially, the Precautionary Principle states that, before you undertake an action, if you have reasonable suspicion that harm may result from it, and if there is scientific uncertainty about it, then you have a duty to act to prevent harm. This can be done by shifting the burden of proof of safety onto those people whose activities raised the suspicion of harm in the first place and by evaluating the available alternatives to find the least harmful way to carry out the activities, using a decision-making process that is open, informed, and democratic and that includes the people who will be affected by the decision. In 2003, San Francisco became the first city in the country to adopt the Precautionary Principle.[24]

The environmental justice framework shifts the burden of proof to polluters and dischargers who do harm, who discriminate, or who do not give equal protection to racial and ethnic minorities. Under the current system, individuals who challenge polluters must prove that they have been harmed, discriminated against, or disproportionately affected. Few affected communities have the resources to hire the lawyers, expert witnesses, and doctors needed to sustain such a challenge. The environmental justice framework requires instead that the parties applying for operating permits for landfills, incinerators, smelters, refineries, chemical plants, and similar operations must prove that their operations are not harmful to human health, will not disproportionately affect racial and ethnic minorities and other protected groups, and are nondiscriminatory.

The environmental justice framework redresses disproportionate impact by targeting action and resources. This strategy targets resources where environmental and health problems are greatest (as determined by some ranking scheme that is not limited to risk assessment). Relying solely on objective science to identify environmental and health problems prevents us from seeing the exploitative way that polluting industries have operated in some communities. It also permits a passive acceptance of the status quo. Human values are involved in determining which geographic areas are worth public investment. Generally, communities occupied by people of color receive lower quality-of-life ratings and thus get fewer dollars, based on these subjective ratings.[25]

The dominant environmental protection paradigm reinforces instead of challenges the stratification of people (according to race, ethnicity, status, power, and so on), places (central cities, suburbs, rural areas, unincorporated areas, Native American reservations, and so on), and types of work (for example, office workers are afforded greater protection than farmworkers). The dominant paradigm exists to manage, regulate, and distribute risks. As a result, the current system has institutionalized unequal enforcement of safety precautions; traded human health for profit; placed the burden of proof on the victims and not the polluting industry; legitimated human exposure to harmful chemicals, pesticides, and hazardous substances; promoted risky technologies such as incinerators; exploited the vulnerability of economically and politically disenfranchised communities; subsidized ecological destruction; created an industry around risk assessment (assessing risk does little to eliminate risks; the risk assessment industry would go out of business if the risks were eliminated); delayed cleanup actions; and failed to develop pollution prevention as the overarching strategy.[26]

The EPA was never designed to address environmental policies and practices that result in unfair, unjust, and inequitable outcomes. It is a regulatory agency, not a health agency. Officials of the EPA and other government agencies are not likely to ask the questions that go to the heart of environmental injustice: What groups are most affected by a specific environmental problem? Why are they affected? Who caused the problem? What can be done to remedy it? How can communities be justly compensated and reparations be paid to individuals harmed by industry and government actions? How could the problem have been prevented? As a result, vulnerable communities, populations, and individuals exposed to environmental problems often fall between the regulatory cracks. They are in many ways invisible communities. The environmental justice movement has served to make these disenfranchised communities visible and vocal.

IMPETUS FOR A PARADIGM SHIFT

Change in the dominant environmental protection paradigm did *not* come from an effort made by regulatory agencies, the polluting industry, academia, or the industry built around risk management. Instead, impetus for the change came from a movement led by a loose alliance of grassroots and national environmental and civil rights leaders who questioned the foundation of the current environmental protection paradigm. The environmental justice movement has changed the way scientists, researchers, policy makers, educators, and government officials go about their daily work. With its bottom-up approach, this movement has redefined the term "environment" to include the places where people live, work, play, and go to school, as well as brought attention to how these things interact with the physical and natural world.

Despite significant improvements in environmental protection over the past thirty-five years, however, millions of Americans continue to live, work, play, and go to school in unsafe and unhealthy physical environments.[27] Over the past three decades, the EPA has not always recognized that many government and industry practices (whether intended or unintended) have had an adverse impact on poor people and people of color. Grassroots community resistance emerged in response to practices, policies, and conditions that residents judged to be unjust, unfair, and illegal. Discrimination is a fact of life in America. Racial discrimination is also illegal.

The EPA is mandated to enforce the nation's environmental laws and regulations equally across the board. It is also required to protect all Americans—not just individuals or groups who can afford lawyers, lobbyists, and experts. Environmental protection is a right, not a privilege reserved for a few who can fend off environmental stressors that address environmental inequities.

Equity may mean different things to different people. Equity can be distilled into three broad categories: procedural, geographic, and social equity. *Procedural equity* refers to the "fairness" question: the extent to which governing rules, regulations, evaluation criteria, and enforcement are applied uniformly across the board. Unequal protection might result from nonscientific and undemocratic decisions, exclusionary practices, public hearings held in remote locations and at inconvenient times, and the use of English alone in communicating information about, and conducting hearings for, the non-English-speaking public. *Geographic equity* refers to location and spatial configuration of communities and their proximity to environmental hazards and locally unwanted land uses such as landfills, incinerators, sewer treatment plants, lead smelters, refineries, and other noxious facilities. For example, unequal protection may result from land-use decisions that determine the location of residential amenities and disamenities. Communities that are unincorporated, poor, and populated by people of color often suffer triple vulnerability to the siting of noxious facilities simply because of these characteristics. *Social equity* assesses the role of sociological factors, such as race, ethnicity, class, culture, lifestyles, political power, and so on, in environmental decision making. Poor people and people of color often work in the most dangerous jobs and live in the most polluted neighborhoods, and their children are exposed to a host of environmental toxins on the playgrounds and in their homes.

As noted earlier, the nation's environmental laws, regulations, and policies are not applied uniformly, resulting in some individuals, neighborhoods, and communities being exposed more than others to elevated health risks. Staff writers in the *National Law Journal* revealed glaring inequities in the way the federal EPA enforces laws:

> There is a racial divide in the way the U.S. government cleans up toxic waste sites and punishes polluters. White communities see faster action, better results and stiffer penalties than communities where blacks, Hispanics and other minorities live. This unequal protection often occurs whether the community is wealthy or poor.[28]

These findings suggest that unequal protection is placing communities of color at special risk. The *National Law Journal* study supplements the findings of earlier studies and reinforces what many grassroots leaders have been saying all along: not only are people of color differentially affected by industrial pollution, but also they can expect different treatment from the government. Environmental decision making operates at the juncture of science, economics, politics, special interests, and ethics. The current environmental model places communities of color at special risk.

ENVIRONMENTAL RACISM

Many of the differences in environmental quality between black and white communities result from institutional racism. Institutional racism influences local land use, the enforcement of environmental regulations, the siting of industrial facilities, and, for people of color, their choice of place to live, work, and play. The roots of institutional racism are deep and have been difficult to eliminate. Discrimination is a manifestation of institutional racism and, because of it, whites and blacks lead very different lives. Racism has historically been, and it continues to be, a major part of the American sociopolitical system. As a result, people of color find themselves at a disadvantage in contemporary society.

Environmental racism is real—as real as the racism found in the housing industry, educational institutions, employment arena, and judicial system.[29] What is it, and how does one recognize it? Environmental racism refers to any policy, practice, or directive that differentially affects or disadvantages (whether intended or unintended) individuals, groups, or communities because of their race or color. Environmental racism in public policies and industry practices results in benefits being provided to whites and costs being shifted to people of color.[30] Environmental racism is reinforced by government, legal, economic, political, and military institutions.[31]

People of color are often victims of land use decisions that mirror the power arrangements of the dominant society. Historically, exclusionary zoning (and rezoning) has been a subtle form of using government authority to foster and perpetuate discriminatory practices, including discriminatory environmental planning practices.[32] Zoning is probably the most widely applied mechanism in regulating urban land use in the United States. Zoning laws broadly define land for residential, commercial, or industrial uses and may impose land use restrictions (for example, minimum and maximum lot size, number of dwellings per acre, maximum square footage per dwelling, maximum height of buildings, and so on).[33] Few people of color participate in writing these zoning laws. In fact, most of the individuals who do participate can be covered by a narrow description. A 2003 report from the National Academy of Public Administration, *Addressing Community Concerns: How Environmental Justice Relates to Land Use Planning and Zoning*, found that members of most planning and zoning boards are men; more than nine out of ten members are white; and most members are forty years old or more. Furthermore, boards contain mostly professionals and few, if any, nonprofessional representatives.[34]

Historically, local land use and zoning policies are "a root enabling cause of disproportionate burdens and environmental injustice" in the United States.[35] Exclusionary zoning has been used to zone *against* something rather than *for* something. Expulsive zoning has pushed out residents and allowed "dirty" industries to invade communities.[36] Largely the poor, people of color, and renters inhabit the most vulnerable communities. Zoning laws are often legal weapons "deployed in the cause of racism" by allowing certain "undesirable" people—such as immigrants, people of color, and poor people—and operations, such as polluting industries, to be excluded from areas.[37]

With or without zoning, deed restrictions or other devices, various groups are unequally able to protect their environmental interests. More often than not, communities made up of people of color get shortchanged in the neighborhood protection game.[38]

Building a multiethnic, multiracial, multi-issue, antiracist movement is not easy. Much work is still needed to develop trust, mutual respect, and principled relationships across racial, ethnic, cultural, gender, and age lines. Internalized racism—the process by which a member of an oppressed group comes to accept and live out the inaccurate myths and stereotypes applied to the group—still keeps oppressed groups from working together, even though they know it is in their best interests to do so.[39] This internalization of negative feelings, images, stereotypes, prejudices, myths, and misinformation promoted by the racist system contributes to self-doubt and mistrust within and among other groups of people of color. For example, as Laura M. Padilla has noted, "patterns of internalized oppression cause us to attack, criticize or have unrealistic expectations of any one of us who has the courage to step forward and take on leadership responsibilities. This leads to a lack of the support that is absolutely necessary for effective leadership to emerge and group strength to grow. It also leads directly to the 'burn out' phenomenon we have all witnessed in, or experienced as, effective . . . leaders."[40]

This problem is not unique to the environmental justice movement, nor will it likely disappear overnight. A cottage industry has emerged around undoing racism.[41] Concerns about racism were around long before the 1991 summit. They were still present at Summit II in 2002. And they continue to permeate the larger society. Language and cultural barriers still hinder communication between the various racial and ethnic groups. It may be unrealistic to expect such a diverse collection of people, groups, organizations, and networks as is found in the environmental justice movement to mirror the mainstream environmental movement. Nevertheless, the strength of the movement lies in the diversity of its constituents and organizations, who are working toward common goals.

Environmental decision-making and policies often mirror the power arrangements of the dominant society and its institutions. Environmental racism disadvantages people of color while providing advantages to whites. A form of illegal exaction forces people of color to pay the costs of environmental benefits for the public at large. The question of who *pays* and who *benefits* from the current environmental and industrial policies is central to this analysis of environmental racism and other systems of domination and exploitation.

Racism influences the likelihood of exposure to environmental and health risks, as well as influences one's access to health care.[42] Many of the nation's environmental policies distribute the costs in a regressive pattern while providing disproportionate benefits for whites and individuals who fall at the upper end of the education and income scale. Numerous studies, dating back to the 1970s, reveal that people of color have borne greater health and environmental risk burdens than the society at large.[43] For example, people of color are subjected to elevated health risks from contaminated fish consumption; from close proximity to municipal landfills, incinerators, and toxic waste dumps; and from toxic schools, toxic housing, and toxic air releases.[44]

THE RIGHT TO BREATHE CLEAN AIR

Clean air is a basic right. Air pollution is not randomly distributed across communities and the landscape, so some populations are at greater risk from dirty air. In a national study done in 1992, National Argonne Laboratory researchers reported that 57 percent of all whites, 65 percent of all African Americans, and 80 percent of all Latinos lived in the 437 counties that failed to meet at least one of the EPA ambient air quality standards.[45] A 2000 study by the American Lung Association shows that children of color are disproportionately represented in areas with high ozone levels.[46] Additionally, 61.3 percent of black children, 69.2 percent of Hispanic children and 67.7 percent of Asian American children live in areas that exceed the ozone standard of .08 parts per million, while only 50.8 percent of white children live in such areas.

Dirty air hurts. Air pollution from vehicle emissions causes significant amounts of illness, hospitalization, and premature death. A 2002 study that was reported in *Lancet* indicates a strong causal link between ozone and asthma.[47] Ground-level ozone may exacerbate health problems such as asthma, nasal congestion, throat irritation, and respiratory tract inflammation; may reduce resistance to infection; and may cause chest pains, lung scarring, loss of lung elasticity, formation of lesions within the lungs, premature aging of lung tissues, and changes in cell function.[48]

Air pollution claims seventy thousand lives a year, nearly twice the number killed in traffic accidents. Emissions from "dirty" diesel vehicles also pose health threats—including premature mortality, aggravation of existing asthma, acute respiratory symptoms, chronic bronchitis, and decreased lung function—to people who live near busy streets and bus depots. Long-term exposure to high levels of diesel exhaust increases the risk of developing lung cancer.[49] Diesel particulate matter alone contributes to 125,000 cancers each year in the United States.[50]

In New York City, six of the Metropolitan Transit Authority's eight diesel bus depots in Manhattan are located in northern Manhattan, a low-income community of color; citywide, twelve of twenty depots are located in communities of color. In addition, five of the depots in northern Manhattan are in residential communities, within two hundred feet of people's homes.[51] Diesel bus fumes from two thousand buses housed in the area inflict life-threatening pollution on West Harlem residents.[52] In 1998, West Harlem Environmental Action, a local environmental justice organization, successfully lobbied to have buses at one depot converted to run on natural gas.

Vehicular traffic along freeways and major thoroughfares produces harmful noise and pollution. Students attending schools close to major thoroughfares have higher incidences of respiratory distress.[53] Adults and children living, working, or attending school within 984.25 feet (300 meters) of major roadways are significantly more likely to get asthma and other respiratory illnesses and leukemia; they may also suffer a higher incidence of cardiovascular disease. Children are at special risk from the ground-level ozone (which is the main ingredient of smog) produced by traffic.[54] One out of four American children lives in an area where the EPA's maximum permissible ozone level is regularly exceeded.[55]

Although it is difficult to establish the dollar cost of air pollution, estimates of its annual cost range from $10 billion to $200 billion.[56] Asthma is the number one reason for childhood emergency room visits in most major cities in the country. The hospitalization rate for African Americans is three to four times the rate for whites. In 2003, the Centers for

Disease Control reported that African Americans had an asthma death rate 200 percent higher than that of whites.[57]

In January and February 2003, the U.S. Commission on Civil Rights held hearings on environmental justice. Experts presented evidence of environmental inequities in communities of color, including disproportionate incidences of environmentally related disease, lead paint in homes, proximity to hazardous waste sites, toxic playgrounds, and schools located near Superfund sites and facilities that release toxic chemicals. In its 2003 report, *Not in My Backyard: Executive Order 12898 and Title VI as Tools for Achieving Environmental Justice,* the commission concluded, "Minority and low-income communities are most often exposed to multiple pollutants and from multiple sources. . . . There is no presumption of adverse health risk from multiple exposures, and no policy on cumulative risk assessment that considers the roles of social, economic, and behavioral factors when assessing risk."[58] The report was distributed to members of Congress and President George W. Bush.

SETTING THE RECORD STRAIGHT

The environmental protection apparatus is broken and must be fixed. The environmental justice movement has set out a clear goal: to fix this protection apparatus by eliminating unequal enforcement of environmental, civil rights, and public health laws. Environmental justice leaders have made a difference in the lives of people and in the physical environment. They have assisted public decision makers in identifying at-risk populations, toxic hot spots, research gaps, and action models in order to correct existing imbalances and prevent future threats. However, affected communities are not waiting for the government and industry to get their acts together. Grassroots groups have taken decisive steps to ensure that government and industry do the right thing.

Communities have begun to organize their own networks and have demanded to be included in public decision making. They have also developed communication channels between themselves and environmental justice leaders, other grassroots groups, professional associations (for example, legal, public health, and education associations), scientific groups, and public policy makers.

As noted earlier, President Clinton issued Executive Order 12898 in 1994. According to a report written by the EPA's Office of the Inspector General, *EPA Needs to Consistently Implement the Intent of the Executive Order on Environmental Justice* (March 2004), the agency earned a

TABLE I.I. TITLE VI COMPLAINTS
FILED WITH THE EPA

Status of Complaint	Number of Complaints
Rejected	75
Dismissed	26
Accepted	16
Suspended	7
Under review	5
Partially dismissed	3
Informally resolved	2
Referred to another federal agency	2
Total	*136*

SOURCE: U.S. Environmental Protection Agency, *Title VI Complaints Filed with EPA* (Washington, D.C.: June 20, 2003).

failing mark on implementing the ten-year-old executive order.[59] Environmental justice advocates are calling for vigorous enforcement of civil rights laws and environmental laws. Many of the hard-won gains in environmental protection are under attack, at the same time that right-wing conservative forces are attempting to dismantle affirmative action, civil rights, and basic civil liberties. But these attacks have the potential to draw environmentalists and human rights advocates closer together.

Grassroots community groups and individuals have continued to file Title VI complaints with the EPA and other federal agencies—even though they have received little sympathy from governmental agencies and even less from the courts. The bulk of the complaints raising environmental justice concerns have been filed with the EPA.[60] From 1993 to June 2003 (the latest figures compiled by the EPA), the agency's Office of Civil Rights received 136 Title VI complaints (see Table 1.1). Most complaints were rejected, dismissed, or suspended. Justice has been incomplete and slow for many environmental justice complainants, whose cases are still pending.[61]

For example, the suit against the Genesee Power Station, *St. Francis Prayer Center v. Michigan Department of Environmental Quality (Genesee Power Station)*, was originally filed in 1992, and it has yet to be decided by the EPA, which handles the administrative Title VI complaints. Nevertheless, the $85-million power station began operation in 1995, burning 365,000 tons of wood a year. The power station is still operating. As recently as 2001, it was reported as "discharging toxic pollutants into the low-income predominantly African American neighborhood, with no determination by the EPA as to whether or not the issuance of that permit violated Title VI."[62] In December 2002, wood chips from thousands of trees infested with fungus were burned at the plant. The Genesee Power Station is one of five wood-burning facilities in Michigan.[63]

JUSTICE DELAYED: WARREN COUNTY, NORTH CAROLINA

In December 2003, after a wait of more than two decades, an environmental justice victory finally came to the residents of Afton, in Warren County, North Carolina. Since 1982, residents of this county—more than 84 percent of whom are black—had lived with the legacy of a 142-acre PCB-filled waste dump. "Midnight dumpers" had illegally dumped PCB-laced oil along roadways in North Carolina in 1978. After the state discovered what had happened, it dug up and removed the contaminated dirt from the roadsides. In 1982, to dispose of the contaminated dirt, the state selected Afton to be the location of a state-owned PCB landfill.

Detoxification work on the dump began in June 2001, and it was completed in late December 2003. State and federal agencies spent $18 million to detoxify or neutralize PCB-contaminated soil stored in the landfill.[64] To detoxify the PCBs, a private contractor hired by the state dug up and burned 81,500 tons of the oil-laced soil in a kiln that reached more than eight hundred degrees Fahrenheit. The soil was then put back in a football-field-size pit at the dump, covered to form a mound, graded, and seeded with grass.

Warren County environmental justice leaders and their allies across the state deserve a gold medal for not giving up the long fight, for pressuring government officials to keep their promise to clean up the mess they created when they authorized the dump. This was no small win, given state deficits, budget cuts, and past broken promises. Residents and officials now must grapple with what to do with the site. The controversial PCB landfill, owned by the North Carolina Department of Environment and Natural Resources, is located about sixty miles northeast of Raleigh off State Road 1604 and U.S. Highway 401. The sign at the entrance to the landfill reads, "PCB Landfill—No Trespassing." Addition of the slogan "Justice Delayed is Justice Denied" might be appropriate.

This toxic-waste dump was forced on the tiny community, helping trigger the national environmental justice movement. While the midnight dumpers who illegally unloaded PCBs along highways in North

Carolina were fined and jailed, members of the innocent Afton community became victims of environmental racism: they were confined to a "toxic prison" created by the state of North Carolina. Warren County was their home, and many did not want to leave or get run out by an act of the state government that placed a landfill near them. The PCB landfill later became the most recognized symbol in the county. Despite the stigma, however, Warren County also became a symbol of the environmental justice movement.

Warren County residents had pleaded for a more permanent solution, rather than a quick fix that would eventually allow the PCBs to leak into the groundwater and wells. Their pleas had fallen on deaf ears. State and federal officials chose landfilling, the cheap way out. By 1993, however, the landfill was failing, and for a decade community leaders pressed the state to decontaminate the site.

Residents of Warren County were searching for a guarantee that the government was not creating a future Superfund site that would later threaten the community. North Carolina state officials and federal EPA officials could give no guarantees, since there is no such thing as a hazardous waste landfill that is 100 percent safe—that will not eventually leak. It all boiled down to trust. Can communities really trust state and federal governments to do the right thing? Recent history is filled with cases in which government has whitewashed real threats to public health.

Even after detoxification, some Warren County residents still question the completeness of the cleanup. They wonder whether contamination may have migrated beyond the 3-acre landfill site, into the 137-acre buffer zone that surrounds the landfill and the nearby creek and outlet basin. PCBs are persistent, bioaccumulative, and highly toxic pollutants. That is, they can build up in the food chain to levels that are harmful to human and ecosystem health. They are probable human carcinogens, cause developmental effects such as low birth weight, and disrupt hormone function.

Warren County is located in eastern North Carolina. The twenty-nine counties in the eastern part of the state are noticeably different from the rest of North Carolina.[65] According to the 2000 census, whites constitute 62 percent of the population in eastern North Carolina and 72 percent statewide. Blacks are concentrated in the northeastern and the central parts of the region. Warren County is one of six counties in the region where blacks constitute a majority: Bertie County (62.3 percent), Hertford (59.6 percent), Northampton (59.4 percent), Edgecombe (57.5 percent), Warren (54.5 percent), and Halifax (52.6 percent). Eastern

North Carolina is also significantly poorer than the rest of the state.[66] In 1999, the per capita income in North Carolina was $26,463, but in the eastern region it was only $18,550.[67]

But there's more to the story. Warren County is not only mostly black, but it is also mostly populated by people who are poor, rural, and politically powerless. The county had a population of 16,232 in 1980. Blacks constituted 63.7 percent of the county population and 24.2 percent of the state population in 1980. The county continues to be economically worse off than the state as a whole, according to all major social indicators. Per capita income for Warren County residents was $6,984 in 1982 compared with $9,283 for the state. Residents earned about 75 percent of the state's per capita income. The county ranked ninety-second out of one hundred counties in median family income in 1980. In the 1990s, the economic gap between Warren County and the rest of the state actually widened. The county's per capita income ranked ninety-eighth in 1990 and ninety-ninth in 2001. One-fourth of Warren County children live in poverty, compared with the state's 15.7 percent poverty rate among children.

The pattern of infrastructure development in this part of North Carolina diverted traffic and economic development away from Warren County. For example, Interstates 85 and 95 run past, not through, Warrenton, the county seat. Generally, development follows along major highways, and, indeed, economic development has bypassed much of the county. Over 19.4 percent of Warren County residents, compared with 12.3 percent of state residents, lived below the poverty level in 1999. The 1999 North Carolina Economic Development Scan gave Warren County a score of two (scores range from one, the lowest, to one hundred, the highest) in relation to its ability to attract new business.

That the state finally detoxified the Warren County PCB landfill, a problem it had created, is a major victory for local residents and the environmental justice movement. However, the surrounding land area and local community must now be made environmentally whole. Soil in the dump still containing low PCB levels is buried at least fifteen feet below the surface. Government officials claim the site is safe and suitable for reuse. Questions remain about the suitable reuse of the site. There is no evidence that the land has been brought back to its pre-1982 condition—where homes with deep basements could have been built and occupied and backyard vegetable gardens grown with little worry about toxic contamination or safety.

The siting of the PCB landfill in Afton is a textbook case of environmental racism. Around the world, environmental racism is defined as a human rights violation. Strong and persuasive arguments have been made for reparations as a remedy for serious human rights abuse. Under traditional human rights law and policy, we expect governments that practice or tolerate racial discrimination to acknowledge and end this human rights violation and compensate the victims. Environmental remediation is *not* the same as reparations. No reparations have been paid for the two decades of economic loss and mental anguish suffered by the Warren County residents.

Justice will not be complete until the twenty thousand Warren County residents receive a public apology and financial reparations from the perpetrators of environmental racism. Determining how much should be paid is problematic, since it is difficult for anyone to put a price tag on peace of mind. At minimum, Warren County residents should be paid reparations equal to the cost of detoxifying the landfill site, or $18 million, to be divided among them. Another reparations formula might include payment of a minimum of $1 million a year for every year the mostly black Afton community hosted the PCB landfill, or $21 million.

It probably would not be difficult for a poor county that lacks a hospital to spend $18 to $21 million. The hospitals nearest to Afton are located in neighboring Vance County (fifteen miles away) and across the state line in South Hill, Virginia (thirty-three miles away). Some people may think the idea of paying monetary damages is farfetched. However, until the community is made whole, the PCB-landfill detoxification victory—won by the tenacity and perseverance of local Warren County residents—remains incomplete.

When it comes to enforcing the rights of poor people and people of color in the United States, government officials often look the other way. Too often they must be prodded to enforce environmental and civil rights laws and regulations without regard to race, color, national origin, and socioeconomic background. Laws, regulations, and executive orders are only as good as their enforcement. In many communities populated by poor people and people of color, unequal enforcement has left a gaping hole in environmental protection. Waiting for government to act is a recipe for disaster.

Environmental justice at the EPA was initiated under the George H. W. Bush administration, but since then it has become all but nonexistent. The title of a March 2004 report by the Office of the Inspector General, *EPA Needs to Consistently Implement the Intent of the Execu-*

tive Order on Environmental Justice, alludes to how environmental justice has fared under President George W. Bush.[68] After ten years, the EPA "has not developed a clear vision or a comprehensive strategic plan, and has not established values, goals, expectations, and performance measurements" for integrating environmental justice into its day-to-day operations.[69]

The solution to environmental injustice lies in the realm of equal protection of all individuals, groups, and communities. No community, rich or poor, urban or suburban, black or white, should be made into a sacrifice zone or dumping ground. However, the officials responsible for issuing permits to hazardous waste facilities and dirty industries have followed the path of least resistance. This is not rocket science, but political science—a question of who gets what, when, why, and how much.

Environmental justice is also about how benefits are distributed and allocated. It is not about poor people being forced to trade their health and the health of their communities for jobs. Poor people and poor communities are given a false choice between having, on the one hand, no jobs and no development and, on the other hand, risky low-paying jobs and pollution. In reality, unemployment and poverty are also hazardous to one's health. This jobs-versus-unemployment scenario is a form of economic blackmail. Poverty makes economic blackmail easy in the United States and abroad, especially in developing countries. Industries and governments, including the military, often exploit the economic vulnerability of poor communities, poor states, poor regions, and poor nations when finding sites for risky operations.

The environmental justice movement challenges toxic colonialism, environmental racism, the international toxics trade, economic blackmail, corporate welfare, and human rights violations at home and abroad. Groups are demanding a clean, safe, just, healthy, and sustainable environment for all. They see this not only as the right thing to do but also as the moral and just path to ensuring our survival.

2

Neighborhoods "Zoned" for Garbage

B efore the rise of the national environmental justice movement, the early research on the connection between race and waste facility siting, begun in Houston, Texas, was undertaken with the assumption that all Americans have a basic right to live, work, play, go to school, and worship in a clean, healthy, sustainable, and just environment. This articulation later became the working definition of environmentalism for many environmental justice activists, academics, and analysts alike.[1]

SOCIOHISTORICAL CONTEXT

Houston is the nation's fourth-largest city. Between 1850 and 2003, it expanded from a mere nine square miles to more than six hundred square miles. The city's black population lives in a broad belt extending from the south central and southeast portion of the city into the northeast and north central area. Henry Allen Bullock, a noted black sociologist, described the concentration of Houston's blacks in the 1950s this way: "Houston's Negro population is very tightly concentrated in a few areas. Although the population has responded to the suburban movement like all other urban populations, tradition has prevented basic changes in the geography of the Negro settlement."[2]

In 1950, two-thirds of Houston's black population was concentrated in three major, segregated neighborhoods—namely, the Third, Fourth, and Fifth Wards. Beginning in the 1960s and accelerating in the 1970s, Houston's black population expanded outward, away from the central city. Even in these outlying areas, the black population remained concentrated, generally in the northeast and southeast quadrants of the city.

During the boom period of the 1970s, Houston was dubbed the "golden buckle" of the Sun Belt and the "petrochemical capital" of the world.[3] The city experienced unparalleled economic expansion and population growth. By 1980, Houston's black population had become further decentralized and now occupied the northeast, northwest, southeast, and southwest corridors. At this time, the city's black community numbered nearly half a million residents, making up 28 percent of the city's total population. However, in both the central city and the suburban neighborhoods, most black Houstonians remained racially segregated: more than 81 percent of the city's blacks lived in mostly black areas. Some formerly segregated white suburban neighborhoods became black neighborhoods. By 1982, Houston had emerged as the nation's fourth-largest city, with a population of 1.7 million persons spread over more than 585 square miles.

Houston's black population forms the largest black community in the South, and this population has increased over the past thirty years. Blacks constituted 21 percent (125,000) of the Houston population in 1960, 26 percent (317,000) in 1970, nearly 28 percent (436,000) in 1980, 28 percent in 1990 (440,000), and 25 percent in 2000 (487,000). However, in 1970 over 90 percent of Houston's blacks lived in city blocks in which blacks were the majority. A decade later, this had changed very little: the 1980 segregation index reveals that some 82 percent of the city's blacks lived in mostly black city blocks.[4]

UNOFFICIALLY "ZONED" FOR GARBAGE

Houston has more than five hundred neighborhoods. It is also the only major American city without zoning laws. This no-zoning policy has allowed for a somewhat erratic land use pattern in the city. In Houston, NIMBY (Not in My Back Yard) was replaced with a PIBBY (Place in Blacks' Back Yards) policy.[5] The all-white, all-male city government and private industry targeted Houston's black neighborhoods for landfills, incinerators, garbage dumps, and garbage transfer stations.

Five decades of this discriminatory practice lowered residents' property values, accelerated the physical deterioration of Houston's black neighborhoods, and increased disinvestment in these neighborhoods. Moreover, the discriminatory siting of solid waste facilities stigmatized the black neighborhoods, making them the "dumping grounds" for a host of other unwanted facilities, including salvage yards, recycling operations, and automobile chop shops.[6] Compared to the larger society, the inhabitants of many of Houston's black residential areas experienced greater health and environmental risks as a result of unregulated growth, ineffective regulation of industrial toxins, and public policy decisions authorizing construction of industrial facilities in the neighborhoods of those without political and economic clout.[7]

Houston's no-zoning policy is characterized by irrational land use planning and infrastructure chaos.[8] In the absence of zoning, developers have used renewable deed restrictions as a means of land use control within subdivisions. Deed restrictions regulate lot sizes; the square footage of structures; the distance that structures must be set back from property lines, street lines, or lot lines; the type and number of structures that may be built on a lot; and whether single or multifamily housing may be built. However, lower income, minority, and older neighborhoods have had difficulty enforcing and renewing deed restrictions.

Renewable deed restrictions were the only tool many residents had at their disposal to regulate nonresidential uses. However, deed restrictions in low-income areas were often allowed to lapse because residents were preoccupied with making a living and lacked the time, energy, or faith in government to get the needed signatures of neighborhood residents to keep their deed restrictions in force. Moreover, the rapid occupancy turnover and large renter population in many Houston inner-city neighborhoods further weakened the efficacy of deed restrictions as a protective device.

Ineffective land use regulations have created a nightmare for many of Houston's neighborhoods—especially the ones that were ill equipped to fend off industrial encroachment. The siting of nonresidential facilities has heightened animosities between the black community and the local government. This is especially true in the case of siting solid waste disposal facilities.

Public officials learn fast that solid waste management can become a volatile political issue. Generally, controversy in Houston centers on charges that disposal sites are not equitably spread in quadrants of the city; equitable siting would distribute the burden and lessen the opposition.[9] Finding suitable sites for sanitary landfills has become a critical

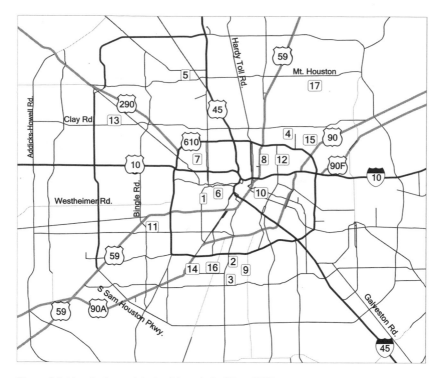

Figure 2.1. Houston's municipal solid waste facilities, 1979.

(1) Fourth Ward Landfill; (2) Sunnyside Landfill; (3) Reed Road Landfill; (4) Kirkpatrick Landfill; (5) West Donovan Landfill; (6) Fourth Ward Incinerator; (7) West End/Cottage Grove Incinerator; (8) Kelly Street Incinerator; (9) Holmes Road Incinerator; (10) Velasco Incinerator; (11) Westpark Mini-Incinerator; (12) Kelly Street Mini-Incinerator; (13) Northwest Service Center Mini-Incinerator; (14) Holmes Road Landfill (1970); (15) McCarty Road Landfill; (16) Holmes Road Landfill (1978); (17) Whispering Pines Landfill

problem mainly because no one wants to have a waste facility as a neighbor. Who wants to live next to a place where household waste—some of which is highly toxic—is legally dumped and where hazardous wastes may be illegally dumped?

Over the past fifty years, the city has used two basic methods to dispose of its solid waste: incineration and landfill. From the 1920s to 1978, a total of seventeen solid waste facilities were built in Houston neighborhoods (see Figure 2.1).

Thirteen solid waste disposal facilities were operated by the city from the late 1920s to 1978: eleven in black areas; one in a Hispanic area; one in a white area. At the same time, there were four additional, privately owned, facilities: three in black areas; one in a white area. The city oper-

TABLE 2.1. CITY OF HOUSTON'S GARBAGE
INCINERATORS AND MUNICIPAL LANDFILLS

Neighborhood	Location	Incinerator or Landfill	Target Area[a]	Ethnicity of Neighborhood[b]
Fourth Ward	Southwest	2	Yes	Black
West End/ Cottage Grove	Northwest	1	Yes	Black
Kashmere Gardens	Northeast	2	Yes	Black
Sunnyside	Southeast	3	Yes	Black
Navigation	Southeast	1	Yes	Hispanic
Larchmont	Southwest	1	No	White
Carverdale	Northwest	1	Yes	Black
Trinity Gardens	Northeast	1	Yes	Black
Acres Homes	Northwest	1	Yes	Black

[a] Target areas are designated neighborhoods under Houston's Community Development Block Grant program.
[b] Ethnicity of neighborhood indicates the racial or ethnic group that constitutes a numerical majority in the census tracts that make up the neighborhood.

ated eight garbage incinerators (five large units and three mini-units): six in mostly black neighborhoods; one in a Hispanic neighborhood; one in a mostly white area (see Table 2.1).

All five of Houston's large garbage incinerators were sited in minority neighborhoods—four black and one Hispanic. One of the oldest city-owned incinerators was located in Houston's Fourth Ward. This site dates back to the 1920s. Other city-owned incinerators included the Patterson Street site, the Kelly Street site, the Holmes Road site, and the Velasco site; the latter was located in the mostly Hispanic Second Ward, or Segundo Barrio. The costs of operating these large incinerators and the problems of pollution generated by these systems were major factors in their closing.

Although blacks made up only about 25 percent of the city's population, the five city-owned landfills (100 percent of the landfills) and six of the eight city-owned incinerators (75 percent of the incinerators) were built in black Houston neighborhoods. From the 1920s through 1978, eleven of thirteen city-owned landfills and incinerators (84.6 percent) were built in black neighborhoods.

In 1972, Houston contracted with the Houston Natural Gas Company, a private company, to conduct a pilot project in which the company built mini-incinerators that were supposed to be more efficient, to cost less to operate, and to burn cleaner. At a cost of $1.9 million, three

TABLE 2.2. PRIVATELY OWNED HOUSTON
SANITARY LANDFILLS PERMITTED BY THE
TEXAS DEPARTMENT OF HEALTH, 1970–1978

Site	Location	Year Permitted	Neighborhood	Ethnicity of Neighborhood
Holmes Road	Southeast	1970	Almeda Plaza	Black
McCarty	Northeast	1971	Chattwood	White
Holmes Road	Southeast	1978	Almeda Plaza	Black
Whispering Pines	Northeast	1978	Northwood Manor	Black

sets of mini-incinerators were installed in the city: on Sommermeyer Road in northwest Houston, on Kelly Street near the North Loop and East-Tex Freeway, and on Westpark Drive in Southwest Houston.

The Sommermeyer incinerator was located at the Northwest Service Center in the mostly black Carverdale neighborhood. The Carverdale neighborhood was also the host community for the first city-owned garbage transfer station. In 1983, the Houston City Council awarded a contract to Waste Management of Houston to haul garbage at the cost of $11.58 per ton; the city appropriated $1 million to pay the contractor.[10]

The Kelly Street mini-incinerator was sited in the mostly black Kashmere Gardens neighborhood, and the Westpark facility was built across the Southwest Freeway, near the mostly white Larchmont neighborhood. Pilot tests of the mini-incinerators found that they were in fact not pollution free: they performed with mixed results. The mini-incinerators did not meet the pollution standards of the Houston Air Quality Control Board and were shut down after a short period of operation in the mid-1970s.

From 1970 to 1978, the Texas Department of Health issued four sanitary landfill permits to private companies for the disposal of Houston's solid waste (see Table 2.2). Privately owned sanitary landfills in Houston followed the pattern established by the city. Three of the four privately owned landfill sites were in black neighborhoods.

Houston's black neighborhoods get dumped on while receiving less than their fair share of residential services, including garbage collection, water, and sewer services. Black Houstonians have gotten used to the neglect. In a 2002 special report on Houston's neglected neighborhoods, *Houston Chronicle* reporter Mike Snyder wrote that hasty annexations by the city left a legacy of blight.[11] Even the best efforts of Houston's Super Neighborhood Program, the cornerstone of Mayor Lee Brown,

Houston's first African American mayor, have done little to reverse the decades of systematic neglect.

Many of these "invisible" black neighborhoods are easily identified by their substandard housing, lack of sewer and water lines, unpaved narrow streets, open ditches, illegal dumps, and lack of sidewalks, curbs, and storm drains. When it rains here, it floods. A sizable share of the mostly black Acres Homes neighborhood, for example, is as impoverished today as it was decades ago. Homoizelle Savoy, a thirty-year resident of Acres Homes, sums up her community's plight: "Thirty years is neglected, isn't it? Ain't no feeling—I know we've been overlooked."[12]

Although Houston has more than five hundred neighborhoods, nine predominately black neighborhoods shouldered the burden for waste disposal sites from the 1920s through 1978. These nine are the Fourth Ward, West End/Cottage Grove, Kashmere Gardens, Sunnyside, Carverdale, Acres Homes, Almeda Plaza, Trinity Gardens, and Northwood Manor.

FOURTH WARD

The oldest black neighborhood in Houston, the Fourth Ward dates back to the 1860s. In 1866, former slaves moved into this neighborhood and founded a community called Freedmen's Town (near the present Jefferson Davis Hospital and Allen Parkway Village public housing project). The neighborhood is often referred to as the "Mother Ward," for many black Houstonians can trace their roots to it. The development that began in the 1860s continued through the mid-1920s. The mid-1920s saw this neighborhood become the center for black culture in Houston: over 95 percent of Houston's black businesses and black professionals were located in the Fourth Ward.

As an economically impoverished neighborhood, the Fourth Ward has experienced extreme pressures from land speculation, expansion of the central business district, and loss of affordable housing, since it lies just west of the downtown area. The Fourth Ward also has a bloody past: the neighborhood was the scene of the city's bloodiest race riot, the Houston Riot of 1917. The city of Houston operated a garbage dump and garbage incinerator in the neighborhood in the 1920s. In 1936, Harris County's Jefferson Davis Hospital was built on the dump site.

The city tore down a large segment of Freedmen's Town as part of its urban renewal and slum clearance program. In its place it constructed a public housing project for whites (called the San Felipe Courts, and later, when blacks moved in, renamed the Allen Parkway Village public housing project) in the early 1940s. The Fourth Ward (census tract 126) was 84 percent black in 1970 and 63 percent black in 1980. With the demolition of the Allen Parkway Village and redevelopment of the property in the 1990s, the neighborhood has experienced an influx of new residents, housing construction, commercial investment, and gentrification. A maintenance facility belonging to the solid waste department was built on the city-owned landfill property, adjacent to Jefferson Davis Hospital.

WEST END/COTTAGE GROVE

This neighborhood contains some of the oldest housing in the city, dating back to the 1880s; over one-third of the housing in the area was constructed prior to 1940. Elderly persons make up a large share of the neighborhood's population. The neighborhood, which constitutes census tract 514, was the site of Houston's Patterson Street incinerator. In 1970, the census tract was over 57 percent black. In more recent years the neighborhood has experienced an in-migration of nonblacks. The 1980 census shows that blacks made up only 42 percent of the tract population. However, blacks remained highly concentrated in 514.02 (a section of tract 514; some of the census tracts were subdivided in 1980 because of population growth), where the incinerator was sited, constituting over 54 percent of the population.

KASHMERE GARDENS

This neighborhood is located just north of Houston's downtown. The neighborhood lies partly in census tract 207, where the Kelly Street incinerator was sited. Land for this area was subdivided in the 1930s; over 57 percent of the housing units were built in the 1940s and 1950s. The racial composition of the neighborhood has undergone little change over the years. Blacks made up 90 percent of the population in 1970 and 89 percent of the population in 1980.

SUNNYSIDE

This neighborhood is located on the periphery of the city, approximately nine miles south of Houston's central business district. Development of the northern part of the neighborhood occurred in the early 1940s along Holmes Road. The 1970 census shows that Sunnyside (which constitutes census tract 329) was over 97 percent black, and it remains a distinctly black area. The neighborhood contains three waste disposal facilities: the Sunnyside landfill, located on Bellfort Street; the Reed Road landfill, located on Reed Road; and the Holmes Road incinerator, located on Bellfort Street off the South Freeway. The latter is adjacent to Sunnyside Park and just one block from Sunnyside Elementary School.

Some of the streets in the neighborhood are gravel roads. Reed Road serves as a commercial strip for the neighborhood, and it features small shops, stores, the public library, and so on. Trash and other debris can be found scattered along Bellfort, which serves as the neighborhood's entrance from the South Freeway. In addition, illegal dumping continues at the entrance to the landfill site on Bellfort Street.

CARVERDALE

Located approximately twelve miles west of the downtown area, this neighborhood covers about 1.5 square miles. The area was developed during 1953 and was annexed by Houston in 1955. The 1970 census indicates that Carverdale had a population of 1,664 residents, of which over 77 percent were black.

The Carverdale neighborhood occupies the northern portion of census tract 528. Over 75 percent of residents are homeowners. Census tract 528 experienced a slight increase in population between 1970 and 1980, growing from 2,033 to 2,106. Carverdale was the site of one of the city's mini-incinerators in the early 1970s. The city-owned garbage transfer station presently located in Carverdale is less than one block from residents' homes.

ACRES HOMES

Located in northwest Houston some nine miles from the central business district, Acres Homes is both rural and suburban in character. Census data reveal that the neighborhood (which constitutes census tract 525) was 75.6 percent black in 1970 and 78.9 percent black in 1980. The neighborhood developed between 1949 and 1953. Over two-thirds of all housing units in the neighborhood are owner occupied.

Some of the older sections in the Acres Homes neighborhood do not have sidewalks or street lighting. The newer sections were developed after 1970 and are occupied mostly by middle-income residents. Two waste disposal facilities are located in this neighborhood, on West Donovan Street and on Nieman Lane.

ALMEDA PLAZA

Located south of Houston's downtown area, this neighborhood lies in the southeastern corner of census tract 332, just south of the Holmes Road landfill. Permits were granted in 1970 and 1978 to operate landfills in the neighborhood. In 1970, the neighborhood was over 58 percent black. All of census tract 332, of which Almeda Plaza is just a part, has undergone a dramatic demographic transition: between 1970 and 1980, the population changed from 26 percent black to over 80 percent black.

Almeda Plaza Park is a major gathering place for youth activities such as basketball and includes a children's playground. Open ditches run along Almeda Plaza and west of the Holmes Road landfill, and standing water in these drainage ditches gives off odors. The ditches may serve as breeding grounds for mosquitoes. Residents in the northern part of the neighborhood have a partial view of the Holmes Road landfill sites. Illegal dumping continues at the landfill even though the sites are closed.

TRINITY GARDENS

This northeast Houston neighborhood was developed in the late 1930s. Its southeast sector lies within census tract 216. The population occupying the majority of the housing units in the southeast sector was 76.3 percent black in 1970 and 90.14 percent black in 1980. There are two public schools in the neighborhood: Kashmere Gardens Senior High School and Houston Gardens Elementary. Trinity Gardens is one of the city's Community Development Target Areas. The Kirkpatrick landfill is located within the Trinity Gardens neighborhood in the general vicinity of the Houston Belt and Terminal Railroad to the north, Hunting Bayou to the south, Homestead Road to the west, and Kirkpatrick Boulevard to the east.

NORTHWOOD MANOR

This suburban neighborhood in northeast Houston consists primarily of single-family working-class and middle-income housing. The subdivision was developed largely in the 1970s. Northwood Manor lies within census tract 224; this tract as a whole had a population of 18,726 in 1980 (over 64.5 percent were black).

The neighborhood conforms roughly to the boundaries of census tract

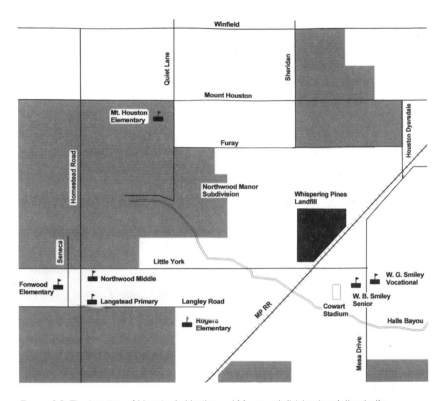

Figure 2.2. The location of Houston's Northwood Manor subdivision in relation to the Whispering Pines Sanitary Landfill.

224.03 (a subdivided part of the larger tract). The total population of this portion of the tract was 8,449 in 1980; blacks constituted over 82.4 percent in 1980. This neighborhood is the site of the contested waste facility named in *Bean v. Southwestern Waste Management Corp.*

Residents in the neighborhood are served by the suburban 17,800-pupil North Forest Independent School District, a district where blacks constitute over 80 percent of the student body. The district administration building is located on East Houston-Dyersdale Road and Little York Road. A total of seven schools of the North Forest district are located in the Northwood Manor area (see Figure 2.2).

The 195-acre Whispering Pines Sanitary Landfill, located at 11800 East Houston-Dyersdale Road, is across the street from the school district's bus facilities, the Smiley High School Complex, and the Jones-Cowart Stadium and athletic fields. The landfill is only fourteen hundred feet from the three-thousand-student Smiley High School complex—which did not have air conditioning in 1982.

As early as 1983, the Whispering Pines landfill mound could be seen rising above the surrounding landscape. A more dramatic and panoramic view of Northwood Manor's "Mount Trashmore," the name given to the landfill by area residents, can be seen from the modern Jones-Cowart Stadium, a outdoor arena where young black high school students practice and play, across the road from the sanitary landfill.

Most of the housing in Northwood Manor is well maintained; over 88 percent of the residents own their homes. Nationally, about 46 percent of blacks own their homes.[13] Throughout the neighborhood, children play in the yards and on the sidewalks; the neighborhood appears to be made up largely of younger families with children.

Farther down East Little York Road, in the direction of East Houston-Dyersdale Road, the streets are littered with various types of debris, such as car tires, paper, boxes, and mattresses. Several schools are located off East Little York Road—a major street that does not have sidewalks. Children who walk to school must walk in the street or along the grassy "trails" beside the road. East Little York Road is the major thoroughfare for the solid waste trucks that dump at the Whispering Pines landfill.

EARLY BLACK RESISTANCE TO DUMPING

Black resistance to the siting and operation of landfills, garbage dumps, and incinerators in black Houston neighborhoods is not new. As early as 1967, black residents picketed the Holmes Road dump, located in the southeast Sunnyside neighborhood, after an eight-year-old black girl drowned there. These protesters joined forces with another protest group, which was marching for equal education. The protesters were later joined by black college students, fueling the conditions that led to the 1967 Texas Southern University riot, the only major civil disturbance that occurred in the city during the turbulent 1960s.[14]

In 1971, the first major controversy that Judson Robinson Jr., Houston's first black city councilman, had to deal with involved a city-owned dump. Councilman Robinson had to quell a near riot at the Kirkpatrick landfill in the mostly black Trinity Gardens neighborhood. Black protesters were demanding that the city close the landfill. After six months of intense protest demonstrations, the city did so.

Controversy surrounding landfill siting peaked in the late 1970s, after the city of Houston received a proposal by Browning Ferris Industries, a company headquartered in Houston, to build the Whispering Pines Sanitary Landfill in the city's mostly black middle-class Northwood Manor neighborhood. As a sociologist at the predominately African American Texas Southern University in Houston, I was asked in 1979 by attorney Linda McKeever Bullard to conduct a study of the spatial location of all municipal solid waste disposal facilities in Houston. The request was part of a class action lawsuit *(Bean v. Southwestern Waste Management Corp.)* that she filed against the city of Houston, the state of Texas, and the locally headquartered Browning Ferris Industries (BFI), at the time the nation's second-largest waste disposal company.

Bean v. Southwestern Waste Management Corp. was the first lawsuit in the United States to charge environmental discrimination in waste-facility siting under the Civil Rights Act. The Northwood Manor neighborhood of single-family homes was an unlikely location for a garbage dump—apparently except for the fact that over 82 percent of its residents were black.

In order to obtain the history of waste facility siting in Houston, I had to manually retrieve government records (city, county, and state documents) because the files were not yet computerized. I also conducted on-site visits, windshield surveys (that is, drove around the community and noted the general distribution of buildings and other structures and the land uses), and informal interviews—playing the role of "sociologist as detective"—as a reliability check.

Significantly, the 1979 Houston case developed and tested a new methodology and legal theory of environmental discrimination without the benefit of any regional or national studies on the subject. The case predated some important landmark studies and events. These include the 1983 study of off-site commercial hazardous waste landfills in the South by the U.S. General Accounting Office; the 1987 release of the report *Toxic Wastes and Race,* authored by the Commission for Racial Justice; the letters written in 1990 by the Gulf Coast Tenants Organization and SouthWest Organizing Project to the "Big Ten" environmental groups accusing them of elitism and racism; the University of Michigan's 1990 conference "Race and the Incidence on Environmental Hazards"; the 1991 First National People of Color Environmental Leadership Summit; and the 1994 Executive Order 12898, which focused on environmental justice, signed by President Bill Clinton.

Locating old landfills in Houston was made easier by the fact that Houston is built on flat terrain, with some areas below sea level. Whenever I encountered a "mountain"—and quite a few were scattered across the urban landscape—I suspected the presence of an old dump site. After collecting the data for *Bean v. Southwestern Waste Management Corp.* and interviewing citizens from other African American neighborhoods, it became apparent to me and my ten graduate sociology students at Texas Southern University that waste facility siting in Houston was not random. Moreover, this was not a chicken or egg (which came first) problem. In all cases, the residential and racial character of the neighborhoods had been established long before the industrial facilities invaded the neighborhoods.

For example, in 1980, the suburban Northwood Manor neighborhood, consisting primarily of single-family homeowners, had a population of 8,449 residents. No major industrial or commercial firms are found in the area. Many Northwood Manor residents thought they were getting a shopping center or new homes in their subdivision when construction of the landfill site commenced. When they learned the truth, they began to organize to stop the dump.

Resident Lonnie Anderson learned of the proposed dump at a community meeting to discuss the drainage, sewage, and rat problem already affecting the area. Anderson and other plaintiffs in the class action lawsuit collected more than two thousand signatures on a petition opposing the dump. Judge Gabrielle McDonald of the U.S. District Court said the petition indicated strong sentiment against the dump, but she ruled that it was inadmissible.[15]

It is ironic than some of the residents who were fighting the construction of the waste facility had moved to Northwood Manor in an effort to escape landfills in their former Houston neighborhoods. Patricia Reaux described her experience with landfills: "About seven years ago, I lived near another dump on Hirsch Road. . . . There were rats so big you had to use a gun to kill them. The smell was awful, and the water sometimes was not drinkable."[16]

To halt the construction of the facility, local residents formed the Northeast Community Action Group, an organization that spun off from the local neighborhood civic association. They later filed a class action lawsuit in federal court to prevent the siting of the landfill in their neighborhood. The residents and their black attorney, Linda McKeever Bullard, charged the Texas Department of Health and BFI, the private disposal company, with racial discrimination in the selection of the Whispering Pines landfill site.[17] Residents were upset because the proposed site was not only near their homes but within fourteen hundred feet of their high school.

Neither Smiley High School nor the other fifteen schools in the North Forest Independent School District are equipped with air conditioning—a significant point in the hot and humid Houston climate. Windows are usually left open while school is in session. Seven North Forest schools are found in Northwood Manor and contiguous neighborhoods. Toley Hart, a North Forest superintendent, testifying in court, expressed his concerns about the Whispering Pines landfill: "I can't see any reason other than racial ones for putting landfills in our area. . . . I worry about how this will affect the attitudes of our schools' young people, whose parents have worked hard to have a nice community and good homes. To have something like this happen is bound to change them."[18]

Hart, who is white, also testified that the district successfully opposed another attempt to site a garbage dump in the area in the 1960s (when the area was 90 percent white), and that the Harris County Commissioners Court, which then licensed all landfills outside the Houston city limits, denied the application after strong protests from the area residents. Hart explained: "About 25 years ago, this area was about 90 percent white, and there were no landfills here. . . . It was not until the early '60s that the first one [dump] was put on Settegast Road in what was then the only minority pocket in the district."[19] The population of Northwood Manor shifted from a majority of whites in 1970 to a majority of blacks in 1980.

The residents and their attorney sought a temporary injunction to prevent the opening of the 195-acre landfill. The suit they filed, in 1979, was the first to be argued in front of Judge Gabrielle McDonald, the only African American female judge in Texas. In December 1979, Judge McDonald denied the temporary injunction. The lawsuit finally went to trial in 1984.

In her written order denying the temporary injunction, Judge McDonald said she "might very well have denied this permit" issued by the Texas Department of Health licensing the landfill site. "It simply does not make sense to put a solid waste site so close to a high school, particularly one with no air conditioning. . . . Nor does it make sense to put the landfill so close to a residential neighborhood. But I am not TDH [the Texas Department of Health]. For all I know, TDH may regularly approve of solid waste sites located near schools and residential areas, as illogical as that may seem."[20] Judge McDonald also described the landfill siting as both "unfortunate and insensitive," but she felt the plaintiffs failed to prove that the permit was motivated by "purposeful racial discrimination."[21]

The case was transferred in 1984 to Judge John Singleton of the U.S. District Court. During my testimony as an expert witness, in which I mapped and described the locations of Houston's black neighborhoods and their proximity to solid waste sites, Judge Singleton repeatedly referred to the black plaintiffs as "nigras" and their neighborhoods as "nigra areas." Most people from the South know that the word "nigra" is a code for "nigger." While sitting in the witness box, I overheard the judge's white clerk softly remind the judge that blacks in his court were offended by his references to them as "nigras."[22] The judge ruled against the residents and the Whispering Pines landfill was built in Northwood Manor.

Though falling short of a legal victory, the class action lawsuit did produce some changes in the way new waste facilities are sited in Houston. The Houston city council, acting under intense political pressure from local residents, passed a resolution in 1980 condemning the siting of the Whispering Pines landfill in the black community and prohibited city-owned trucks from carrying Houston solid waste to the controversial landfill.[23] The city also gave Northwood Manor residents a park. The only problem with this is that the park, East Little York Park, is built next to the Whispering Pines landfill.

The Texas Department of Health updated its landfill permit requirement: applications must now include detailed land use, economic, and sociodemographic data on areas where applicants propose to site standard sanitary landfills. Black Houstonians sent a clear signal to the Texas Department of Health, city government, and private waste disposal companies, informing them that they would resist any future proposals to site waste facilities in their neighborhoods. The landfill question appears to have galvanized and politicized a part of the Houston community, the black community, which for years had been inactive on environmental issues.

DIRTY TRICKS AND CORRUPT POLITICS

The Whispering Pines landfill was mired in dirty politics long before the facility was permitted. Ordinarily, most Americans expect their elected officials to protect their community interests; they do not expect them to arrange for garbage dumps to be sited in their neighborhoods without their knowledge or consent. Yet the Texas senator Jack Ogg did exactly that. Ogg, a white politician who represented residents in northeast Houston and Harris County (part of the district lies in Harris County outside the Houston city limits), and his two law partners acquired the land for the Whispering Pines landfill. They later sold it to BFI in 1978.[24] After learning of Ogg's ownership of the land, protesters picketed the waste facility with signs that read, "Welcome to the land of Ogg. Compliments of Senator Jack Ogg."

BFI contracted with Image Transition and Ed Shannon, two local black public relations firms. The *Bean* plaintiffs' lawyer discovered this when a briefcase full of memoranda, invoices, and correspondences was mysteriously dropped off at her office—a sort of "Deep Throat" drop. The two public relations firms were to conduct an "image enhancement" campaign to counter the "negative image problems that have emerged from conflict with factions of North-east Houston Black community."[25] The campaign strategy included profiling key black leaders from north-east Houston and determining their expected position on the Whispering Pines landfill. A sampling of the profiles that they created includes:

- Aaron Jackson: "Jackson is a member of the North Forest Independent School District and is considered by many to be the unofficial political boss in the Northeast area."
- Ernest McGowen: "City Councilman McGowen is considered effective by many Northside residents. He talks very *black*, but is inclined to go with the prevailing winds."
- Senfronia Thompson (state representative) and El Franco Lee (state representative): "Both of these state representative persons are strong in their own right. They will fight, if they feel the issue of 'landfill' will hurt re-election chances."
- Rev. C. L. Williams: "He is a powerful human rights conduit in that community and is considered to be on the cutting edge of the new political thrust within the Northeast community. His position on the landfill is soft."[26]

BFI hired the law firm of Fulbright and Jaworski to represent it in *Bean v. Southwestern Waste Management Corp.* As is customary in legal cases, Judge McDonald instructed both sides to explore a possible settlement. The settlement proposal offered by the plaintiffs' lawyer, which was supposed to be kept confidential, was given to City Councilman Ernest McGowen. Councilman McGowen went on the popular "Sunday Morning" radio show on the FM radio station Magic 102 and gave details of the confidential settlement proposal. The plaintiffs' lawyer brought this breach of confidentiality to the attention of the court. Judge

McDonald found BFI's attorney, Simeon Lake, in contempt of court and ordered him not to discuss with, or divulge to, the councilman any information related to the *Bean* case.

It also came to light that BFI had made a campaign contribution to Councilman McGowen's political action committee. When the councilman was asked about the contribution, his position was that the money was "an investment in good government." On the other hand, many Northwood Manor residents, who were fighting BFI's landfill, saw the contribution as "influence money." While it may have been legal for the councilman to take money from BFI, it did not sit well with the Northwood Manor residents who were asking all—including Houston's black elected officials—to form a united front against the landfill.

Houston's waste disposal facilities tended to be built in low-income people of color neighborhoods. Many of the low-income Houston neighborhoods inhabited by people of color in which waste disposal facilities were built were later designated as Community Development Block Grant neighborhoods, targeted to receive federal funds. The environmental stressors associated with waste disposal compound the myriad social ills found in these neighborhoods, such as crowding, crime, poverty, drugs, unemployment, congestion, and infrastructure deterioration.

Houston's waste facility siting was not mere classism. It was a case of slam-dunk, in-your-face environmental racism. Landfills attract garbage. They also attract illegal dumping on adjacent streets, lots, and wooded areas. Once a Houston neighborhood received a dump, it often became a dumping ground for all kinds of throwaways. In practice, black Houston neighborhoods became throwaway communities regarded as having fewer rights to environmental protection than their white counterparts.

Limited housing and residential options, combined with discriminatory facility-siting practices, contributed to the imposition of all types of toxins on African American neighborhoods. The builders of garbage landfills, incinerators, and transfer stations have generally followed the path of least resistance, which has led to placement of their facilities in economically poor and politically powerless communities.

Low-income African American communities are not the only victims of siting disparities and environmental discrimination, however. Middle-income African American communities are confronted with many of the same land-use disputes and environmental threats as their lower income counterparts. Increased income has enabled few African Americans to escape the threat of unwanted land uses and potentially harmful environmental pollutants. Racial segregation is the dominant residential pattern in America, and racial discrimination is the leading cause of segregated housing. Since affluent, middle-income, and poor African American Houstonians live in close proximity to one another, the question of environmental justice can hardly be reduced to a "poverty" issue. Among those making environmental and industrial land use decisions, African American communities, regardless of their class status, have been considered compatible with garbage dumps, transfer stations, incinerators, and other waste disposal facilities.

Although the 1979 *Bean* lawsuit did not prevail in court, it remains a watershed case because it was the first instance in U.S. history in which Americans challenged environmental racism using civil rights law. It was also a turning point for black Houston, which decided to end its role as the dumping grounds for other people's garbage.

3

Women Warriors of Color on the Front Line

W omen of color have been on the front lines of the environmental justice movement, doing groundbreaking work to make environmental justice a part of daily life. These leaders and thousands of other women of color are the unsung heroes of the environmental justice movement. Their work is beginning to receive international recognition. For example, Peggy Shepard, an African American who directs West Harlem Environmental Action, won the 2003 Heinz Award for the Environment. In 2004, Margie Richard of Concerned Citizens of Norco, Louisiana, became the first African American to win the prestigious Goldman Environmental Prize. And in October 2004, Wangari Maathai, an environmental justice activist from Kenya, became the first African woman to win the Nobel Peace Prize. Professor Maathai founded the Green Belt Movement, and, during the past thirty years, she has mobilized poor women to plant 30 million trees.[1]

We highlight here the indispensable role of women in planning the Second National People of Color Environmental Leadership Summit (Summit II), which took place in Washington, D.C., October 23 to 26, 2002. We offer selected voices of women of color who tell their stories of struggle and triumph.

WOMEN WARRIORS TAKE CONTROL

The four-day Summit II was held together by a few hardworking, fearless, and dedicated women of color.[2] Men were actively involved and played an important role in planning the meeting, but women were the ones who kept the complex event together. Women chaired Summit II and all but one of its key subcommittees, where the real work occurred. The First National People of Color Environmental Leadership Summit (Summit I), which had been planned primarily by men, took place in 1991. In just a decade, women made the second summit happen.

When Summit II needed a sponsor, Beverly Wright of the Deep South Center for Environmental Justice at Xavier University in New Orleans, who served as Summit II's chair (Wright became chair after several male cochairs resigned), went to Washington and secured the Reverends Adora Iris Lee and Bernice Powell Jackson of the United Church of Christ. The church, under the leadership of the Reverend Benjamin Chavis, sponsored Summit I in 1991. Wright also took on the responsibility of finding office space for Summit II in the nation's capital. She was able to cajole McKinney and Associates (a black, female-owned public relations firm) into renting space to house the national office. A little over a decade earlier, Gwen McKinney and her partners had served as the public relations firm for Summit I.

Under Wright's disciplined leadership, the Summit II planning team began to take shape. On the recommendation of Peggy Shepard, Summit II planners hired Zenaida Mendez, a New Yorker of Dominican extraction. Mendez proved to be an outstanding manager, organizer, and fundraiser. In fund-raising especially, Mendez proved to be a jewel.

The planners made a special effort to attract young people to the gathering. Summit I planners had been criticized for the meager participation by youth. Bhoupa Toumaly, a young Thai American, was hired as youth coordinator, and, under her capable leadership, young people were given a separate budget and encouraged to develop their own program priorities. Toumaly teamed with Torkwase Karame, a young female African American volunteer from Savannah, Georgia, to attract a record two hundred students and other young people to the meeting. Karame, who also served as a youth delegate on the executive committee, provided energy, youth perspectives, and insights from the hip-hop generation.

Mildred McClain of Citizens for Environmental Justice mentored the youth leaders, often using songs, prayer, and her uplifting personality to imbue the spirit of *harambe* (let's pull together) in closed-door sessions and open meetings. That McClain has a doctorate from Harvard is camouflaged by her grassroots community-based work, which focuses on federal facilities, such as military installations, and communities affected by radioactive waste, such as those near the U.S. Department of Energy's nuclear energy production site on the Savannah River.

Peggy Shepard chaired the program committee, along with Pam Tau Lee of the Asian Pacific Environmental Network and Beverly Wright. These three women, while managing their responsibilities to their families and nursing sick parents and friends, generated more than 120 workshop proposals. Several dozen of the proposed workshops and hands-on training sessions had to be merged. Women chaired, moderated, or presented in over half of the eventual 86 workshops and training sessions that emerged from the proposals.

Donele Wilkins, who heads Detroiters Working for Environmental Justice, chaired the Outreach Subcommittee. Under Donele's leadership, Summit II swelled from a meeting planned for only five hundred people to one with more than fourteen hundred attendees. Cipriana Jurado Herrera, who chaired the International Subcommittee, directs the nonprofit Center for Worker Research and Solidarity based in Ciudad Juárez, Mexico. She added an international focus to the outreach. Herrera has worked on issues concerning environmental and economic justice, worker rights, and women's rights on both sides of the Mexico-U.S. border. Although six months pregnant, she made her way from Mexico to attend Summit II. Other international delegates came from more than a dozen foreign countries throughout North, Central, and South America, the Pacific Islands, Asia, and Africa.

A year earlier, some Summit II planners had considered an estimate of five hundred participants to be overly ambitious. They were dead wrong. The bandwagon effect kicked in as Summit II drew closer and as it became apparent that no roadblocks would deter these women from making Summit II a reality. Maintaining a laser focus and a no-nonsense work ethic proved to be an unstoppable strategy for these women warriors.

Summit II made a special effort to honor women leaders in the movement at the Crowning Women Awards Dinner. Honorees included Charon Asetoyer of the Native American Women's Health Education Resource Center; Rose Augustine of Tucsonians for a Clean Environment; Dolly Burwell of Concerned Citizens of Warren County; Faye

Bush of the Newtown Florist Club; Mayor Emma R. Gresham of Keysville, Georgia; Hazel Johnson of People for Community Recovery; Pam Tau Lee of the Asian Pacific Environmental Network; Alicia Marentes of the Farm Worker Network for Economic and Environmental Justice; Margie Richard of Concerned Citizens of Norco; Gloria Weaver Roberts and Emelda West of St. James Citizens for Jobs and the Environment; Peggy Shepard of West Harlem Environmental Action; and Margaret Williams of Citizens against Nuclear Waste.[3]

The event honoring women was the brainchild of Beverly Wright. She made it clear to all that the awards dinner was going to happen even if no other food was to be served at Summit II. Some people took this as a joke, but those of us who know Wright knew it was no joke or idle threat. Because of limited funds for refreshments—the bulk of the money raised was allocated to getting grassroots delegates to the meeting—the Reverend Adora Lee related to us a nightmare she had had about "food fights." There were no food fights, and the long-overdue Crowning Women Awards Dinner proved to be the highlight of the international gathering.

The leadership displayed by Cipriana Jurado Herrera, Bernice Powell Jackson, Torkwase Karame, Adora Iris Lee, Pam Tau Lee, Mildred McClain, Zenaida Mendez, Peggy Shepard, Bhoupa Toumaly, Donele Wilkins, and Beverly Wright demonstrates that, without these women and others like them, we likely would not have an environmental justice movement today.

WOMEN SPEAKING FOR THEMSELVES

The following vignettes concerning women on the front line tell a lot about the environmental justice movement and its future. Their stories provide insights into the on-the-ground struggle for basic human rights, environmental and economic justice, and sustainability.[4] It is important that these women's stories be told in their own words, in keeping with the environmental justice principle that demands that people be allowed to speak for themselves. The late Dana Alston knew this in 1990 when she edited the book *We Speak for Ourselves: Social Justice, Race, and Environment*.[5] The same holds true today.

The voices of these environmental leaders must be heard and respected. These women represent the heart and soul of the modern environmental justice movement and provide a vision for environmentalism in the new millennium.

MARGARET WILLIAMS: RELOCATION FROM "MOUNT DIOXIN"

I am a retired Pensacola, Florida, schoolteacher. For the past five years my community has been involved in a campaign to relocate our residents away from the environmental and health hazards posed by the nation's third-largest Superfund site, the former location of a private wood-treating company in Escambia County. The site is located in a mixed industrial and residential area in north central Pensacola, Florida. In the past six years, in my community of only 358 families, some fifty people have died of cancer. This has been a good community in which to live, but we've paid a terrible price.[6]

The Escambia Treating Company operated from 1943 to 1982, using creosote and pentachlorophenol to treat wood for use as utility poles and foundation pilings. Few environmental precautions were taken. Wastes were placed in an unlined landfill, in an unlined containment pond, and in unlabeled drums. Former workers have told us that the treatment cylinders (pressure cookers used to saturate the wood with pentachlorophenol) would sometimes fly open, releasing hundreds of gallons of toxic solution. They have told of being sent to pump out creosote and pentachlorophenol that had pooled in yards north of the plant after heavy rains flooded the waste ponds and to distribute sand over the contaminated areas.

The U.S. Environmental Protection Agency (EPA) data confirms that dangerous amounts of dioxin have migrated into some residents' yards. The elevation of the wood-treating site is more than sixty feet above much of downtown Pensacola. During the plant's operation, storm runoff often carried contaminants well beyond the residential neighborhoods closest to the plant.

After the plant ceased operations in 1982, it was abandoned and left in disarray. Leaking drums, a lab full of broken equipment and open containers, an overturned electrical transformer, and crumbling asbestos insulation wrapped around a boiler littered the site. The company also left behind soil, sludge, and groundwater contamination from forty years of wood-preserving activities. By the mid-1980s, the extent of the contamination had become obvious and the company underwent bankruptcy proceedings in 1991.

The Escambia site was dubbed "Mount Dioxin" because of the sixty-foot-high mound of contaminated soil that the EPA dug up from the neighborhood. The contaminated mountain of dirt was covered with black plastic wrap. The L-shaped mound holds 255,000 cubic yards of soil contaminated with dioxins, one of the most dangerous compounds ever made.

Citizens against Toxic Exposure (CATE), a neighborhood organization formed in order to fight for funds to pay for residents' relocation, battled with EPA officials over the relocation plan. CATE demanded the relocation of all residents in the affected neighborhood. The EPA had first proposed to move only the 66 households most affected by the site. After prodding by CATE, the agency then added 35 more households, bring relocation costs to a total of $7.54 million. However, this plan would have left out some 257 households, including those in an apartment complex. CATE refused to accept any relocation plan unless everyone was moved. A partial relocation plan would have been tantamount to partial justice. CATE took its campaign on the road to the EPA's National Environmental Justice Advisory Council.

CATE was successful in getting the council's Waste Subcommittee to hold a Superfund Relocation Roundtable in Pensacola in May 1995. At this meeting, CATE's plan for total neighborhood relocation won the backing of more than one hundred grassroots organizations. The EPA designated the Escambia site as the focus of the agency's pilot program, one that would help the agency develop a nationally consistent relocation policy. The policy would be designed to consider not only toxic levels but also welfare issues such as residents' property values, quality of life, health, and safety.

On October 3, 1996, EPA officials agreed to move all 358 households from the contaminated site, at an estimated cost of $18 million. EPA officials deemed the mass relocation as "cost-efficient" after city planners decided to redevelop the area for light industry rather than clean the site to residential standards. This decision marked the first time that an African American community was relocated under the EPA's giant Superfund program. It was hailed as a landmark victory for environmental justice.

By November 1999, some families had successfully negotiated purchase prices for their property and moved into homes in uncontaminated neighborhoods. Many, however, felt pressured to accept inadequate compensation for their homes and to settle for shabby or even unsafe replacement homes. The EPA had hired contractors to appraise the homes, and it had agreed to discount the presence of the Escambia Treating Company site in the appraisals. However, the EPA refused to tell owners the appraised values of their homes, and refused to tell homeowners who had not yet sold their homes the prices paid for their neighbors' homes. Low buyout offers indicated that the neighborhood's industrial setting, nearby sources of pollution, and racial segregation affected the valuations.

Homeowners who had already moved for health reasons were financially penalized. Moreover, lack of upkeep for contaminated—therefore noncreditworthy—homes by (often ill) owners was unfairly reflected in buyout offers that should have covered replacement housing. CATE was eager to see the relocation process completed, but the group was also determined to make sure that residents received enough to acquire equivalent homes without financial loss. CATE prevented the cleanup from proceeding until all were relocated and until the group was certain that the remediation procedures protected public health from all possible routes of exposure. In particular, the condition of the cover on "Mount Dioxin" was of critical concern, not only for those in the relocation neighborhood but also for the rest of Pensacola.

The Escambia relocation, completed in 2001, was the third-largest relocation of people from a Superfund site in U.S. history. The abandoned homes were finally demolished in November 2003. The $146,000 demolition project was funded by the Escambia County Commission and the city of Pensacola, with assistance from the U.S. Army Corps of Engineers, the EPA, and the Florida Department of Environmental Protection.[7]

CATE will continue to be actively involved in the Escambia Treating Company cleanup site. The cleanup process is profoundly important to area surface water and drinking water sources. CATE will also continue seeking health care for exposed residents, especially preventive care.

EMELDA WEST: ST. JAMES CITIZENS DEFEAT SHINTECH

I am a seventy-nine-year-old great-grandmother, environmental activist, and longtime resident of Convent, Louisiana. My home, community, and environment are under siege from industrial polluters who have turned the eighty-five-mile stretch along the Lower Mississippi River into a toxic wasteland. From my home in Convent, located on the winding Mississippi River Road, I have witnessed my community undergo a transformation: from one made up primarily of sugar cane plantations to one heavily dominated, and devastated, by the petrochemical industry.

Convent is an unincorporated community in St. James Parish. More than 80 percent of Convent residents are African Americans. Over two thousand people live here. The community gets its name from the Convent

of Sacred Heart, a Catholic school for the daughters of plantation owners that existed in the 1800s. St. James Parish was established on March 31, 1807, and was one of the first nineteen parishes in the state. During the 1800s, the chief economic source in St. James was agriculture developed by slave labor. Today, only a few sugar cane fields remain, and the sites of many of the old plantations are now occupied by industrial facilities. The plantation system has been replaced with one of industrial plants.

St. James Parish is located in the center of Louisiana's infamous "Cancer Alley," an area along the Mississippi River that stretches from Baton Rouge to New Orleans. Over the years, dozens of companies have moved into my community while promising jobs to local residents. Many of my neighbors could actually walk to work, because the plants are so close to their homes. However, few community African American residents are actually hired. The community has an extremely high unemployment rate. The average annual income of local residents is only $6,000. Over 40 percent of the population of Convent lives below the poverty line.[8]

In 2002, more than 160 industrial facilities in the twelve-parish Cancer Alley area accounted for 62 percent of all the toxic pollution produced in the state, which totaled 209,339,389 pounds annually.[9] Eight industrial facilities in St. James Parish released or transferred more than 6.1 million pounds of toxics. Over 60 percent of the toxic pollution in St. James Parish comes from four facilities. These facilities are some of the biggest polluters in the parish, and all operate within three miles of Convent residents: IMC-Agrico-Faustina, IMC-Agrico-Uncle Sam, Star Enterprise (now Motiva), and Chevron Chemical. On the northern border of St. James Parish is Ascension Parish, the parish with the highest release of toxic pollution in the state (23.8 million pounds annually).

Today, the Mississippi River is so polluted that the fish are not safe to eat. Although our drinking water comes from the Mississippi River, residents who can afford to buy bottled water and install filters do so. However, this added expense places a hardship on the region's low-income residents. Industrial pollution has also kept many of us from gathering fruits and planting vegetable gardens. These losses have created more poverty, because, in a community with high unemployment, we are now forced to rely solely on wage income.

In addition to dealing with toxic pollution released every day, we have no protection against chemical accidents. There are thirty-six residential streets in Convent that are within three miles of six industrial plants. All these streets are dead-end streets. Evacuation is a problem because there is usually only one way in and one way out, and the streets are poorly paved and not much wider than a vehicle. The streets are so narrow that several trailer homes have burned because the fire trucks were too wide for the streets and could not be driven to the trailer homes. In addition, the fire department is staffed by volunteers. Volunteers have to leave their jobs in order to respond to an emergency.

We are very concerned about the children who attend our two elementary schools, Romeville Elementary School and Fifth Ward Elementary. Romeville is less than a mile away from the Zen-Noh Grain Corporation's grain elevator, and both schools are within three miles of most of the largest industrial polluters in the parish. Each school has more than three hundred students, most of whom are African American. School buses pass by several plants twice a day. Our children, who live and go to school in Convent, are exposed daily to grain-dust pollution, which poses a health hazard to nearby residents, especially individuals with asthma and other respiratory diseases. They are also threatened by the risk of a chemical accident.

St. James Citizens for Jobs and the Environment was formed in the home of Clifford Roberts and Gloria Weaver Roberts in September 1996. Before the organization was formed, I received a phone call from Pat Melancon informing me that the Shintech Corporation, the U.S. subsidiary of a Japanese multinational, had proposed to purchase the last three plantations in Convent (Wilton, St. Rose, and Helvetia) consisting of 3,500 acres. The land was needed for the proposed $700-million Shintech complex, which would manufacture polyvinyl chloride plastics. The addition of this complex would contribute six hundred thousand additional pounds of airborne toxins to the area annually and discharge over 8 million gallons of wastewater into the Mississippi River daily.

The grassroots struggle against Shintech began with a community organization made up of working-poor residents from Convent, a town in the industrially devastated St. James Parish. The parish residents, mainly African Americans, decided to use the courts to block the Shintech Corporation from constructing the plant in their community. Polyvinyl chloride is associated with the production of dioxin, considered one of the most lethal synthetic chemicals known.

I joined the struggle against the Japanese company because environmental justice in Convent was long overdue. The Shintech struggle was an environmental justice case because African Americans and poor people in Convent would be disproportionately affected by the plant siting. The confrontation between the community and Shintech took on an added dimension when Louisiana's Governor Murphy J. "Mike" Foster became involved. The governor criticized the community's efforts to block Shintech and claimed that they were undermining his administration's efforts to bring economic development to poor communities in the state.

The community argued that, despite the governor's good intentions, they did not want the pollution. They also pointed to the fact that they were not given a guarantee that St. James residents would be used to fill those jobs. The residents cited previous industrial development efforts that had not resulted in jobs for the local community. The governor expressed his determination to see the Shintech project go through. The St. James residents, unable to afford private legal counsel, sought the services of Tulane University's Environmental Law Clinic, the only environmental law clinic in the state and one of only two in the South.

Local residents concentrated their efforts on addressing environmental racism. Since the mid-1980s, environmental and civil rights activists have charged that polluting industries have deliberately selected poor communities of color for their operations. The lower Mississippi River corridor (between Baton Rouge and New Orleans) is home to a heavy concentration of industrial waste dump sites, chemical factories, sanitary landfills, industrial waste incinerators, grain elevators, and a host of other hazards.

President Bill Clinton issued Executive Order 12898 in 1994 to ensure that low-income and minority communities are not disproportionately and adversely affected by environmental pollution. The Shintech case was a litmus test for the Clinton administration's policy. It indicated to the nation how strenuously the administration intended to enforce its ban on environmental racism. The relentless community pressure forced the EPA to conduct its own equity analysis. The community, however, did not rely on the government for its information. Professor Beverly Wright of the Deep South Center for Environmental Justice at Xavier University conducted an independent study for Convent residents.

The heroes of the struggle are individual leaders who live in communities in Cancer Alley. They stood with us and never gave up. These leaders included black and white residents working together. Community activists such as Pat Melancon, Dee Simmons, Gloria Roberts, and Amos Favorite kept the issue on the community's radar. We also had assistance from attorneys and environmental advocates such as Bob Kuehn of Tulane and Mary Lee Orr of Louisiana Environmental Action Now. We were able to galvanize the support of a national environmental organization (Greenpeace), a civil rights organization (the Commission for

Racial Justice), entertainers (Bonnie Raitt, Danny Glover, Aaron Neville, and Stevie Wonder), and a political organization (the Congressional Black Caucus) in our struggle against Shintech.

In June of 1998, after ongoing pressure by the Louisiana Association of Business and Industry, the state Supreme Court, which regulates the state's university law clinics, issued a highly controversial ruling seen as undermining the legal rights of working poor people in the state. The court ruled that university law clinics were now barred from representing any community organization unless 51 percent of its members were indigent (that is, they made less than $16,000 per year for a family of four). The law clinics were also barred from providing representation if the community organization happened to be affiliated with a national organization.

Since most community organizations are not made up of a majority of indigent families, this ruling makes it difficult, if not impossible, for the working poor to obtain lawyers to defend themselves. In effect, this ruling blocks their access to the legal system. A huge outcry condemning the decision was heard across the state from public interest lawyers and civil rights and environmental activists, as well as from a variety of journalists and politicians. The decision was compared in the press to similar decisions made during the early civil rights era, decisions that blocked the NAACP from bringing civil rights cases to court.

In Louisiana, as around the country, seeking help from university law clinics is among the most common ways for working poor people to obtain legal representation. The student lawyers in these clinics, under the careful supervision of their law professors, represent persons and community organizations that otherwise would not be able to afford attorneys. Because the cases they bring have the potential to drag on for years, hiring private attorneys would cost tens of thousands of dollars, if not hundreds of thousands. Legal clinics have become essential to working poor people who want to defend their rights in court. They are now an essential component of American democracy, because they safeguard and enhance the principle of equal protection under law.

In spite of the court's decision, the St. James Citizens for Jobs and the Environment continued the fight. In June 1998, a three-member delegation—two Louisiana residents (I was one of the delegates) and a Greenpeace representative—visited the Shintech headquarters in Tokyo to submit protest documents. We accused the Shin-Etsu Chemical Company, Shintech's parent company, of environmental racism. We argued that the industrial complex would pose a health hazard, exacerbating damage to an already overly polluted region. The group filed a Title VI administrative complaint with the EPA against the company.

On September 18, 1998, just under three years after its initial announcement, Shintech withdrew its plan to build the polyvinyl chloride plastics plant in St. James Parish. This was a major victory for the citizens and the environmental justice movement. Environmental justice activists vowed to continue the fight to keep the plastics industry from expanding in Louisiana.

SUSANA R. ALMANZA AND SYLVIA HERRERA: THE COLOR PURPLE AND LAND USE POLITICS IN EAST AUSTIN

We are the cofounders of People Organized in Defense of Earth and Her Resources (PODER), and we live in East Austin, a neighborhood in Austin, Texas. The group was formed in May 1991 by Chicana and Chicano activists and community leaders living in East Austin. The goal of the group is to increase East Austin residents' participation in corporate and governmental decisions related to economic development, environmental hazards, and their effects on our neighborhoods. PODER has helped form neighborhood associations and coalitions to address injustices in our neighborhoods.

Janie Rangel, a member of the Gardens Neighborhood Association, lives with the daily indignity of residing next to a trash-recycling facility, which handles materials that come from over 350,000 Austin residents. Josephine Zamarripa, a member of the Brooke Neighborhood Association, lives across the street from a warehouse that is sandwiched into a residential area and that brings eighteen-wheelers into a designated school zone. Fidelina Rivera can step out into her yard and smell odors coming from a nearby tank farm (a gasoline storage tank facility). Robert Donley has to live with the noisy, polluting Holly Power Plant adjacent to his neighborhood. Nola Chase lives with the odors coming from the city's garbage truck facility.

These neighborhoods have one thing in common—the color purple, which the city of Austin uses to designate industrial zoning. East Austin has more than its fair share of zoning for industrial uses. Although Austin has been promoted as a liberal city, it is, like other cities with segregated communities, plagued with a variety of social, economic, and environmental problems. Many of these problems disproportionately affect low-income people and people of color.

Austin completed its city plan in 1928. This plan, which has been the primary guide to the city's growth, indicates why people in East Austin—primarily African Americans and Latinos—live next to hazardous industries. The plan designated East Austin as a "Negro district" in order to solve what was called "the race segregation problem." East Austin was singled out to be the site of the industrial district, as well as the location of homes, schools, and parks for people of color. The 1928 plan became the blueprint for Austin's first zoning map, issued in 1931, and it designated East Austin as the dumping ground for hazardous industries.

Since PODER was formed, it has worked with many other community groups and residents to address various zoning, permitting, environmental, and economic issues affecting East Austin. These include revisions of the city's enterprise zone–tax abatement ordinance, relocation of the tank farm, closure of the city's garbage truck facility on Hargrave Street, and the closure and relocation of the Robert Mueller Municipal Airport. The group fought against the proposed establishment of a high-tech corridor adjacent to the Montopolis community and against the permitting of the Balcones Recycling plant in the Hidalgo neighborhood. It supported relocation of the Browning Ferris Industries recycling plant, closure of the Holly Power Plant, and development of a long-term solution to the industrial zoning problem in East Austin. It is clear that the core causes of these injustices in East Austin are discriminatory land use and economic development policies.

In November 1996, various East Austin community groups and neighborhood associations formed El Pueblo Network (the People's Network) to change racist land policies that have plagued East Austin. El Pueblo met with the members of the city of Austin's environmental board, planning commission, and city council to address overdue zoning changes.

As a result, on December 12, 1996, the Austin City Council made two major landmark decisions. First, it passed an ordinance prohibiting acceptance of Commercial General Services (CS) or Commercial Liquor Sales (CS-1) zoning designations within the East Austin area (bounded by I-35 on the west, by Airport Boulevard on the east and north, and by Town Lake on the south). Second, it directed the city manager to undertake a land use study of the area.

PODER, by means of El Pueblo Network, worked with city officials to establish a process by which to down-zone industrial sites in East Austin. PODER and El Pueblo scored a big victory when the city council voted on July 17, 1997, to place a conditional overlay (a set of special development considerations adopted by the local planning commission, added to the existing ordinance's land use regulations) on selected industrial and commercial lots in East Austin that were part of the land use study. This overlay is called the East Austin Overlay Combining District Ordinance. For the first time, East Austin neighborhood residents, registered neighborhood associations, and community groups must be notified any time certain industrial and commercial facilities seek to locate or expand their operations in East Austin. Residents now have a right to a public hearing process.

Even though the East Austin Overlay was a major victory for the community, the residents realized that many other facilities were not covered under the ordinance and that amendments were needed. On April 15, 1999, at the urging of PODER and other community groups, the city council approved a moratorium in East Austin on all site development permits, building permits, and other site plan exemptions until May 31, 1999, in order to amend the East Austin Overlay Combining District Ordinance.

On May 31, 1999, East Austin experienced another victory that opened doors to a process and privilege that many Austin residents west of I-35 have always enjoyed. The East Austin Overlay was amended to include additional commercial, industrial, and civic land uses as "conditional uses." A "conditional use" is a land use not approved administratively by city staff, but that is allowed on a discretionary and conditional basis by the planning commission or, if appealed, the city council. A public hearing must be held and a notice of the hearing sent to registered neighborhood associations and property owners within three hundred feet of the property.

More important, because of the overlay, developers are realizing that they must invite area residents and community groups to sit at the table if they want to build or expand their businesses in East Austin. Residents are using the overlay to regulate unwanted land uses in their neighborhood. East Austin residents are now beginning to enjoy a quality of life never experienced before the changing of the color purple.

GAIL SMALL: VOICES FROM NORTHERN CHEYENNE INDIAN COUNTRY

I am a member of the Northern Cheyenne tribe. I am an environmental attorney, an activist, and the founder of Native Action, one of the few grassroots environmental groups based on a reservation. The five-hundred-thousand-acre Northern Cheyenne reservation is located in the beautiful ponderosa pine country of southeastern Montana. Our reservation is rapidly being surrounded by the largest coal strip mines in this country.

Founded in 1984, Native Action has been at the forefront in fighting for environmental and economic justice for Northern Cheyenne. I have been involved in the fight to protect our reservation and southeastern Montana from coal mining since the 1970s, when I was in high school. It was then that the Cheyenne learned the horrifying news that the U.S. Bureau of Indian Affairs had leased over half of our reservation for strip mining, at the paltry rate of seventeen cents per ton, with no environmental safeguards included in the leases.

I was one of several young Cheyenne sent by the tribe to investigate coal mines in Navaho country and Wyoming. After college, I served on the tribal committee charged with voiding the leases—the only member with a college degree. It took almost fifteen years of sacrifice by the people before the Northern Cheyenne convinced Congress to void the coal leases.

The Northern Cheyenne are not the only Indians who face such problems. Tribes across the country find their lands aggressively sought after for their energy resources and for use as dumping grounds for America's waste. Indian tribes own over a third of the low-sulfur coal west of the Mississippi River, as much as half of the privately owned uranium in the country, and sizable reserves of oil, natural gas, and oil shale. The instability and depletion of world energy supplies—along with the 1990 Clean Air Act Amendments, which favor low-sulfur coal—have prompted the increase in pressure exerted by companies who want to mine these reserves.

As self-governing entities, tribes have the legal authority for environmental regulation and enforcement of tribal environmental laws; they also have the proprietary and police powers necessary for environmental protection. Why, then, is it so difficult for Indian tribes to protect their environments? One reason is that, as the Northern Cheyenne found when we fought the coal leases in court during the 1970s and 1980s, it is extremely difficult for Indian tribes to sue our federal trustees for breach of trust. Moreover, there has been only token federal assistance to tribes to develop the infrastructure necessary for environmental protection.

In 1977, for example, my tribe petitioned the EPA for the right to designate our air quality as Class I, as among the cleanest in the country, and to adopt the most stringent air quality standards. The Northern Cheyenne tribe was the first government entity to take this step, but we had to lead the EPA by the hand for more than ten years before it acknowledged that we were a government, one with the right to funding and enforcement authority under the Clean Air Act. Almost twenty years later, the Northern Cheyenne are still fighting this battle.

My tribe has refused extravagant offers from the coal companies and has directed every resource we have to the legal battles against coal mining on nearby lands. The people have forgone indoor plumbing, roads, and schools for the sake of the environmental integrity of this region. The elderly man who lives next door to my office must use an outhouse, and as I write, the temperature here is twenty degrees below zero.

Many younger Cheyenne regard the EPA's failure to fund tribal environmental protection as institutional racism. We have also seen such racism in white environmental organizations, which failed to respond to our calls for help in fighting mining in the region—even though the mines are destroying pristine wilderness on federal lands. It was my idea to make these requests to the environmental groups, and when they went unanswered, our tribal president told me I was young and naïve, and that I had to learn to live with the fact that we have few allies. And indeed, it has been my experience that most Americans would rather fight for a rain forest five thousand miles away than join the battle being waged by native peoples right here in their own backyards.

Indians believe in the spiritual nature of the environment. The federal agencies charged with helping us protect our physical surroundings cannot do so unless they understand the interdependence of environment, culture, and religion in the tribal way of life. When I worked as a tribal sociologist some years ago, I once took a draft tribal water code to the five villages of my reservation for public input. I found that protection of water spirits was a preeminent concern throughout the reservation and that the identity of the spirits varied, depending on whether the water source was a river, lake, or spring. I reported my findings to the attorneys who had been contracted by the U.S. government to draw up the code, and they laughed at my findings.

But it was no laughing matter a few years later, when an elderly Cheyenne man with a rifle held off an ARCO drilling team that had planned to lay lines of dynamite across his spring. This archaic practice was no longer being used in most drilling operations outside Indian reservations. "Today is a good day to die," he said, holding his hunting rifle before him. I represented him in tribal court the next morning, seeking a restraining order against ARCO. And I cried with him as he told me how the water spirits sometimes came out and danced at his spring. Eventually, we saved the spring.

As I write this, the coal fight is beginning again on my reservation, as it has every year for the past three decades. Another coal contract is before the tribal council; the coal company is promising to make every Cheyenne a millionaire, and some are arguing that we must cut off the toe to save the body—that we should lease a small part of the reservation, because we need the white man's money in order to give our children a way out of poverty.

Native Action has been busy exploring strategies to improve environmental and economic conditions on the reservation. In December 1991, for example, the Board of Governors of the Federal Reserve System shocked the banking industry by denying an interstate bank merger application based solely on an appeal filed by Native Action under the Community Reinvestment Act. On September 18, 1992, Native Action was able to negotiate a precedent-setting agreement with First Interstate Bank under the Community Reinvestment Act. The bank agreed to a $4-million lending goal over five years. The objective of the lending goal was to stimulate the local reservation economy and to provide a tool for evaluation. The bank also agreed to appoint a Cheyenne to its board of directors; install an automated teller machine in Lame Deer; hold frequent liaison meetings; offer technical assistance; and make a commitment to hiring and training qualified tribal members for banking positions, including management positions.

Twenty months after the agreement went into practice, it was evaluated, and we were excited to learn that, during this time, First Interstate Bank had loaned approximately $3.9 million to residents of the Northern Cheyenne Reservation. About $2 million of this money was loaned to young people working to establish ranches and farms on our reservation. Before the agreement, a total of less than half a million dollars had ever been loaned, by all banks, to members of the reservation.

Native Action also began drafting tribal codes and statutes to implement our community-organizing work. In 1993, a model Plains Indian Water Code was successfully drafted and disseminated to Indian tribes in the Northern Great Plains. Native Action is also working to inform the public about the Toxic and Solid Waste Code, Tribal Facilities Siting Act, Tribal Environmental Policy Act, Tribal Surface Mining and Reclamation Act, and Tribal Culture Preservation Act.

So far, the work of Native Action has paid off. There are no coal mines on my reservation yet, and no coal leases have been signed. But every year the mines on nearby lands come closer. Like many Cheyenne, I feel as if I have already lived a lifetime of fighting strip mining. We live in fear, anger, and urgency. And we long for a better life for our tribe. I've been told that if we mined our coal, we'd be millionaires. We want to keep our homeland, to keep it intact.[10]

CASSANDRA ROBERTS: COMBATING "TOXIC TERROR" IN ANNISTON, ALABAMA

I have lived in the Sweet Valley–Cobb Town neighborhood for forty-four years, practically all of my life. This community was always filled with plenty of houses, open space, and gardens. My father raised fruit trees. This was a real neighborhood, where people cared about each other. Everybody knew each other. Over the years, the community started to deteriorate. People started moving out. The community has a bad flooding problem. The houses started to deteriorate because the community was in such a bad flood area. We didn't know why they were deteriorating. People just started moving out. We hadn't figured out why houses were deteriorating. I know now that, in the area where the contamination was coming in, that's the reason why.

The majority of the houses flooded. My house didn't. My father built the house that I lived in higher than the other houses in the area. Only a few of the houses didn't flood. Sometimes people couldn't go out of their houses for two or three days, until the water and mud went down. Then we'd all get together in the community and help clean the mud out of the houses when the water went down.[11]

My neighborhood is not a neighborhood anymore, because Monsanto bought the community out. They bought all the property in the area. People are scattered. Our neighborhood is dead. Toxic contamination killed my community. My community was mostly African American. The neighborhood that I lived in was one of the first communities contaminated. It's the only community that Monsanto acknowledged was contaminated.

I've done some research on the history of Monsanto in the area. Monsanto moved in while my parents were still there. One of the elderly people in the neighborhood spoke about the community when the company first moved in. She spoke about how her father and grandfather cleaned out the property for Monsanto to move in. They used to play softball on the property where Monsanto is now. It is a racial issue. There is a white community that sits right behind Monsanto, a poor white community. Monsanto bought some of the white families out when I was a little child. They got the whites out early. This place is dangerous. I remember hearing explosions. The area also smelled bad, like rotten eggs. It was a shame when we'd have company over to our house. People would ask, "What's that smell?" The smell was worse for us because we were closest to it.

You would have to live here to know the problem. When it rains, it floods. Monsanto sits across the street. When it rained, floodwater would come into our community, and we would have to get out in the yard and clean out all the debris. We would have paper and cans. We had everybody's trash. Sometimes they'd have to get boats to get people out of their houses.

I had gotten married and moved from the area. I owned property near Monsanto that my mother had given my husband and me as a wedding present. Monsanto wrote us a letter. The letter asked our permission to test our property for PCBs, and they said that they would give us the results. When the testing was completed, they called a meeting with residents, which was held at one of the local community churches. When they called this meeting they said there was a small amount of PCBs in the area, and that's when they offered a buyout.

It was our option to take the buyout or stay in the community. We were told that it was just a small amount of contamination. I was curious, and I asked the plant manager how much PCB was found on my property, and they wouldn't tell me. I was told that I had to call a telephone number to get the information. But when I called the number, I still couldn't get any information. It was like a bell went off in my head. I thought that something was not right about this. It was around October 2001 that they brought the information to us, and it was around Christmastime that people started to sell their property. I tried to express to them that they should not take the first offer without negotiating for the best deal possible, but a lot of people needed the money and they wanted to get out of the area.

My father was exposed to a lot of contaminants because he built houses in the area and dug foundations for them. After several community health surveys, we learned that there were a lot of kidney failures. We've had five kidney transplants among residents of this neighborhood in the past five years. We've also had a lot of liver disease and cancer in the neighborhood. One of the young children was diagnosed with leukemia when she was thirteen, and she died when she was sixteen. We had another child who was also diagnosed with leukemia. All sorts of diseases were reported on the health survey. Kidney disease was particularly bad. We had a lot of heart attacks here too. We don't know all the health impacts of PCBs, but we do know that this stuff is not making us any healthier.

I have never been the type to protest or demonstrate. I pretty much attended to my own business. But after seeing the danger that my mother was in because she was still living there, I felt like I had to fight it. I felt like I had to fight it because the company was too bold about it. I felt that Monsanto was not being honest with the people. After people started selling houses, the company began tearing them down. Then the Southern Organizing Committee came in.

We had no idea what PCBs would do to you. When Monsanto had its meeting, they didn't tell us about the effects of PCBs. When the Southern Organizing Committee came in, they brought brochures. They brought a scientist and lawyers to explain what PCBs could cause. That's when I felt that I had to fight them, because of what they were offering people for their homes. I wanted my mother to move, but she is over sixty years old and was on a fixed income. She couldn't move because she had no money for paying a mortgage on a new place. I knew that she couldn't stay there, though, because of the contamination, and because the house was falling apart. By that time it was well publicized that the community was contaminated, and she couldn't get money to repair it. My main reason was to get her out of harm's way.

Before the Southern Organizing Committee came in, I didn't know anything about environmental issues or task forces. But when the committee came in, they told us what we needed to do. And that's what we did. We organized the night that they came in and brought all the lawyers. We had about ten community people there to talk to them, so we could find out about the PCBs. We organized that night. The people at this meeting became our official board.

I didn't know that we could win. I just felt like I could make them move my mother and others like her. When we started dealing with lawyers, I learned that we could file a lawsuit and possibly win some money. I was mainly trying to get my mother and other people out of the community to keep them from continuing to be exposed. We finally got my mother and others out of the area, and Monsanto ended up giving them more money than those who had already moved. They moved my mother and others into temporary housing for two or three years until they found the houses that they wanted. Monsanto paid all of their bills. After the testing, and before the lawsuit, Monsanto was calling my mother's house every day asking if we wanted to sell. My mother was too old to deal with this. I had to do something. I was the only one there. It fell on my shoulders. Who wouldn't fight a company to save one's mother?

We went to trial for two weeks in federal court. After two weeks, Monsanto decided to throw in the towel.[12]

We had tried to negotiate with them for three months prior to trial, but they had refused. The judge ordered them to settle, but they refused. They settled after two weeks of testimony—expert testimony, because we only had one community person who had a chance to testify. It was a holiday weekend, and I was due to testify on Monday. They settled on the Saturday before I was scheduled to give my testimony. The community had picked five people to work on the settlement for the community. We also had very good lawyers who, along with the committee, kept the community abreast of developments with the litigation and settlement process.

I wish that we had not settled. I wanted to take the case to a jury. One thing that I had to consider, though, was the importance of getting the older people out of the community. It wasn't just my decision to settle. Everything was taken back to the community for a decision to be made on the settlement. The lawyers called a community meeting of all the clients that they had, before anything could be approved. If it had been up to me, we would not have settled.

I think that this buyout and relocation part was the best thing that Monsanto did. As far as the settlement, they couldn't have given us enough money. I would have liked to see more done for the community. Nobody expected we could have gotten this far. Our win is a victory for environmental justice. No amount of money can repair the damage caused by exposure of generations to toxic chemicals, but we are happy to get some compensation.[13]

MARGIE EUGENE RICHARD: TAKING OUR HUMAN RIGHTS STRUGGLE TO GENEVA

I am the president of Concerned Citizens of Norco. My hometown is located in the southeastern section of Louisiana along the Mississippi River. In 1926 the Royal Dutch/Shell Group purchased 460 acres of the town called Sellers and began building its oil refinery. When Shell purchased the town of Sellers, which is now Norco, they displaced African American families from one section to another.

We are now surrounded by twenty-seven petrochemical and oil refineries, refineries like the one from which Norco received its name: Norco is an acronym for New Orleans Refinery Company. Our town is approximately one mile in diameter and is home to five thousand residents. The four streets near the Shell plants are occupied by African

Americans; these streets are Washington, Cathy, Diamond, and East. My house is located on Washington Street and is only twenty-five feet away from the fence line of the fifteen-acre Shell chemical plant that expanded in 1955. Norco is situated between Shell's refinery on the east and Shell's chemical plant on the west. The entire town of Norco is only half the size of the oil refinery and chemical plant combined.

Nearly everyone in the community suffers from health problems caused by industry pollution. The air is contaminated with bad odors from carcinogens, and toxic chemicals such as benzene, toluene, sulfuric acid, ammonia, xylene, and propylene.

My sister died at the age of forty-three from an allergenic disease called sarcoidosis. This disease affects one in one thousand people in the United States, yet in Norco there are at least five known cases in fewer than five hundred people of color. My youngest daughter and her son suffer from severe asthma; my mother has breathing problems and must use a breathing machine daily. Many of the residents suffer from chronically sore muscles and cardiovascular, liver, and kidney diseases. Many die prematurely from poor health caused by pollution from toxic chemicals.

Please indulge me while I share with you a few stories that express some of our fears, because these tragedies can happen at any moment, without notice. In 1973, a Shell pipeline exploded, killing Helen Washington and Joseph Jones. Washington was inside her home asleep and her neighbor, Jones, was cutting grass in his backyard; they both died from burns sustained from the explosion.[14]

In 1988, an explosion at the Shell oil refinery created a nightmare. Houses collapsed. Afterward, people suffered from numerous health problems. The Shell explosion affected people up to thirty-seven miles away. In 1994, the oil refinery had a major acid spill. On May 10, 1998, a lime truck inside the company's chemical plant exploded and spilled the lime into the community. And on December 8, 1998, the chemical plant spilled methyl ethyl ketone into the community. Over the past decade, Shell has released over 2 million pounds of toxic chemicals each year.[15]

Daily, we smell foul odors, hear loud noises, and see blazing flares and black smoke that emanates from those foul flares. The ongoing noisy operations and the endless traffic of huge trucks contribute to the discomfort of Norco citizens. We know that Shell and the U.S. government are responsible for the environmental racism in our community and other communities in the United States and many communities throughout this world. There must be an end to industrial pollution and environmental racism.

Even though we are U.S. citizens, our government does not protect us from environmental racism in the United States. I would like to see justice in action and an end to this struggle. Norco and many other communities of color across our nation suffer the same ills. We are not treated as citizens with equal rights according to U.S. law and international human rights law, especially the United Nations' International Convention on the Elimination of All Forms of Racial Discrimination, which our government ratified as the law of the land in 1994. I bring these issues before you to end support for these human rights violations by the United States. I propose that we take action to protect communities of color from being dumping places for industrial waste, because these deadly toxic substances cause poor health and a degraded environment. I also propose that we change the way human beings are mistreated by multinational corporations worldwide.[16]

On July 5, 2002, Concerned Citizens of Norco celebrated the buyout of our community by Shell. Thirty years of intense community struggle culminated in sit-down meetings with Shell, in which the company finally built trust with local residents and produced a buyout plan for all families who wanted to move away from the company's plant in Norco. The plan is a model of respect for human dignity and community choice that Shell can and should replicate in all other troubled areas where it does business.

The environmental justice movement is made up largely of small, democratically run grassroots groups. It is important to note that women of color lead the vast majority of the grassroots environmental justice groups—a significant deviation from the leadership of national environmental and conservation organizations. Most women activists were pressed into duty because of environmental threats to their families, homes, communities, and workplaces.[17] With meager financial resources, these women warriors have defied all odds. They have stayed focused, they have persevered, and, in many instances, they have won their battles. Their leadership emerged despite the racism and sexism that permeate the larger society and the environmental movement.

PART TWO

THE ASSAULT ON FENCE-LINE COMMUNITIES

POLLUTING INDUSTRIES ARE NOT RANDOMLY SCATTERED across the urban and rural landscape. Often the science of siting and permitting locally unwanted land uses has little to do with toxicology, epidemiology, and hydrology, but everything to do with political science. Historically, those who build polluting industries have followed the path of least resistance. If a community happens to be poor, politically powerless, or inhabited largely by people of color, then its residents are often viewed as expendable and they receive less protection than affluent whites and political elites do. In reality, the politics of pollution create vulnerable communities and environmental sacrifice zones inhabited largely by poor people, people of color, and other individuals who lack health insurance and access to affordable, good-quality medical facilities.

Polluting industries often promise poor communities jobs as a trade-off for the right to locate among them. The promise of a job is different from an actual job, however. Promises are routinely broken: there is little correlation between living next to a polluting factory and the employment of fence-line neighbors. Government is part of the problem, not the solution. Government has helped create many environmental sacrifice zones through corporate welfare policies, such as tax breaks, and related incentives and giveaway programs. Polluting industries use economic blackmail—threats to relocate—as a weapon to extract concessions from government. Dismantling this state-corporate collusion is a central focus for many environmental justice activists and legal practitioners.

4

Living and Dying in Louisiana's "Cancer Alley"

A history of human slavery spawned environmental racism in the United States. Environmental racism is also a by-product of the racial segregation and discrimination legitimated in the southern United States by Jim Crow laws (enacted between 1877 and 1954, when the U.S. Supreme Court, in *Brown v. Board of Education*, struck down "separate but equal" laws) that made all forms of segregation and discrimination legal. Customs and practices in other areas of the United States as well permitted segregation and discrimination, even without laws specifically authorizing them.

The disenfranchisement of an entire race of people was the law in the southern States. But it was practiced throughout the country, and its forms included discrimination in housing, education, and public transportation as well as in the availability of recreational facilities and restaurant service. Environmental racism is merely one vestige of the overall pattern and practice of racism in the United States.

FROM PLANTATIONS TO PLANTS

The South has long been an important battleground in African Americans' struggle for social justice. During the 1990s, southern activists added environmental justice to their agenda. Up until the turn of the twentieth century, over 90 percent of African Americans lived in the southern states. At the beginning of World War I, and again at the beginning of World War II, blacks began to migrate from the small rural southern towns to the Northeast, Midwest, and West.

All across the South, a steady stream of men, women, and children pulled up stakes and embarked on a new life away from the cotton fields, sugar cane plantations, and sharecropped farms. This migration was stimulated by both the "push" of Jim Crow laws and the "pull" of economic and political freedom that the migrants expected to find outside the region.[1] Not until the mid-1970s was this exodus reversed. Today, more than 54 percent of all African Americans live in the South.

The South has always been regarded as backward because of its social, economic, political, and environmental policies. By default, the region became an environmental sacrifice zone, a dump for the rest of the nation's toxic waste.[2] A colonial mentality exists in the South, where local governments and big business take advantage of people who are politically and economically powerless. This mentality emerged from the region's earlier marriage to slavery and the plantation system—a brutal system that exploited both humans and the land.[3]

The Deep South is stuck with its legacy of slavery, Jim Crow segregation, and whites' resistance to equal justice for all. This legacy affects race relations and the region's ecology. Southerners, black and white, have less education, lower incomes, higher infant mortality, and lower life expectancy than Americans elsewhere. It should be no surprise that the environmental quality southerners enjoy is markedly different from that of other regions of the country.[4]

The South is characterized by "look-the-other-way environmental policies and giveaway tax breaks."[5] It is our nation's Third World, where "political bosses encourage outsiders to buy the region's human and natural resources at bargain prices."[6] Lax enforcement of environmental regulations has left the region's air, water, and land the most industry-befouled in the United States.

When one thinks of examples of corruption in government in the south, one state races to the top of the list: Louisiana. As a result of such notable politicians as the legendary Governor Earl K. Long and Governor Edwin Edwards (who was convicted in 2000 for racketeering and incarcerated in 2004), corruption in government appears to be woven into the culture and political fabric of Louisiana.[7] Adding to these circumstances the state's history of slavery, discrimination, and racism yields a dangerous mix for minorities and the poor, human health, and the environment.

Louisiana is consistently ranked as one of the most polluted states in the nation, and it has a high poverty rate. The national poverty rate in 2004 was 12.1 percent. With an overall poverty rate of 17.5 percent, Louisiana ranked fourth highest in the nation and third highest in the South. The percentage of the state's children in poverty (26.4 percent) was second highest in the nation.[8] Only ten states have a higher percentage of working poor, defined as those who earn less than one and a half times the poverty level. In 1999, the weighted average poverty threshold for a family of three was $13,290. Nearly 39 percent of Louisiana households earn less than $25,000 dollars a year.

The Mississippi River chemical corridor in Louisiana, better known as Cancer Alley, challenges nearly every environmental policy and regulation in this nation. The struggles of communities in the corridor exemplify many of the environmental conflicts fought by numerous communities in this country and abroad. Louisiana's overdependency on petrochemical production has placed its economy and the health of Louisiana's citizens and its environment in dire straits.[9]

LOUISIANA'S UNHOLY ALLIANCE

No place better exemplifies the deleterious effects of the incestuous relationship between government and the petrochemical and chemical industry than Louisiana. The unholy alliance between government and industry has been unbreakable, and the people of Louisiana have suffered its consequences.

Louisiana is rich in natural resources, almost to its detriment. These rich resources have served as the most influential factors in the state's development. Over three hundred years ago, the French recognized the economic potential of Louisiana's location at the mouth of the Mississippi River. The river was a means of connecting the state with both the nation and the world. Four of the eleven largest ports in America are located in Louisiana, and each year forty-five hundred seagoing vessels and a hundred thousand barges travel the state's waterways. The Mississippi River is the heart and soul of the Louisiana economy, linking the state and much of the nation with 191 countries around the world.[10]

Louisiana's economic policies were first established by the French, but the state has continued to focus on enticing international trade and service businesses to set up shop along the river. Domestic exporters recog-

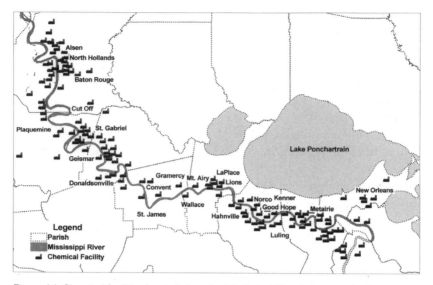

Figure 4.1. Chemical facilities located along the Mississippi River in Louisiana's "Cancer Alley," 1991.

nized the benefits of locating along the Mississippi, which served as an easy means of transport for heavy industries.

With the collapse of the sugar plantation system after World War II, Louisiana became a prime setting for the petrochemical industry. Access to oil fields in the Gulf of Mexico catapulted Louisiana to its position as the second-largest producer of refined oil in the United States. Louisiana can boast of having 11 percent of the petroleum reserves in the country. Some 135 petrochemical plants line the eighty-five-mile stretch of the river from Baton Rouge to New Orleans (see Figure 4.1). Louisiana's petroleum industry is extremely important to the state and the nation. The state's nineteen refineries produce approximately 17 billion gallons of gasoline annually.[11]

Petrochemical industries have made significant economic contributions to the state for decades. The fact that their fate is tied to the state's economic and political climate is not lost on the industries' managers. Corporations have been absolutely shameless in using their power to ensure that their interests are fully represented in the state legislature.

Corporations in Louisiana are extremely well organized. The Louisiana Association of Business and Industry is arguably the most powerful lobby in the state. Its power is the result of implementation of a skillfully chartered plan to support political candidates who support the association's interests. The association embraces what could be described as a cradle-to-grave approach to political lobbying. Behaving much like a political organization, the association actively "recruit[s] and train[s] potential candidates throughout the state."[12] It does not limit itself to grooming and training potential candidates, however, but also expends energy to establish connections with rising politicians. And, by allying itself with other industry-specific political coalitions, such as the powerful Louisiana Chemical Association, it augments its efforts to influence and promote a pro-industry economic development model that supports the industry's expansion.[13]

In 1991, a New Orleans newspaper reported that "Louisiana and other oil states are in a position to grow faster than any other part of the economy in coming years."[14] But in the early years of the twenty-first century, it is obvious that this new prosperity is a dream deferred. Louisiana has failed to grow at the projected rate and has failed miserably in its efforts to diversify the economy. The state government has chosen to remain committed to old economic development plans that look to the petroleum industry as the means of growing the economy.

Although several factors have combined to undercut Louisiana's economy, the Industrial Property Tax Exemption Program is by far the most important one. This program is the result of a marriage of ideas about economic development between corporations and politicians and constitutes the largest of all tax incentives offered by the Louisiana government. Businesses normally must pay property taxes to the parishes (counties), but the exemption program gives manufacturing corporations property-tax relief on buildings, machinery, and equipment for up to ten years. Following the exemption period, corporations pay property taxes at a reduced rate. From the program's inception in 1936 to 1988, eleven thousand exemptions were granted. From 1988 to 1998, $2.5 billion in exemptions were granted.[15]

This tax exemption program could best be described as a corporate welfare program paid for by the poor of Louisiana. Since the exemption relieves businesses of local property taxes, local governments do not receive sufficient operating funds to maintain local roads, parks, libraries, and schools. "We're the only state in the United States of America that lets education subsidize businesses," explained Cleo Fields, a state senator from Baton Rouge.[16]

There have been numerous attempts to introduce bills in the legislature to repeal the tax exemption program, including legislation that would give parishes a local option to exclude education taxes from the program. To date, all of these efforts have failed; most bills have not even gotten out of committee. The majority of credit for the defeat of these efforts goes to the Louisiana Association of Business and Industry and its political action committee. This powerful lobby has been extremely successful in its campaign against what it describes as "anti-business special interest groups":

> The Louisiana Association of Business and Industry (LABI) is the largest and most effective business lobbying group in Louisiana. Each year, many groups attempt to persuade the Louisiana Legislature to enact laws that favor their special interests, and their best interest is often directly opposed to your best interest. Most companies cannot afford to spend the time or money and hire the personnel necessary to keep up with the many issues that affect their business income and then successfully lobby their position to state government. Joining LABI means they unite with their peers from around the state to accomplish their objectives with much less expense.[17]

Negative headlines on stories describing the state's corporate tax exemptions are not unusual, for the program has gained national attention. In 1998, *Time* magazine published a three-part exposé on what it described as American corporate welfare. In that issue Louisiana took top billing.[18] This also means that Louisiana ranks number one in providing tax subsidies to corporate polluters.[19]

But the state can ill afford these subsidies. Louisiana has the fourth-lowest per capita taxes in the country. Nevertheless, it gives industry more than $350 million in tax breaks annually while ranking consistently near the bottom in environmental performance. In jobs and incomes, the state usually ranks behind states that assess higher taxes and demand greater environmental responsibility from businesses. The bulk of Louisiana's $350-million subsidy goes to heavy polluting manufacturers, who provide only 10 percent of the jobs in the state.[20]

THE MISSISSIPPI RIVER CHEMICAL CORRIDOR

This industrial corridor produces one-fifth of the United States' petrochemicals. The air, ground, and water along the corridor were so full of carcinogens that it was once described as a massive human experiment. This eighty-five-mile stretch of chemical plants and oil refineries transformed one of the poorest, slowest-growing sections of Louisiana into communities of brick houses and shopping centers. But at what price to the people living there, especially to the communities that emerged from the old plantation system, who were there long before the plants came?

The Mississippi River was a pull factor for petrochemical companies because it furnished access by barges and a ready disposal site for chemical waste. In the 1940s, the state's population began taking up jobs created by this new oil-based economy. By 1956, 87,200 Louisianans were directly employed by the petrochemical industry. In the 1990s, the number was smaller: 59,600 held such jobs in July 1998. By February 2004, the number of jobs in Louisiana's petrochemical industry dropped to 47,300.[21]

The industrial inducements program implemented by Governor John McKeithen in the 1960s attracted petrochemical companies to the state. By the 1970s the Mississippi River chemical corridor was lined with 136 petrochemical plants and seven oil refineries, or nearly one plant or refinery for every half mile of river.

Ever since the EPA introduced the Toxic Release Inventory in 1989, Louisiana has consistently ranked highest in the nation in toxic environmental releases and waste generation. The 2000 *Gold and Green Report,* compiled by the Institute for Southern Studies, ranked Louisiana fiftieth in the country in environmental quality.[22] The state ranked second in the country (after Texas) in the number of chemical accidents involving member companies of the American Chemistry Council, with 5,375 accidents reported between 1990 and 2003.[23] In 2002, the state ranked third in the country in the number of facilities (sixty-six) storing more than one hundred thousand pounds of an extremely hazardous substance other than ammonia.[24] Louisiana State University professor Paul Templet has analyzed all fifty states and found that those with lax environmental enforcement have the poorest economies. Louisiana residential consumers pay four times as much per unit of energy as industrial users pay. Templet observes:

> The energy subsidy . . . reduces the cost of obtaining a natural resource. There is no particular reason that industry should enjoy drastically cheaper energy than the public does. . . . The huge price differences in certain states reflect political power. Eliminating the energy subsidy would return the appropriated natural assets to citizens in the form of reduced pollution and more equitable prices. It would also promote more efficient use of energy and enhance public health. Citizens could spend less on energy, and more on education or other needs.[25]

Templet also found that states doling out the largest subsidies to polluters, energy guzzlers, and the rich are the same states that have the weakest environmental protection policies and the most polluted environments. Louisiana leads the pack of twenty-five states whose total subsidies to polluters are larger than the national average. Other states in this category are (in descending order of subsidy size) Utah, Florida, Tennessee, Mississippi, Alabama, Washington, Nevada, Texas, Arizona, New Mexico, Oklahoma, Hawaii, West Virginia, Arkansas, South Carolina, North Dakota, Indiana, South Dakota, Virginia, Kansas, Missouri, North Carolina, Alaska, and Georgia.

In the end, all three subsidy categories—pollution, energy, and tax—foster inequality. Subsidies diminish productivity, disposable income, health, and quality of life for those who bear the costs. Subsidies also enhance the political power of those who are subsidized, allowing them to manipulate markets and the political process to further their own interests. And subsidies deprive governments of revenues that they could otherwise use for education, health care, and similar programs that serve citizens.[26]

In 1980, Louisiana's Mississippi River chemical corridor emitted as much as 700 million pounds of toxic chemicals into the air, water, and soil. The total releases and transfers reported by facilities listed in the Louisiana Toxic Release Inventory for 1995 were 185,102,963 pounds. Air releases amounted to 84,671,835 pounds; water discharges, 28,269,936 pounds; land discharges, 4,660,001 pounds; and releases by deep well injection, 54,494,453 pounds.

In 1995, ten parishes' combined releases and transfers made up 85.81 percent of the state total reported in the Toxic Release Inventory. The state's remaining parishes combined contributed less than 15 percent of the total releases and transfers reported. It is clear from these data that some areas in Louisiana have greater toxic emissions than others. In 2002, the year when the most recent government statistics were published, the top ten parishes emitted over 169 million pounds of the total 209 million pounds, or 80.9 percent of the releases and transfers statewide (see Table 4.1).[27]

Louisiana ranks low in almost all quality of life indicators. However, it ranks first in the nation in per capita toxic releases to the environment. Moreover, it ranks second in the nation in total chemical releases and wastes injected into the ground, and third in air releases.[28] The pollution burdens for the citizens of Louisiana are immense, but these burdens are greatest for those who inhabit the chemical corridor. As noted earlier, most of the communities in the corridor existed long before the plants made it their home.

A geographic information systems analysis of facilities that report their releases to the Toxic Release Inventory determined the relationship between race and facility siting within nine parishes along the Mississippi River chemical corridor. The analysis shows the proximity of minority

TABLE 4.1. TOXIC RELEASES IN PARISHES
IN THE MISSISSIPPI RIVER CHEMICAL
CORRIDOR, 2002

Rank	Parish	Total Releases	Total Releases and Transfers
1	Ascension	23,819,331	34,106,806
2	Calcasieu	15,682,029	39,940,692
3	St. Charles	12,440,542	27,523,765
4	De Soto	9,795,836	9,881,440
5	Jefferson	9,580,099	10,634,137
6	East Baton Rouge	9,295,708	14,833,194
7	Ouachita	9,125,945	9,407,255
8	Iberville	5,486,067	10,340,489
9	St. James	4,667,076	6,108,469
10	St. John the Baptist	2,975,831	6,682,090
Total		*102,868,464*	*169,458,337*

SOURCE: U.S. Environmental Protection Agency, *Toxic Release Inventory*, 2002, 2004, www.epa.gov/triexplorer/geography.htm.

communities (specifically, African Americans) to toxic facilities, and it compares this to the proximity of whites to such facilities. The nine parishes included in the analysis are Ascension, Jefferson, St. James, St. Charles, East Baton Rouge, Iberville, St. John, West Baton Rouge, and Orleans.[29]

According to the analysis, all nine parishes have clusters of air-polluting facilities largely located in areas with high concentrations of African Americans. Approximately 80 percent of the total African American community in the nine parishes lives within three miles of a polluting facility. A clearly discernible pattern of discrimination is evident.

TOXIC NEIGHBORS

Communities in the chemical corridor are sandwiched between numerous and various toxic facilities. Many of the homes are built on top of landfills, and residents must battle frequent attempts by companies to build yet more toxic-spewing facilities in their communities. This is life in the corridor. There have been many environmental justice struggles in the corridor. This chapter focuses on the battles in Norco, at the Agriculture Street Landfill, and in Convent, which represent the environmental nightmares of African Americans and other people of color living with the impact of environmental toxics.

NORCO, LOUISIANA

Norco is located in St. Charles Parish, approximately forty miles northwest of New Orleans. The town's name is derived from the New Orleans Refinery Company. The Diamond community, which is part of the town of Norco, is more than a hundred years old. As a result of the Shell Oil Company's industrial expansion, the size of this community has been reduced, and it now consists of only four streets. The community was graphically described in a 1999 *New Orleans Times-Picayune* article:

> The residents of the Diamond Community in Norco, Louisiana, are sandwiched between the Shell Chemical Plant and the Shell/Motiva Refinery. Loud noises, noxious odors and deadly chemicals are the constant neighbors of the citizens of Norco. The view from their front windows is of the pipes, storage tanks, and production towers of a petrochemical plant. Flares erupt noisily and unpredictably, sometimes roaring through the night. Delivery trucks and vehicles servicing the chemical plant move deadly chemicals through their communities. Unexplained booming noises shake their homes in the night. Strange smells waft into their homes, producing headaches and breathing difficulties.[30]

The residents of the Diamond community live in a manufacturing complex that, in the 1997 Toxic Release Inventory, reported releasing over 2 million pounds of toxic emissions to the air. This represents over 50 percent of the toxic air releases in the entire parish. Within the petroleum industry, the Shell oil refinery is Louisiana's second-largest emitter of toxic chemicals to the air. The refinery also releases more recognized carcinogens to the air than any other refinery.[31]

In the 1950s, the Shell Norco Refining Company, which began operations in 1955, purchased part of the Diamond Plantation and drafted plans to build a new wing for its chemical plant. The community that occupied this part of the old Diamond Plantation was displaced and relocated on a small plot of land elsewhere on the plantation grounds, between the oil refinery and the chemical plant. A simple fence was, and is, the only separation between the community and the plant.

Before the displacement of the Diamond Plantation residents, the predominantly African American community was prosperous. Although the community shares a fence line with the plant, only a few residents acquired jobs at the plant. All that remains of the original community on the Diamond Plantation is a cemetery for African American soldiers who fought during the Civil War. The displacement and relocation of this small community marked the beginning of economic strife and environmental injustice in the Norco area.[32]

In the aftermath of a tragic explosion in May 1988 at the Norco refinery, which killed 8 workers, injured 20 others, and caused the evacuation of 4,500 people, a group of 250 Diamond residents sued Shell. On October 5, 1993, the Concerned Citizens of Norco convened to plan another lawsuit to force Shell to buy out and relocate the Diamond residents. The community was experiencing an unusually high death rate and high rates of respiratory ailments. However, in 1997, the jury's verdict in the original case filed in 1988 favored the defendants.

The community organization then appointed as their president Margie Eugene Richard, a lifetime resident of the Norco community who had grown up in a home just twenty-five feet from the plant's fence line.[33] Members of the organization remained convinced that the incidences of disease and death in their community were unusually high and very likely related to emissions from the Shell plants. Margie Richard is a dynamic and powerful spokesperson. She remembers that, before the original plant was built, the Diamond neighborhood was a happy and peaceful community that hosted frequent outdoor picnics. After Shell came in, and as it expanded, the community became bigger, noisier, and uglier, with more steam, fires, and flares and no fresh air. Her wish was uncomplicated: "to be relocated to an area where she can once again experience the simple pleasures of life, such as clean air and a quiet environment."

Margie's small trailer facing the expansive plant was no match for her neighbor in size or value, but her spirit and tenacity were inspiring. She had lost her sister to the rare disease sarcoidosis, and this strengthened her conviction that the plant was dangerous and was disabling and killing the people of Norco.

After years of struggling to force Shell to pay for relocation of the Diamond residents away from Shell facilities, Concerned Citizens of Norco achieved an environmental justice victory. On June 9, 2002, the group and Shell announced to the Diamond community the "Diamond Options Program," which would allow residents the choice of either relocating away from Shell's facilities or remaining in the Diamond community with assistance from Shell's home improvement and community development program.

Shell's original relocation offer was an agreement to purchase the homes on only two of the five streets shadowed by the chemical plant. The residents' struggle, however, grabbed national attention and was supported by a diverse coalition of supporters. Congresswomen Maxine Waters (D-CA) and eleven other members of the Congressional Black Caucus wrote a letter to Shell officials in 2002 urging them to consider buying out all Diamond residents. Shell reversed itself and stated, "We have come to recognize the Diamond neighborhood is truly unique. The community is like an extended family, and we realize now that our previous efforts to create a greenbelt around our facilities may have created difficulties for some families and caregivers in the Diamond neighborhood. While our first preference is to preserve the historic fabric of the Diamond neighborhood, we believe it is important to give residents the choice of determining what is best for their families."[34]

The Diamond program allowed residents who wanted to stay in Diamond to receive a no-interest home improvement loan of up to $25,000 that would be forgiven if residents continued to own their home for five years. Residents who wanted to relocate could sell their homes at the appraised value; there was to be a minimum price of $80,000 paid for each house and $50,000 paid for each mobile home. A minimum price of $17,500 was set for each vacant lot. In addition, some residents would be eligible for a $5,000 moving allowance, a $500 professional-service allowance for consultation with financial and other experts, and a miscellaneous-expense allowance of $15,000. People living on Cathy and Washington Streets, the first two streets included in the relocation offer, who had rejected Shell's original offer could be a part of the expanded program. The relocation plan ended years of heated arguments between Shell and the residents of the Diamond community.[35]

AGRICULTURE STREET LANDFILL

Located in New Orleans, the subdivisions of Press Park and Gordon Plaza were built on a portion of land that had been used as a municipal landfill for more than fifty years. The Agriculture Street Landfill, covering approximately 190 acres, had been designated as a city dump as early as 1910. Municipal records indicate that, after 1950, the landfill was mostly used to discard large solid objects, including trees and lumber, and it was a major site for dumping debris from the destructive 1965 Hurricane Betsy. Notably, the landfill was classified as a solid waste site and not a hazardous waste site.

In 1969, the federal government created a home ownership program to encourage lower income families to purchase their first homes. Press Park in New Orleans was the program's first subsidized housing project.

The federal program allowed tenants to apply 30 percent of their monthly rental payments toward the purchase of a family home. (In 1987, seventeen years later, the first purchase was completed.) In 1977, construction began on a second subdivision, Gordon Plaza. This development was planned, controlled, and constructed by the U.S. Department of Housing and Urban Development and the Housing Authority of New Orleans. Gordon Plaza consists of approximately sixty-seven single-family homes.

In 1983, the Orleans Parish School Board bought a portion of the Agriculture Street Landfill as a site for a school. The fact that it had previously been part of a municipal dump prompted concerns about the suitability of the site for a school. The board contracted engineering firms to survey the site and assess it for contamination by hazardous materials. Heavy metals and organics were detected at the site.

In May 1986, the U.S. Environmental Protection Agency (EPA) performed a site inspection in the community built on the Agriculture Street Landfill. Lead, zinc, mercury, cadmium, and arsenic were found there. However, the score of three assigned to the site, based on the Hazard Ranking System model used at that time, was not high enough to place the community on the EPA's National Priorities List for cleanup. Despite this and the warnings issued by the engineering firms that had surveyed the site, the Moton Elementary School, an $8 million, state-of-the-art public school was constructed. It opened in 1989 with 421 students.

On December 14, 1990, the EPA published a revised Hazard Ranking System model in response to the Superfund Amendment and Reauthorization Act of 1986. Upon request by community leaders, the EPA conducted a expanded site inspection of the Agriculture Street Landfill area in September 1993. On December 16, 1994, the community was given a new score of fifty and placed on the National Priorities List.

This community is home to approximately nine hundred African Americans. The average family income here is $25,000 a year, and adults typically have a high school education or above. Community members pushed for a buyout of their properties and relocation. However, this was not the EPA's resolution of choice. Instead it ordered a cleanup at a cost of $20 million; the community buyout would have cost only $14 million. The actual cleanup began in 1998 and was completed in 2001.[36]

Following the cleanup, an existing citizens group called the Concerned Citizens of Agriculture Street Landfill filed a class action suit against the city of New Orleans for damages and relocation costs. It has taken nine years to bring this case to court. The last court date has been postponed, and the community anxiously awaits its final day in court.

CONVENT, LOUISIANA

An environmental problem in Convent catapulted Louisiana to the top of the list in every discussion on environmental racism and how it relates to the siting of facilities that pollute. In 1996, the people of Convent became involved in a fight for their lives and the life of their community as they knew it. The Japanese-owned Shintech Corporation made plans to build in this town the world's largest polyvinyl chloride plastics production facility. Convent, in St. James Parish, is a rural town of approximately two thousand people. At the time, the makeup of the part of town closest to the proposed Shintech site was 82 percent African American.

The plant was to be a massive operation composed of three chemical-processing units, a hazardous waste incinerator, and a number of on-site storage tanks. The plant's toxic releases, too, were to be enormous. An estimated six hundred thousand pounds of toxic chemicals would be released into the air each year, and 8 million gallons of wastewater would be pumped into the Mississippi River each day. This vinyl production facility would also emit dioxin, a by-product of polyvinyl chloride production formed in processes involving the use of chlorine and heat. Significantly, the EPA ranks dioxin as a major health threat, even in small amounts, and links the substance to human hormone disruption, cancers, reproductive damage, and other serious illnesses.

The community of Convent, especially the area near the proposed construction site, was already inundated with chemical plants and toxic emissions. Within a three-mile radius stood six operating plants. Construction was also under way for three new iron mills. Convent residents, if employed, could literally walk to work; ironically, however, the unemployment rate in this area is over 60 percent. Plants such as these have a record of rarely hiring their neighbors, particularly their poor black neighbors.

The residents of Convent bitterly complained about the pollution in their community. They reported numerous health problems such as asthma, respiratory problems, cancers, and other diseases they associated with the chemicals spewing from the many plants in the neighborhood. Tired of the pollution, a large and vocal group of Convent citizens saw the Shintech Corporation as the last straw. After local politicians refused to assist these citizens with the matter, the group formed the St. James

Citizens for Jobs and the Environment, which aggressively undertook a legal battle to stop construction of the Shintech plant.

On April 2, 1997, Greenpeace and the Tulane University Environmental Law Clinic, representing Convent residents and sixteen environmental and public interest organizations, filed a citizens' petition, or administrative complaint, under Title V (the permitting program) of the Clean Air Act. They demanded that the EPA object to air permits that the state of Louisiana proposed to issue to Shintech. On May 21, 1997, Greenpeace and the Tulane University Environmental Law Clinic filed an amended petition with the EPA that provided the agency with additional grounds for objection to Shintech's air permits. Among these were the contention that the community of Convent was protected by the president's Executive Order 12898, which addresses environmental justice. Public hearings were held on the Title V environmental justice issues in January 1998.

On September 10, 1998, as the result of pressure from St. James Citizens for Jobs and the Environment and its allies, Carol Browner, the EPA's administrator, in a precedent-setting action rejected Shintech's application for a permit on technical grounds but also rejected the environmental justice arguments in the Title V petition. The EPA found fifty technical deficiencies in Shintech's permit application. This was the first time the EPA had accepted a citizen complaint under Title V. In an accompanying advisory letter, Browner also asked that the Louisiana Department of Environmental Quality address environmental justice issues through a public hearing as part of the procedure of reopening the permit process. Moreover, she indicated that the EPA had accepted for further investigation a Title VI complaint on behalf of African American residents under the Civil Rights Act of 1964, which bars racial discrimination by entities receiving federal funds. The Louisiana Department of Environmental Quality receives federal funds to administer its delegated authority to issue permits under the Title V Clean Air Act permitting program. The Title VI complaint, filed by the Tulane University Environmental Law Clinic, contended that a permit issued to Shintech would be racially discriminatory according to the definition given in Title VI.

The EPA's Office of Civil Rights launched an investigation of this complaint, and its decision was expected to be handed down in June 1998. However, the lawsuit never went to trial, and the EPA never rendered a decision about this complaint, because on September 18, 1998, Shintech announced that it had scrapped its plans to build a plant in Convent and had decided instead to move about twenty-five miles upriver to Plaquemine, Louisiana, near Baton Rouge. Moreover, the size of the plant would be drastically reduced. The Plaquemine Shintech plant would create, according to Shintech representatives, only a third of the jobs anticipated at the plant proposed for Convent and a third of the expected emissions. Ironically, the Shintech victory was not a legal one, although the legal process was extremely important in influencing the outcome. Citizen activism, organization, grassroots mobilization, and national support were the defining qualities of the struggle that led to this victory.

Two leaders of the Shintech movement were lifelong residents of Convent: Emelda West and Gloria Roberts, both seventy-nine-year-old retired grandmothers. Emelda West, by far, stands out as the vocal leader of this struggle. She brought to the struggle the energy of a much younger person and a powerful moral voice. Gloria Roberts, a retired schoolteacher who considers West to be one of her closet friends, served as the quiet but dangerous self-described "worker bee." She collected all the facts, wrote the reports, and developed the ammunition to fight Shintech. The two made a powerful duo. West noted that she uttered a prayer every time she passed the proposed Shintech site, saying, "In the name of Jesus, I promise you, Shintech, you will *not* build here!" The Shintech case has been described as being as important to the environmental justice movement as *Brown v. the Board of Education* was to the civil rights movement.

CASUALTIES OF CHEMICAL POLLUTION

As noted earlier, the Mississippi River chemical corridor produces one-fifth of the nation's petrochemicals. Louisiana holds 11 percent of the petroleum reserves in the United States. The state's nineteen refineries produce approximately 17 billion gallons of gasoline annually. Louisiana's petroleum industries are extremely important to the state and the nation: for decades, these industries have made significant economic contributions to the state. The pollution burdens created by these industries, however, are immense.

Corridor residents have to endure greater health risks and sometimes die from diseases they believe are related to chemical exposure. An even more sinister consequence of the growth of the corridor has been the loss of historic lands and communities. For African Americans, this means the loss of land owned by their ancestors who were former slaves. Louisiana's chemical corridor has become a graveyard for the African American communities of Morrisonville, Reveilletown, and Sunrise.[37] All three communities were intrinsically tied to African Americans' freedom from slavery. Blacks survived the horrors of slavery, but some of the homesteads of their offspring were destroyed by the modern petrochemical industry.

MORRISONVILLE, LOUISIANA

Founded in the 1870s by slaves freed from the Australian Plantation, Morrisonville stood on the banks of the Mississippi River just north of Plaquemine. The people of Morrisonville formed a tightly knit community of relatives and friends who could trace back their ancestry in this community for more than a century. The town's founder, Robert Morrison, was a preacher who had struggled to create this community around the church that he led, the Nazarene Baptist Church, and the God-fearing faith of freed slaves.

The town had endured many hardships and had even managed to survive a government-ordered relocation, in 1931, when the town was ordered to move a mile and a half west after the U.S. Army Corps of Engineers refused to continue maintaining the levees that protected the town from the Mississippi River. But surviving the Dow Chemical Company was a task far too difficult. Many Morrisonville residents can still recall when the land that the Dow plant stands on was part of a huge sugar cane empire owned by the Mayflower and Union Plantation. The plantation house is still standing and can be seen inside the fence surrounding land owned by Dow.

In 1959, the community sold some land to Dow. Most see this transaction as the mistake that marked the beginning of their demise as a community. The land sold created a greenbelt, but Dow then expanded, building on the greenbelt land right up to the fence lines of Morrisonville residents. The once serene rural community, which covers two hundred acres, found itself situated along the eastern boundary of Dow's third-largest plant, which covers eighteen hundred acres.

In May 1989, Dow began buying out the residents of Morrisonville in what was called the Morrisonville Plan. Landowners reportedly were offered $20,000 an acre, and homeowners between $50,000 and $200,000. Dow also offered a minimum of $10,000 to resettle the families who were renting homes in the town. A subdivision nearly four miles downriver was built to house some families in new brick homes and establish another community. Most families accepted the money, but only twelve chose to move to the new subdivision, named Morrisonville Estates.

In less than two years, Dow spent more than $10 million dollars in a voluntary buyout of Morrisonville and got nearly everyone to relocate. The town's estimated 250 residents moved away to various places. Morrisonville as a community is gone except for a church and two graveyards. Community members return every Sunday to worship in the Nazarene Baptist Church, their only means of remaining connected.

The voluntary buyout of the community, Dow's Morrisonville Plan, represents the first time a company attempted to buy out a town near its property line without a lawsuit. Dow's approach to solve the "too close neighbor" situation, which affects many companies, has been closely watched by other chemical companies in the corridor and around the country to see if it presented a workable solution and if other fence-line communities would also demand relocation.

REVEILLETOWN, LOUISIANA

Reveilletown is located across the Mississippi River from Baton Rouge and stands five miles south of Morrisonville and the Dow Chemical Company's plant. The town's history is not unlike Morrisonville's. Reveilletown too was founded in the 1870s by freed slaves, and a large chemical-producing plant—the Georgia Gulf Corporation—stands alongside it. The company's main products are plastic consumer items such as computer parts, vinyl window frames and siding, automotive trim, and medical and surgical supplies, as well as commodity chemicals and the polyvinyl chloride resins used as industrial raw materials.

In producing plastics, the plant emits vinyl chloride, a poison that can cause liver disease. After traces of vinyl chloride were found in the blood of local children in 1987, thirteen Reveilletown property owners filed suit against the company. The case was settled about a year later, and the property owners who had sued moved away. Twenty other families subsequently agreed to sell to Georgia Gulf for a total of $1.2 million. Twelve of these families moved two miles north to a subdivision near Morrisonville Estates that is popularly called New Reveilletown. The Georgia Gulf Corporation completed a program in 1990 that paid for the relocation of these thirty-three property owners and seventeen others—a total of fifty families—away from its vinyl chloride plant. As in Morristown, the move marked the death of a community that had been founded by freed slaves. Reveilletown is now a six-acre grove of oaks and pecan trees.

SUNRISE, LOUISIANA

The community of Sunrise was established on land purchased in 1874 from a white landowner by Alexander Banes, a former slave. The property changed hands in 1904, when Mr. Banes sold the property to Benjamin Mayer, a white businessman from Baton Rouge. Mr. Mayer subsequently subdivided some of the land and sold parcels to individuals.

In the 1930s, Sunrise was inhabited mostly by white residents. According to the 1970 census, Sunrise had become about 17 percent white and 83 percent black. The census data also show that, on the streets closest to a highly polluting industrial plant, Placid Refining Company, 48 percent of the residents were white and 52 percent were black. The racial mix and socioeconomic status of Sunrise residents have varied significantly over time.

Placid is a private independent oil-refining and marketing company that takes crude oil and material resources produced in Louisiana and converts them into gasoline, diesel, and jet fuel. The products are utilized by consumers in Louisiana and throughout the southern United States in cars, trucks, buses, and farm machines, to name a few. The company sells its jet fuel to the U.S. Navy and other branches of the military. In 1979, the Placid Refining Company initiated a program to buy out Sunrise community members. The program resulted in Placid acquiring more than one hundred parcels of land—about one-third of the lots in Sunrise.

By 1985, Placid had purchased $947,000 worth of property in Sunrise. However, the African Americans left in Sunrise were not part of the buyout. Only the properties of white residents were purchased. Some African American property owners in Sunrise were told at this time that the company would get back to them. This did not occur. The remaining members of the Sunrise community filed suit against the company in 1990. The suit listed 241 individuals as plaintiffs, including 89 renters and the owners of 36 houses.

In response to the suit filed against the company, Placid offered in March 1991 to buy homes of any homeowners in Sunrise who were not plaintiffs in the lawsuit. The company offered to purchase homes at prices that would allow owners to build new homes the same size as, and made of the same kind of materials used in, the ones they owned in Sunrise. In addition to the purchase price, owners would receive $5,000 per household. The program resulted in Placid acquiring more than 90 percent of the homes not owned by plaintiffs. Plaintiffs indicated no desire to participate in the Sunrise program. They and the company finally reached an out-of-court settlement under which Placid purchased all property of the plaintiffs.

The towns of Reveilletown, Morrisonville, and Sunrise, built by former slaves on the plantations on which they had lived as slaves, no longer exist. All three communities were swallowed up by nearby chemical facilities. We have yet to see the end of this trend.

The citizens of Louisiana have not conceded defeat to the chemical industry in the corridor. Since about 1990, a concerted effort has been made by various facets of the environmental movement, including labor, to resist the industry's assault on human health and the environment. As a group, we in the environmental movement have been greatly disappointed by the assault, but we have also experienced some amazing victories.

Information that came to light during the battle against Shintech in Convent highlights the powerful relationships between state governments and industry. Environmental justice organizations have not forgotten the unmitigated gall of the administrator of the Louisiana Department of Environmental Quality and staff who shamelessly flouted the law to protect the interests of Shintech and carelessly disregarded the rights of the citizens of Convent.

The victory over Shell in Norco highlights the insidious nature of racism and its long-lasting effects on communities, and it demonstrates how industry and government may collude. The citizens of Norco experienced the disruption of their community through forced evacuations and relocations and, finally, encroachment as Shell built out to their fence lines. What could warrant such an invasion of a community by industry? What city government would allow this to happen to its citizens? The answer is simple. Only a reckless and racist disregard for black citizens would allow the political structure to curry favor with a rich and powerful industry and to abandon its responsibility to protect its constituents.

The Agriculture Street Landfill case in New Orleans similarly highlights the racism that supported segregation and dictated the inferior services provided to blacks. The city of New Orleans, the Housing Authority of New Orleans, the Department of Housing and Urban Development, and the EPA all worked together to create Press Park and Gordon Plaza. The homes in these developments were built for working-class African Americans on land that had been a city dump.

How could so many agencies be involved in a seemingly worthwhile project that had such a damaging outcome? Who decided that this land was safe to build homes on? Who would consider toxic land to be satisfactory for lower-income African Americans to live on? Oddly enough, it is hard to identify a sinister plot to endanger the lives of African Americans, but they have been injured nonetheless. No one bothered to ask the obvious questions. No one took the precautions that would have been taken for richer and more powerful citizens. The real estate and construction industries profited from the deal. If these industries asked no questions about safety, where was the EPA?

The greater insult to this community has been the response of all liable parties (the community originally sought remedies from the Department of Housing and Urban Development and the subdivision's developer). After nearly a decade of fighting, the community is still waiting for a settlement. Residents agree that this would not be the case if the plaintiffs had been white or wealthy.

Over the past ten years the environmental justice coalition in Louisiana has grown to include academicians, grassroots organizations, lawyers, environmentalists and environmental organizations, labor, faith-based organizations, environmental legal clinics, physicians, singers, and actors. In all of our victories, we have had the support of these others, and it has been our cooperation that has made the difference. We have learned valuable lessons in the long struggle for environmental justice, and they are truly simple: together we can win. We can change the way industry and government operate in our community. Finally, it is important to recognize that governments seldom initiate action to address environmental problems. Governments generally respond to outside pressure, and this pressure must be applied over an extended period of time to achieve lasting results.

MANUEL PASTOR JR., JAMES L. SADD,
AND RACHEL MORELLO-FROSCH

5

Environmental Inequity in Metropolitan Los Angeles

Over the past half decade, we have participated in an academic-community collaboration in which we have conducted research on environmental disparities in the Los Angeles metropolitan area and worked to help correct these disparities. When we first embarked on this work, Manuel Pastor proudly told his aunt that he was part of a team investigating environmental inequity. After expressing pride in her researcher-nephew's tremendous accomplishments and future plans, his aunt asked a straightforward question: What is environmental inequity? The researcher explained that environmental hazards are disproportionately located in low-income neighborhoods and communities of color and that the pattern seems to be connected more closely to a community's political power than to market dynamics. His aunt's beaming smile slowly gave way to a quizzical look. She gazed sadly into her nephew's eyes and, as though letting him in on a long-held secret—and perhaps gently warning him that it would soon be discovered that he was wasting his time—she told him, "But Manuelito, everyone knows that."

In fact, everyone does know that, and we acknowledge both the strength of community wisdom in this regard and the fact that the battle for healthy communities will largely be fought and won in the numerous community struggles detailed in this and other volumes.[1] However, it is also clear that the environmental justice movement has often existed in a symbiotic relationship with research and researchers. It was the landmark 1982 protest in Warren County, North Carolina, against the creation of a landfill for disposal of polychlorinated biphenyls in a largely African American community, that prompted a 1983 study by the U.S. General Accounting Office confirming that hazardous waste landfills in the southern United States were disproportionately located in black communities.[2] A subsequent, pathbreaking study by the United Church of Christ Commission for Racial Justice established a broader case, showing that the siting of disposal facilities designed for hazardous and toxic wastes was positively related to the proportion of people of color residing within the same zip code area.[3] This work was indispensable, both because it triggered further systematic and detailed research into similar questions of environmental justice and because it established the credibility of the burgeoning movement engaged in creating new environmental politics and new environmental policies.

In the early to mid-1990s, the environmental justice movement began to gain traction at the political and policy levels. In particular, the movement persuaded the Clinton administration to issue its mandate on environmental justice: the president's now famous 1994 Executive Order 12898. Unfortunately, at the same time, a series of academic studies challenged the fundamental premises of advocates. Some critics, such as Douglas Anderton and his colleagues, argued that there were no statistically significant differences between population groups with regard to their proximity to certain hazardous facilities, after accounting for other possible determinants of facility location. Other critics, such as William Bowen, began to question whether any racial disparities that might be observed were truly consequential for human health and well-being. Christopher Foreman went so far as to suggest that the focus on race, and the introduction of political economy and discrimination frameworks to explain the patterns, was intended to contribute to the building of a new political movement more than to the development of good science and environmental policy.[4]

Our work has focused on understanding whether there is, in fact, environmental injustice in the Los Angeles area. In our research approach, we have maintained a regional focus partly because of the methodological reasons we lay out below, but also because of our close relationship with, and our desire to support, a regionally based partner, Communities for a Better Environment.

The evidence of environmental injustice that we have found is consistent with what Manuel's aunt—now known to everyone on our team as the prescient Tía Dalia—claimed to be common knowledge: there are sharp inequalities in environmental exposures, these differences are largely the product of broad social forces, and they have real consequences for people's health and lives. The question is: What implications do this research and these patterns have for policy making, organizing, and future research?

DATA JUDO IN THE RESEARCH WORLD

Ongoing debates about environmental inequality among policy makers, environmental advocates, and industry have fueled a surge of academic inquiry into whether and how discrimination creates disparities in the distribution of environmental hazards among diverse communities in the United States. Research on environmental inequality varies widely, ranging from descriptive and qualitative studies to statistical modeling that seeks to quantify the extent to which race and class are significantly associated with environmental exposures.[5] Although the results of this research have by no means been unequivocal, much evidence points to a trend in which, in many areas of the United States, environmental hazards are more likely to be situated in communities inhabited by people of color and the poor. Disparities often persist across income strata.

Nevertheless, as the environmental justice movement has gained momentum, several researchers have offered methodologically sophisticated studies challenging the view that environmental injustice not only is related to race but also is a significant problem. One frequent criticism is that an observed positive association between two variables—minority presence and environmental hazards—does not necessarily suggest discrimination per se.[6] If the underlying factor in hazard siting is land value, and this is correlated with income and therefore minority presence, the disproportionate exposure of communities of color and the poor to hazards may not be the result of discriminatory action but could simply reflect market dynamics.[7]

In the mid-1990s, a new wave of studies attempted to address this question by using statistical techniques that could account for the separate effects of income, proximity to industry, composition of the local workforce, and other factors. These early studies, generally national in scope, suggested that race did not significantly determine where hazards were sited, especially when one took into account the proportion of local residents employed in manufacturing (based on the hypothesis that firms might choose to locate near potential employees).[8] However, these national-level results have been criticized for both methodological reasons—particularly for excluding from the comparative analysis certain metropolitan areas with no hazardous sites—and data difficulties, particularly for attempting to find hazardous sites by using the addresses of businesses' headquarters and for unrealistically making simplistic assumptions regarding the geography of potential exposure.[9] Moreover, a broad national study launched by three researchers initially skeptical of environmental justice claims did find evidence of disparities by race and class, depending on the geographic scale used.[10]

The issue of scale has itself become a subject of analysis and debate. Several researchers have argued that the distribution of hazards is mostly related to localized land-use patterns and economic development decisions that shape the landscape of regional industrial clusters; therefore, analysis should focus on the pattern of hazard distribution *within* a region. In this view the furniture-making and metal-plating industries in Los Angeles are not likely to drift up to Seattle, and Microsoft is not likely to move south to Hollywood, and it is the relative equity of the distribution of toxics within a particular region that matters.[11]

As a result, some researchers have begun to examine environmental hazard distributions at the metropolitan and regional levels, yielding mixed results on the equity question.[12] However, a national study has attempted to take on both the broad national picture and the local regional effects by trying to see whether patterns of unequal impact exist region by region.[13] That is, the study attempted to generalize from the region up, rather than from the nation down. The results indicate sharp disparities for both African Americans and Latinos, even after researchers controlled for—that is, accounted for—income and other variables. These results lend credence to the notion that one must look at a regional level for concrete patterns, effects, and possibilities.

BUILDING A REGIONAL COLLABORATIVE FOR ENVIRONMENTAL HEALTH AND JUSTICE

In 1998, the authors of this chapter, along with our community partner, Communities for a Better Environment (CBE), formed a research and action collaborative to address environmental justice issues facing people of color and low-income communities in Southern California. The work of this academic-community partnership came at a time when CBE's organizing and policy advocacy efforts in Southern California had significantly expanded and had yielded some impressive results.

In the past few years, for example, the organization has successfully compelled the regional air quality authority South Coast Air Quality Management District to (1) halt a special emissions-credit-trading system, in which businesses were able to purchase older cars and take them off the road rather than clean up toxic hotspots in a predominantly Latino community; (2) adopt a new set of environmental justice principles to guide its regulatory and enforcement activities; and (3) strengthen its pollution standard for new industrial facilities (known as Rule 1402) to significantly restrict additional cancer risks associated with emissions. The organization's other victories include preventing the construction of a power plant in an already overburdened Latino community, and, as part of a broader community effort, minimizing the expansion of the Los Angeles International Airport.

The research partners in this collaborative have provided direct and indirect support for several of these initiatives, including analyses, newspaper opinion articles, and participation in training programs for organizers and community members. We have also supplied basic research on the general pattern of disproportionate exposures to environmental hazards in the Los Angeles region. Our decision to focus our efforts on this issue was collective. Within the collaborative, our research priorities and project development choices are decided in a way that is relevant to community organizing and environmental policy making.

CBE works from an organizing framework that combines science, organizing, and policy, and it has generally focused on work that addresses some of the persistent methodological challenges in the field of environmental justice research. Their view is that neighborhood-by-neighborhood work, while essential for building a base, will add up to environmental change only if the movement can scale up to the regional level. Understanding whether there is indeed a commonality of disparity on a regional level—and why and how it exists—could therefore help the movement's progress. This long view of research has allowed us to develop, step-by-step, a case demonstrating environmental inequity in the region.

We have focused on Southern California partly because this is where CBE was doing its work, but there are also several academic or research justifications for this focus. First, the region has a unique regulatory history: it has mounted an ongoing struggle to solve some of the worst air pollution problems in the country, even as it balances that with the need to promote economic growth. Second, Southern California, whose population majority is already made up of people of color, is rapidly becoming a bellwether for demographic and socioeconomic change for the state as well as the nation. Third, a regional focus on environmental justice research squares with the notion that industrial clusters, transportation planning, and economic development decisions are often regionally rooted, and so the question about equity is: How are the social and environmental health effects of urban economic development distributed within the regions and among the communities that host industrial and other facilities?

MAKING THE CASE: RESEARCH AND RESULTS

Following the lead of early watershed studies on environmental inequality, we chose in our first study in Southern California to examine the location of hazardous waste treatment, storage, and disposal facilities (TSDFs) in Los Angeles County. In the second of our studies, we also examined facilities in all of Southern California that were listed on the U.S. Environmental Protection Agency's Toxic Release Inventory (TRI facilities).[14] The first study found significant demographic differences between census tracts (or neighborhoods) that had TSDFs and tracts that did not.[15] In particular, tracts that hosted a TSDF or were located within a one-mile radius of a TSDF had significantly higher percentages of residents of color (particularly Latinos), lower per capita and household incomes, and a lower proportion of registered voters. Because of the interpretive limits of the study—we could make only simple correlations between two variables—we also used more sophisticated statistical procedures to ask whether the relationships were statistically significant in light of the other variables: that is, does race still matter once one controls for, say, zoning or neighborhood income?

The specific statistical technique was called "logistical regression"— a process in which a binary outcome (does the census tract host or not host a facility) is tested against a series of factors to see which ones influence the probability of that outcome. Table 5.1 shows the regression results. The most statistically significant variables are land use and percentage of residents of color.[16] Perhaps surprisingly to some, we found that the relationship between income and the presence of TSDFs is mixed: the relationship follows an inverted U-shaped curve in which extremely poor tracts have fewer facilities, as do wealthier communities. We believe the first relationship emerges because poorer areas have less economic and industrial activity, and therefore fewer facilities producing hazardous emissions, and that the latter relationship results because

TABLE 5.1. REGRESSION RESULTS SHOWING THE
ASSOCIATION BETWEEN THE LOCATION OF TSDF
FACILITIES AND RACE OR ETHNICITY, ECONOMIC,
AND LAND USE VARIABLES IN LOS ANGELES COUNTY
(N = 1,636 tracts)

Independent Variables	Direction of Effect	Statistical Significance
% Residents of color	+	***
Population density	+	ns
% Employment in manufacturing	+	**
Per capita income	+	***
Per capita income^2 (squared)	(−)	***
% Industrial land use	+	***

*** = highly significant (at the 1% level); ** = very significant (at the 5% level); ns = not significant

greater wealth supplies the political power necessary for neighborhoods to resist any efforts to site such facilities among them. The Los Angeles County neighborhoods with the highest probability of having TSDFs were working-class communities of color—the same communities that CBE and other environmental justice advocates in the Los Angeles area have been organizing politically.

In our second locational study, we broadened our regional scope to include the South Coast Air Quality Management District (composed of Ventura, Los Angeles, Orange, San Bernardino, and Riverside counties). In this study, we examined the distribution of facilities that are required to report their air emissions to the U.S. Environmental Protection Agency for inclusion in the Toxic Release Inventory.[17] The study distinguished between such facilities in general and the ones that release the class of pollutants that the EPA most wants to see reduced; the latter facilities are included in the agency's 33/50 Program.[18] Our study results indicated that, compared to Anglo residents, Latinos were twice as likely to live in a tract with a facility that released chemicals named in the 33/50 Program; Latinos were followed closely by African Americans. Even after we tried to control for the level of area income, the percentage of local land devoted to industrial land use, and the density of the population—all factors that might influence facility location—we found that the likelihood of living within one mile of a facility releasing toxic emissions was significantly associated with the proportion of residents of color (see Table 5.2). In this study, we also

TABLE 5.2. REGRESSION RESULTS SHOWING THE
ASSOCIATION BETWEEN THE LOCATION OF TRI
FACILITIES AND RACE OR ETHNICITY, ECONOMIC,
AND LAND USE VARIABLES IN SOUTHERN CALIFORNIA
(N = 2,567 tracts)

Independent Variables	Direction of Effect	Statistical Significance
% Residents of color	+	***
Population density	(−)	***
% Employment in manufacturing	+	***
Per capita income	+	***
Per capita income^2 (squared)	(−)	***
% Industrial land use	+	***

*** = highly significant (at the 1% level)

found a similar relationship between the siting of such facilities and the neighboring residents' incomes.

Although our first two preliminary studies focused on the siting of potentially hazardous facilities, we also sought to assess the implications of outdoor air pollution for potential disparities in individuals' estimated lifetime cancer risks.[19] In doing so, we were driven by the internal logic of research—academics often seek new methodological challenges and improvements in research techniques. But we were also driven by the fact that Communities for a Better Environment wanted to understand whether measuring people's cumulative exposure could uncover high levels of disparity in community health outcomes and, therefore, prompt local agencies to act.

Given the paucity of epidemiological data at a local level, we attempted a different approach to cumulative exposure, one based on the techniques of risk assessment.[20] While risk assessment remains a controversial topic for activists and policy makers alike, it can serve as a useful comparative framework when epidemiological data is not available and time-sensitive decisions about unequal impact must be made. For example, risk assessments have been used in the judicial and administrative examination of complaints filed under Title VI of the Civil Rights Act of 1964, which prohibits discriminatory practices in programs receiving federal funds.[21]

Making use of a study undertaken by the Environmental Protection Agency's Cumulative Exposure Project, our research combined estimated long-term, annual average outdoor concentrations of 148 haz-

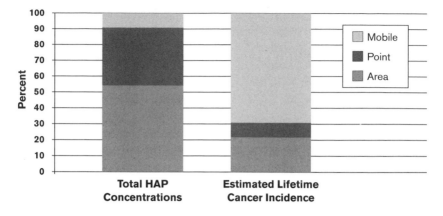

Figure 5.1. Sources of air pollution, and the estimated lifetime cancer incidence in the South Coast Air Basin, 1990.

ardous air pollutants listed under the 1990 federal Clean Air Act Amendments.[22] This made our study of air pollutants broader in scope than previous environmental justice studies, mostly because we incorporated outdoor concentrations of hazardous air pollutants originating from mobile sources (for example, cars), as well as pollutants from industrial manufacturing facilities, municipal waste combustors, small service industries, and other area emitters. By combining concentration estimates with cancer toxicity information, we derived tract-level estimates of lifetime cancer risks and analyzed their distribution among populations in the region.

The estimated lifetime cancer risks associated with exposure to toxic chemicals in outdoor air in the South Coast Air Basin were found to be ubiquitously high, often exceeding, by between one and three orders of magnitude, the goal of the Clean Air Act.[23] Figure 5.1 presents the contributions of different mobile, point, and area sources to total concentrations of toxic chemicals in the air and to total estimated excess lifetime cancer incidence.[24] Mobile sources include on-road and offroad vehicles, area sources include small manufacturing and nonmanufacturing facilities, and point sources include large manufacturing facilities such as those listed in the EPA's Toxic Release Inventory. Interestingly, area and point emissions account for over 90 percent of total estimated concentrations of hazardous air pollutants, but mobile sources are the biggest cause of estimated excess cancer incidence, accounting for 70 percent of the estimated excess cancer incidence associated with outdoor concentrations of hazardous air pollutants from these three source categories.

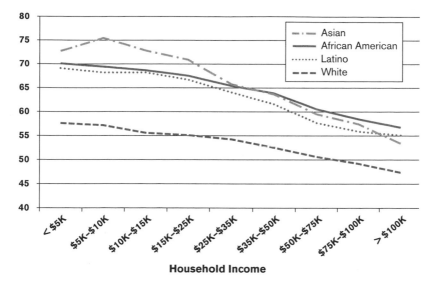

Figure 5.2. Estimated lifetime cancer risks from exposure to air pollution in the South Coast Air Basin, by race or ethnicity and income.

While some critics have taken this result to suggest that the focus should be shifted from large corporate polluters, like refineries, to the average driver, we urge caution in making such an interpretation. Although, at a regional level, point sources do not appear to contribute substantially to concentration estimates and predicted cancer risks, there are several neighborhoods (tracts) in the South Coast Basin where point-source contributions to both concentration and risk estimates are dominant.

Figure 5.2 shows how the racial and ethnic disparities in estimated cancer risks persist across household income strata. The vertical axis shows the estimated individual excess cancer risk for five racial and economic categories, and the horizontal axis shows nine annual household income categories. Asians, African Americans, and Latinos have the highest estimated population cancer risks, with risks nearly 50 percent higher than for Anglos. Although risk levels tend to decline for all groups as household income increases, the gap between residents of color and Anglos is fairly consistent across income strata.

Part of what produces these differences is location: African Americans, Latinos, and Asian residents are concentrated mainly in the urban core, where pollution levels and risks tend to be higher, while Anglos live primarily in less urban areas, where risks are lower. However, Table 5.3 indicates that, even after we controlled our results for well-known

TABLE 5.3. REGRESSION RESULTS SHOWING THE
ASSOCIATION BETWEEN CANCER RISKS LINKED WITH
AIR TOXICS AND RACE OR ETHNICITY, ECONOMIC,
AND LAND USE VARIABLES

(N = 2,495)

Independent Variables	Model 1		Model 2	
	Direction of Effect	Statistical Significance	Direction of Effect	Statistical Significance
% Residents of color	+	***	—	—
Population density	+	***	+	***
% Home ownership	(−)	ns	(−)	ns
Median housing value	+	***	+	***
Median household income	+	***	+	***
Median household income^2 (squared)	(−)	***	(−)	***
% Transportation land use	+	***	+	***
% Industrial land use	+	***	+	***
% Commercial land use	+	***	+	***
% African American	—	—	+	***
% Latino	—	—	+	***
% Asian	—	—	+	***

*** = highly significant (at the 1% level); ns = not significant

location-based causes of pollution such as land use (industrial, commercial, and transportation), as well as for income and for property values and home ownership, which together act as a proxy for assets and political power, race was consistently shown to be positively associated with higher cancer risks. The one way that our study differed from the previous locational studies is in the positive and significant effect of the population density variable. It differed primarily because some of the sources of ambient air pollution, including both traffic and small manufacturing and non-manufacturing facilities, are often concentrated in crowded urban areas.

DEMOGRAPHIC TRANSITION AND THE SITING OF ENVIRONMENTAL HAZARDS

Although both locational and health risk studies suggest that environmental hazards have a great effect on communities of color in Southern California, the fact that these results compare communities at a single point in time has led some commentators to argue that we cannot assess the causal sequence of facility siting. That is, we do not know whether facilities were sited in communities of color, or whether residents of color moved into neighborhoods after the siting of facilities decreased property values and neighborhood desirability.

We have termed the latter the "field of bad dreams" argument: build it and they will come. Many in the environmental justice community suggest that the question of which came first should not to be taken seriously; after all, the critical question is whether health disparities exist. But policy makers do, in fact, use the potential hypothesis of "minority move-in" to justify inaction, and Communities for a Better Environment was interested in investigating this question in the Southern California setting.

We therefore undertook a detailed study, compiling data on the siting and location of TSDFs from 1970 to 1990.[25] The results indicated that the proportion of residents of color living within a one-mile radius of a TSDF increased from less than 9 percent in 1970 to nearly 22 percent in 1990, while the percentage of Anglo residents living within a one-mile radius of a TSDF went from around 4 percent in 1970 to 7.6 percent in 1990; the latter increase is smaller both as a percentage of the population and as a growth rate. Since this disproportionate increase in exposure could indicate *either* a discriminatory placement of TSDFs or a "minority move-in," we decided to look at tracts receiving TSDFs between 1970 and 1990 and the changes that occurred after the facilities were sited.

As it turns out, the neighborhoods in which the facilities were built had a higher proportion of residents of color, were poorer, had more blue-collar workers, had lower initial home values and rents, and had significantly fewer homeowners. The number of residents of color in these neighborhoods did increase after the TSDFs were built—but no faster than in other neighborhoods in the rapidly changing Los Angeles area. More sophisticated statistical analysis, in which we tried to model both the siting and moving processes, confirmed that there was little evidence of a so-called minority move-in within neighborhoods where TSDFs had previously been sited. But our analysis did show that there were significant indications of disproportionate siting in communities of color, even after we had controlled for income and other measures.

Finally, we sought to examine something not usually considered in studies by either the proponents or the critics of the environmental justice movement: whether neighborhoods that had undergone rapid demographic transitions in their ethnic and racial composition were more vulnerable to subsequent TSDF siting. Our argument was that rapid changes

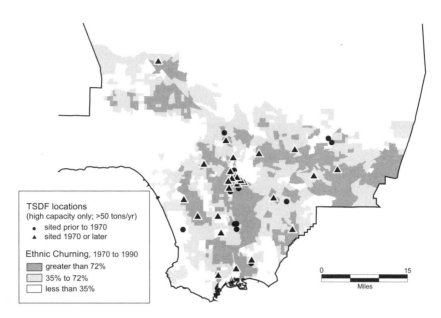

Figure 5.3. Locations of high-capacity hazardous waste treatment, storage, and disposal facilities in relation to ethnic churning in Los Angeles, 1970–1990.

of this sort could weaken the social and political networks that undergird a community's capacity to organize and influence siting decisions. We were not arguing that such change could be avoided, but rather that such areas might require special attention from policy makers and organizers alike.

Also unique in our analysis was that we were not simply considering the transition from Anglos to non-Anglos. We recognized that beneath a stable percentage of people of color can be a rapidly changing mix of African Americans, Latinos, and Asian Pacific-Islanders. Such has been the story in South Central Los Angeles, which has seen a rapid black-to-Latino transition over the past three decades. The usual approach to demographic transition, which focuses on a white-centered view of population loss and gain, would miss this important trend. We thus constructed a measure of "ethnic churning" that took the absolute sum of racial demographic change between 1970 and 1990. Figure 5.3 maps this ethnic-churning variable in Los Angeles in relation to the siting of TSDFs during the 1970s and 1980s.

The apparent visual correlation between high demographic transition and TSDF siting is striking. But we also tested it with a modeling approach that once again attempted to capture the dynamics of siting and of moving. Results revealed that this ethnic churning predicted the siting of a TSDF in a significant number of cases, and did so even after we controlled our results for the impacts of economic and other demographic indicators (not shown). Thus, a potentially hazardous facility is less likely to be sited in historically or uniformly "ethnic" areas—perhaps because residents have common bonds of race, language, and historical experience—than in locations where the proportion of residents of color is high but split and is changing between African American and Latino groups. Indeed, our results suggest that over this time period a peak level of vulnerability in Los Angeles County occurred when the mix was 44 percent African American and 48 percent Latino. The pattern suggests that one of the environmental justice movement's key strategic directions—its focus on creating multiracial coalitions of people of color—not only is good politics but also is essential to building power and protecting community health.

IMPLICATIONS FOR ORGANIZING AND POLICY

Taken together, the evidence from our research in Southern California yields a consistent picture of disproportionate burdens borne by communities of color: a greater number of TSDFs and facilities listed on the Toxic Release Inventory are hosted by these communities, and members of these communities have higher lifetime cancer risks associated with exposure to outdoor air toxic chemicals. Results—looking at the process over time—challenge the "field of bad dreams" argument: they indicate that the disproportionate location of hazardous waste treatment, storage, and disposal facilities in communities of color is the result of facility siting decisions and not simply a market-induced move-in of poor residents of color to lower-rent areas that are already affected by environmental hazards. Finally, we have identified the fact that communities undergoing rapid demographic transition seem more vulnerable to the future imposition of environmental hazards.

Like CBE, other leading community-based organizations have begun to address the pattern of environmental inequity confirmed by this research. The Labor/Community Strategy Center, for example, has battled oil refineries in low-income neighborhoods and led an ongoing struggle to keep bus fares low and public transportation accessible.[26] Earlier, Concerned Citizens of South Central Los Angeles and the Mothers of East Los Angeles successfully resisted the siting of an incinerator near their neighborhoods, forging the black-Latino unity our research suggests is essential. A coalition of community groups, aided by intermediaries like the Center for Law in the Public Interest, managed to force a developer to reconsider plans for an industrial complex in the largely Asian and Latino neighborhoods immediately north of downtown Los Angeles and to instead set aside the land for a park to meet the needs of residents starved for open space.[27] These and other organizing victories have reverberated in the policy arena as well. In 1999, the California legislature passed Senate Bill 115, a measure that directs the state's Office of Planning and Research to coordinate environmental justice initiatives with the federal government and across state agencies, including the California Environmental Protection Agency. This initiative has resulted in several state assembly and senate bills dealing with children's health, cumulative exposure, and other matters.

In light of these political gains, state agencies increasingly have been looking for feedback from environmental justice groups on how to identify issues and solutions. Ensuring meaningful community participation in these efforts requires extensive preparatory work on the part of government agencies. They must assess communities' language needs and scientific literacy and conduct extensive outreach efforts via existing social networks, schools, churches, and civic organizations. The communities themselves must build their members' capacity to understand the issues at stake. Over the past several years, for example, CBE and the Liberty Hill Foundation have run a summer institute in Los Angeles to provide training for between forty and sixty community members and members of grassroots organizations each year. The institute's workshops offer information about the scientific issues related to environmental health and train people to use geographical information systems, access Web-based data resources, and develop strategies for effective policy advocacy.

There have been similar efforts elsewhere in the state. CBE in Northern California trained youth in Richmond's Bayo Vista neighborhood to conduct community surveys on asthma and air pollution and drew the attention of public health officials, who were persuaded to more closely examine and address the high prevalence of childhood asthma in this community. The Environmental Health Coalition in San Diego has trained immigrant Latinas on issues of environmental health and air pollution and thereby enabled them to document the extent of respiratory illness and lead poisoning among children in Barrio Logan. The Asian Pacific Environmental Network has utilized similar strategies in its work with the Laotian community in Richmond.

But even though empowering communities to engage in the environmental-policy-making and regulatory arenas is critical, we should also strive to determine and enforce baseline standards that can protect groups who may not be in a position, due to a lack of political power or organization, to effectively defend their own interests. Moreover, hazard-by-hazard organizing can drain community resources and lock organizing efforts into a reactive rather than a proactive mode. State- and regional-level rules that are automatically invoked could ensure a more level playing field in the siting process.

At minimum, any development project that would worsen environmental inequities should at least trigger a more comprehensive review that could be incorporated into an environmental impact statement. In addition to assessing the existing cumulative exposure to pollution and associated health risks in an affected area, such an analysis would also require consideration of the demographic composition and linguistic capabilities of the surrounding community. It would also require data on land use patterns and proximity of schools, hospitals, and other facilities used by populations particularly vulnerable to environmental pollution.

In order to build a case to support these and other environmental justice policy initiatives, more research will be necessary. With the increased availability of ambient air pollution data, toxicity data, and information on exposure through various other media—such as food and water—future research must emphasize a cumulative-exposure approach to understanding inequalities in the susceptibility of communities to toxics and their potential link to disparities in health outcomes such as cancer, respiratory illness, and immunotoxic effects. Supporting existing and new community-academic collaboratives to conduct such sensitive research will be key to this effort, as scientists, activists, and policy makers work to develop, implement, and prioritize future environmental initiatives aimed at protecting the health of particularly vulnerable populations.

As the environmental justice movement proceeds with both research and organizing, we should stress that our goal is not simply the protection of those who are currently overexposed. Preliminary research in California and other areas suggests that residential segregation and disparities in political power influence not only who bears the net costs and benefits of environment-degrading services but also the overall magnitude of environmental degradation (for example, air pollution) and health risks (such as individual estimated lifetime cancer risks).[28] When hazards can no longer be placed in the backyards of south Los Angeles, new efforts to reduce facilities' emissions and to avoid everyone's back-yard become politically more feasible.

Ultimately, the broader goal of organizing for environmental justice is not simply to equitably reallocate environmental hazards to higher income white neighborhoods, but rather to envision and build a future in which industry, government, and society at large are compelled to adopt viable strategies for pollution prevention that benefit everyone. In the years to come, universalizing the message and securing an even broader constituency, one that understands the deep connections between justice and the environment, will be key to achieving both racial equity and environmental sustainability. Meanwhile, environmental disparities exist in the Los Angeles metropolitan area. And these environmental dispari-ties and environmental exposures adversely affect individuals' health and lives.

6

Toxic Racism on a New Jersey Waterfront

esidents of Camden, New Jersey, have struggled against environmental racism for decades, with little tangible success.[1] County and
state officials repeatedly have allowed waste facilities and heavy
industry to locate in Camden's low-income communities of color, despite
intense neighborhood resistance. But in 2000, a high-profile federal civil
rights suit challenging the permit issued to a cement-grinding facility in
Waterfront South, a heavily environmentally contaminated Camden
neighborhood, brought national attention to the plight of this community.

A small, politically powerless, low-income community waged a battle
against a corporate giant and a state bureaucracy without the benefit of
any financial resources. The precedent-setting lawsuit and the related
community organizing efforts and advocacy raised public awareness
about environmental justice issues, fostered the development of local
leadership, and gave rise to new coalitions and alliances. The struggle
also made evident, however, that little had changed in Camden despite
years of environmental justice advocacy on the national level.

The legal tools available to fight this blatant environmental injustice
proved to be grossly inadequate. In Waterfront South, a community that
had become an environmental sacrifice zone, residents faced considerable
trouble in enforcing their fundamental civil rights, health, and safety.

125

CAMDEN AND THE WATERFRONT SOUTH NEIGHBORHOOD

Camden is a struggling city of close to eighty thousand residents who persevere in their efforts to maintain a decent quality of life and sense of community in the face of severe adversity. As in many other former industrial centers, the manufacturing businesses that at one time provided well-paying jobs went out of business or moved out of town, leaving behind polluted land and abandoned factories. After decades of white flight to the neighboring suburban communities, the city is now home to an almost exclusively African American and Latino population.[2] Camden is the poorest city in New Jersey and one of the poorest in the nation, and it shows all the signs of urban blight. Per capita income is less than $10,000, which is less than half the county and state income levels. The citywide poverty rate is over 30 percent. Infant mortality rates equal those of undeveloped nations.[3] The murder rate and the school dropout rate are the highest in the state. Virtually every block in the city contains vacant and abandoned houses.

Waterfront South is a particularly devastated and environmentally degraded neighborhood in the southern part of the city. It extends east to west, from an interstate highway to the Delaware River, and it encompasses most of the South Jersey Port, the former base for a major shipbuilding company, as well as a small historic residential core, a deteriorated commercial corridor, and numerous industrial sites situated alongside schools, homes, and churches.

Within the small Waterfront South neighborhood, which measures less than one square mile, stand two federal Superfund sites. The first, the General Gas Mantle Corporation site, contains radioactive thorium, the by-product of a gas-lantern-mantle manufacturing business that operated in the neighborhood from 1915 until 1940. For many years after the factory closed, the property was used as a warehouse. Workers using the building exposed themselves to radon gas and tracked contaminated materials through the surrounding neighborhoods. Although the New Jersey Department of Environmental Protection first discovered the radioactivity in 1981, it took no action for eleven years. In 1992 the warehouse business was finally relocated; almost ten years later, the building was torn down.

Today, more than twenty years after the contamination at the site was discovered, the radioactive soil there and in hot spots in nearby backyards and basements has still not been removed. Until the summer of 2002, families lived in homes with backyards that backed against the

Superfund site. That year a new state administration finally took the initiative to relocate them. The U.S. Environmental Protection Agency (EPA) has estimated that long-term exposure to low-level radiation has increased, by 1.8 percent, the cancer risk of residents whose homes were next to the Superfund site.[4]

The other Superfund site, Martin Aaron, Incorporated, was created by a hazardous drum recycler who cleaned the drums by flushing their contents into drainage basins on the property, eventually contaminating the entire property and the groundwater with carcinogens and other toxins, including volatile organic compounds, polychlorinated biphenyls, arsenic, and barium. The site narrative on the EPA's National Priorities List reports:

> Leaking roll-off containers and drums have been observed on site. Reports indicate that holes were dug throughout the property for the disposal of wastes, and that liquid and solid wastes and 200 to 1,000 containers of waste were buried on the property. New Jersey Department of Environmental Protection (NJDEP) has confirmed the reports of disposal, observed buried drums of hazardous waste and found contaminated soils at depths below the water table. NJDEP reports that chemical wastes were illegally deposited on the site in March 1999.[5]

This site is still waiting its turn for cleanup by the EPA. Given the limited funding available for Superfund cleanups, and the unwillingness of the Bush administration to speed up the process, the wait will be a long one.[6]

There are also thirteen other known contaminated sites in Waterfront South. These contain soil full of lead, mercury, tetrachloroethylene, trichloroethylene, and other dangerous contaminants. In addition, many active industries in the area are generating yet more pollution. The neighborhood has four junkyards, a petroleum coke transfer station, a scrap metal recycler, several auto body shops, a paint and varnish company, a chemical manufacturing company, three food-processing plants, and numerous other heavy industrial businesses. Just north of the neighborhood is the large and dusty G-P Gypsum Corporation plant. All these businesses rely on diesel trucks to transport their materials, which in turn further pollute the air by emitting carcinogenic fumes.

Even as the proliferation of polluting businesses continues, county and state officials have imposed additional unwanted and dangerous facilities into Waterfront South. In the early 1980s, when Camden County was required to upgrade its sewage treatment system, it selected the small city sewage plant in Waterfront South for expansion in order to process there all the sewage from thirty-five mostly affluent, white, and suburban municipalities. The county then constructed an open-air sewage-sludge-composting facility in close vicinity to the treatment plant. Next came the regional trash-to-steam incinerator, one of the largest in the state, less than a mile from the sewage treatment plant. In the early 1990s, Waterfront South was chosen as the site for a cogeneration power plant. The New Jersey Department of Environmental Protection (DEP) freely granted permits for all of these facilities over strong community opposition.

Despite its industrial history, Waterfront South was a reasonably livable community before it became a dumping ground for undesirable and polluting facilities. The family of the longtime resident and community leader Phyllis Holmes was the first African American household to move onto her block thirty years ago. She recalls enjoying her nice neighbors and the friendly atmosphere of the community. The sewage plant, incinerator, and other major polluters, however, along with years of neglect by government enforcement officials, have taken their toll on the community. For years, Waterfront South residents have been forced to endure toxic fumes, dust, horrific odors, and noise. Truck drivers frequently violate traffic codes by taking shortcuts down residential streets. The eighteen- and twenty-four-wheelers barrel past, endangering young children playing outside, drowning out conversations, damaging the foundations of houses and streets, and leaving residents choking for air.

The incinerator, power plant, local licorice plant, and gypsum plant all emit many tons of fine, inhalable particulates. Inhalable particulates are known to cause lung cancer; aggravate respiratory illnesses such as asthma, emphysema, and bronchitis; trigger cardiovascular symptoms; and bring on premature death. These particulates, combined with the air pollution generated by refineries and other industries in nearby Philadelphia, result in severely unhealthful air quality. The Waterfront South area has the state's highest readings for inhalable particulate pollution.[7] In addition, in Camden, as in most areas in New Jersey, the ozone levels significantly exceed federal air quality standards.[8]

In January 2004, with a $100,000 grant from the EPA, the New Jersey Department of Environmental Protection launched an Air Toxics Pilot Project in the Waterfront South area because of known sources of air toxics emissions in and near the residential community. This pilot project supplements the DEP's existing air monitoring efforts with more detailed information about air toxics and particulate matter emitted by individual facilities in this neighborhood. One component of the larger Air Toxics Pilot Project in Camden is the "Bucket Brigade" project, which trains local residents to collect air samples and measure pollution exposure in their neighborhoods. DEP-trained citizens use a simple five-gallon plastic bucket to collect an air sample in a plastic bag. The residents take the samples over a four-minute period during odor episodes or other times of concern. These samples are then analyzed for odorous, sulfur-containing substances and volatile organic compounds such as benzene. Two community groups are participating in the Bucket Brigade: South Camden Citizens in Action and the Antioch Community Development Corporation.[9] Only limited information has been collected on the actual inhalation of emissions by citizens living in the neighborhood.

The Air Toxics Pilot Project focuses on industrial and manufacturing sources of air pollution and the particulate emissions from diesel trucks. Most of the sources are located within the boundaries of Camden's Waterfront South neighborhood, but the project also includes some large facilities or sources of special concern located near the neighborhood. Of the more than fifty facilities considered for the pilot project, twenty-seven were selected and subjected to dispersion-modeling analysis. Dispersion modeling is a mathematical calculation that predicts how far, how fast, and in what direction certain gases or particulate matter will move into the air from any given location.

Not surprisingly, the rates for asthma and other respiratory problems have risen dramatically in Waterfront South in the past decade. An odor study showed that 61 percent of residents experienced some type of respiratory symptoms, compared to 35 percent in a different Camden neighborhood.[11] Administrators at a local elementary school report that almost one-quarter of the students have asthma. Bonnie Sanders, a long-time resident and leader in community environmental struggles, is raising a granddaughter and a foster child in the row house she owns in Waterfront South's residential core. Both girls have developed respiratory ailments. The children wake during the night when the air is still and dusty and they must sit up in order to breathe comfortably.

Although the pollution it produces is perhaps less dangerous than the other air pollution in the area, the sewage treatment plant has had the most obvious blighting effect on the neighborhood. The strong smell of raw sewage constantly permeates the area. According to the local school principal, children thought, because of the odor, they were being punished if they were told to play outside during recess. Residents stopped sitting in their backyards and on stoops on hot summer days. Industrial odors stigmatized the community and many families became embarrassed to invite friends and relatives to visit. Moreover, "when rating the intensity of sewage plant odors, people who live near them tended to rate the lower concentrations of those odors as much, much weaker, and some couldn't discern them at all."[12] Having lived with noxious odors, a form of pollution, for years, their sense of smell had become dulled.

Although most sections of Camden experienced increasing blight from 1970 to 1990 due to many factors, Waterfront South was especially devastated. Residents who could afford to move left the neighborhood. Businesses relocated to more desirable areas in the city and suburbs. City services decreased. Housing values dropped dramatically, and, for the remaining households, moving out became increasingly difficult. Waterfront South now has close to two thousand residents.[13] Almost half of them are children, who are the most vulnerable to pollution.

CREATING A VOICE FOR THE COMMUNITY

Camden has a proud history of activism. In the early part of the century, the city's union leaders fought to protect the rights of workers. Civil rights activists during the 1960s and 1970s battled city hall and the federal government over housing discrimination policies and the forced displacement of African American families. Residents organized strong neighborhood opposition to the siting of a prison and an incinerator in the city during the 1980s and 1990s. Camden's environmental justice struggle against St. Lawrence Cement was initiated and led by a group of Waterfront South residents known as South Camden Citizens in Action (SCCIA).

The SCCIA was formed in 1997 after a local nonprofit organization in Waterfront South decided to sponsor a grassroots neighborhood planning project and brought together residents to explore how living conditions could be improved. A core group of these residents decided to create the SCCIA. These new community leaders were not experienced or trained activists. They were mostly African American women, all low-income, and some in poor health. They were also longtime residents of Camden, and all shared a commitment to making their community more livable and safe.

The SCCIA did not define itself as an environmental justice organization; it worked on many neighborhood issues. From the beginning, however, environmental problems dominated the discussions. At the first open community meeting, residents quickly decided by consensus that the problem they most wanted to tackle was the odor from the sewage plant. The SCCIA organized a campaign to develop a record of odor violations and get local officials' support. After the DEP failed to address their complaints, the group recruited a public interest lawyer to bring a citizen lawsuit to enforce the odor regulations.[14]

The SCCIA obtained a settlement requiring the facility to upgrade its odor controls. While the litigation was pending, an EPA representative came to Camden to inform residents about one of the Superfund sites in their neighborhood. Many residents heard for the first time about the abandoned warehouse and scattered hot spots throughout the residential neighborhood that had been emitting low-level radiation for more than eighty years. SCCIA members evaluated the EPA's remediation plans, and the agency accepted the group's recommendation that all contaminated materials be removed.

Newly aware of these environmental hazards, the SCCIA made strong demands on behalf of the residents, quickly acquiring a reputation for being assertive in tackling government and other entities. Soon after its formation and initial successes, however, the SCCIA lost the support of its sponsoring nonprofit organization. Lacking any other organizational support or resources, it began to function as an exclusively volunteer organization. Its leaders continued to meet in one another's living rooms and donate their own money for refreshments and supplies. In 1999 this fragile group had to confront a new major environmental justice struggle: the coming of the St. Lawrence Cement Company (SLC) to Waterfront South.

THE FIGHT AGAINST ST. LAWRENCE CEMENT

Based in Canada, and a member of the Swiss Holderbank Group (now called Holcim), the SLC is one of the world's largest manufacturers of cement. In March 1999 the company negotiated a lease with the South Jersey Port Corporation, a state agency, for twelve acres of land along the Delaware River at the port's Broadway terminal in Waterfront South to construct a cement-grinding facility. It would ship in blast-furnace slag from Italy by barge to a docking facility in Camden, truck it three miles to the facility in Waterfront South, and grind it into a very fine powder for use as a cement additive. The product then would be distributed throughout the northeastern United States. The cement company's operations would generate an estimated seventy-seven thousand diesel truck trips and emit one hundred tons of pollutants per year.[15] Almost sixty tons of this would be made up of inhalable particulates, or PM-10.[16] A significant amount would be composed of the very smallest, and therefore most dangerous, particulates, PM-2.5.[17]

Because its facility is located on state land, the SLC would pay no property taxes and would offer no host benefits to Camden. The cement-grinding operations would be highly mechanized and produce only fifteen jobs. Opponents of environmental justice like to point to the need for business investment in communities such as Waterfront South, and they fault advocates for "discouraging" such investment. However, the cement company is typical of the type of industry that seeks to locate in these communities. All too often, polluting industries supply few jobs and their blighting effect on the area only discourages other, more desirable and labor-intensive businesses from locating nearby.[18] The proliferation of waste disposal and recycling facilities, transfer stations, and heavy industry in Waterfront South has not alleviated Camden's high unemployment and poverty rates, which continue to rise along with pollution levels.

The SLC used a proactive strategy to try to defuse community opposition and obtain needed political and government support. The company hired a public relations consultant in Camden to assist it in its efforts; it also paid for lobbyists in the state capital, Trenton, and in Washington, D.C. Shortly after executing the lease, the SLC began a series of meetings with the DEP to discuss its plans for the facility. Because port land is exempt from zoning and planning, the company did not have to obtain any local board approvals or to involve city officials. In August 1999 the company submitted its permit application to the DEP and made its plans known to the community. Although the DEP did not require community outreach of the company, the SLC conducted an aggressive public relations campaign to obtain the support of local churches, nonprofit organizations, and community groups. It held several community meetings and organized a community advisory panel. It even paid for experts, whom the advisory panel selected, to review the permit application. This campaign underscored an aspect typical of environmental justice controversies: communities without any resources become pitted in David-versus-Goliath struggles against corporate giants that can use their extensive financial and other resources to influence public opinion and undermine community organizing efforts.

From the start, SCCIA members were suspicious of the cement company's tactics. Eventually the SCCIA refused to participate in the community advisory panel because the members saw that the company was trying to use the participation of neighborhood organizations to demonstrate that it had community support. Instead the SCCIA engaged in an organizing effort to oppose the cement company through petitions, letters, neighborhood speak-outs, and meetings with DEP officials.

The DEP evaluated the SLC's permit in accordance with New Jersey air quality regulations and the federal Clean Air Act.[19] It analyzed the company's estimated emissions and determined that they would not exceed the National Ambient Air Quality Standards.[20] In doing so, the DEP applied the 1987 PM-10 standard, which is still in effect today, even though, as has been well established, this standard is inadequate to protect human health.[21] By relying exclusively on six narrow environmental criteria (the air quality standards), the DEP was able to avoid looking at the real effects of the facility. The agency did not investigate or consider the cement company's more dangerous PM-2.5 emissions. In addition, the DEP did not consider the effects of the diesel truck fumes on air quality because the Clean Air Act does not include such "mobile source emissions" in permitting review. Moreover, the DEP did not consider the local conditions in Waterfront South, the potential cumulative and synergistic effects of all the pollution in the area, the residents' poor health, or the facility's effects on the overall quality of life. Most significantly, the DEP did not consider whether it was disproportionately burdening African American and Latino residents with more than their fair share of environmental hazards.

Because of the peculiarities of New Jersey law, the DEP allowed the SLC to construct the $50 million facility "at risk"—that is, before the agency even issued the permit.[22] By the time the DEP did issue a draft permit and schedule the first and only public hearing, in the summer of 2000, construction was more than 50 percent complete. Some residents, seeing construction of the massive cement plant in progress, viewed the SCCIA's campaign against the facility as futile and the public hearing process as meaningless. Nevertheless, more than 120 persons appeared at the public hearing. Most of them testified in opposition to the plant and raised both civil rights and health concerns. However, as the SCCIA's president, Bonnie Sanders, later told a DEP official, "There was a public hearing, but no one got heard." The DEP did not take any steps to address the residents' concerns.

In October 2000, the SCCIA filed administrative civil rights complaints with both the DEP and the EPA, noting that the facility would have a discriminatory effect on African American and Latino residents. Both the DEP and the EPA ignored these complaints. On October 31, 2000, the DEP issued the final permits to the cement company, and litigation became the only option for continuing the struggle.

The SCCIA filed a lawsuit in the U.S. District Court on February 13, 2001, and simultaneously requested a preliminary injunction to prevent the SLC from starting operations. Unlike many other environmental justice cases, the SCCIA's lawsuit rested exclusively on civil rights rather than environmental claims. Given the inadequacy of the PM-10 standard, proving a technical violation of the Clean Air Act seemed impossible. The DEP's actions were egregious, according to the SCCIA, not because the agency had misapplied environmental criteria, but because it had failed to consider the discriminatory effects of the permit, knowingly perpetuating the environmental racism to which Waterfront South residents had been repeatedly subjected. Therefore, the SCCIA's primary claim was racial discrimination in violation of the regulations enacted under Title VI of the Civil Rights Act of 1964.[23] The SCCIA also alleged that the agency had violated the Fair Housing Act[24] and had intentionally discriminated against the neighborhood in violation of Title VI and the equal protection clause of the U.S. Constitution.

The first issue addressed by the court was the SCCIA's request for an injunction, which was based entirely on the discriminatory impact claim brought under the Title VI regulations. On April 19, 2001, Judge Stephen Orlofsky issued his first ruling. In a 140-page published decision, he agreed with the SCCIA that the DEP had violated the Title VI regulations by relying exclusively on environmental standards and failing to make a "disparate impact analysis" before issuing a permit.[25] He ordered the DEP to conduct such an analysis within thirty days. The judge made extensive factual findings about the environmental and health conditions in Waterfront South and the harm likely to result from the cement company's operations, concluding that the SCCIA was likely to prevail on the merits of the case. Most important, he enjoined operation of the facility.[26]

This was the first time in U.S. history that a court found a permitting agency to have violated civil rights law, and it was a major victory for environmental justice advocacy. It was also one of the rare instances in which civil rights plaintiffs succeeded in proving disparate impact. This decision put a multimillion-dollar investment at risk and drew national attention to the case. However, only five days later, while the SCCIA was just starting to enjoy its victory and appreciate its new fame, the U.S. Supreme Court decided *Alexander v. Sandoval,* holding that private citizens did not have a right to enforce Title VI regulations, which were the heart of the SCCIA's case.[27]

Judge Orlofsky kept the injunction in place despite the *Sandoval* decision. He allowed the SCCIA to amend its complaint to include a claim under section 1983, a different provision of the civil rights statutes. In May he issued a second decision, allowing plaintiffs to use section 1983 to enforce the Title VI regulations.[28] This was the first court decision to interpret *Sandoval,* and it offered a temporary road map for civil rights litigants nationally.[29]

Many environmental justice battles are won when a company decides that the legal and political struggles are not worth the trouble and leaves town. But the SLC had already invested so much money in constructing its cement-grinding plant in Camden that the SCCIA had no illusions that it would walk away from the facility. Both the cement company and the DEP appealed the two trial court decisions in the Third Circuit Court of Appeals. In June of 2001, in a severe blow to the community's morale, the court stayed the injunction and allowed the cement company to start operations. Later that year, in December, the court ruled two to one to reverse Judge Orlofsky's second decision, and it held that Title VI regulations were not enforceable through section 1983.[30] The SCCIA's requests for rehearing by the full Third Circuit Court and for a review by the U.S. Supreme Court were denied.

The Third Circuit Court's decision thus placed the SCCIA in the peculiar position of having obtained a ruling, still in effect, that the state environmental agency's practices violated civil rights, and of having no ability to benefit from that ruling. Meanwhile, the cement company continues to operate, releasing invisible but dangerous particulates from its smoke stacks. On windy days, dust from its sixty-foot-high, uncovered slag piles blows around in the streets. Its diesel trucks circle the neighborhood. The air quality in Waterfront South remains severely unhealthful.

WINNING BEYOND THE COURTS

Despite the legal setbacks, the *South Camden Citizens in Action v. NJ DEP* litigation has significantly furthered environmental justice advocacy on the local, state, and national levels. The court action gave the community leverage that it would not otherwise have enjoyed. The two-month delay in the start of the cement company's operations cost the company millions of dollars, sending a shock wave through the regulated business community and requiring them to reconsider whether supposedly powerless communities like Waterfront South are safe to exploit. Judge Orlofsky's findings about the unfair environmental burden that had been placed upon the Waterfront South community gave new credibility to the arguments of environmental justice advocates and a sense of entitlement to Camden residents.

The high profile of the case generated a great deal of attention, and SCCIA members emerged as community spokespeople and leaders. SCCIA leaders held numerous press interviews, obtaining favorable coverage in major news media such as the *New York Times*, *Business Week*, National Public Radio, the *National Law Journal*, and the *Philadelphia Inquirer*. This publicity raised public awareness about environmental justice and the plight of communities such as Waterfront South. Because of their visibility, SCCIA members were able both to connect with longtime environmental justice advocates and to interest other activists in environmental justice issues.

In Camden, the SCCIA, working together with other area activists, organized numerous neighborhood educational events, protests, and petition campaigns. Realizing that environmental justice problems extended beyond their neighborhood, they banded together with nearby supporters to form the citywide Camden Environmental Justice Coalition. They gained the support of some local officials, and the Camden City Council passed a resolution opposing the cement company's operations. The county, state, and national branches of the National Association for the Advancement of Colored People all publicly expressed support for the SCCIA's struggle.

Camden residents also engaged in statewide efforts to change the DEP's permitting procedures and prevent further instances of siting disproportionate numbers of polluters in communities of color. The SCCIA and Camden Environmental Justice Coalition members were joined by environmental and civil rights activists from around the state at a rally they organized at the DEP's headquarters in October 2001 to protest the department's refusal to address civil rights. In March of 2002, the new DEP commissioner accepted the SCCIA's invitation to visit Camden and spent several hours touring the city and speaking to residents about environmental problems. The immediate results of his visit included the enforcement of truck traffic restrictions by state police, testing of

Camden's drinking water, relocation of five families living immediately adjacent to the radioactive Superfund site, and a comprehensive enforcement initiative that focused on industrial companies in the Waterfront South community that had a history of pollution violations.

The SCCIA and the coalition also played a lead role in bringing together environmental and civil rights groups to respond to the DEP's newly proposed "environmental equity" permitting regulations. These weak regulations added public participation requirements for certain types of permits, but did nothing to change the standards for issuing permits. In written comments and during testimony at a public hearing, the community leaders stressed the need to strengthen the regulations to prevent the continued siting of polluters in already overburdened communities. The DEP has reevaluated, and decided not to proceed with, the proposed regulations.[31]

As a result of the litigation and the organizing efforts, the SCCIA and other Camden activists also have participated in national environmental justice advocacy. This has included taking part in a press conference at the U.S. Senate concerning judicial appointments, the Second National People of Color Environmental Leadership Summit, the National Strategy Conference to Stop the Rollback of Civil Rights, and the U.S. Commission on Civil Rights environmental justice hearings.

In addition, the SCCIA has used its setbacks in court to educate legislators about the need for stronger protection for residents who have suffered from environmental racism. SCCIA members have met with city, state, and federal elected officials to describe the health and quality-of-life problems in Waterfront South and to urge legislators to fashion remedies that could help such communities.

At the same time, the new connections among advocates and a greater knowledge about local environmental hazards has increased awareness among Camden residents about environmental racism and strengthened their commitment to continue the fight. As new environmental justice problems come to light in Camden, residents have been able to take on these struggles with greater unity and strength. For example, in the spring of 2002, residents learned that they had been provided with severely contaminated drinking water for more than twenty years from what is now a Superfund site. In addition to pursuing toxic tort litigation, community activists initiated a campaign to inform the public, ensure that the current water supply was safe, plan a health impact study, and monitor cleanup of the Superfund site. Later that year, a proposal to dispose of radioactive wastewater by discharging it into Camden's sewage system generated a high level of public opposition from many affected communities. The issue brought together suburban and city environmental activists. The public outrage expressed by the community forced officials to reconsider the plan.

Unfortunately, however, Camden activists have faced significant obstacles in their organizing work, limiting their ability to take full advantage of the opportunities presented by the litigation and making it harder to win their environmental justice campaign against the cement company. Lack of resources and organizational capacity have been major hurdles. There are no stable, established, and well-funded community organizations in Camden that can undertake or support an environmental justice campaign. It is left up to emerging community groups such as the SCCIA and the Camden Environmental Justice Coalition to wage these battles, even though they may have limited organizational strength.

The SCCIA has had to depend largely on volunteers with little or no formal training or experience. These neighborhood residents are forced to take time out of busy schedules and to balance competing demands of family and work. Some residents inevitably have grown tired of the need to constantly join battles, against one environmental insult after another, in which there have been so few successes. The hardships of living with limited income under egregiously bad conditions in a community such as Waterfront South make organizing efforts yet more difficult. Knowing financial support is needed, the group has tried to raise funds to hire staff. There has been no one who could conduct aggressive fund-raising on the SCCIA's behalf, however, and it has proved difficult to obtain financial support despite the group's high visibility.

In spite of these difficulties, SCCIA members and other Camden residents continue to bravely fight to increase the role of residents in decision making and to secure clean and safe communities. They know that the health and safety of their children, their parents, and their neighbors are at stake, and they see no choice.

CAMDEN LESSONS AND ENVIRONMENTAL JUSTICE ADVOCACY

Camden's struggles clearly show how much remains to be done to achieve environmental justice. First, the conditions in Waterfront South illustrate the extent to which environmentally overburdened, impoverished urban communities of color still experience discrimination in siting decisions, enforcement efforts, and allocation of resources by environmental and other government agencies. In addition, the story of Camden's environmental justice campaign demonstrates two crucial needs: the need to support grassroots groups and help them increase their capacity and strength, and the need to secure more effective legal tools for protecting vulnerable communities. While environmental justice leaders have recognized and attempted to address both issues, the experiences of Camden's residents show that they have not yet realized these goals.

There is no question that Camden's struggle benefited from years of environmental justice advocacy, which has led to greater public knowledge about environmental racism, the formation of supportive national and regional environmental justice networks, and research and analysis by specialized experts. Nevertheless, from a Camden perspective, it is hard to see any tangible improvements in local conditions in the past decade since the environmental justice movement gained prominence. Residents of communities such as Waterfront South continue to experience racial discrimination, live in concentrated poverty, and be subject to severe environmental degradation. Without resources and political clout, they find it hard to exercise control, or even significant influence, over decisions affecting their communities. While resorting to legal action can enhance a community's leverage, courts can do little to redress environmental discrimination under current laws.

The need to build stronger grassroots organizations is obvious. Environmental justice advocates have long recognized that environmental justice can be achieved only if residents of affected neighborhoods come together to exercise their collective power. Advocates also appreciate that strong local institutions are needed to achieve the goal of collective power. Frequently, however, residents of neighborhoods like Waterfront South are not well organized and have little institutional support.

Very few funders support organizing activities. In addition, environmental justice advocacy challenges many of our most powerful and wealthy institutions, such as multinational corporations and state and local governments. As the Camden story exemplifies, environmental justice campaigns are therefore often highly controversial. More established organizations may shy away from becoming involved for fear of damage to their reputations or funding. If the environmental justice community does not find a way to channel financial resources quickly to grassroots groups and provide them with technical support when needed, many environmental justice campaigns are likely to be lost on the local level.

Camden's effort also underscores the need for legislative and administrative advocacy. Effective legal tools, combined with ready access to legal assistance, can sometimes bolster a community struggle. Even the threat of litigation can increase a community's leverage in bargaining, while administrative proceedings and court battles can delay or stop an unwanted project.[32]

The *South Camden Citizens in Action v. NJ DEP* litigation clearly demonstrates the current limitations of legal administrative and court remedies. The SCCIA's administrative Title VI complaints were ignored. Even though a federal judge ruled that the DEP had violated Title VI, residents lost hope—given past performances by the EPA and DEP in this and in other cases—that either agency would act on that ruling. The grounds for a civil rights lawsuit—after the *Sandoval, South Camden,* and *Gonzaga University* Supreme Court decisions—are limited.[33]

Creative lawyers will continue to pursue the legal avenues that remain, such as intentional discrimination claims under federal law, state law claims, and environmental statutes. Although challenges based on environmental laws have proven most fruitful thus far in environmental justice litigation, they offer limited relief to communities like Waterfront South. Environmental litigation is costly and highly technical, and many communities lack the resources to pursue it. Courts defer to the expertise of environmental agencies, so the standard for challenging an agency's decision to issue a permit is a difficult one to meet.

Most important, environmental laws alone cannot address the disparity in environmental burdens imposed upon low-income and nonwhite communities. Without civil rights remedies, a hundred more businesses could be sited in one community such as Waterfront South, and all polluting facilities in the state could be located in communities of color. Even such extreme disparity in apportioning the burdens of pollution does not provide a legal basis for stopping an agency from continuing to grant permits under environmental laws. It is only a matter of time before another polluter announces plans to open a new facility in Waterfront South, and residents worry that there will be no legal avenue for stopping the project.

Environmental justice and other civil rights and environmental advocates must continue to push federal and state legislators, administrative agencies, and elected officials to create more legal tools for environmentally overburdened communities and other groups suffering from discrimination.[34] The future success of the environmental justice movement depends on fundamental social change, including the investment of affected communities such as Waterfront South with greater decision-making power. Environmental justice advocacy should be directed toward creating stronger neighborhood institutions, building leadership, and helping organizations acquire needed resources, technical assistance, and legal tools, which will enable groups like the SCCIA to reclaim and rebuild their communities.

PART THREE

LAND RIGHTS AND SUSTAINABLE DEVELOPMENT

THIS SECTION EXAMINES LAND USE, land rights, sovereignty, resource extraction, and sustainable development conflicts. Many sustainable development struggles around the world revolve around land and how it is defined and used. We are unlikely to achieve sustainability in the world without addressing key equity issues, including access to land and redistributive land reform.

Land and resource rights are fundamentally important to indigenous peoples around the world because these rights constitute the basis of their economic livelihood and their spiritual, cultural, and social identity. Land rights, human rights, and sustainability are intertwined. Corporate greed and corrupt governments have spawned resource wars and turned thousands of indigenous peoples and local residents into resource rebels—groups who are fighting for their basic survival and way of life.

Land, green space, and nature are also important in the urban landscape, which is dominated by glass, steel, and concrete structures. Race and class factors influence the distribution of parklands. Communities made up of people of color suffer the greatest negative consequences of being park-poor. The struggle against this inequity gave birth to the urban parks movement.

Parks can address a multitude of urban challenges: they can spur economic development, address environmental issues, and offer educational and youth development services. A park and its surrounding area can be not only a place to understand and relate to nature but also a place for social and cultural exchange.

7

Anatomy of the Urban Parks Movement
Equal Justice, Democracy, and Livability in Los Angeles

The urban parks movement is building community and diversifying democracy from the ground up by giving people a sense of their own power in deciding the future of their city, their lives, and their children's lives. People who have not participated in government before are fighting city hall and wealthy developers—and winning.

The movement is making Los Angeles, for example, a greener, more just, and more sustainable community for all.[1] Case studies from grassroots struggles there, in which people of color and low-income communities have partnered with public interest lawyers, show how people have gained access to parks, other green space, beaches, school playgrounds, and ultimately, the good life.

WHY PARKS MATTER: THE VALUES AT STAKE

The United Nations recognizes a child's right to play as a fundamental human right.[2] The simple joys of playing in the park go hand in hand with health, recreation, and other values discussed below.

Access to parks and recreation is about community health. The human need for parks, school yards, and active recreation, and its implications for human health, are profound.[3] If current trends in obesity,

145

inactivity, and disease continue, today's youth will be the first generation in this nation's history to face a life expectancy shorter than that of their parents.[4] The health crisis costs the United States over $100 billion each year.[5] The epidemic of obesity, inactivity, and related diseases like diabetes is shortening children's lives and destroying the quality of their lives.

In California, 27 percent of children are overweight and 40 percent are unfit.[6] Only 24 percent of the state's fifth, seventh, and ninth graders met minimal physical fitness standards in 2003.[7] The numbers are even lower within the Los Angeles Unified School District, where just 17 percent of fifth graders, 16 percent of seventh graders, and less than 11 percent of ninth graders met all six of the minimum fitness standards in 2003.[8] State assembly districts with the highest proportion of overweight children also have the highest concentrations of people of color.[9]

Overweight and unfit children face a greater risk of developing lung disease, diabetes, asthma, and cancer.[10] Type 2 diabetes, formerly known as adult-onset diabetes, now affects millions of overweight and inactive children at younger and younger ages.[11] As a result, children are more likely to suffer long-range effects from diabetes, including loss of limbs, blindness, and death. As a result of shrinking budgets and demands for improved standardized academic test scores, physical education is being squeezed out of the school day.[12]

Time spent outdoors promotes physical activity, good health, and the full development of the child. The Center for Health Policy Research at the University of California, Los Angeles, recommends increased funding for physical activity programs offered before, during, and after school in order to reduce rates of diabetes among young people.[13] Recreation programs provide alternatives to gangs, drugs, violence, crime, and teen sex.[14] In the aftermath of the riots and rebellion that followed the acquittal of the police officers in the state trial involving the Rodney King beating, gang members issued a manifesto calling for peace and listing the shortage of parks and open spaces as one of their major concerns.[15]

Parks and green space cool the city, clean the air and ground, and help reduce polluted storm water runoff.[16] Parks can raise property values, increase tourism, promote the economic revitalization of neighboring communities, create jobs, and reduce health care costs. When cities create greenways in or near downtown areas, property values rise and the number of businesses and jobs grows.[17]

Parks are democratic commons that bring people together as equals, as the first landscape architect, Frederick Law Olmsted, recognized when

designing Central Park in New York City.[18] People from different racial
and ethnic groups use parks differently, constructing meaning for public
open space based on their own values, cultures, histories, and traditions,
according to a study by the University of California, Los Angeles, that
examined cultural differences in the use of urban parks.[19] New Latino
immigrants do not organize politically. Rather, they first organize soccer
leagues and then use those same organizing skills to go on to organize
politically.[20] For Hispanics, the park is primarily a social gathering place.
African Americans, more than any other racial group, engage in sports.
Sports and recreation programs help bring society together. Jackie
Robinson broke down color barriers seven years before *Brown v. Board
of Education* declared "separate but equal" to be unconstitutional.[21]
Spiritual and social justice values inspire faith-based support for parks
and natural lands. Articulating the values at stake to appeal to different
stakeholders in the urban park movement is consistent with Professor
George Lakoff's call for a progressive movement built around the shared
values that define who progressives are, and that encompasses the efforts
by groups working on many different issue areas and programs.[22]

RACE, ETHNICITY, AND UNEQUAL ACCESS TO PARKS

Los Angeles, with a population of 3.7 million people in 2000, is the second-largest city in the United States. About 69 percent of its population
is made up of people of color, and only 31 percent is non-Hispanic white;
45 percent of the city's population is Hispanic.[23] The sprawling city covers more than 469.3 square miles and has 15,600 acres of parkland,
including the 4,217 acres of Griffith Park, the largest municipal park in
the United States. According to the *Los Angeles Almanac*, the city has
382 public parks, 123 recreation centers, 52 pools, 28 senior citizen centers, 13 golf courses, 18 child care centers, and 7 camps.[24] Los Angeles is
park poor, however, with fewer acres of park per resident than any other
major city in the United States. When a city lacks enough parks and
recreation facilities, all communities within the city suffer, but low-
income people of color suffer first and worst. In Los Angeles, there are
unfair disparities in access to parklands, playgrounds, beaches, and recreation based on race, ethnicity, and class.[25]

The lack of parks in communities of color in Los Angeles is not an
accident of unplanned growth, but the result of a history and pattern of
discriminatory land use planning, racially restrictive housing covenants,
discriminatory funding formulas, and other practices. People of color did

not simply choose to live in ethnic enclaves in Los Angeles—Latinos in East L.A., Chinese in Old and New Chinatown, Japanese in Little Tokyo, and African Americans in South Central—they were forbidden from living in other places.[26]

Though the practice was not codified in law, public space in Los Angeles was "tacitly racialized."[27] For example, blacks were not allowed in the pool in many municipal parks, and in other parks they were allowed to swim only on the day before the pool was cleaned. Public pools continued to be segregated into the 1940s. Lincoln Park in East Los Angeles was a popular destination for black youth from South Central and Latino youth from East Los Angeles, who could take the Pacific Electric railroad to reach the park where they were not feared and despised.[28]

The city of Los Angeles virtually abandoned parks, school construction, and public recreation in the wake of Proposition 13 in 1978, the taxpayers' revolt that cut funding for local services, including parks and schools. Poorer communities in the inner city have been historically shortchanged by city funding formulas for parks and recreation programs, according to former Los Angeles mayor Richard Riordan, a wealthy Republican businessman, in an interview in the *Wall Street Journal*. Money for parks and recreation, for example, is not invested throughout the city based on need, but is distributed equally among the fifteen city council districts regardless of need.[29] Many urban parks are more heavily used than suburban parks and require more staff.

The city's Department of Recreation and Parks has long recognized the inequities in park funding. According to the department's director of planning and development in 1998, "It's a pattern we all understand. The urban areas of Los Angeles have fewer park facilities than the new areas or outlying areas, where ordinances require that parks be developed when housing developments go in."[30] Because there has been little new construction in poorer neighborhoods, those areas benefit little from the state's Quimby Act, which requires developers to set aside money to create parks near their new projects. New projects are disproportionately built in disproportionately wealthy white communities, which benefit from the Quimby funds.

The city of Los Angeles also encourages parks to operate like businesses and collect user fees. People pay to play. Since the wealthier and whiter areas of the city have more park space and fee-generating facilities and programs, such as tennis courts, racquetball courts, golf courses, Little League, and other organized team sports, this has created a regressive distribution of park resources. Inner-city communities do not have fee-generating amenities, and residents could not afford to pay for them even if they did.

Local park bond funds are distributed in ways that exacerbate rather than alleviate the inequities in access to parks and recreation.[31] Each of the criteria and methods of administration discussed above fail to account for the needs of the poorest neighborhoods, which are disproportionately inhabited by people of color.

The lack of parks in inner-city communities is exacerbated by the disappearance of school yards where children could play and join recreation programs. Due to the epic overcrowding at public schools in Los Angeles and the concomitant use of portable classrooms that devour playground space, school yards at existing schools are disappearing. Already ill-served by an overburdened school system, low-income youth fare even worse after school, in the absence of school yards and parks.

According to a survey on Californians and the environment by the influential California Public Policy Institute, 64 percent of Californians say that poorer communities have less than their fair share of well-maintained parks and recreational facilities. Latinos are far more likely than non-Hispanic whites (72 percent compared to 60 percent) to say that poorer communities do not receive their fair share of these environmental benefits. A majority of residents (58 percent) agree that compared to wealthier neighborhoods, lower-income and minority neighborhoods bear more than their fair share of the environmental burdens of toxic waste and polluting facilities.[32]

Los Angeles has less than an acre of park per thousand residents, compared to the six to ten acres per thousand residents that is the National Recreation and Park Association standard. And, as noted earlier, there are unfair disparities in access to the parks and recreation facilities that do exist in Los Angeles as a whole. In the inner city, there are .3 acre of park per thousand residents, compared to 1.7 acres in the disproportionately white and relatively wealthy parts of Los Angeles.[33]

The paucity of parkland is matched by the lack of recreational facilities. For example, within Baldwin Hills State Park (or within a five-mile radius of it), which lies at the historical heart of African American Los Angeles, there is one picnic table for every 10,000 people, one playground for every 23,000 children, one soccer field for every 30,000 people, and one basketball court for every 36,000 people.[34]

These figures do not take into account the privatization of public space. Los Angeles' population has increased dramatically since 1990—

with little change in public park space. Families in more affluent white communities have backyards, swimming pools, basketball hoops over the driveway, access to country clubs and private beaches, and vacation resorts. Families in low-income communities of color do not. The children in these neighborhoods lack adequate access to cars or to a decent transit system to reach parks in other neighborhoods and in wilderness areas.

Although—or because—communities of color and low-income communities are disproportionately denied the benefits of parks and recreation, these communities were the biggest supporters of California's Proposition 40, which was the largest resource bond in United States history. This state proposition provided $2.6 billion for parks, clean water, and clean air. Proposition 40 passed in March 2002 with the support of 77 percent of black voters, 74 percent of Latino voters, 60 percent of Asian voters, and 56 percent of non-Hispanic white voters. Seventy-five percent of voters with an annual family income below $20,000 and 61 percent with a high school diploma or less supported Proposition 40— the highest among any income or education levels.[35]

Proposition 40 demolished the myth that the environment is a luxury that communities of color and low-income communities cannot afford or are not willing to pay for. The steering committee of the organization Yes on Prop 40 engaged in strategic outreach to diverse communities. The campaign targeted half a million voters with direct mail in English and Spanish, the Web site of the group Yes on Prop 40 included materials in English and Spanish, and a get-out-the-vote drive targeted diverse communities. African American ministers called on their congregations to support Proposition 40 from the pulpit the Sunday before the election, and Cardinal Roger Mahony endorsed Proposition 40.[36]

OLMSTED'S VISION YESTERDAY AND TODAY

In 1930, the firm started by the sons of Central Park's designer, Frederick Law Olmsted, proposed a network of parks, playgrounds, schools, beaches, forests, and transportation to promote the social, economic, and environmental vitality of Los Angeles and the health of its people. According to the Olmsted Report:

> Continued prosperity [in Los Angeles] will depend on providing needed parks, because, with the growth of a great metropolis here, the absence of parks will make living conditions less and less attractive, less and less wholesome. . . . In so far, therefore, as the people fail to show the

understanding, courage, and organizing ability necessary at this crisis, the growth of the Region will tend to strangle itself.[37]

These words remain true today. The Olmsted Report proposed the joint use of parks, playgrounds, and schools to make optimal use of land and public resources, and it called for doubling the public beach frontage. The report recommended a massive program that would create 71,000 acres of parkland, with another 91,000 acres in outlying areas. The heart of the program was 214 miles of interconnecting parkways, including a parkway along the Los Angeles River. Implementing the recommendations would have cost $233 million in 1930 dollars, taken forty to fifty years to complete, and required the creation of a regional park authority that could have levied fees to pay for parks and open space.[38]

Implementing the Olmsted vision would have made Los Angeles one of the most beautiful and livable regions in the world. Powerful private interests and civic leaders demonstrated a tragic lack of vision and judgment when they killed the Olmsted Report. Just two hundred copies were printed, only enough for the members of the blue ribbon commission that oversaw the report. Civic leaders killed the report because of politics, bureaucracy, and greed in a triumph of private power over public space and social democracy.[39] The recommendations have yet to be implemented.

THE BATTLE FOR THE CORNFIELD

The Cornfield lies just south of the confluence of the fifty-one-mile Los Angeles River and the twenty-two-mile Arroyo Seco (dry canyon), in one of Los Angeles' most culturally, historically, and ethnically diverse communities. The reason the site is called the Cornfield is not clear. In the first written description of the area that later became El Pueblo de Los Angeles, Father Juan Crespí, a member of the 1769 Spanish expedition led by Captain Gaspar de Portolá, described the trees and green bottomlands that spread out along the banks of the Los Angeles River as "looking from afar like nothing so much as cornfields."[40] The area has been used to grow different crops including grapes, vegetables, fruits, nuts, and corn. According to State Park officials, railroad workers first nicknamed the site the Cornfield in the mid-1900s. Now a rail yard that has been abandoned since about 1992, the Cornfield is located downtown, between Chinatown on the west and the river on the east, within walking distance of city hall, just down the hill from Dodger Stadium. As this book goes to press, the California Department of Parks and Recreation has recommended that the new park on the site be called the Los Angeles State Historic Park.

The site presents a once-in-a-century opportunity to create a world-class park in one of the region's most diverse and park-poor communities. Most of the people who live near the site today are people of color who live in poverty, have no access to a car, and have limited education. The community within a five-mile radius is 68 percent Latino, 14 percent Asian, 11 percent non-Hispanic white, and 4 percent African American. Thirty percent of the population lives in poverty, compared to 14 percent for the state of California as a whole, and compared to 18 percent for Los Angeles County.[41]

The median household income in this community is $28,908—just 60 percent of the $47,493 median household income in the state. Fully 29 percent of households have no access to a car—an astonishing figure in Los Angeles, the car capital of the world. Only 9 percent of households in California and 13 percent of households in Los Angeles County are without cars. Fewer than half the people over age twenty-five who live nearby (49 percent) have completed high school, and just 15 percent have a bachelor's degree. In contrast, 77 percent of Californians and 70 percent of County residents over age twenty-five have high school diplomas; 27 percent of Californians and 25 percent of county residents have bachelor's degrees. There are 993,047 people, including 282,967 children (representing 28 percent of the total population), within five miles of the site.[42] A park built on the site would not only create playing fields and open space in a neighborhood that has none, it would also help improve the quality of life, create quality jobs, increase tourism, increase property values, promote economic revitalization of the community, and preserve invaluable cultural and historic resources in the birthplace of Los Angeles.

"On a deserted railroad yard north of Chinatown, one of Los Angeles's most powerful and tenacious real estate developers, Ed Roski, Jr., of Majestic Realty Co., met his match," according to a front-page article in the *Los Angeles Times*.[43] In 2001, members of the citizens group Chinatown Yard Alliance stopped payment of federal subsidies earmarked for an $80 million warehouse project that had been planned by Majestic and the city of Los Angeles without a full environmental review. The group then secured state funding to create the park in the Cornfield. Advocates obtained the support of the community, a cardinal of the

Catholic Church, Nobel peace laureate Rigoberta Menchú of Guatemala, a cabinet member in the Clinton administration, Governor Gray Davis, and the state legislative leadership to make the dream of a park come true.

Many experts advised the alliance that their fight against city hall and Majestic was hopeless. But the alliance pressed ahead with a "sophisticated political, legal and media blitz" that put legal and political obstacles in the path of the warehouses and secured support for a park.[44] "They tried to present it as a done deal from the beginning," said Lewis MacAdams, founder of Friends of the Los Angeles River, a key organizer of the Chinatown Yard Alliance, and a poet. "We said, 'No, it's not a done deal.' We were good at presenting options."[45]

Previously, Chinatown has had no park, and it still has no middle school or high school with playgrounds, playing fields, or green space of any kind. The only elementary school in the neighborhood does not have a single blade of grass. William Mead Homes, one of the earliest and largest public housing projects in Los Angeles, is located directly east of the Cornfield.

The Cornfield area is the Ellis Island of Los Angeles. The original Native American village of Yangna is nearby, marked today by nothing more than a center divider on the Hollywood Freeway. The Cornfield was a part of the original Pueblo de Los Angeles. The first settlers were Spaniards, including Catholic missionaries; Native Americans; and blacks. Mexicans and Californios further established the city before statehood. Today El Pueblo Historic Park, lined with historic buildings, is a few blocks south of the Cornfield. Chinese began arriving in 1850 in search of gold and ended up working on the railroad and in domestic jobs. The site of the Chinatown massacre of 1871, which first brought Los Angeles to international attention, is now a traffic light. The city forcibly evicted the Chinese and razed Old Chinatown in order to build Union Station in the 1930s. During World War II, the Japanese of Little Tokyo a few blocks further south were forced into concentration camps. Biddy Mason, a former slave freed in the 1850s, became a major landowner downtown and a founder of First AME, a major black church in Los Angeles. Blacks in the twentieth century were forced into South Central by discriminatory land use policies. Italian and French immigrants, some of whom planted vineyards that graced the area, assimilated into the broader culture.[46]

Remnants of the historic Zanja Madre, the "mother trench," the lifeline that first brought water from the Los Angeles River to El Pueblo in

1781, have been found on the Cornfield. Los Angeles became the most important city in Southern California in large part because of its water supply. The Zanja Madre provided water for residential, agricultural, and industrial use from 1781 until 1904. The *zanja* system permitted early Los Angeles to develop an agricultural economy with vineyards, citrus groves, vegetable gardens, and later, fields of flowers.[47]

The Juan Bautista de Anza National Historic Trail, which marks the trail that Spaniards and Catholic missionaries used to reach northern California, runs near the Cornfield. The nearby communities are also crisscrossed by Native American trails, railroads, trolley lines, and freeways. The Native American Tongva, or Gabrieleño, village of Yangna was located near the confluence of several Native American trails. Today four freeways slice through the surrounding communities, while almost a third of the people have no access to a car. With the opening of the Los Angeles Metropolitan Transit Authority's Gold Line light rail and connecting bus service, the Cornfield is more accessible to surrounding communities and visitors.

The new state parks in the Cornfield and Taylor Yard, another former Union Pacific rail yard, are essential components in revitalizing the Los Angeles River. Many public leaders see the river corridor as a key to the economic and environmental enhancement of Los Angeles, and its enhancement as a means to provide Los Angeles with a greater sense of community. As one writer put it:

> The Los Angeles River has always been at the heart of whichever human community is in the basin: Gabrielino village, Spanish outpost, Mexican pueblo, American city. The river has been asked to play many roles. It has supplied the residents of the city and basin with water to drink and spread amidst their grapes, oranges, and other crops. It has been an instrument by which people could locate themselves on the landscape. It has been a critical dividing line, not only between east and west, north and south, but between races, classes, neighborhoods. . . . The river has also been a place where ideas and beliefs about the past, present, and future of Los Angeles have been raised and contested.[48]

THE CHINATOWN YARD ALLIANCE

One of the central lessons of the struggle for the Cornfield is the importance of building a diverse coalition that appeals to a variety of interests while staying focused on unifying goals: here, to create the park and stop the warehouse project. The Chinatown Yard Alliance offered a vision for a positive alternative use of the land, in addition to opposing the warehouse project, and it secured the resources to make that dream a reality. The alliance brought together an unprecedented group of over thirty-five community, civil rights, traditional environmental, environmental justice, religious, business, and civic organizations and leaders. The alliance met regularly over dim sum at a restaurant in Chinatown to plan strategy and maintained an e-mail network to keep the community posted on developments in the Cornfield project.

Different stakeholders had different but overlapping motivations, and they kept their eyes on the prize: the creation of a park. The desperate need for parks was a primary motivation for the people in the community. Equal access to parks inspired social and racial justice advocates. The Center for Law in the Public Interest organized a civil rights challenge on the grounds that the warehouse project was the result of discriminatory land use policies that had long deprived minority neighborhoods of parks. Protecting open space, clean air, and clean water, and cleaning up a brownfield, appealed to traditional environmentalists. The intersection of civil rights and environmental issues attracted environmental justice advocates, including Concerned Citizens of South Central Los Angeles. Moral, spiritual, and social justice facets of the project engaged the religious community, including the Catholic Archdiocese of Los Angeles and the politically active African American religious community. An awareness of how parks and active recreation influence wellness motivated the health community. The National Park Service called for a full environmental review to protect cultural and historical resources. A number of elected officials provided leadership, while others responded to the demands of their constituents.

Lewis MacAdams of Friends of the Los Angeles River was instrumental in helping to achieve inclusiveness and consensus within the alliance. Architect Arthur Golding drew up the conceptual plan for a park that the alliance used to marshal supporters to attend public hearings and organize presentations. Chinatown activist Chi Mui worked with MacAdams and Golding to build the alliance. Robert García from the Center for Law in the Public Interest, Joel Reynolds, and a private attorney led the legal and advocacy team.

The alliance waged the battle for the Cornfield on multiple fronts for almost a year, from November 1999 through September 2000, trying to persuade then mayor Richard Riordan, city planners, the city council, Majestic, and federal authorities to adopt the park alternative or, at a minimum, to prepare a full environmental impact report for the warehouse proposal that would enable the community to decide between a park and the warehouses.

Attorneys for the alliance submitted to local and federal officials the first letters challenging the warehouse project in November 1999, about thirty days before Majestic was scheduled to close escrow on the purchase of the Cornfield from the Union Pacific Railroad. The alliance challenged the warehouse proposal on the grounds that the city and Majestic had failed to prepare a full environmental impact report or statement, failed to consider the park alternative, failed to analyze the effects of the project on low-income people of color, and failed to adequately consider the air pollution, traffic congestion, noise, land use conflicts, and flood hazards that would result, as well as the project's effects on water quality, historic resources, and aesthetics. The initial result was to delay the closing. The alliance used the time to organize community support for the park; refine legal strategies; develop additional evidence through public record requests, historical research, demographic analyses, and other factual investigations; meet privately and publicly with city officials; engage in a strategic media campaign; and build a record at each successive hearing to prepare for the possibility of litigation.

Majestic countered by donating money to Chinatown organizations and publishing a glossy color brochure in English and Chinese. Majestic extended invitations to local leaders to watch basketball and hockey games from its luxury suite at Staples Center. "They did a good job getting the business community to support them," noted Chi Mui. "They tried to fracture the coalition."[49]

Despite the opposition by the alliance, the city and Majestic moved the warehouse project through the planning process without a full environmental impact report or statement. The city approved the project based instead on a mitigated negative declaration. The city's planning department approved the warehouses in May 2000. The Central Area Planning Commission approved the warehouses in July 2000. The city council approved the warehouses after just a ten-minute hearing on August 15, 2000.

In the meantime, in March of 2000, the voters of California had passed Proposition 12, a $2.4-billion statewide park bond that could provide the funds to buy the Cornfield for a park, but only if there were a willing seller. Majestic was not yet a willing seller. The alliance's strategy was to make Majestic into a willing seller.

At public forums on or about September 14, 2000, the alliance persuaded every major candidate for mayor to endorse a park in the Cornfield. "Candidates did not want to be seen as favoring a rich developer over park-deprived central city residents," reported the *Los Angeles Times*.[50] This was a significant turning point in the battle for the Cornfield. If full environmental review were required, that would delay any final action until after June 2001, when the new mayor could still pull the plug on the warehouse project.

Attorneys for alliance members filed a petition in state court seeking a full environmental impact report under California law on September 6, 2000. The California attorney general filed an amicus brief supporting their position. The alliance also used a combination of formal administrative proceedings and a network of connections to persuade the U.S. Department of Housing and Urban Development to reconsider its financial subsidies for the project. The alliance submitted to federal officials the first letter challenging the warehouses in November 1999, supplementing it with additional submissions as evidence developed.

Strategic telephone calls and letters from such figures as then state senator Tom Hayden and the Justice and Peace Commission of the Catholic Archdiocese of Los Angeles attracted the attention of Secretary Andrew Cuomo of the Department of Housing and Urban Development. On July 7, 2000, a delegation of the agency's top officials traveled from Washington to Los Angeles, where the alliance briefed them on the park alternative and the opposition to the warehouse project.

Attorneys filed an administrative complaint with the Departments of Housing and Urban Development, Commerce, and Justice on September 21, 2000, challenging the federal subsidies to Majestic on grounds of federal civil rights, environmental, and historic preservation. During a visit to Los Angeles on September 25, 2000, Cuomo "dropped a bombshell."[51] He announced that he would not release $12 million in federal subsidies earmarked for urban development without a "full-blown" environmental impact statement that analyzed the likely effect of the warehouse proposal on communities of color and on the environment, considered the park alternative, and enabled full and fair public participation in deciding the future of the Cornfield.[52]

While the community was elated, the reaction at city hall was very different. They were "shocked and disappointed," according to Deputy Mayor Rocky Delgadillo.[53] Attorneys for Majestic sat down at the settlement table with attorneys for the alliance on September 28, 2000. The federal administrative complaint and the state litigation were stayed;

both were ultimately dismissed when the parties reached a settlement after six months of negotiations.

SETTLEMENT

The park in the Cornfield is not the result of any court order but of a creative solution agreed upon between the parties. On March 12, 2001, the parties announced a settlement: If the alliance could persuade Governor Davis and the state legislature to buy the site for a state park during that budget year, using proceeds from Proposition 12, Majestic would abandon the warehouse proposal. Majestic would even support the purchase of the site for a state park. If the state did not buy the site within that time frame, the alliance would withdraw its opposition to the warehouse proposal.

The alliance organized support for the state's purchase of the Cornfield. Cardinal Roger Mahony personally wrote to Governor Davis and state legislative leaders urging the purchase of the Cornfield for a state park. The Los Angeles City Council reversed its earlier position and unanimously passed a resolution supporting construction of a park in the Cornfield.

In the summer of 2001, Governor Davis and the state legislature allocated $35 million to create the park, despite the claimed energy crisis and the softening of the economy. On December 21, 2001, Davis stood arm in arm with children from the community to celebrate the purchase of the Cornfield and Taylor Yard as the first state parks in the heart of Los Angeles. The audience rose to its feet in a standing ovation as Davis arrived at the celebration, and dozens of soccer players from the Anahuak Youth Soccer Association chanted his name. One woman held a sign reading, "Gracias Santa Davis." "Now, instead of playing in the street, the children will have a place to play," said Santo Palacios, a coach who brought a gaggle of young players to the event.[54] "We do not have a place to play soccer, and when we go to nearby parks to practice they kick us out," Coach Palacios told *La Opinion*. "Today our children's dreams of having their own place to play soccer have come true, and the struggle is over after so many years."[55]

It was a victory for the community. "Nothing like this has ever happened in Chinatown before," stated Chi Mui. "We've never had such a victory. And now, every time people walk with their children down to that park, they'll see that great things can happen when folks come together and speak up. We can renew our community one dream at a time."[56]

The day after the governor's reelection in November 2002, state parks officials announced for the first time that there would be no playing fields in the Cornfield or Taylor Yard, but rather, only passive recreation or a park with only historical elements.[57] In response, the Center for Law in the Public Interest published *Dreams of Fields*, a report outlining the policy and legal justifications for sports in urban parks and organized a campaign to support active recreation. The report notes that the state parks agency provides fields for soccer, polo, baseball, softball, and other organized sports in wealthy white areas like the Malibu Bluffs, Will Rogers, and Pfeiffer State Parks, as well as golf courses in Lake Tahoe and Moro Bay. Simple justice, it points out, requires balanced parks with playing fields in the Cornfield and Taylor Yard.[58] The Cornfield Advisory Committee, a citizens group created by state legislation, also published a report recommending that the park in the Cornfield incorporate four central themes: connectivity, cultural-historical, recreation, and transportation.[59]

The struggle continues. As this book goes to press, the state parks department has responded to the community and unveiled the conceptual plan for the Cornfield that includes historical elements and playing fields.

GROWING A DIVERSE MOVEMENT

The *Los Angeles Times* called the Cornfield victory "a heroic monument" and "a symbol of hope."[60] But it is not the only major victory by environmental justice and urban parks advocates in the Los Angeles area. Drawing on the lessons of the Cornfield, a community alliance stopped a commercial project slated for Taylor Yard, a former Union Pacific rail yard, mentioned earlier, in favor of a forty-acre park, one portion of a planned 103-acre park. This project is part of the greening of the fifty-one-mile Los Angeles River. Another community alliance helped thwart a power plant and a city dump in the Baldwin Hills, located in the historic heart of African American Los Angeles, so that a two-square-mile park can be built instead. It will be the largest urban park constructed in the United States in over a century—bigger than Central Park in New York City or Golden Gate Park in San Francisco.

The urban parks movement extends beyond Los Angeles. With an unprecedented level of support among communities of color and low-income communities, urban parks advocates have helped pass statewide park, air, and water bonds that target funds to underserved communities.

The California Coastal Commission has required the wealthy enclave of Malibu to maximize public access to the beach while ensuring the fair treatment of people of all races, cultures, and incomes, helping to keep California's public beaches free for all—thereby setting a precedent for other communities around the world. State and local school construction bonds provide incentives for the joint use of schools, playgrounds, and parks to make optimal use of scarce land and public resources.

Support is growing to create a Heritage Parkscape—like the Freedom Trail in Boston—that will link the Cornfield, Taylor Yard, and the Los Angeles River with one hundred other cultural, historical, recreational, and environmental resources in the heart of Los Angeles.[61] Public art projects—including murals, photography exhibitions, school art projects, oral histories, and theater—will be part of this living legacy.

The Heritage Parkscape will serve as a "family album" to commemorate the struggles, hopes, and triumphs of the natives, settlers, and later immigrants who came to Los Angeles and settled in this area. The parkscape project illustrates the power of place: "the power of ordinary urban landscapes to nurture citizens' public memory, to encompass shared time in the form of shared territory. . . . And even bitter experiences and fights [that] communities have lost need to be remembered—so as not to diminish their importance."[62] The park space within the Heritage Parkscape coincides closely with the Olmsted vision for downtown. Through their many different efforts, advocates are taking the opportunity today to restore a part of the Olmsted vision and the lost beauty of Los Angeles.

Public transit will take children and their families and friends from the Heritage Parkscape to the beach, mountains, forest, and other recreation areas. The people who live in neighborhoods without parks and playgrounds also lack cars and a decent transit system to take them to the neighborhoods where the parks and playgrounds are. It is necessary to bring open space to the people, and take people to the open space.[63]

The Center for Law in the Public Interest is also working to diversify access to and support for the four national forests in Southern California, inspired in part by the Olmsted vision for incorporating the national forests into the park and recreation system for the region.[64] The Southern California forests are among the most urban-influenced forests in the National Park Service system, serving over 20 million people who live within an hour's drive of the four forests.[65] Nevertheless, between 77 and 83 percent of visitors to the Angeles, Cleveland, and Los Padres National Forests are non-Hispanic whites,[66] in a region that is disproportionately composed of people of color and in a state in which non-Hispanic whites are in the minority. Fully 93 percent of visitors to wilderness areas in Los Padres are non-Hispanic whites.[67]

BALDWIN HILLS

A diverse coalition worked together to prevent the construction of a power plant and a garbage dump to save the community by saving the state park proposed for the Baldwin Hills, a two-square-mile area that is now slated to become the nation's biggest natural urban park designed in over a hundred years. Within a three-mile radius of the Baldwin Hills, the population is 36 percent African American, 29 percent Latino, 8 percent Asian, and 23 percent non-Hispanic white.[68]

Easily accessible to millions of people, and with stunning views of the Los Angeles basin, the Pacific Ocean, and surrounding mountains, the Baldwin Hills offer an extraordinary opportunity to create a world-class park and green space. A remarkable variety of native plants and wildlife persist in this natural island in the Los Angeles sea of humanity. More than 160 bird species have been found in the hills, and foxes, raccoons, and other wildlife thrive within sight of downtown Los Angeles.

The Baldwin Hills have a long history of abuse. For decades the hills have been the site of an oilfield, and miles of pipeline and pumping stations litter the landscape. But the oil development has also been the area's salvation, because it has precluded other urban development. During the claimed energy crisis in 2000, a developer proposed building a new power plant in the heart of the Baldwin Hills under state emergency orders allowing fast-tracking of new power plants, which meant there would be limited environmental review and public input. The plant would have exacerbated the serious air pollution in the area and would have deprived the people of the park.

Given less than thirty days to fight the plant, advocates organized the community and mobilized legal resources. Hundreds of people attended the first hearing on the plant; an overflow crowd of hundreds more was turned away. In a truly remarkable outpouring of support, more than a thousand people turned out to protest the plant when the California Energy Commission held an unprecedented second hearing two weeks later. A professor from the University of Southern California testified that the power plant was too little, too late, too expensive, and not necessary to help solve the claimed energy crisis. The head of the South Coast Air Quality Management District testified that the agency could not expedite issuance of the air permit for the plant.

Over sixty organizations and community leaders opposed the plant, including every major African American church and the Catholic Archdiocese of Los Angeles, homeowners associations, and civil rights activists. The *Los Angeles Times* twice editorialized against the plant and in support of the Baldwin Hills park. Less than twenty-four hours before the final hearing in Sacramento, and at the strong urging of every local elected African American official, the energy company proposing the plant withdrew its application.

Although no lawsuit was ever filed to stop the power plant, at the press conference announcing the victory a county supervisor told an attorney from the Center for Law in the Public Interest, "You have no idea how scared you had state officials with the legal team you put together." The legal team included the Center for Law in the Public Interest, Johnnie Cochran, the Natural Resources Defense Council, and a private law firm. In the summer of 2003, an alliance once again saved the community and the park in the Baldwin Hills when they persuaded the city of Los Angeles to abandon plans for a garbage dump there.

The Baldwin Hills area has played a unique role in the history of African Americans in Los Angeles, across the state, and across the nation. The Baldwin Hills area became a center of excellence and affluence for African Americans in the 1950s and 1960s, a position it still holds today. African Americans in this community were generally much better educated than in other parts of Los Angeles, which translated into greater job opportunities for them. Perhaps the greatest advantage of living here was the superior quality of the public schools. In 1971, the Los Angeles Department of City Planning described Baldwin Hills public schools as "the best schools of any city area inhabited primarily by black people" and "on par with those in West Los Angeles and the San Fernando Valley."[69] Public schools in Baldwin Hills were also more racially integrated. In addition to superior jobs, education, and housing, residents of the Baldwin Hills and the nearby Leimert Park and Crenshaw areas also enjoyed more conveniences as consumers. The Crenshaw Shopping Center opened in 1947, one of the first planned suburban malls in the United States. The Baldwin Hills Center and the Ladera Center opened during the 1960s, offering greater selection and convenience. Baldwin Hills households had greater access to cars than other black residents had in other areas, such as Watts.[70]

Yet, the struggle never ends. As this book goes to press, Governor Arnold Schwarzenegger's California Performance Review Commission has proposed eliminating the Baldwin Hills Conservancy to save money.

At the same time, the governor has signed legislation to create a new conservancy for the Sierra Nevada that could cost the state $10 million per year to benefit nonurban, disproportionately wealthy and white counties. According to the governor's press release, the new conservancy will promote resource conservation and economic benefits in those counties. The secretary of the California Resources Agency says that people living within those counties will be able to protect the environment in which they live while influencing the prosperity of their communities. State officials cannot justifiably provide those benefits to some communities, while taking them away from the diverse Baldwin Hills communities. The solution is not to pit one conservancy against another, but to fairly distribute the benefits for all. The Center for Law in the Public Interest has submitted comments opposing the abolition of the Baldwin Hills Conservancy on behalf of a diverse alliance.[71]

TAYLOR YARD

About two miles up the Los Angeles River from the Cornfield lies Taylor Yard, a former Union Pacific rail yard that opened in the 1920s. A Florida developer wanted to turn a forty-acre parcel there into an industrial park without filing a full environmental impact report. The Coalition for a State Park at Taylor Yard, drawing on the lessons of the campaign for the Cornfield, exhausted the city planning process, and members then filed a lawsuit demanding a full environmental impact report under state law. The superior court ruled that a full environmental impact report was required, which would determine the likely effects of the industrial and retail development on air and water and on a nearby bicycle path. The ruling led to a settlement, resulting in the state's purchase of the site for a park. Purchase of the 40-acre parcel is the first step toward the development of an anticipated 103-acre state park at Taylor Yard. The state and the city of Los Angeles have announced plans to jointly develop a balanced park, one with playing fields as well as passive recreation. The Los Angeles Unified School District is also considering building a school there to make joint use of the green space.

The community within a five-mile radius of Taylor Yard is 56 percent Latino, 17 percent Asian, 20 percent non-Hispanic white, and 4 percent black. Twenty-seven percent of the population lives in poverty. The median household income is $32,863, just 69 percent of that for the state. There are 235,000 children within five miles of Taylor Yard.[72]

The state parks at the Cornfield and Taylor Yard are not even finished yet, and they are already threatened by state and federal proposals for a high-speed train from San Francisco to San Diego that could run through twenty to forty state parks throughout the state. On behalf of a diverse alliance, the Center for Law in the Public Interest has filed comments against having the proposed high-speed train run through the state parks, on civil rights, environmental justice, and environmental grounds.[73]

EQUAL ACCESS TO THE BEACH

The eleven-hundred-mile California coast belongs to all the people. The city of Malibu and media mogul David Geffen nevertheless have filed suit to cut off public access in a case that could affect the entire California coast. Malibu is 89 percent white, and 25 percent of the households have incomes of $200,000 or more per year. Locked gates and barbed wire keep people off the beach, as "Blacks Prohibited" signs did throughout Southern California during much of the twentieth century. In the 1920s and 1930s, the city of Manhattan Beach forcibly evicted the black residents around Bruces' Beach, the only black beach resort in the Los Angeles region.

A diverse alliance organized by the Center for Law in the Public Interest influenced the California Coastal Commission to adopt a plan requiring Malibu to maximize access to the beach while ensuring the fair treatment of people of all cultures, races, and incomes. This is the first time an agency has implemented the state definition of environmental justice. This action sets a precedent for other communities and government agencies. The alliance raised claims concerning discrimination, environmental justice, and environmental quality, as well as the First Amendment right to public access to the beach.[74] This work has drawn international attention and has even been featured in the comic strip *Doonesbury,* by Garry Trudeau. Maximizing access to the beach evokes the Olmsted Report's recommendation that public beach frontage be doubled.

JOINT USE OF SCHOOLS, PLAYGROUNDS, AND PARKS

Los Angeles is building schools and playgrounds for virtually the first time in over thirty years, since Proposition 13—the taxpayers' revolt—cut off funds for local services, including schools and parks. The Los Angeles Unified School District is investing over $14 billion in school construction, modernization, and repair. The district has over eight hundred schools for students attending kindergarten through twelfth grade, with about 2,000 acres of playgrounds. According to the district, 240 acres of open space will be added in the first phase of construction.

An anticipated $45 to $55 billion will be available statewide for school construction and repair, including some incentives for the joint use of schools, playgrounds, parks, and green space for active recreation to make optimal use of scarce land and public resources.[75] Schools will serve as centers of their communities, with playgrounds and playing fields remaining open after school and on weekends. New construction and modernization will create local jobs for local workers and stimulate the Los Angeles economy: the school construction program will create 174,000 jobs, $9 billion in wages, and $900 million in local and state taxes. The school district is focusing on small businesses and local workers to ensure they receive a fair share of these benefits. The school yards of Los Angeles could finally begin to reflect the vision of the Olmsted Report.[76]

EQUAL JUSTICE AFTER *SANDOVAL*

Equal access to public resources, including parks, playgrounds, schools, and beaches, remains as important today as ever. In *Alexander v. Sandoval,* a conservative five-to-four majority in the U.S. Supreme Court took a step toward closing the courthouse door to individuals and community organizations challenging practices that adversely and unjustifiably affect people of color,[77] such as unequal access to parks and recreation, transportation inequities, police abuse, and racial profiling of drivers on the highway. The majority, led by Justice Antonin Scalia, held that the Title VI regulations create no right for private individuals like José Citizen and groups like the Chinatown Yard Alliance to enforce the discriminatory-impact regulations issued by federal agencies under the Title VI statute.

Although the *Sandoval* ruling is a serious blow to civil rights enforcement, it is more important to keep in mind that intentional discrimination and unjustified discriminatory effects are just as unlawful after *Sandoval* as before. Recipients of federal funds, like the city of Los Angeles, remain obligated to prohibit both. Even now, after *Sandoval,* individuals still can sue a recipient of federal funds under Title VI to challenge intentionally discriminatory practices. Known discriminatory impact—whether known in advance or after the fact—continues to be among the most important evidence leading to a finding of discriminatory intent.

Private lawsuits are not the only way to enforce discriminatory-impact regulations. Recipients of federal funds, bound by Title VI regulations, sign a contract to enforce these regulations as a condition of receiving federal funds. This provides an important opportunity to use the planning and administrative processes to resolve discriminatory-impact issues, as the Chinatown Yard Alliance did in the Cornfield case.

There are important strategic considerations in the quest for equal justice after *Sandoval*. Elected officials should be increasingly sensitive to and held accountable for the effects of their actions on communities of color, especially now that people of color constitute the majority in forty-eight of the one hundred largest cities in the United States.[78] Increasingly, people of color are being elected to positions of power or otherwise holding positions of authority. Additionally, Congress should pass legislation to reinstate the right of private individuals and groups to file lawsuits to enforce the discriminatory-impact standard under Title VI regulations.

Ballot items like Propositions 12 and 40 and school bond measures can be crafted to provide resources for underserved communities. State civil rights protections can be enforced and strengthened, as the California Coastal Commission did in applying the definition of environmental justice in Malibu. Claims demonstrating civil rights and environmental injustices can be combined in future cases in the wake of the Cornfield effort and *Sandoval*. Similar kinds of evidence are relevant in proving both discriminatory intent and discriminatory impact. The same kinds of evidence can be as persuasive in the planning process, administrative arena, and court of public opinion as in a court of law, as illustrated by the Baldwin Hills victories, which shut out the power plant and the garbage dump.

The complexities of achieving equal justice after *Sandoval* require far-reaching strategies that include—in addition to litigation—building multicultural alliances; pursuing legislative and political advocacy and strategic media campaigns; undertaking multidisciplinary research and analyses of financial, demographic, and historical data; and strengthening democratic involvement in the public decision-making process. Societal structures and patterns and practices of discrimination are significant causes of racial injustice and should be principal targets of reform.

Issues of racial and ethnic justice continue to be among the most intractable problems in our society. Among the lessons of the urban parks movement is the message that we must revive the forgotten history of Los Angeles—we must not be confrontational and divisive but, on the contrary, must overcome interracial differences. As the victories represented by Proposition 40, the Cornfield, Taylor Yard, and the Baldwin Hills park demonstrate, understanding and championing equal justice, like creating great urban parks, is a greater win for all of Los Angeles.[79]

8

Resource Wars against Native Peoples

N ative peoples are under assault on every continent because their lands contain a wide variety of valuable resources needed for industrial and military production.[1] This chapter examines three cases where mining and oil investments have encroached upon resource-rich native lands, in the Philippines, Colombia, and the state of Wisconsin. These are not instances where the natives have been helpless victims of progress. In all three cases, native communities organized themselves and made alliances with a wide variety of groups to publicize their situation and apply pressure on multinational corporations, holding them accountable for their behavior toward native peoples.

Multinational mining, oil, and logging corporations are now using advanced exploration technology, including remote sensing and satellite photography, to identify resources in the most isolated and previously inaccessible parts of the world's tropical rain forests, mountains, deserts, and frozen tundras. What the satellites don't reveal is the fact that native peoples occupy much of the land containing these resources.[2]

Forty percent of the world's countries (72 of 184) contain peoples defined as native or indigenous. Worldwide, there are over 350 million indigenous people representing some 5,250 nations.[3] The invasion of these resource frontiers by multinational corporations and nation-states has resulted in the systematic displacement, dispossession, and, in some cases, destruction of native communities. These conflicts go largely unreported in the mass media, except when they erupt in violence and civil war, as in Sierra Leone or Papua New Guinea. However, the systematic human rights abuses against native peoples, including mass killings, arbitrary executions, and destruction of their food supplies, are rarely covered in the mass media.

For the most part the dominant media have stereotyped native peoples as fighting a losing battle against the onslaught of industrial civilization. The basic assumption of U.S. energy and resource policies, which is hardly ever questioned, is that other societies, whether they be in the Third World or on native lands in the advanced capitalist countries, should give up control of their own resources because the United States and other industrial societies refuse to control their own cultures of consumption.[4]

This process has frequently been described as modernization but is more accurately characterized as developmental genocide for those who stand in the way of the economic exploitation of valuable resources.[5] The basic element of this process is the devaluation of the victims, which makes them seem inferior or worthless. Native communities who occupy lands containing untapped resources are frequently described as primitives, savages, or obstacles.

Faced with the Occidental Petroleum Corporation's invasion of their traditional lands, the five thousand members of the U'wa Nation in Colombia have been organizing to prevent the company from drilling on sacred U'wa land. However, a former minister of mines in Colombia dismissed the objections of the U'wa by saying, "You can't compare the interests of 38 million Colombians with the worries of an indigenous community."[6] Another variant of this discourse of dominance is the portrayal of state and corporate efforts to take native resources as acts of economic development undertaken for the sake of the natives.[7] Such justification usually involves ignoring or belittling the existing subsistence-based economies of native communities. For example, when the Exxon Minerals Company was trying to develop a large zinc-copper mine next to the Mole Lake Ojibwe reservation in northern Wisconsin, they sent one of their biologists to investigate why the tribe was so concerned about the proximity of the mine to a lake where they harvested wild rice. But all the Exxon biologist could see was "a bunch of lake weeds."[8] As far as he was concerned, the Chippewa's wild-rice-based subsistence economy was nonexistent.

Beneath all the rationalizations about progress and economic development lies the insatiable consumption of minerals and energy by the world's leading industrial economies. The United States, which consumes more raw materials of all kinds than all other countries, has experienced an eighteenfold increase in materials consumption since 1900. While people in the industrial countries make up roughly 20 percent of global population, they consume far more materials and products than people in the developing nations, using, for example, 84 percent of the world's paper and 87 percent of the cars each year.[9] As the demand for minerals and fuels has increased exponentially in the leading industrial economies, there has been a renewed emphasis on mineral and oil investments. Under pressure by the International Monetary Fund and the World Bank, half of the world's states have changed their mining laws to make themselves more attractive to foreign investment.[10]

THE PHILIPPINES: MINING CODES VERSUS NATIVE LAND RIGHTS

In 1995 Philippine president Fidel Ramos signed into law a new mining code, drafted by multinational mining companies, that effectively gave away a quarter of the country to multinational corporations. If a similar deal had been done in the United States, an area as large as that stretching from Maine to Minnesota and south to Virginia and Kansas would be under corporate control. In the Philippines, multinational corporations can claim blocks of land of up to two hundred thousand acres, compared to a maximum of forty thousand allowed to Philippine companies. The mining code permits 100 percent foreign ownership of projects, rather than the previous 40 percent maximum; accelerated depreciation on fixed assets; 100 percent repatriation of profits; and fifty years' worth of exclusive rights to exploration and development within a large concession area. The new code also lowers environmental standards by permitting increased open pit mining, for example, and gives companies the right to evict villagers from houses, farms, or other "obstacles" to their operations.[11] All these measures have been promoted as part of the Structural Adjustments Program imposed by the International Monetary Fund and World Bank to stabilize the Philippine economy by encouraging mineral exports and reducing the country's $39 billion debt.[12]

Since passage of the mining code, seventy mining applications have been filed, for operations covering 16.5 million acres, or 23 percent of the country's total land area. The 1991 *International Mining Annual*

Review reports that, in terms of minable minerals per acre, the Philippines ranks second in the world for gold production and third for copper.[13] Unsurprisingly, despite the fact that most of the land proposed for mining forms part of their ancestral territories, the country's 8 million tribal peoples were never consulted when the law was being drafted. Tribal peoples, who make up about 12 percent of the population and occupy 20 percent of the country's land area, were especially offended at the swift passage of the law. They have been lobbying for almost ten years for an Ancestral Domain Law that would recognize ownership and management rights to their land, as promised in the 1987 Constitution. The same congress that passed the Mining Act of 1995 shelved the Ancestral Domain Law. The London-based international native rights organization Survival International has called the new code "the greatest of all threats to the future of tribal communities in the Philippines."[14]

Most of the new mining claims focus on gold, which is found in extensive low-grade deposits. Because the grade of ore is lower than that mined in the past, more ore must be mined at a faster rate to maintain profits, and more waste is generated for every ton of ore that is mined. The most profitable method to extract the gold is the open pit mining technique, in which large quantities of rock are blasted, bulldozed, and pulverized so that the gold can be extracted by means of cyanide and other toxic chemicals that separate the minerals. With this method, gold production can be profitable, even if it produces as little as one gram of gold per ton of rock.

This may be cost-effective for the mining companies, but it is devastating to the local people, who find their lands and waters ruined by silt and toxic discharges from the millions of tons of tailings (mine wastes) left over from this type of mining. According to the Center for Environmental Concerns in Manila, around 160,000 tons of chemical-laced tailings are dumped into Philippine rivers and lakes every day.[15]

In Benguet province, which has been the Philippines' most important gold and copper mining region, runoff from the tailings has contaminated rice fields, killed biological life in the Itogon River, and led to severe health problems among the Igorot native people.[16] While the government protects the large mining companies, no such concern is shown for the mining rights of the small-scale miners, which include up to a hundred thousand of the Igorot in Benguet province. "Igorot" means "people of the mountains." It is the collective term for all the native peoples of the Cordillera region, which constitute seven major ethnolinguistic groups.[17] The Igorot have their own long-established mining practices, which are communally controlled and do not entail dangerous chemicals like cyanide in the processing of the minerals. Proceeds from the mining are shared in the community.[18] However, under the provisions of the 1991 Small-Scale Mining Act, small-scale miners must have prior approval in order to mine, and approval procedures are controlled by the large mining companies.

As one large company, the Benguet Corporation, expanded its open pit operations, it encroached upon the diggings of the Igorot small-scale miners. The Cordillera People's Alliance, a confederation of indigenous peoples of the Cordillera, took the lead in opposing Benguet's expansion. The alliance was formed in 1984 out of the successful native struggles against the Chico River Dam Project and commercial logging. According to Joan Carling, who is the alliance's secretary-general and a Kankana-ey from Benguet province, "We are promoting indigenous people's rights and working for the recognition and defense of these rights, especially now in the face of globalization, with people's resources and territories being taken over by multinational companies."[19] When the Igorot barricaded the roads around the mine and demanded an environmental study, the government sent troops to clear the roads. The troops have remained to protect the assets of the Benguet Corporation, Asia's largest gold producer.[20]

As native and environmental protests against the 1995 mining code continued to mount, the most serious mine disaster in Philippine history occurred on the island of Marinduque, one hundred miles south of Manila. In March 1996 a concrete plug in an old drainage tunnel at the Mount Tapian mine operated by the Marcopper Mining Corporation burst and spilled an estimated 4 million tons of mine tailings into the Boac and Makulapnit rivers.[21] The tailings, which consisted of water and fine particles including sand, mud, and traces of copper material, escaped from an open pit used to hold the liquid waste. The spill clogged river channels that the local people relied on for fish for their food and their livelihood. The Marcopper labor union reported that the spill affected fourteen villages and threatened another twenty villages.[22] It took four months for the company to plug the leak. The Philippine government declared a forty-mile stretch of the Boac River biologically dead five days after the accident.[23]

Initial blame was placed equally on Marcopper, 40 percent of which is owned by Placer Dome of Canada, and on the Philippine Department of Environment, for its failure to regulate and monitor the site. The plug had been known to be leaking several months prior to the disaster. The

Philippine government, which owns a 48 percent share in the mine, has filed criminal charges against Marcopper executives and suspended Placer Dome's applications for new projects.

Grassroots native and environmental activists mobilized national outrage at the mine disaster to oppose the Mining Act and large-scale mining in general. In April 1996, the Cordillera People's Alliance helped organize a People's Regional Mining Conference in the Cordillera region, which brought together native and environmental grassroots organizations, along with church social-action networks, to discuss what to do about mining.[24] Tribal elders from all provinces of the Cordillera signed a unity pact "vowing to oppose the entry of mining companies in collective defense of their land, livelihood, and resources."[25] A traveling campaign caravan brought the same discussion to other mining regions throughout the Philippines. Several provincial governments have enacted mining bans for periods of fifteen to twenty-five years. Such bans are inconsistent with the Mining Act but have nevertheless brought mining exploration to a halt.[26]

The international mining industry responded to public criticism of the mining code by openly warning the Philippine government against imposing stricter environmental standards on the industry. Twenty companies, led by the Newmont Mining Corporation of the United States and the Western Mining Corporation of Australia, signed a letter to the government protesting any changes in the mining code as "inappropriate and impractical." An editorial in the London-based *Mining Journal* pointed to the favorable investment climate in Indonesia and warned the Philippine government of a possible loss of investment if it delayed implementation of the mining code.[27]

Despite the threat of economic blackmail, the continuing problems at the Marcopper mine have contributed to a growing antimining movement in the Philippines.[28] Philippine president Gloria Macapagal has accused Placer Dome of running away from an environmental and human disaster waiting to happen on Marinduque. In 1997, Placer Dome abandoned the mining project by selling its 39 percent share in Marcopper to a local mining company, making the local company responsible for the unfinished cleanup.[29] The local company hired experts to assess the safety of the mine's infrastructure and was told that another accident could happen at the Marcopper mine while downstream residents were still suffering from health problems related to the 1996 disaster.

At the 2002 Placer Dome annual meeting in Vancouver, Canada, Ted

Alcuitas, of the Marinduque Council for Environmental Concerns, an organization based in the Philippines, and Catherine Coumans, Mining Watch Canada's research coordinator, demanded that the company take full responsibility for the Marcopper mine disaster: "In December 2001, without warning or consultation, Placer Dome Technical Services pulled out of the Philippines, leaving behind toxic mine tailings in the Boac River, the threat of five dangerously unstable mine structures, and the incomplete compensation of Marinduquenos affected by the 1996 spill."[30] The company's refusal to take responsibility for the mining disaster has created a public relations nightmare for the industry and sustained protests from native communities against new mining projects. "We are not against development per se," says Joan Carling of the Cordillera People's Alliance. "We are against development that is being imposed on us and is not consistent with the practice of our indigenous way of life, which is more sustainable and meets the needs of the people."[31]

COLOMBIA: OIL AND VIOLENCE

As the international oil industry explores the frontier regions of the globe for new supplies, it inevitably comes into contact with the native peoples who occupy the world's remaining forests, wetlands, tundra, and deserts. According to the Rainforest Action Network and Project Underground, "The high correlation between petroleum basins and indigenous communities on every continent tells a story of increasing pressure on indigenous peoples and their homelands to feed the industrialized world's growing appetite for oil and gas."[32]

The close connection between native peoples and their land has made them particularly vulnerable to changes in their ecosystems. Because of their direct dependence on the earth for subsistence, they suffer more acutely than others when toxic materials pollute their lands. Moreover, in the case of oil and mineral extraction in Colombia, there is an inseparable connection between the assault on the environment and the assault on human rights. A recent study by Oxfam America, an international antipoverty agency, suggests that oil and mineral extraction in the Third World is more likely to promote violence and lawlessness than economic and political stability.[33] Michael Renner, of the Worldwatch Institute, an environmental think tank based in Washington, D.C., says that a quarter of the armed conflicts around the world during 2000 "had a strong

resource dimension—in the sense that legal or illegal resource exploitation helped trigger or exacerbate violent conflict or financed its continu-
ation."[34] Political scientists call this "the resource curse."[35]

The first native organization in Colombia emerged in the southern
part of the country (Cauca Province) in 1971. Since then, government
security forces, drug traffickers, leftist guerrillas, and paramilitary groups
in the pay of landowners have killed more than five hundred native leaders in a country where the total native population is approximately eight
hundred thousand.[36] Why have native people suffered some of the most
intense levels of violence over the past three decades of Colombia's internal war? They suffer from the same developmental genocide that has
affected others who are considered obstacles to progress in the Philippines and elsewhere. In June 2001 the Latin American Association for
Human Rights estimated that half of Colombia's native peoples face
annihilation from encroaching violence associated with land invasion, oil
operations, and mega development projects.[37]

Approximately a quarter of Colombian territory is legally recognized
indigenous territory, and a significant part of the country's oil reserves
are on indigenous land. A major study of the impact of large projects on
native land singled out the oil industry as especially harmful:

> The activities of the oil industry on indigenous territories, both now and in
> the past, have regularly caused a significant fall in the indigenous population
> living in the territory concerned. This fall in population has been due to the
> sudden collapse in the physical, cultural and spiritual aspects of the indige-
> nous way of life and the coercion of the affected groups in a situation in
> which they are unable to defend themselves against [the] surrounding so-
> ciety. In certain cases, the arrival of the oil industry could have caused the
> extinction of indigenous groups.[38]

But the violence is not directed only at native peoples. Under the
Colombian doctrine of national security, the war against "subversives"
justifies killing peasant and labor leaders, journalists, priests, nuns,
human rights workers, and unarmed citizens. The Colombian army publicly stated that 85 percent of the "subversives" they must attack are
engaged in a "political war," not combat.[39] Human rights groups estimate that there are between three thousand and four thousand political
killings a year, with over 70 percent attributed to right-wing paramilitary
groups and their military allies.[40] The other 30 percent of killings are
done by guerrillas and drug traffickers. An estimated 2 million Colombians are refugees of the violence.[41] Since 2000 the United States has pro-

vided Colombia with $3 billion in military assistance by means of a pro-
gram known as "Plan Colombia," which has only escalated the killing
along with the numbers of refugees from the violence.

The putative purpose of most of the aid package is to assist Colombia's corrupt military in its war against the "narco-guerrillas" of the
Revolutionary Armed Forces of Colombia and the National Liberation
Army. Roberto Perez, president of the U'wa Traditional Authority, challenges the idea that Plan Colombia is about fighting a war on drugs:

> Plan Colombia is a plan for violence. The Colombian government says its
> purpose is to eradicate coca production, but that's not the case. It is directed
> against the guerrillas and against the people. The money the United States is
> spending in Plan Colombia will go to protecting the international companies
> by purchasing arms, more sophisticated equipment, and to constructing mil-
> itary bases in the richest zones. And when they say they will eradicate the
> coca crops by aerial fumigation, they are contaminating the environment,
> the rivers, and the [agricultural] cultivations for consumption. When you
> analyze the regions where they have chosen to apply those resources, their
> first priority is Putumayo, because it's rich in natural resources. Second is
> the Colombian Amazon; third, the northeastern forests where our territory
> is located; and fourth is the Pacific coast. Those are the strategic areas, and
> that is where they will construct military bases.[42]

It is no accident that some of the first victims of the current escalation of
the "drug war" are native people resisting oil drilling on their land.

OXY INVADES U'WA LANDS

Shortly after President Bill Clinton announced the Plan Colombia funding, four U.S.-supplied helicopters carrying Colombian National Police
forces attacked a group of U'wa Indians who had been peacefully
blockading the road leading to the Gibraltar 1 drilling site, owned by the
Los Angeles–based Occidental Petroleum Corporation (Oxy). Hundreds
of police attacked the U'wa with riot batons, bulldozers, and tear gas.
Three U'wa children drowned when police forced them into the fast-
flowing Cubujon River.[43] According to the U'wa, the governor of
Northern Santander, in northeast Colombia, where the Gibraltar site is
located, said, "Those animal Indians have to be evicted violently." The
military forces declared that "the oil will be extracted even over and
above the U'wa people."[44]

The most intense resistance to new oil development comes from the
U'wa, a native community of five thousand members, who live in the
cloud forest of the Sierra Nevada de Cocuy in northeastern Colombia,

near the Venezuelan border. Since 1992, the U'wa have resisted attempts to explore for oil in their traditional territory, known to the oil industry as the Siriri oil block (formerly called Samore). The U'wa believe that the project will only bring the violence that they have seen in other oil regions. The consortium pushing the oil exploration project includes Oxy and the Royal Dutch/Shell Group, each of which holds a 37.5 percent share, and Ecopetrol, the state-owned oil company, which has a 25 percent share. The Siriri oilfield is estimated to contain 1.5 billion barrels, amounting to no more than three months' worth of oil for U.S. consumers.[45]

The U'wa have threatened to commit mass suicide if Oxy and Shell go ahead with exploration plans, preferring to die "with dignity, as opposed to slowly."[46] The U'wa have a long history of resisting colonial domination. When the Spanish conquistadors were enslaving native peoples to dig for gold, the U'wa retreated into the mountains. Rather than endure subjugation, a portion of the tribe plunged to their deaths over a fourteen-hundred-foot cliff.[47] Today, the U'wa see their very existence threatened by Oxy and the Colombian government, who "are insisting on ignoring our territorial rights over land we have occupied for thousands of years. We are the owners of the territory on which they aim to exploit petroleum, without recognizing the constitutional rights of community lands for our ethnic group which are inalienable, non-negotiable, and irremovable, protected by public laws over collective property."[48]

The U'wa reserve, which is a small fraction of their ancestral territory, lies at the headwaters of the critical Orinoco River basin. Inside the U'wa territory are multiple lakes and underground reservoirs that feed national parks; rivers that begin here lead to surrounding inhabited regions.[49] The U'wa believe that "oil is the blood of Mother Earth" and that to take the oil is "worse than killing your own mother."[50] The U'wa have already seen the consequences of oil extraction just north of their reserve, where guerrilla attacks on oil pipelines have spilled over 1.7 million barrels of crude oil into the soil and rivers (the *Exxon Valdez* spill involved only 36,000 barrels).[51]

The U'wa have turned to both national and international law to preserve their land from oil exploitation. The Colombian Constitution of 1991, in which indigenous leaders played a critical role, for the first time recognized indigenous territorial, political, economic development, administrative, social, and cultural rights.[52] When the U'wa filed suit in Constitutional Court to stop oil exploration on their land, the court cited these rights in ruling that the U'wa must be fully consulted before the government could approve the project. One month later, this decision was overruled by the Council of State, which asserted state ownership of mineral rights above all other considerations. The U'wa then took their case to the Organization of American States. The National Indigenous Organizations of Colombia, along with the Earthjustice Legal Defense Fund and the Coalition for Amazonian Peoples and Their Environment, presented the U'wa case in Washington, D.C., in 1997. The Organization of American States issued a report recommending an immediate and unconditional suspension of all oil activities in the Samore (Siriri) block and legal recognition of the entire territory of the U'wa.[53]

PETRO-VIOLENCE

Since the first major oil field at Cano Limon was discovered in 1984 by Oxy, there have been over five hundred pipeline bombings by the National Liberation Army, which is committed to disrupting foreign oil companies and which favors nationalization of the industry.[54] The growth of the oil industry and of the guerrilla armies has gone hand in hand. The Colombian government has responded "by militarizing these areas and terrorizing the local population, whom they presume to be guerrilla supporters."[55]

Human rights abuses have risen dramatically in the areas with the most intense oil activity. Illegal detentions are a serious problem in the province of Arauca, where the large Cusiana oil deposit mined by the BP Exploration Company is located, while forced disappearances have risen in the province of Northern Santander, site of the Cano Limon–Covenas pipeline.[56] Native communities in these oil-producing areas have been caught in the crossfire among Colombian armed forces, leftist guerrillas, and right-wing paramilitary groups. Both Colombian and U.S. government officials deny that they have any connection to or responsibility for the activities of the paramilitaries. However, since 1991 the Colombian military has worked with a team from the U.S. Defense Department and Central Intelligence Agency to create "killer networks that identified and killed civilians suspected of supporting guerrillas."[57]

Part of the government's militarization of the oil production and pipeline zones involved a "war tax" of $1 per barrel on foreign oil companies to pay indirectly for the protection of the armed forces. Currently, one in four Colombian soldiers is assigned to protecting oil installations.[58] In addition, BP and Oxy have negotiated protection agreements directly with the military and private security firms. In February 2000, Oxy's vice president Lawrence Meriage testified before the U.S. Congress on the military aid package to Colombia. Meriage suggested that Colombian guerrillas were using the U'wa for their own purposes. The suggestion that the U'wa are "dupes" is an important aspect of the discourse of dominance that justifies taking native lands. In the culture of the colonizer, there is no room for the idea that native peoples are capable of managing their own natural resources or responding to attempts to separate them from their lands and culture.

The U'wa demanded that Oxy withdraw the charges of their being guerrilla sympathizers, because it put U'wa leaders and supporters in grave danger of arrest, torture, and murder in an already militarized region around the Siriri oil block. In October 2000, the Colombian Agrarian Reform Institute declared the five-hundred-meter area surrounding the company's drill site a "petroleum reserve zone," and military personnel have placed land mines around the Gibraltar 1 drilling site to keep the U'wa and other protesters from blockading drilling rigs.[59] Up to three thousand Colombian soldiers occupied U'wa lands to defend oil drilling machinery in 2001.[60]

THE OCCIDENTAL CAMPAIGN

International attention was focused on the U'wa people's struggle when three international indigenous rights activists—Terence Freitas of Los Angeles; Ingrid Washinawatok, a Menominee Indian from Wisconsin; and Lahe'ane'e Gay of Hawaii—were murdered by guerrillas from the Revolutionary Armed Forces of Colombia in March 1999. Terry Freitas was one of the founders of the U'wa Defense Working Group and had devoted the last two years of his life to supporting the U'wa in their campaign to stop Oxy's oil project. Ingrid Washinawatok and Lahe'ane'e Gay were assisting the U'wa in setting up an educational program to maintain and promote their traditional culture.

In April 1999, the U'wa Defense Working Group, a coalition of nongovernmental environmental, human rights and native rights organizations, coordinated an "International Week of Action for the U'wa," which included protests at Oxy headquarters, press events, and the appearance of U'wa leaders at Oxy's annual shareholders meeting. The *Wall Street Journal* commented on how effectively the coalition put Oxy in a difficult position: "By personalizing the global fight over natural resource extraction with the brooding faces of the U'wa[,] . . . environmentalists are tugging at heartstrings like never before."[61] Shell had already announced its intent to sell off its share of the Siriri project the previous year.

In Colombia, the U'wa won a temporary victory in March 2000, when a Colombian court ordered Oxy to halt all construction work on the drill site because it was on the sacred ancestral land of the tribe. But the Colombian high court overturned this ruling in May. By September the Boston-based Fidelity Investments, one of Oxy's largest investors, had sold more than 60 percent of its holdings of Oxy stock, totaling $400 million. This followed a ten-month campaign by the Rainforest Action Network, Amazon Watch, and other environmental groups involving ongoing demonstrations at Fidelity's corporate headquarters and protests around the world involving thousands of people demonstrating at over seventy-five Fidelity offices, creating a public relations nightmare.[62] From the perspective of the global oil industry, the outcome of the U'wa-Oxy conflict could affect the ability of the industry "to explore for and develop oil and gas resources in the sociopolitically high-stakes arena that is Latin America's rainforest."[63]

While Colombian soldiers protected Oxy's drilling rigs on U'wa land, guerrilla attacks on Oxy's Cano Limon pipeline cut oil production to less than half the 1999 level. Moreover, the company's reliance on the Colombian army for security was quickly becoming "the most contentious issue" for the company, according to the *Wall Street Journal*.[64] In April 2003, the International Labor Rights Fund and the Center for Human Rights at the Northwestern University School of Law filed a class action suit against Oxy and its security contractor, AirScan, for their role in the murder of innocent civilians in the hamlet of Santo Domingo, Colombia, in December 1998. The suit charged that both Oxy and AirScan helped conduct the attack, by providing key strategic information as well as ground and air support to the Colombian military in the bombing raid on the town. Oxy has denied providing "lethal aid to Colombia's armed forces." Whatever the outcome of the suit, Oxy's complicity in Colombia's violence has drawn unwanted public attention. "Even if the firm does indeed prove not to have provided 'lethal aid,'" say the editors of the *Economist*, "it faces a high-profile trial exposing its relationship with a regime with an, ahem, uneven record on human rights."[65]

In January 2003 the U.S. State Department cut off U.S. funding to the Colombian Air Force unit responsible for this raid. However, this did not signal a shift in U.S. support for the Colombian military, which continues to carry out similar human rights abuses. U.S. lawmakers granted $131 million in U.S. military aid in 2003 for U.S. military forces in Columbia and for the training of Colombian military forces, and up to

$147 million is proposed in 2004 for the protection of Oxy's Cano Limon pipeline.[66] While Oxy welcomed the pipeline protection funds, they nonetheless announced at their May 2002 annual shareholder meeting their plans to return to the Colombian government the controversial Siriri oil block, located in the traditional territory of the U'wa people.[67] Oxy immediately tried to downplay the significance of the U'wa resistance in their decision by pointing to the exploratory drilling that had come up dry the previous summer. However, in October 2002, the U'wa reported that Ecopetrol, Colombia's state oil company, was resuming oil test drilling at the site, under heavy military protection.[68] In March 2003, Ecopetrol announced that exploratory drilling close to the Colombia-Venezuela border, within the ancestral territory of the U'wa, had located reserves of up to 200 million barrels of light crude oil. The U'wa have reminded Ecopetrol that they will never negotiate or sell their mother earth.[69]

WISCONSIN, U.S.A.: NATIVE RESISTANCE TO MULTINATIONAL MINING CORPORATIONS

One of the crucial differences between the situation of native peoples in postcolonial nation-states like the Philippines and advanced capitalist countries like the United States, Canada, and Australia is the existence of legal structures that can be and have been used by native peoples to assert tribal sovereignty over land and natural resources and to oppose destructive mining projects. For the past twenty-eight years, one of the smallest and poorest Native American nations in the United States has successfully prevented some of the most powerful multinational mining corporations in the world from constructing a large mine next to its tiny, eighteen-hundred-acre reservation at the headwaters of the Wolf River in northeastern Wisconsin. The determination of the Sokaogon Ojibwe Nation, one of the six bands of the Lake Superior Ojibwe Nation, to resist unwanted mining has developed into a multiracial antimining movement that "can provide a model not only to environmental alliances, but to grassroots education and organizing campaigns that operate without large staffs and funding proposals," showing how "imagination and community support can outfox the world's largest multinational corporations."[70]

Native resistance to multinational mining corporations in Wisconsin has been growing for more than two decades. It started in 1975, when the Exxon Corporation discovered the large Crandon zinc-copper sulfide deposit in Forest County, one mile upstream of the wild-rice beds of the

Mole Lake Ojibwe Reservation, five miles downwind of the Forest County Potawatomi Reservation, and forty miles upstream (via the Wolf River) of the Menominee Nation.

As local opposition intensified in the mid-1980s, Exxon withdrew from the project, citing low metal prices. But the company returned in 1993, this time with a new partner, the Canadian-based Rio Algom Mining Corporation. Much had changed since Exxon first proposed the mine. The Mole Lake Ojibwe, Menominee, Potawatomi, and Mohican (Stockbridge-Munsee) nations had opened casinos,[71] generating income that enabled them to fight more effectively against mining companies in the courts and in the arena of public opinion. The four tribes formed the Nii Win Intertribal Council (*nii win* is the Ojibwe word for "four"), which immediately began hiring lawyers and technical experts to challenge Exxon and Rio Algom's mine permit application. The Oneida Nation, which is downstream from the mine site near Green Bay, also joined the opposition. Today the Crandon mine still has not opened.

THE MOLE LAKE OJIBWE AND WILD RICE

The economic, cultural, and spiritual center for the Mole Lake Ojibwe is their wild-rice lake. The rice, called *manomin* (gift from the creator), is an essential part of the Ojibwe diet, an important cash crop, and a sacred part of the band's religious rituals. The proposed mine would generate sulfuric acid wastes, use toxic chemicals in ore processing (including up to twenty tons of cyanide a month), and reduce groundwater tables in the area because of the constant dewatering of the proposed underground mine.

The construction at the headwaters of the pristine Wolf River of the largest toxic waste dump in state history would pose an unacceptable risk to the downstream tourist industry on this trout stream designated Class I by the U.S. Environmental Protection Agency (EPA). Frances Van Zile, a tribal elder and leader of the opposition to mining, says, "These people [from the mining company] don't care about us. They don't care if we live or die. All they want is that copper and zinc."[72]

To protect tribal resources and assert tribal sovereignty, the Mole Lake Ojibwe have developed a multifaceted strategy that includes (1) developing tribal water regulatory authority under the provisions of the federal Clean Water Act, (2) joining with their non-Indian neighbors in the town of Nashville to oppose the mine and develop economic alternatives to mining jobs, and (3) developing statewide and international antimining alliances.

TRIBAL WATER REGULATORY AUTHORITY

Tribal lands were ignored in the original versions of many federal laws of the 1970s, including the Clean Air Act and the Clean Water Act. To remedy this exclusion, amendments to these laws have been enacted to give tribes the authority to enforce environmental standards. In 1995 the Mole Lake Ojibwe became the first Wisconsin tribe granted independent authority by the EPA to regulate water quality on their reservation. The tribe's wild-rice beds are just a mile downstream from the proposed Crandon mine. Tribal regulatory authority affects all upstream industrial and municipal facilities, including the proposed mine. Because Swamp Creek flows into the tribe's rice lake, the tribe has to give approval for any upstream discharges that might degrade their wild-rice beds.

Within a week after the EPA gave the Mole Lake Ojibwe authority over water quality, Wisconsin's Attorney General James Doyle sued the EPA and the tribe in federal court, demanding that the federal government reverse its decision.[73] A petition urging Doyle to drop the lawsuit was signed by twenty-six environmental groups, two neighboring townships, and 454 people from 121 communities around the state. In April 1999, the U.S. District Court in Milwaukee dismissed the Wisconsin lawsuit and upheld the tribe's right to establish water quality standards to protect its wild-rice beds. The state appealed this decision to the U.S. Supreme Court. Four townships downstream from the proposed mine signed on as friends of the court for the EPA and the tribe. In June 2002, the U.S. Supreme Court let stand the lower court decision that upheld the right of the tribe to set water quality standards that are higher than those of the state.[74]

Meanwhile, after five years of opposition from the state of Wisconsin and the state's largest business lobby, the Forest County Potawatomi Tribe won the EPA's approval of their Class 1 air quality designation. This decision allows the tribe to designate their eleven thousand acres as Class 1, the highest air quality designation possible. No new facilities that release more than 250 tons of particulate per year will be permitted. Air modeling by the state shows that, by operating the mine, the mining partnership would violate these air standards. If either tribal air or water quality standards would be violated by the proposed mine, the tribes can deny air or water quality permits necessary for mine approval.

BUILDING MULTIRACIAL ALLIANCES

After the recognition of Chippewa treaty rights in 1983, white sportsmen held sometimes violent protests against Chippewa off-reservation spear-fishing. Antitreaty groups, opposed to the exercise of any treaty rights, accused the Chippewa of destroying the fish and the local tourism economy, even though the tribes never took more than 3 percent of the fish.[75] By 1992, increased cultural education, a federal court injunction against anti-Indian harassment, and a Witness for Nonviolence monitoring program lessened the violence.[76]

Because antitreaty groups refused to oppose the mining companies, they began to lose their environmental image. The tribes saw this development as an opportunity to build bridges with certain sportfishing groups. Even at the height of the spearing clashes, the late Red Cliff Ojibwe activist Walter Bresette predicted a realization by non-Indian northerners that environmental and economic problems are more of a threat to their lifestyle than Indians who go out and spear fish. He said, "We have more in common with the anti-Indian people than we do with the state of Wisconsin."[77]

By 1996, the Wolf Watershed Educational Project (founded by the Midwest Treaty Network) began to coordinate a series of antimine speaking tours around the state, bringing tribal representatives to communities that had never heard a Native American speak publicly. Fishing organizations and sportsmen's clubs began to strongly oppose both the Crandon mine and the metallic-mining district proposed by pro-mine interests.[78] Mining companies had perhaps felt that sportfishing groups would never join hands with the tribes, yet the "inconceivable" came to pass: sportfishers realized that, if metallic sulfide mines were allowed to contaminate rivers with heavy metals, there might be nothing left to argue about.

The same year, the Mole Lake Ojibwe joined with their non-Indian neighbors in the town of Nashville (which covers half of the mine site and includes the reservation) not only to fight the mine proposal but also to chart economic alternatives to mining development. In December 1996, the Nashville town board signed a local mining agreement with Exxon and Rio Algom following a number of illegally closed meetings and despite the objection of a majority of township residents.[79] The town board was replaced in the April 1997 election by an antimining board that included a Mole Lake tribal member. In September 1998 the new town board rescinded the local agreement. Without this agreement, the state could not grant a mining permit. The mining company sued the town for violation of contract. The township countersued, charging that the local agreement "resulted from a conspiracy by the mining company and the town's former attorneys to defraud the town of its zoning authority over the proposed mining operations."[80] To raise funds for its defense, the town set up its own Web site to explain how people can donate money to a legal defense fund in what the town called a "David and Goliath" showdown. In January 2002 a state appeals court upheld the 1996 local agreement.[81]

Cooperative relations between the town and the Mole Lake tribe had been further strengthened in 1999 when the town and tribe received a $2.5 million grant from the federal government to promote long-term sustainable jobs in this impoverished community. Together with surrounding townships, the Menominee Nation, the Lac du Flambeau Ojibwe Tribe, and the Mole Lake Ojibwe formed the Northwoods NiiJii Enterprise Community. (*NiiJii* is the Ojibwe word for "friends.") Now Indians and non-Indians are working together to provide a clear alternative to the unstable boom-and-bust cycle that mining would bring to their communities. If successful, the unique project could bring in an additional $7 to 10 million to these communities over the next decade. This effort, combined with the casinos that have made the tribes the largest employers in Forest County, has dampened the appeal of mining jobs for many local residents. Indian gaming, while not providing an economic panacea for many tribes, has enabled them to finance legal and public relations fights against mining companies.

STATEWIDE AND INTERNATIONAL ALLIANCES

The Crandon project appeared doomed in 1998 when the state legislature passed a "mining moratorium" law requiring mining companies to show a single example of a "safe" metallic sulfide mine elsewhere in North America, but the law was subsequently undermined by the state Department of Natural Resources.[82] The concurrent upsurge in environmental activism around the state, however, convinced Exxon to turn the Crandon project over to its partner, Rio Algom, which then changed the name of the operating subsidiary from the Crandon Mining Company to the Nicolet Minerals Company. In October 2000, the London-based South African company Billiton, PLC, purchased Rio Algom. In March 2001, Billiton merged with the Australian Broken Hill Proprietary to create the world's largest mining company: BHP Billiton. Company spokesman Marc Gonsalves soon reported that the company had received an "endless stream of e-mails" from Crandon mine opponents around the world.[83]

Beginning in December 2000, the Wolf Watershed Educational Project had demanded that BHP Billiton withdraw applications for mining projects; open a dialogue with state, tribal, and local governments; and eventually turn over the site to the public. In June 2002, the company communicated to mine opponents a willingness to consider a public purchase of the site. An alliance of environmental and conservation organizations and local and tribal governments released a detailed proposal calling for public acquisition of the Crandon mine site (nearly five thousand acres of land and its mineral rights) as a conservation area devoted to sustainable land management practices, tribal cultural values, and tourism suitable to this environmentally sensitive area. The main goal of the purchase would be to permanently end the controversy over permitting the Crandon mine by taking the land out of the hands of mining companies and guaranteeing that no mineral extraction would ever take place at the site.

When the state failed to make a financial commitment to purchase the site, the Sokaogon Ojibwe and the Forest County Potawatomi pursued their own negotiations and worked out a deal to pay $16.5 million for the land, assets, and mineral rights of the proposed Crandon mine. In October 2003, the two tribes held a press conference at the state capitol and announced that they were the new owners of the mine site. The tribes split the cost: the Potawatomi spent $8.5 million from their gaming revenues; and the Sokaogon Ojibwe paid $8 million in borrowed money and assumed ownership of the mining applicant, the Nicolet Minerals Company.[84]

As the new owners of the company, their first priority was to notify the state Department of Natural Resources that they were withdrawing the permit application to mine the Crandon deposit. After twenty-eight years, a grassroots movement of Native American nations, sportfishing groups, environmentalists, unionists, rural residents, and urban students not only defeated some of the most powerful multinational mining corporations but also acquired control over the mine site.

The successful conclusion of the Crandon mine conflict was not simply the result of casino revenues coming to the rescue of the tribes and the local community. By the time BHP Billiton had sold the project to a Crandon lumber firm, the company had given up the idea of ever receiving a mine permit.[85] In explaining why he sold the Nicolet Minerals

Company to the tribes, project manager Gordon Connor Jr. said he had searched throughout the world for venture capitalists or mining partners, but none wanted anything to do with Wisconsin.[86] The international industry journal *North American Mining* in 1998 discussed Wisconsin as one of the industry's main global battlegrounds, where "the increasingly sophisticated political maneuvering by environmental and special interest groups [has] made permitting a mine . . . an impossibility."[87] The journal of the National Mining Association had earlier complained that Wisconsin "barbarians in cyberspace" were disseminating anticorporate tactics around the world through the Internet.[88] The *Mining Environmental Management* magazine in 2000 portrayed the Wolf Watershed Educational Project as an "example of what is becoming a very real threat to the global mining industry."[89]

The assault on native lands and cultures by multinational mining and energy corporations has been met by grassroots organization of local, national, regional, and international alliances in defense of native communities. Thanks to instantaneous communication through the Internet, fax, and e-mail, native struggles for survival can no longer be ignored in powerful places. The same mining and oil industry journals that once dismissed native resistance as "backward looking" now recognize the power of native rights movements to affect corporate profits and market position. In all of the cases described in this chapter, native resistance movements have asserted collective rights to their land, their resources, and their own development paths. As the globalization process accelerates the assault on native lands, we can expect native peoples to seek to enforce norms of conduct for multinational corporations through such vehicles as the recently established United Nations Permanent Forum on Indigenous Issues and through international protest campaigns.

9

Tierra y Vida
Chicano Environmental Justice Struggles in the Southwest

Since the early 1980s, people of Mexican origin have made vital contributions to the environmental justice movement. Chicana and Chicano activists founded organizations like the SouthWest Organizing Project, established in 1981, and the Southwest Network for Environmental and Economic Justice, established in 1990. Over the past decade, grassroots activists have created hundreds of local, regional, and multinational organizations. The Coalition for Justice in the Maquiladoras, Farm Worker Network for Economic and Environmental Justice, People Organized to Demand Environmental and Economic Rights, Ganados del Valle, Taos Valley Acequia Association, Colorado Acequia Association, Fuerza Unida, and Labor/Community Strategy Center are a few examples of these community-based organizations. Grassroots activists have connected hundreds of local organizations, neighborhoods, and communities through the regional and multinational environmental justice networks. The Southwest Network links hundreds of local grassroots affiliates in communities across the Southwest (Arizona, California, New Mexico, and Texas) and Mexico. The Farm Worker Network connects affiliates based in New York, New Jersey, Florida, Texas, Ohio, California, Washington, Puerto Rico, and the Dominican Republic.

Chicana and Chicano activists contributed to the First National

People of Color Environmental Leadership Summit and the drafting of the Principles of Environmental Justice in 1991. They played key roles in subsequent campaigns against environmental racism in the U.S. Environmental Protection Agency (EPA) and the Group of Ten mainstream environmental organizations. Activists were members of the multiracial coalition that pressured the Clinton administration to develop and implement Executive Order 12898, which addressed environmental injustice, and worked with congressional representatives on legislation to implement the Principles of Environmental Justice. Since the inception of the National Environmental Justice Advisory Council in 1993, Chicana and Chicano grassroots activists and organizers have participated in this council and in policy debates related to the inequitable politics of environmental risk assessment.[1] Mexican-origin communities continue to generate significant grassroots environmental justice struggles. Farmworkers, factory workers, land grant heirs, acequia farmers, urban barrio residents, and rural *colonia* residents are among the social forces underlying this movement.[2]

FARMWORKERS

There are more than 4 million farmworkers in the United States today, including 100,000 minor children. At least two-thirds of these workers are immigrants, and 80 percent are from Mexico.[3] The struggles of farmworkers for environmental justice extend beyond resisting the environmental racism that results in poor working and living conditions to embrace the struggle for sustainable and equitable agriculture. Since the 1960s and 1970s, farmworkers have sought democratic change through the power of collective bargaining. They have fought for workers' control of production as the basis for attaining environmental and economic justice. Their vision of workplace democracy, environmental protection, and economic justice endures in contemporary farmworker-organizing struggles.

Farmworkers face a legacy of generations of exposure to toxic chemicals. But the range of problems they must cope with extends beyond the issue of pesticides and other toxins. They experience health problems related to inadequate housing, malnutrition, and lack of access to medical care.[4] According to the Occupational Health and Safety Administration, Latina and Latino immigrants experience a disproportionate number of workplace fatalities.[5] The EPA reports at least 300,000 pesticide poisonings among farmworkers each year, and this is considered an unrealistically low estimate.[6] The death rate among farmworkers in 1996 was estimated at 20.9 per 100,000, compared to the average for all industries of 3.9 per 100,000 workers.[7]

Not all states have adequate laws to protect farmworkers from exposure to toxins. Even in the states with regulatory statutes, the laws are not readily or consistently enforced. In California, the law sets penalties for violations related to exposure of workers to toxins and failure to provide training and safety equipment to protect workers. Yet in more than half of all incidents, growers were not fined and instead faced meaningless "notices of violation."[8] Not surprisingly, farmworkers have a life expectancy of forty-nine years. The rates for infectious and chronic diseases, malnutrition, and infant and maternal mortality among United States farmworkers by far exceed national averages.

Conditions in labor camps and other housing present aspects of environmental racism and social injustice. Crowded and unsanitary conditions in labor camps are a persistent feature of corporate agriculture. Farmworkers and their families are often forced to live in one-room shacks without heating, running water, or toilet facilities.[9] In Southern California's Imperial Valley, some farmworkers live in caves or holes dug out of cliff sides with nothing more than tattered plastic tarps and tin scraps for roofing held in place by rocks, dirt, and discarded tires.[10]

Commercial agricultural biotechnology is an issue of emerging concern. One type of agricultural biotechnology involves the production of genetically engineered organisms, also known as transgenic crops. Many of these transgenic crops have been engineered for increased resistance to herbicides and other agroindustrial chemical agents.[11] The implications are too obvious: farmworkers will bear a disproportionate burden of higher-level toxic exposures in fields planted with genetically engineered organisms.[12]

Since the 1970s, farmworker movements have integrated environmental justice concerns into organizing campaigns. The Farm Worker Network for Economic and Environmental Justice is an example of this tendency. Organizations like this one subsume environmental concerns within their demands for workplace democracy and workers' control of production. Quality-of-life concerns like adequate housing, nutrition, and health care are integrated into a strategy that emphasizes gaining collective bargaining agreements to deal with all these issues in a holistic manner. The environmentalism of everyday life does not divide the environment into disembodied parts like "nature," "work," and "home."

Environmental issues are not separate from working and living conditions. The Farm Worker Network embodies this holistic approach to organizing.[13] The network's mission statement declares that the organization exists to "improve farm worker safety, health, and economic well-being; strengthen and build farm worker organizations and communities as a means of self-representation for workers and families; [and] support the sustainability of . . . agriculture."[14]

Campaigns for sustainable agriculture involve the creation of worker cooperatives. The United Farm Workers of America promoted strawberry cooperatives in California during the 1970s and 1980s.[15] These efforts were largely successful, and the number of cooperatives dedicated to other crops continues to grow. An increasing number of Mexican and Chicana and Chicano farmworkers are making the transition from farm labor to farm ownership and operation. While white family farms continue to decrease, the number of farms owned and operated by Latinas and Latinos is increasing at a dramatic pace. Between 1987 and 1997, the number increased by more than 40 percent.[16] There are now Latina and Latino farmers in every state, although approximately 72 percent are concentrated in five states: California, Colorado, Florida, New Mexico, and Texas. About 80 percent of these farmers are of Mexican origin, and many are immigrants and former farmworkers.

INDUSTRIAL WORKERS

Work-related injuries, mutilations, and deaths remain high in manufacturing sectors characterized by concentrations of people of color, including Mexican and other immigrant workers.[17] These patterns of injury and death correlate to environmental racism in the internal organization of the workplaces. Chicanos and other workers of color are disproportionately concentrated in occupations and industries that "pose greater risks of work-related injuries, unsafe working conditions, and environmental hazards."[18] Inside the factories, the division of labor delegates Mexican workers to lower-waged, higher-risk jobs.[19]

Workers face multiple workplace health and safety hazards, including exposure to toxic chemicals and fumes, assembly line speed-up, inadequate ventilation and lighting, poor ergonomic design, hazardous machinery, and persistent patterns of racial and sexual or sexist harassment. This is the case in the microelectronics sector, which presents itself as a "clean" and "light" industry. Assembly workers in microelectronics, the majority of them Chicanas and other women of color, are dispro-portionately exposed to some of the most dangerous chemicals used in production. These chemicals are clearly associated with a wide variety of diseases, including cancers, cardiovascular illnesses, and respiratory and reproductive system disorders.

There are numerous examples of worker struggles against environ-mental racism in the microelectronics and semiconductor industries. An important example took place at GTE-Lenkurt, a telephone electronic switchboard assembly plant that was based in Albuquerque, New Mexico. In 1987, the company agreed to a paltry $2.5-million settlement with workers as compensation for a history of workplace contamination. Most of the 225 workers were women of color, and two-thirds were Chicanas or *mexicanas*. The corporation then relocated assembly opera-tions to Juárez, Mexico, to escape a well-organized workforce. Since the plant closed and relocated, at least twenty-five former workers have died from work-related illnesses.[20]

Patterns of environmental racism subject workers to a higher risk of injury, illness, or death in the workplace. "El desgaste obrero," the "wasting of workers," is the result of a combination of hazardous con-ditions, not the least of which is the incessant pressure to produce more efficiently.[21] Studies of industrial accidents demonstrate that Mexican workers suffer higher rates of injury and death as a result of working conditions. The advent of the North American Free Trade Agreement has only worsened attacks on health and safety standards in the industrial workplace.[22] Mexican workers in meatpacking, food processing, and confined-animal-feeding operations; road and building construction trades; transportation; and other industries face similar patterns of envi-ronmental racism. Globalization of production poses significant chal-lenges to environmental justice organizing campaigns.

Economic blackmail is another terrain of struggle that unifies workers and local communities. The threat of plant closings by corporations is a recurring problem for the environmental justice movement. The case of Fuerza Unida illustrates the importance of the struggle against the geo-political mobility of corporate capital in the age of globalization. Fuerza Unida was established in 1990 when workers at Levi Strauss and Company in San Antonio, most of them Chicanas, organized an inde-pendent union to fight plant closings and layoffs; 10,400 people and fifty-eight plants were affected by the company's eventual relocation of production to Costa Rica and Mexico.[23] Workers were pressured to make wage concessions or face the risk of further plant closings and relocations. The Fuerza Unida struggle was an important precursor to the struggles against the North American Free Trade Agreement, which increased corporate mobility in the global flows of production and undermined traditional, locally based working-class organizing.[24]

Workers and communities have resisted the imposition of a choice between jobs and environmental protection. One example of this involves the Campaign for a Just Transition. This is a joint organizing project of the Oil, Chemical, and Atomic Workers Union, the Indigenous Environmental Network, and the Southwest Network for Environmental and Economic Justice. This fusion of labor unions and environmental justice networks builds bridges between union organizers, who work to create safe and sustainable workplaces, and community organizers, who work to create safe and sustainable neighborhoods.[25] The fusion is significant because it widens and shifts the focus of the environmental justice movement from the critique of environmental racism to a search for alternative visions of sustainable development.

LAND GRANT COMMUNITIES

The resurgence of land grant struggles since the 1980s signals a persistent memory of place. It is a strong sense of place, a fierce cultural attachment to, and identity based on, a direct relationship with the land and water, and it clearly defines the ecological politics of the Mexican-origin land grant communities of the Rio Arriba bioregion.[26] There are nearly three hundred Spanish and Mexican land grants in New Mexico and Colorado, and dozens more in Texas, Arizona, and California. For decades, many land grant communities have sustained active campaigns to restore the traditional use rights of Chicana and Chicano families with multi-generational ties to these ancestral lands.

The land grants were lost to an unjust enclosure—some were appropriated and then incorporated into national forests—driven by the U.S. government in its rush, after 1891, to establish the national forests. Significant land grants were also lost to theft and unethical partitioning by unscrupulous lawyers, land barons, and federal bureaucrats. Of an estimated 35 million acres, only 2.05 million acres of these land grants were patented or confirmed. According to a 2001 report by the congressional General Accounting Office, New Mexico has a total of 295 Spanish and Mexican land grants. The report identifies 152 of these as "community land grants," which are "land grants that set aside common lands for the use of the entire community."[27]

The restoration of community land grants to the Mexican-origin heirs remains a priority of the movement, but now activists have embraced a wider range of struggles. These include efforts to organize communities to demand direct local participation in forest planning and grassroots comanagement of national forest and rangelands. In their endeavor to increase local control, land grant activists have often clashed with government foresters and environmentalists in northern New Mexico.

One important struggle is centered in the Vallecitos Federal Sustained Yield Unit, located northwest of Taos, New Mexico. The Vallecitos Unit was carved out of a section of the Kit Carson National Forest that had been part of the common lands of the Vallecitos de Lovato land grant, erroneously rejected by the surveyor-general in 1886.[28] The Vallecitos Unit was established by an act of Congress in 1948 as part of a federal policy for sustained-yield timber management (the 1944 Sustained Yield Forest Management Act). The 1944 act has been criticized for favoring monopoly timber interests, and the policy was eventually modified to include among its goals the reduction of rural poverty and the enhancement of the economic and social stability of forest-dependent communities.[29]

In the 1970s and 1980s, local forest workers fought difficult battles against the U.S. Forest Service and timber companies over the volume of timber cuts, which the local community viewed as excessive and unsustainable.[30] The local forest workers opposed a succession of timber harvest agents that consistently failed to hire local people in logging operations. In 1985, the local community called on La Floresta (the Forest Service) to adopt a policy favoring small contracts for "thinning and for harvesting of forest products (such as firewood, vigas, Christmas trees, fenceposts, and the removal of landscape trees)."[31]

Local pressure led the district ranger to adopt a policy favoring small local operators and contractors over the large and mostly out-of-state timber corporations. The local forest workers established La Madera Forest Products Association in 1988, a worker-owned wood products cooperative. However, the group was "stymied by a lack of equipment, buildings, and organizational capability among its members."[32] In 1990, the Chicano loggers founded a second organization, called La Compañía Ocho. This organization worked for years to gain certification as a responsible operator and to obtain a timber sale from the Forest Service.

In 1997, La Compañía Ocho was awarded a small cut named "La Manga Timber Sale." A radical environmental group, the Forest Guardians, opposed the timber sale, alleging the cut would destroy one of the "last old growth" ponderosa pine stands in northern New Mexico within the historic habitat range of the Mexican spotted owl.[33] La Compañía Ocho finally won its timber contract, but the conflict with the Forest Guardians deepened divisions between land grant communities and environmentalists. In 1998, numerous New Mexico activists joined a multicultural pledge group to declare public support for the principle of "inhabited wilderness" in order to bring such conflicts to an end and unify the land grant and environmental communities.[34]

Similar conflicts over the management of enclosed land grants pitted environmentalists against land grant activists in other Rio Arriba communities. Ganados del Valle (Livestock of the Valley) and Tierra Wools are well-known grassroots organizations that redefined the land grant movement in the 1980s and 1990s. The community-owned livestock and artisan weaver's cooperatives are based in Los Ojos, New Mexico. A conflict with environmentalists developed after Chicano sheepherders launched a civil disobedience campaign to protest the lack of access to traditional grazing range on the enclosed Tierra Amarilla land grant.[35]

Ganados was the latest in a long line of grassroots activist organizations that had struggled over the Tierra Amarilla land grant for more than a hundred years.[36] As in other areas of rural northern New Mexico, "poverty was highly racialized" in Tierra Amarilla.[37] Laura Pulido has written that the conflict between Ganados and environmentalists over grazing rights on public lands revolved around the struggle to reestablish the "ecological legitimacy" of a traditional land-based local culture. The livestock cooperative adopted an ecosystem management model for its proposed grazing and range restoration plans.

Many environmentalists and state land managers erroneously viewed Ganados as ill equipped to manage the land. The legitimation of traditional livestock producers as sustainable stewards of the land was in fact stymied by the arrogance and political power of state wildlife managers and environmentalists who viewed the sheepherders through the racialized lens of their white, middle-class, or managerial positions: The "Hispanic" grazers were "quaint" but "ignorant" ecological thugs.[38] Ganados responded by strategically romanticizing their relationship to the land and representing themselves as an endangered local culture. This type of cultural essentialism allowed Ganados to gain the ecological legitimacy it badly needed to be an effective actor in this struggle.

Sylvia Rodríguez and others have noted how timber cutting, road building, grazing, hunting, fishing, hiking, and other multiple uses degraded the environment of the land grants and their watersheds.[39] Struggles over watershed protection in land grant communities certainly involve resistance to toxic racism, or environmental racism, caused by mining and other industries. However, an increasing number of communities are facing displacement and ecological devastation from another source, the "amenity" industries. Toxic racism is combined with exotic racism, which arises with the "new" economy based on global village tourism and nature-culture appreciation industries.

Exotic racism threatens to consume the landscapes and cultures of rural communities inhabited by Chicanas and Chicanos, by turning them into commodities for the amusement and enjoyment of tourists. The new economy of tourism is driven by the growing consumer demand for natural and cultural spectacles. The bucolic scenery and "quaint" local cultures are the basis of this new economy, but the economic system tends to undermine that which it would celebrate as an "exotic other."[40] A highly speculative market for second homes has emerged, and the acequia-irrigated orchards and pastures have become overpriced in a globalized real estate market that ruthlessly commodifies ancestral landscapes at $80,000 to $100,000 an acre.[41] The pressure to sell increases, as do the property taxes. The land-rich but cash-strapped locals are slowly being displaced by the new economy of "multicultural" landscapes.[42]

Some of the most intense land grant struggles have occurred in the context of private enclosures of community lands. An important example of this is the long-standing land rights struggle of the heirs of a land grant in southern Colorado's San Luis Valley. This struggle involves a historic land rights case against the so-called Taylor Ranch, a private enclosure of the eighty-thousand-acre common lands of the Sangre de Cristo land grant (decreed in 1844 and settled in 1851). The Taylor family of New Bern, North Carolina, ending more than one hundred years of local use and access under customary law and edict, purchased and enclosed these common lands in 1960. The local land grant heirs filed a lawsuit in 1979, *Rael v. Taylor,* in an effort to restore the historic use rights to the common lands.[43]

By the mid-1990s, many acequia farmers and land grant activists believed the lawsuit would not succeed and, in any case, would fail to restore community ownership of the grant. Many activists felt that the lawsuit did not go far enough to protect the watershed. Even if *Rael v. Taylor* restored use rights, the Taylor Ranch could retain the rights to log, mine, or subdivide the land. Between 1993 and 1998, the local community worked with governmental and nongovernmental organizations to arrange the purchase of the ranch. The acquisition would include a comanagement agreement between the local community and the state of Colorado, and it would restore the historic use rights of the land grant heirs to graze, hunt, fish, gather wood, and collect wild plants.[44] In April 1998, the Taylor family rejected a final offer by the state of Colorado and the local community to purchase a fifty-five-thousand-acre portion for $18 million. A few months later, the Taylor family sold the land to Lou Pai, the chief executive officer of Enron Energy Services.

Between 1995 and 2000, the Taylor Ranch was subject to massive industrial-scale logging of the relatively undisturbed subalpine and montane forests. The logging involved an estimated 210 million board feet on the thirty-four thousand acres of land stocked with what was deemed to be "merchantable timber." The timber operations were met by an intense antilogging campaign characterized by the *New York Times* as the "hottest environmental dispute in the southern Rockies."[45] The Taylor Ranch antilogging campaign was a historically significant watershed in the history of American environmentalism because it marked the occasion of a coalition of acequia farmers and ranchers, land grant activists, environmental justice activists, and radical environmentalists.[46] This partnership, called the Culebra Coalition, included white ecoactivists from Earth First!, Greenpeace, and Ancient Forest Rescue, among other radical organizations.[47] It offered a positive contrast to the experiences of land grant activists who had dealt with environmentalists in the Vallecitos and Ganados del Valle struggles. The Culebra Coalition sustained a direct-action campaign for five years. More than a hundred protestors were arrested, including local women and children who participated in the logging road blockades and lockdowns.

ACEQUIA FARMERS

Acequia farmers are part of the growing movement for sustainable agriculture and the struggle to strengthen traditional systems of local food security.[48] They have developed programs to certify local producers of organically grown foods, provide cooperative economic development opportunities to farmers with limited resources, and train farmers in ecologically sound land and water management practices.

In the town of Questa, New Mexico, local acequia farmers have struggled since the mid-1980s against the contamination of their water supplies by tailings and spills associated with acid mine drainage from the Molycorp molybdenum strip mine. This is an important example of environmental racism in the Rio Arriba. This case involves damage from large-scale industrial mining in an enclosed common land that is threatening the very livelihoods of the traditional farming and ranching community.

A similar struggle occurred some forty miles north of Questa in San Luis, Colorado. The case of the *San Luis Peoples Ditch v. Battle Mountain Gold, Inc.* remains one of the premier examples of organizing for environmental justice in the Rio Arriba area.[49] The farmers who use the Culebra River watershed acequias were solidly opposed to the Battle Mountain Gold Company's proposed strip mine and gold-processing mill that would use the cyanide-vat leaching technique.[50] The acequias hired lawyers, hydrologists, and ecologists as part of an expert legal and scientific team to argue their case in the district water court. Local acequia farmers testified knowledgeably about problems with the reclamation and monitoring plans.[51]

The unending wave of environmental and economic threats to the acequia farms of the Culebra watershed led to the creation in 1998 of the Colorado Acequia Association. This association has roots in the activism of the 1990s antilogging campaign against the Taylor Ranch and in the efforts by La Sierra Foundation to plan for the eventual acquisition and comanagement of the land grant. The Colorado Acequia Association was also more deeply rooted in the ancient traditions of customary law that have governed this form of watershed democracy for generations. It led efforts to create the county land use planning commission. It also contributed to the development of a land use code and a watershed protection ordinance based on the work of conservation biologists and proponents of the biological reserve design.[52]

The Colorado Acequia Association is establishing a land and water trust to acquire and protect historic farmlands, sensitive watershed areas, wildlife habitat, and open space. This strategy builds on the natural and cultural assets of the community. It values the ecosystem services provided by the acequia system: for example, the conservation of soil, water quality, wildlife habitat, and heirloom varieties of land race crops, the native cultivars adapted to the local environmental conditions. The association exists to protect acequias from encroachment by developers who covet the water rights of the irrigation municipality.

In New Mexico, the Taos Valley Acequia Association was established in 1988 to address the growing threats to the water rights to the sixty-six acequias in the Taos region. Now the acequia communities have organized the New Mexico Acequia Association and the Congreso de Acequias (the Acequia Congress). In New Mexico, the customary law governing the acequia enjoys status equal to that of the Doctrine of Prior Appropriation (the Anglo water law: first in use, first in right); in Colorado the customary law is subordinated under the prior appropriation law.[53]

Acequias are increasingly using their authority to regulate land use activities to promote the environmental protection of the watersheds and ditch networks. For example, in 1995 the association Acequia de San Antonio in Valdéz, New Mexico, posted a public sign on crossings over the *acequia madre* (main irrigation ditch, or "mother" ditch) declaring its authority to regulate land uses that could threaten the operation of the traditional acequia system.[54] Over the past twenty years, the acequias in the Taos area have faced increasing damage from the expansion of the Taos Ski Valley resort and the construction of condominiums and second homes in the foothills of the Sangre de Cristo Mountains. Roads constructed to reach these new homes damage acequias as a result of illegal culverts, poor design, and sedimentation caused by erosion from road surfaces.

Two major issues for New Mexico and Colorado acequias are the readjudication of water rights, and the conflicts between customary acequia water law and other legal doctrines like prior appropriation. In the process of readjudication, water rights are subject to a technical and legal review and reconfigured in light of historical use patterns and other criteria determined by the legislature and the State Engineer's Office. This has been a difficult process for most acequias, but they have managed to preserve and protect most of their water rights. They have successfully defended their priority status and avoided being listed as having "abandoned water rights," a designation often used during the early 1900s to strip acequias of their water rights.[55]

There are conflicts between customary law and Anglo American legal doctrines such as the system of prior appropriation.[56] The customary local law of the acequia can be said to embrace the right of thirst, an Islamic principle that establishes a right to water for all living things with thirst, including plants and animals.[57] This concept is associated with certain traditional principles of ditch management, including the principle that scarce water must be shared during droughts. It is also evident in the flourishing of riparian corridors and anthropogenic wetlands created by acequias and their subirrigation of the broader landscape.

The Doctrine of Prior Appropriation (first in use, first in right) treats surface water as a commodity that can be separated from the land and sold to other users. It also requires an assignment of priority that must be strictly honored in making water allocations by starting with the most senior (the earliest established) and moving down the list to the most junior (the most recently established) water rights. This means that scarcity is not shared. In a drought, those with senior rights get water, but those with junior rights may not. These legal conflicts deserve further study.[58]

POLITICAL ECOLOGY OF THE BARRIO

Today, Mexican-origin people are at the center of a demographic transition called Latinization, a dramatic rise in population that is remaking the major urban centers of the United States.[59] A Latina and Latino urban core has emerged and consists of more than 22 million people living in the five most populous cities (Los Angeles, San Antonio, New York, San Diego, and Phoenix).[60] This Latina and Latino urban core is "reinventing the United States big city."[61] Mexican-origin communities have borne the brunt of environmental racism perpetuated by land use planning and environmental protection regimes that privilege private property rights and corporate profits over the ecological integrity of neighborhoods and entire communities. The largest concentration of hazardous waste landfills in the United States is in the South Side of Chicago, in communities and neighborhoods with predominantly African American and Latina and Latino populations. Chicana and Chicano children, and other children of color, are more likely to live in housing with lead paint and other toxics. Their families cannot afford to move to safer housing, so abatement is an ongoing struggle.

In this urban context, social movements have embraced an expanded definition of environmentalism. The SouthWest Organizing Project is a good example of an environmentalism of everyday life. It resulted from a collective response by the Mexican American community in Albuquerque to an urban environment characterized by pervasive patterns of discrimination and police brutality.[62] People of color lack access to urban ecological "amenities" like clean, uncrowded housing; open space, parks, and recreational facilities; and unpolluted neighborhoods. Their communities are often surrounded by toxic brownfields, polluting industries, and deteriorating housing stocks. Such ecologically degraded urban neighborhoods are often treated as sacrifice zones, which are geographically distinct areas defined as expendable in terms of the protection of environmental quality.[63] The fortress of police power further encapsulates the ecology of the barrio. Thus, environmental justice activists have viewed the urban built environment as a force that at once dehumanizes and punishes residents under a regime of constant surveillance and spatial control of the "grid" (that is, segregation by class, race, and national origin).

Communities are shifting from reactive struggles against environmental injustices to proactive campaigns for healthy, livable cities. Mexican-origin people are playing a pivotal role in new social movements for housing, community-based health care, alternative economic development, urban horticulture, and local food security. The concept of the urban habitat has been championed as an important basis for the development of ecological, sustainable, and socially just communities. People are organizing to demand and reclaim community space, the public common places that promote conviviality and locally oriented economic development. The reclamation of urban community space often involves self-help housing projects, urban gardens, and the cleanup of brownfields and other contaminated soils.

The antitoxics campaign waged by El Pueblo para el Aire y Agua Limpio (People for Clean Air and Water) in semirural Kettleman City, located in Central California's San Joaquin Valley, is an important example of the grassroots environmental justice movement in Mexican-origin communities.[64] This struggle implicated the EPA and a large corporation in excluding a local community from lawful participation in the process of environmental review. The predominantly Mexican and Mexican American community in Kettleman City confronted state and federal regulatory bureaucracies that had consistently remained insensitive to the health risks posed by an existing hazardous waste facility. In fact, the site, hidden from the town by a hill, had been established without the local people's knowledge or consent. For decades, the community was denied equitable access to the scoping, research, and public commentary processes that are required under the National Environmental Policy Act of 1969 for all federal environmental impact statements.

The Kettleman City case illustrates the legacy of environmental racism inside the EPA. El Pueblo waged a successful five-year campaign to defeat the proposed hazardous waste facility. This struggle set the tone and direction for the young environmental justice movement by demanding nothing less than prevention instead of mere mitigation of the environmental risks of hazardous wastes.

In south Tucson, a similar process unfolded involving Mexican-origin and Tohono O'Odham communities in a struggle over environmental risk and damage caused by the infamous Hughes (now Raytheon) Air Force Missile Plant No. 44.[65] This case involves a struggle that spanned more than a decade. The local grassroots mobilization, which began in the mid-1980s, eventually resulted in a multimillion-dollar settlement for affected families and the designation of the site as a Superfund site.

Between 1955 and 1977, Hughes Aircraft Corporation dumped large amounts of trichloroethylene (TCE), a highly toxic and confirmed carcinogen, and other untreated chemicals into the arroyos surrounding the missile plant at Tucson International Airport. This practice resulted in a six-mile-long, mile-and-a-half-wide toxic waste problem that Tucsonians call the "TCE plume."[66] In 1981, without informing the public or explaining the rationale, Pima County officials started closing domestic drinking-water wells in the area of south Tucson affected by the TCE plume.[67] In 1987, Native and Mexican Americans organized Tucsonians for a Clean Environment. The grassroots activists mobilized sixteen hundred affected families to file suit against Hughes Aircraft and the U.S. Air Force. In 1991, Tucsonians for a Clean Environment agreed to an out-of-court settlement of $85 million, at the time the largest award for a water pollution case in the history of the United States.[68]

A similar process unfolded in East Los Angeles. Established in 1985, Madres del Este de Los Angeles (Mothers of East Los Angeles) is one of the oldest organizations in the Chicano environmental justice movement. Activists in this organization are mainly Mexican American women who have used their position as mothers to wage ecological struggles. Aurora Castillo and Juana Gutiérrez were among the early organizers of this grassroots environmental justice organization, which they developed in concert with a local Catholic parish priest. Madres del Este de Los Angeles successfully led opposition to proposals for a toxic waste incinerator, state prison, and fuel pipeline, and they redefined ecological politics by challenging the widespread practice that imposed locally unwanted land uses on low-income communities of color.[69]

The organization came to symbolize the central role of women in the environmental justice movement. Feminist theorists have debated the wisdom of the organization's identity politics, which emphasized motherhood, but Mary Pardo has pointed to its significance as an example of the strategic use of an identity that is imbued with moral authority and respect. This is another case of cultural or strategic essentialism: The activist women of Madres del Este de Los Angeles recognized that as Mexican Americans they would be marginalized and ignored by politicians and decision makers. Presenting a public face as "mothers," they were less likely to be rejected or disrespected in the political discourse. This strategy clearly placed the organization before the public in a manner that strengthened and legitimized the movement's claims and grievances.[70]

Environmental justice struggles in the urban areas include New Mexico's courting of the Intel Corporation, which has raised environmental justice concerns in the context of large-scale economic development projects. The Intel plant was built in 1983 and expanded several times, in 1984, 1995, and 2000. The Southwest Network for Environmental and Economic Justice launched a campaign to deal with Intel because industrial subsidies, site development, and manufacturing operations all posed significant risks to workers, their communities, and the environment. The plant manufactures microchips and uses a wide range of toxic and carcinogenic substances. Environmental justice activists were opposed to the granting of subsidies and tax breaks; they felt this policy rewarded a corporation that was already responsible for three Superfund sites in California's Silicon Valley.[71]

The Intel plant uses 2 to 3 million gallons of water a day. Albuquerque is located in an arid environment, and water resources are already stretched beyond carrying capacity. Intel "mines" the local groundwater aquifer at the rate of 1.5 billion gallons or 4,500 acre-feet per year and purchases additional supplies from industrial, municipal, and agricultural sources.[72] This has already lowered the water table, since Intel's rate of withdrawal exceeds the recharge capacity of the aquifer's watershed. Under New Mexico law, the neighboring water well users will have to pay their own way to follow the declining depth of the aquifer as Intel's cone of depression begins to alter the hydrology of the area. In November 1997, the New Mexico State Engineer's Office rejected Intel's bid to resurrect water rights on agricultural lands south of Socorro, Texas, some sixty miles from Albuquerque.[73] Intel's search for water to "augment" losses to the Rio Grande from its groundwater withdrawals remains a threat to acequia farmers and rural householders in the region.

Los Angeles has also emerged as a major site for multiracial environmental justice organizing. The Labor/Community Strategy Center in Los Angeles has been at the heart of the environmental justice movement in Southern California since the mid-1980s. The center is a multiracial and anticorporate "think tank/act tank."[74] It has a long history of involvement in struggles across the environmental justice spectrum. The center has organized and supported workers' struggles against industrial hazards and environmental risks; it has supported labor- and union-organizing campaigns among janitors and other workers. Its activists are connected to community groups waging struggles over air and water quality, fair and safe housing, sustainable jobs, and the organization and defense of immigrants. The center's pathbreaking research revealed how regional antipollution policies in the Los Angeles basin discriminate on the basis of race and class.[75]

Among the many important grassroots environmental justice campaigns connected to the center is the Bus Riders Union, a multiracial organization that has waged a decade-long struggle against transit racism and for equitable and sustainable mass transit. This organization has been involved in a series of civil rights lawsuits against the Los Angeles Metropolitan Transit Authority. The agency built a light rail transit system to serve the predominantly white suburbs in the Los Angeles basin, in part by cutting back on the budget for the street bus system. This policy shift led to a Title VI lawsuit and a settlement requiring the transit authority to restore and expand the bus system.

The Labor/Community Strategy Center has outlined and pursued a political program that includes a "Superfund" for workers (to invest in detoxification and the containment of toxics at the point of production); state and federal restrictions on capital flight; opposition to the use of the Third World as a toxics dumping ground by U.S. corporations; development of less polluting auto transportation; low-fare, convenient, and safe public transportation; reduction of the total number of cars on the road through van and car pools paid for by employers; independent community economic-development programs that reinvest in local neighborhoods; progressive taxation of corporations; and consumer action to demand environmentally safe products and workplaces.[76] This represents a shift in the environmental justice movement toward a proactive strategy emphasizing the quest for justice and sustainability.

Urban communities made up of Chicanas and Chicanos are contributing to the development of the urban agriculture movement. This movement addresses the need for local food production systems that can deliver fresh, organic produce to low-income, inner-city families and communities. Raquel Pinderhughes has clarified the connection between urban food self-sufficiency and environmental justice: "Urban agriculture has the potential to transform blighted, vacant lots into vibrant green community spaces. . . . It . . . brings people together to create safe, open spaces that facilitate community social networks and interactions."[77] Low-income communities of color have limited access to land for urban agriculture. Pinderhughes and other activists emphasize the effectiveness of grassroots organizing campaigns that pressure elected officials to increase the amount of land designated for this use (as opposed to industrial, commercial, or housing developments).[78] The environmental justice movement must develop strategies involving the innovative use of land trusts, conservation easements, or compensation to landowners for the transfer of development rights to support access to land for agriculture among low-income urban communities of color.

This movement can also contribute to local food security among low-income families that are "marginalized by the mainstream food system."[79] In contrast to "hunger relief," the urban agriculture movement increases local peoples' capacity to be more food self-sufficient.[80] This movement builds on the tradition among many Mexican immigrants to engage in home gardening. Zapoteca and Mixteca immigrants from Oaxaca maintain urban horticultural spaces in thousands of back- and front yards, vacant lots, and even alleys and street medians across the Los Angeles basin.[81] This grassroots subsistence horticulture is evident in other United States rural and metropolitan areas where Native *mexicanos* have settled over the past twenty years. The extraordinary ethnobotanical and agroecological knowledge of Oaxacalifornios could be tapped as part of a broader campaign to link the urban agriculture and environmental justice movements.

RURAL COLONIAS

The struggles of colonia residents for basic services like water and sanitation is intertwined with their struggles for human dignity and environmental justice. Colonias are usually characterized as rural or semirural slums inhabited mostly by Mexican-origin immigrants and Mexican Americans. In the United States-Mexico border region, colonias are low-income subdivisions built without legal protections for residents and homeowners. According to one observer, "Colonias are constructed on tracts of newly subdivided land outside city limits which were purchased on contracts for deed."[82] Along the Texas-Mexico border, where many of these settlements are located, the laws regulating subdivisions did not apply to colonias until new reforms were enacted after communities, environmental justice activists, and legal counsel exerted pressure.[83] Official estimates (for Texas alone) count 1,471 colonias.[84]

Colonia residents face many difficult social, economic, and environmental problems. Most colonias lack both water and sanitation systems. These conditions contribute to high rates of waterborne diseases among colonia residents, including dysentery and chronic diarrhea. Often, the only potable water for residents comes from *piperos*, the fly-by-night commercial retailers who sell water from tanker trucks in the colonias. However, the water the *piperos* deliver is itself often contaminated by toxic chemicals. In one case, *piperos* were found drawing their water from municipal wells polluted with industrial solvents used in the maquiladora industry.[85] Colonias also contribute to border environmental problems wherever untreated human wastes *(aguas negras)* leach into surface streams and groundwater aquifers.[86]

Texas border colonia residents are organizing a movement to demand access to potable water, sanitation systems, and health care facilities. Colonia residents are coordinating projects to support housing construction cooperatives that draw on the strong self-help and mutual-aid traditions commonly followed by urban "squatters" in Mexico and other Third World countries. On the Mexican side of the border in Ciudad Juárez, Sociedad Cooperativa de Seleccionadores de Materiales, the municipal dump workers' cooperative, offers an inspiring model of the possibilities of autonomous economic and political self-organization among colonia residents.[87] The El Paso Interreligious Sponsoring Organization, a Catholic community-based group, played a critical role in supporting colonia struggles during the late 1970s and 1980s. The organization pressed for water and sanitation facilities in the colonias, attracting the support of public figures like the political commentator Jim Hightower and the attention of the mass media and elected officials.[88]

Colonia residents remain underserved by water and sanitation districts, lack access to public health care facilities (even clinics are rare), and have serious problems related to toxic contamination of soils on home lots and surrounding lands. Their communities are captive to the larger forces surrounding water development politics in Texas and the rest of the Southwest. The lack of political will among elected officials is accentuated by the political power of the real estate and subdivision development interests that are able to continuously lobby state legislators to avoid "overregulating" private property and "developers' rights."[89]

The Chicano environmental justice movement presents a remarkably diverse and active social force in contemporary ecological politics. The movement is shifting from the struggle against environmental racism to the building of sustainable and just alternatives to political, economic, and ecological injustice. Increasingly, the search for sustainable alternatives will define the environmental justice movement as it enters a third decade of mobilization and organization.

PART FOUR

HUMAN RIGHTS AND GLOBAL JUSTICE

THE FINAL SECTION OF THE BOOK examines human rights and globalization. Ecological sustainability is key to realizing global peace and prosperity. Ecological inequalities, and repressive regimes trample human rights and threaten world security. Environmental racism is a human rights issue. Environmental racism also exacerbates poverty and threatens public health. The gap between the world's haves and have-nots is growing. Global poverty cannot be alleviated without economic opportunity.

Globalization has placed a special strain on the economies and ecosystems of many poor communities and poor nations inhabited largely by people of color and indigenous peoples. Polluting industries, including the military, have endangered the health of nearby residents and turned many poor communities in toxic wastelands. Global resource extraction industries such as oil, timber, and minerals have left a trail of poverty, pollution, human rights violations, illnesses, and death.

Recent antiglobalization struggles have been anchored in the age-old quest for social justice, human rights, and democracy; they have not been driven by some external "terrorist" network. Poverty and the violation of human rights are both national security threats. Globalization has made it easier for transnational corporations and capital to flee to areas with the least environmental regulations, best tax incentives, cheapest labor, and highest profits. Globalization is subsidized by multilateral and regional economic institutions, multilateral and regional free trade and investment agreements, transnational corporations, large investment and banking institutions, national export promotion agencies, corporate affinity groups, and pro-business academics and think tanks.

10

Environmental Reparations

ntiurban attitudes, covert and institutionalized or normalized racism, and conscious ignorance can undo efforts to resolve nearly any contemporary environmental problem. Cities are where waste streams meet and accumulate. Cities are also becoming increasingly brown and black in their demographic composition. And cities are where the voters necessary for changing governmental policies are located. The profoundly antiurban messages of many U.S. environmentalists and their grounding in racist ideology; parochial land use practices; and the resistance of scientific elites to confronting the phenomenon of multiple, chronic, cumulative, and bioaccumulative toxins in the risk decisions they make, all threaten human health and living systems on which we depend.

Largely without support from the mainstream environmental groups and scientific elites, environmental justice communities are struggling against these barriers to build the framework for a reparative, restorative environmental policy based on justice first, then sustainability. Antiurban and racist values have left critical gaps in our approaches to environmental justice, protection, and sustainability. This antiurban attitude within mainstream environmentalism masks an unconscious racism that threatens to replicate racist outcomes even without conscious intent.

All environmental problems are local in some sense. They can be local in terms of the cause, source, or impact of the waste stream, including all emissions, discharges, and pollution. As waste streams increase and accumulate, environmental problems have begun to affect areas outside of the immediate locations where waste streams are created. This is particularly true of urban environments. Urban environments are complex. They became the sites of industrialism years before any governmental regulation, and the main sites for human habitat years before knowledge about the human health risks of industrialism. They are also important aspects of ecosystems and bioregions. As wastes, emissions, discharges, and pollution have accumulated in our cities, they have begun to affect air sheds and watersheds of ecosystems near and far from the sources of the pollution. As both wastes and human population increase, they are brought closer together, increasing conflict over environmental decisions. This conflict can take many different forms, such as land use disputes, industrial permitting decisions, court cases, or conflicts over public mass transit projects.

In addition, urban dwellers increasingly are people of color who define environment and environmental concern much more holistically than the general population does. This broader approach to environmentalism is at odds with the approaches of mainstream environmental groups, which evolved out of a wilderness-conservation political agenda.[1] The U.S. environmental movement has operated to exclude the concerns of urban dwellers and people of color from the environmental movement and to exclude urban dwellers and people of color from the traditional posts within government devoted to environmental concerns.[2] The exclusion of people of color is repeated over and over again, as government and environmentalists react to social concerns about the deteriorating environment.

Urban environments in particular have been ignored in the U.S. environmental movement and in governmental policies developed to address the environment.[3] Traditionally, mainstream environmental activists, public policy officials, and researchers have narrowly conceptualized environmental concerns. Their vision tends to be limited to the media of pollution—air, water, and land—and it ignores public health indicators. This vision shaped the form of current environmental protection agencies, creating artificial barriers to protection with racist and antiurban consequences. According to Robert Bullard, "When we restrict the boundary conditions of 'environmental concern' to include only environmental impacts related to air, water, land, . . . we tend to ignore critical impacts to sociocultural and cultural systems."[4]

Further, assigning public health and the various environmental indicators to different federal, state, and local agencies decreases our ability to look at the picture of environmental and community health indicators together. It introduces turf battles between agencies into the basic activities of gathering data and making risk management decisions regarding this fragmented data. This disconnection between public health and environmental indicators is repeated at all levels of government.

Environmentalists themselves have not seriously examined their own negative attitudes toward cities generally and toward African Americans specifically. From the very beginning of our history in the United States, our political leaders thought of cities as having negative effects on people and as having a corrupting force on democracy. Thomas Jefferson thought of cities as "pestilential to the morals, the health and the liberties of man."[5] He went on to write,

> The mobs of great cities add just so much to the support of pure government, as sores do to the strength of the human body. It is the manner and spirit of a people which preserve a republic in vigor. A degeneracy in these [cities] is a canker which so eats to the heart of its laws and constitution.[6]

In the early 1900s, people began to refer to cities as "jungles" and "wilderness." Later, whites were called "urban pioneers" when they moved back into the cities they had abandoned for suburbs. This potent metaphor of the city as frontier or jungle reveals a certain attitude toward African Americans. It implies that cities can become civilized only when whites are the majority population. This attitude pervades the contemporary environmental movement in countless unexamined ways. Waste sites called "brownfields" are the domain of brown and black city dwellers, while "greenfields" remain predominantly white, suburban, nonindustrialized spaces. Zero population activists and anti-immigration environmental policies continue to promote a vision of land dominated by white culture as the standard and as worthy of having environmental protection. In their discourses, most advocates of sustainability segregate communities of color and ignore them, making exceptions only for token references to Native Americans as the only people of color possessing an authentic environmental ethic. Sustainable policies must be the first exception to the normative rule of exclusionary environmental decision making.

Racism is real and has consequences for the environment. Nature may not countenance race or racism, but we do. At the turn of the twentieth century, William E. B. DuBois observed that the color line in America establishes the standard for acceptance.[7] The power of skin color over the psyche and behavior of Americans influences all public policy, program planning, and implementation. Environmentalists must consider what happens when racist attitudes form the basis of contemporary environmental policy and programs, whether sustainability or "green urbanism" or "smart growth." After six hundred years of colonization, removals, industrialization, slavery, and segregation, tremendous disparities in economic, physical, and environmental well-being remain in places where African Americans and Native Americans have been concentrated by governmental policies and programs. As long as these disparities remained in the cities, where they were portrayed as "black" problems, or on reservations, where they were invisible, they were an acceptable price of industrial development. But environmental policy must now engage and embrace burdened people and places in order to repair and restore whole living systems that have been sacrificed to toxins and neglected. This is especially true of any environmental policy that embraces "sustainability." It will be difficult because "racism poisons all United States urban and social planning."[8] Communities of color are speaking for themselves in order to protect themselves from accumulated wastes, emissions, and discharges. They are changing land use planning processes and introducing environmental criteria.[9]

There is no "separate but equal" in nature, no "separate but equal" way to solve the issue of sustainability. There are no allowable sacrifice zones, human or otherwise, in our ecological interconnectedness, and there is no exit. Racist views and practices, both individually and institutionally, produce at least two outcomes in the environmental movement. First, whites ignore or discount the distinctively different orientations of people of color to nature and the environment as less important than those presented by whites. For example, when asked to define environment and nature, people of color across many ranges of ethnicity include a broad range of phenomena: the creations of nature, living and dead, contemporary and future, flora and fauna, where we live, work, learn, and play. The conservation-based environmental movement focuses instead on so-called wilderness, wild places, and wild things. Second, there is unproductive racial confrontation as marginalized urban communities and communities of color are forced to challenge the predominantly white, male, upper-class elite who dominate the environmental movement and government regulators.

Illusory political constructs such as race, land as exclusively private property, and profit as a proxy for social good deny the ecological physics of our natural universe. These concepts were constructed for political ends and deny that we are part of one closed system that makes what we put into it return to us. Pollution loading in communities results in pollution loading in the land. The places where our waste has accumulated now have a human face on them, and when we reject that human face, we cannot restore the land. Privilege preserves illusions that support an unsustainable mode of living, working, and thinking.

The illusion of racial differences, which we now know scientifically to be false, allows the privileged to feel unconnected to the consequences that their conduct has for other people, whom they do not have to encounter or engage. Feeling unconnected enables a full range of irresponsible, dangerous, and foolish conduct toward people and our living systems, as revealed in a spectrum of human rights violations ranging from lynching to genocide.[10] The illusion of private ownership of land allows the privileged to feel unconnected to the consequences of their conduct toward the living systems of which those lands are a part. As the gap grows between rich and poor, between people of color and others, the greater grows the separation between environmentally privileged communities and those on the receiving end of pollution and racism.

Privileged societies and persons who are disenfranchised, especially societies based upon natural resource consumption, will view any attempt at regulation as an intrusion on their property and freedom. But land as private property, like other natural resources, may have to be subordinated to the common good. For example, land use law evolved to recognize that a property owner cannot do as she pleases with the built environment regardless of the consequences. Similarly, under contemporary environmental law, a landowner cannot simply allow illegal pollution. These rules of land and environment have limited individuals' real property rights in favor of the common good. The challenge now facing us is whether we will revisit past infringements on basic liberty, which were visited upon oppressed and marginalized people. These infringements are being questioned by the contemporary descendants of slaves as part of the nascent reparations movement. These infringements were also visited upon nature: the extinction of species, loss of the long views from our national parks, migratory disruptions, and ecosystem destruction, to name a few. When we make environmental decisions about the commons, we must, in order to achieve true sustainability, consider past, present, and future stakeholders not currently represented in the decision making processes.

We must embrace the city. As government seeks to prevent pollution and clean up the environment, government is inescapably being brought back into urban environments, because that is where the pollution streams converge. Urban environments are politically and environmentally more volatile. Communities whose majorities are made up of people of color and poor people are saturated with the ubiquitous, "normal" by-products of the industrial and chemical boom. Multiple pathways of chemical and toxic exposure, and possible synergistic interactions between substances, have not been studied by scientific elites, who are only now trying to accommodate popular demand by communities for information and analysis. Urban communities can be quickly organized and mobilized around environmental and public health concerns, and they demand meaningful participation in the environmental decisions that affect them.

CUMULATIVE RISK: A BASELINE FOR JUSTICE AND SUSTAINABILITY

People with the greatest exposures suffer the most when risk assessment does not take into account all the effects of exposure. Minorities and some low-income communities face greater exposure to environmental contaminants, and the failure of past and current risk assessments to account for multiple and cumulative exposures affects these populations most immediately. Although narrowly defined risk assessment paradigms might not be intentionally biased against people of color or low-income groups, the failure to account for the higher exposures experienced by these communities results in a lower level of environmental and human health protection, precaution, and remediation.

Scientific understanding of human and species vulnerability, response variability, and susceptibility to environmental agents is woefully incomplete. People are exposed to myriad pollutants from many sources, but scientific methodologies for environmental risks currently assume single pathways of exposure. These methodologies fail entirely to account for possible synergistic interactions. Moreover, the actual frequency of multiple chemical exposures is unstudied. Less than 2 percent of chemicals in commerce have been fully tested for health effects, and no data whatsoever is available for 70 percent of commercial chemicals. About 79,120 chemicals are listed on the Toxic Substances Control Act Inventory, and about 19,533 of these are pesticide products currently on the market. The U.S. Environmental Protection Agency's Toxic Release Inventory covers about 660 chemicals commonly released into the environment. Increasing the Toxic Release Inventory to include information about additional synthetic chemicals, and enacting additional local laws concerning the local right to know, like that enacted in Eugene, Oregon, will enable a better measurement of cumulative and synergistic impacts by communities with the capacity to speak for themselves.

Communities have been rankled by the fact that science, industry, and government have ignored their concerns and allowed toxic chemicals to escape into the environment and accumulate. As conflict increases, affected stakeholders arm themselves with knowledge about these decisions and accumulating impacts, including quality-of-life indicators where they live, work, play, and learn. They seek solutions for their protection. Many environmental justice representatives distrust science and scientists as a political constituency. This distrust of science is deeply embedded in our environmental law. According to one observer:

> Science has been the thorn in the side of environmental policymakers since the dawn of environmental law. Sound environmental policy cannot be developed without some kind of scientific basis; yet attempts to incorporate science into environmental regulations have met with failure. Reduced public participation, excessive regulatory delays, and the incomplete and inaccurate incorporation of science have plagued science-based environmental regulations for nearly three decades.[11]

Many community residents view the delegation of decisions about whether to protect their health to scientists as a betrayal of their fundamental right to participate in the decisions that most affect them and their families.

Communities, especially urban communities populated with people of color, face the inevitability of accumulated risk through environmental exposure. Cumulative risk assessment is becoming important to communities considering environmental issues. Cumulative risk entails the combined risks from aggregate exposures to multiple agents or stressors.

Assessments involving a single chemical or stressor are simply not cumulative risk assessments. Agents and stressors can be chemicals, but they also can be biological and physical agents. A proper assessment of risk caused by multiple agents must consider them when they are combined and then accumulated. The interaction of the chemicals, whether synergistic or antagonistic, must be studied. As of this writing, most risks from exposures to chemicals are simply added together. These are not cumulative risk assessments. Aggregate assessments of risk are better than nothing, but they are only the beginning of a cumulative risk assessment. In the transition from traditional risk assessment to cumulative risk assessment, the principle of additivity must be clearly stated as a default position. This principle adds the risks of chemicals together when they are combined; many chemicals increase the risk of other chemicals in a compound by means of synergy. When community stakeholders become aware of the potential for synergistic and bioaccumulative effects, they may want to take precautions, especially if they are uncertain about the level of public risk and danger. Here precaution simply means making decisions to pursue economic development more slowly when the risk to human health and living systems is unknown. Although our focus here is the United States, it is important to note that other countries have more experience with cumulative risk assessment and management and the implementation of the Precautionary Principle.[12]

The EPA is just beginning to combine aspects of ecological risk assessment with human health risk assessment. Cumulative risk assessment is becoming population driven and human focused. In this way, the EPA is grappling with concepts of vulnerability. It is including both qualitative approaches—community-based environmental planning—and traditional quantitative approaches. The Superfund program, used to clean up our cities, issued new guidance on risk assessment. Recent, positive developments in the program include new policies that actually examine cumulative and ecological risk when dealing with polluted sites.

The EPA's Office of Pesticide Programs has developed guidelines for conducting cumulative risk assessments for pesticides. It has also prepared a preliminary risk assessment for organophosphorous pesticides. Other federal and state agencies are beginning to study the unavoidable issue of accumulating impacts and their consequences for all environmental programs, especially those focused on sustainability. However, because of the limitations of current science, cumulative risk assessments will not be able to answer all questions concerning risks to community residents. The growth of ecological epidemiology and an increased use of biomarkers—chemicals that accumulate in organisms—and public health data are also necessary to measure the true state of health of people and their ecology.

Meaningful community involvement is absolutely necessary in determining the social, economic, and cultural parameters of any cumulative risk assessment. The factors that we must include if we are to improve cumulative risk assessment are also the factors necessary for sustainable urban planning.[13] Communities point to the need for certain kinds of data and may also identify which chemicals and exposure pathways should be monitored. Cumulative risk assessments can answer some questions, they can help us pose better questions, and they can help establish the environmental baselines necessary for the development of a policy of sustainability. They can help to define areas of uncertainty where social values should be explicitly considered in decision making. Nonetheless, we will still need to make environmental decisions when our social values are in gridlock. If the values of the nation as a whole include environmental sustainability, then we must embrace the city to prevent further irreparable harm to all of us. What we are losing, and will continue to lose, by following an unexamined trajectory of urban development is irreplaceable. We can't make water or fabricate air. We can't replace the services these natural systems provide.

THE CASE FOR ENVIRONMENTAL SUSTAINABILITY AND JUSTICE REPARATIONS

The general argument that the country owes reparations to African Americans is well developed.[14] The shocking gaps in health, income, education, justice, and housing that remain between African Americans and whites are linked explicitly to slavery. The fact that these gaps have remained constant over time—and that they are pervasive, predictable, and lethal, despite the expressed good intentions of individuals within the health, income, education, justice, and housing systems—is evidence that the cause of these gaps is structural racism, so pervasive that it has become normal regardless of professed values.

We engage in political and legal debates about intentionality, racism, and public policy, and in scientific debates about accumulating toxic exposures. Meanwhile, the reality of burdened land and burdened people is rapidly overwhelming the flimsy barriers of privilege and private property. Centuries of racist, exploitive public policy have confined the detritus of industrial development to places defined by the race and income of the people living there. But nature is not interested in the politics of externalities or deceived by the rhetoric of intentions. The exposures and injuries are reflected in the watersheds, air sheds, and lands that connect entire bioregions. They are reflected in the mothers' milk and babies' bones of all humanity now.

The urgency of the need to repair the most impacted places on earth is based not simply on claims for justice, but on recognition of the common dependence of all living things on heavily affected living systems. It would be right to do what is just and then to find ways to make that sustainable. But it is now critical that we do what is just if we truly want to be sustainable. Whether the urgently needed environmental reparations in urban communities of color should be accompanied by an apology, or by acknowledgment of harm done, is an issue that demands attention, but the urgency itself is not debatable. The benefits of environmental reparations to these areas would have the effect of revitalizing the living systems on which all living things in the bioregions encompassing them depend.

Environmental justice reparations may take many forms: the uncompromised cleanup of air, water, and land poisoned by industrial users. Reparations might entail making a commitment to monitor certain toxins and exposure pathways. They might entail making a commitment to convert polluting industries to industries that use clean production technologies. Environmental reparations to some communities might encompass an entire bioregion. For example, in an African American community with a history of exposure to hazardous chemicals emanating from industrial sites, the location of those sites may be of key importance to a regional water quality testing program and a water quality improvement program, especially if the wastes have migrated into the water table. Who better to include when tracking the migration of wastes than the local community? Underground storage tanks, either never regulated or conveniently forgotten, are remembered by both the environment and the people who have lived, worked, played, and learned there. Moreover, making environmental reparations to that African American community by locating waste sites and cleaning them up, by adaptive reuse, and by instituting environmental monitoring in the area will benefit the water quality of the entire region.[15] The safety of American drinking water is declining, its use is increasing, and waiting for improvement could have irreparable consequences, especially for vulnerable populations like children.

By reparations, we do not mean parks. "Parks" are separate land uses, often banked as land to develop later, and, therefore, inadequate as reparations. We propose the designation of environmental preservation districts as reparations.[16] The allocation of land, and not capital, as reparations is not a new idea, as former colonies have already reasserted land claims at the World Conference against Racism in 2002.[17] Preservation districts themselves are not a radical concept; already, an entire legal and policy framework at the local, state, and federal levels exists to implement historic preservation districts. As noted earlier, environmental preservation districts could be modeled on current historic district land use ordinances.

There are over thirty-five hundred historic listings in the U.S. National Register of Historic Places. Federal law requires federal agencies to take historic resources into account in environmental impact statements. Historic district programs are widespread at the state and local level. The Fifth Amendment to the U.S. Constitution allows for the exercise of the power of eminent domain by the state if done for a public purpose and if fair compensation is paid to the property owner. Most cities prefer not to pay for these takings of private property, and they develop land use regulations to avoid such takings. Historic districts highlight the edge of land use actions that are not quite takings, but that nonetheless greatly restrict the use of private property. For the common cultural good, historic districts create rigid criteria for the built environment.

Environmental preservation districts are as legally defensible as historic preservation districts, which are well grounded in urban law and policy. Like historic preservation districts, environmental preservation districts would not allow a property owner to demolish her property in order to put it to more profitable use, would require her to restore the ecosystem if damaged, and would require her to go through a hearing before an environmental review board, similar to the hearings conducted by architectural review boards to address properties in historic districts. The concept of average reciprocity of value could be incorporated by measuring environmental benefits and burdens, instead of, or together with, property value preservation.[18] Environmental preservation districts would still increase wealth over time for private property owners.

Health has intrinsic value at the community level, no matter how the word "health" is defined. The environmental benefits and burdens of a land use regulation would raise questions about the carrying capacity of the land. Just as in a land use plan in which build-out occurs when every zone reaches its maximum allowed density, carrying-capacity analyses would examine the "build-out" of an ecosystem. While it is probably a good policy to know ecosystem capacity, to plan to grow to the point of capacity may violate the Precautionary Principle, which would call for slowing development when environmental impacts are unknown and potentially threatening. This will become a pointed and inescapable policy issue when cumulative risk assessments are developed and implemented. Environmental preservation districts would help establish urban environmental baselines, which are sorely missing from U.S. cities. These districts would be especially effective and appropriate in communities already engaged in land use decisions by introducing environmental criteria. Reparations to oppressed people in ravaged land will help the nation become sustainable.

The basic constitutional underpinning of historic districts is the concept of average reciprocity of property value. All landowners in a given historic district are burdened by the restrictive nature of the historic district, but all also benefit from the protection of property values that the historic district ordinance provides. This is also a foundation of zoning and allows for the creation of wealth for private property owners over time. Again, the purposes and goals that animate the land use planning processes help preserve the value of private property. Environmental preservation districts would ecologically and culturally restore ecosystems and communities, and the purposes and goals that would animate the restoration process would be community inclusion and precautionary development.

This is not an idealistic pipe dream. Land is actually becoming available in our dense urban areas that have large populations of people of color, like Detroit, New York City, and Boston. For example, when the world's largest municipal garbage dump closed in New York City, it contained twenty-five hundred acres of urban public land. Boston covered over a landfill in the West Roxbury community to create a park bigger than the Boston Common and Boston Public Garden combined, which it named Millennium Park. These landfills are expected to settle a few feet per year and will continue to ooze leachate and emit gases for years. Unlike industrial brownfields and Superfund sites, however, these former municipal dumps have not been cleaned so much as contained while the trash rots.

Both New York and Boston are noted for their neighborhood planning processes, which are much more inclusive than most in the United States. Neighborhoods in these communities have organized and mobilized to address a variety of issues and are effective stakeholders in processes of equal decision making—that is, they are allowed to speak for themselves, have adequate resources and capacity, and otherwise meaningfully participate. We propose that the newly available urban lands—the sixty to seventy municipal landfills in urban areas that are closing, predominantly in East Coast cities—be designated as environmental preservation districts and not simply as more parks, golf courses, subdivisions, schools, roads, airports, warehouses, or prisons.

Some communities will need additional capacity building to become effective participants in these processes. This additional community capacity-building work is an intrinsic part of environmental justice reparations to land and people. Communities must be prepared to participate in decision making, and so they will require environmental education and education about the basic processes of democracy.[19] Government must embrace citizen involvement in its processes. It must take on the task of environmental citizenship building, in part to compensate for the historical exclusion of people of color from environmental policy and decision making.

Environmental reparations represent a bridge to sustainability and equity. Even if environmental reparations are limited to monitoring and measuring environmental impacts and their accumulation, at least we can begin the process of establishing an environmental baseline in our urban areas and begin to manage some of the current uncertainty that bedevils environmental decisions. In this way, we can begin to repair the worst damage that has been bequeathed to us and future generations. Reparations are both spiritual and environmental medicine for healing and reconciliation. They are legally possible, and they form the path to both justice and restoration of living systems on which we all depend. Even talking about environmental reparations is a first step toward a fair transition to a sustainable future, a necessary first step in preparing ourselves for more meaningful and inclusive dialogue.

11

Vieques
The Land, the People, the Struggle, the Future

In recent years, the sixty-year struggle to stop the U.S. Navy from bombing the island of Vieques, Puerto Rico, and to end its occupation of three-quarters of the island, has made international headlines. This "David versus Goliath" story, replete with accounts of powerful, creative, and nonviolent resistance to continuing environmental and social degradation, has attracted attention from environmental justice, antimilitary, and human rights activists and gathered support from government officials and religious leaders in Puerto Rico, the United States, and the world.

This powerful struggle to demilitarize Vieques extends beyond simply stopping the bombing, to what might happen once the navy leaves. Understanding the complex forces involved in the ongoing struggle for control of the land requires a historical overview, as well as a discussion of the competing plans—whether public or private, community-based or driven by outside interests. This analysis necessarily considers how racism and colonialism have been used to justify sacrificing people and lands for the national security of others, and how they continue to flavor the mainstream vision of what Vieques might become after the navy leaves.[1] The struggle for Vieques is an antiracist struggle, for it involves the efforts of long-oppressed people of color to stand up to their oppressor and play a deciding role in the future of their community.

The significance of the Vieques struggle also reaches far beyond anti-military concerns and the contentious issue of U.S.–Puerto Rican relations. The eventual fate of the lands should interest all who seek to understand the relationship between a community's survival and the degree of its control over planning and resource use. The Vieques struggle offers a powerful example of a movement that opposes the separation of communities from the environment that sustains them and which they must protect—and for which they require the means to do so. Yet Vieques speaks not only of resistance but also of affirmation—the affirmation of basic human dignity, of the responsibility to care for one's people and environment, and of peaceful, sustainable alternatives to the dominant culture of violence, oppression, and destruction. This story of one community's struggle for survival, today and in the future, holds a lesson for us all.

THE LAND AND THE PEOPLE

The island of Vieques lies six miles off the southeastern coast of Puerto Rico. It extends twenty-one miles from southwest to northeast, is six miles wide at its widest point, and covers 33,119 acres. Rolling hills run east to west through the island's center, and the highest, Mount Pirata (elevation twelve hundred feet) stands in the west. There is a variety of parent rocks and soils, including loam throughout the island and clay in the eastern half. The 1910 *Encyclopaedia Britannica* aptly refers to the "fertile island of Vieques." From the nineteenth century until World War II, export agriculture was dominated by sugar cane production, and ranching produced some of the best beef in the Caribbean.

Historically, farming the land produced staples such as root crops, peppers, rice, and plantains, as well as commercially grown items such as coffee, coconuts, and pineapples. The climate on the island is drier than in Puerto Rico as a whole, yet rainfall is adequate to maintain several permanent streams, lagoons, and underground water supplies. Native vegetation includes diverse forests, ranging from mangroves to mahogany. Fish have always been abundant, as the island is surrounded by productive coral reefs, sea grasses (*Thalassia* spp.), and mangroves. Land crabs were so numerous that Vieques was once known as "Crab Island."[2]

Some of the earliest human remains found in the Caribbean—more than four thousand years old—were discovered in Vieques; in fact, among the earliest artifacts are items of Andean origin. Archaeologists believe that Vieques may hold an important key to understanding Caribbean pre-Columbian history. While hundreds of archaeological sites have been identified on the island, few have been adequately studied, because of military restrictions.[3] At the time of Columbus, both the island and Boriquén (the "big island," now Puerto Rico) were ruled by Arawak-speaking Taínos, who called the island Bieke ("little island"). The little island, one of many autonomous Taíno settlements, was led by two brothers, Cacimar and Yaureibo. When Cacimar was killed in 1513 while fighting the Spanish invasion of Boriquén, his brother avenged his death by attacking Spanish positions there. The Spanish pursued him back to Bieke, where he also fell in battle.

Yet Bieke resisted full Spanish control and settlement until the nineteenth century. In fact, this officially "unpopulated" Spanish possession was home to peoples in resistance: native Caribs and Africans escaping slavery, as well as pirates—many of whom earned the name for conducting trade outside of Spanish control. The island was constantly attacked by other European powers and was visited by Simón Bolívar during his campaigns to end Spanish colonial rule in America.[4]

Following the loss of nearly all its American colonies during the early nineteenth century, the Spanish government determined that it would have to intensify the settlement and development of its remaining possessions, Cuba and Puerto Rico. In order to consolidate its hold on Vieques—the strategic eastern gateway to Puerto Rico—Spain offered land grants to settlers who invested in sugar cane production. Not only Spaniards but also French and Danish planters settled in Vieques, bringing both slaves and free workers from eastern Caribbean islands.

Expansion of the sugar cane industry also attracted laborers from eastern Puerto Rico. Spain's policy encouraged settlement by anyone possessing the needed skills or capital, while expelling (or sending into hiding) "unofficial" residents who resisted the new settlers' claims to land grants. These unofficial—that is, uncounted—residents resisted Spanish control, taxes, labor drafts, and so on by hiding in the more inaccessible areas of Puerto Rico, such as caves, mangroves, swamplands, and mountainous areas without roads.[5] Rural settlements in Vieques were generally spread far apart, although the western lands were more densely settled. Workers in Vieques were offered usufruct rights on the land where they built their homes, according to a Spanish law still in force in Puerto Rico today; their orchards, garden plots, and fishing helped reduce dependence on plantation company stores. However, by the end of Spanish rule in 1898, only 15 percent of the Vieques population held legal title to their land. During the first forty years of U.S. rule, this decreased to 5 percent; in fact, by 1940 at least 70 percent of the island was owned by only two entities, one of which was part of a New York–based sugar conglomerate.[6]

Vieques's first Spanish census counted close to two hundred inhabitants in 1828; more than half were listed either as *peónes* or slaves. By 1839, some eight hundred people were counted, more than half of whom were considered "free people of color." Most were born in Puerto Rico and Vieques, but there were also French, Danish, and English subjects. The 1867 Spanish census counted four thousand residents, and by the end of the nineteenth century nearly six thousand were registered. U.S. census records show that Vieques's population nearly doubled between 1899 and 1910, to over ten thousand, twelve years after the United States' invasion and occupation of Puerto Rico and the resulting expansion of the sugar industry. And while the 1910–1940 U.S. censuses counted between ten and eleven thousand residents, locals claim that many living in isolated areas or temporarily working off-island were missed. As Vieques grew in population, its resistance to exploitation also grew. Troops were used to put down insurrections by plantation workers on more than one occasion, both before and after the U.S. takeover.[7]

THE STRUGGLE

The U.S. Navy had been interested in establishing bases in Puerto Rico, including the islands of Vieques and Culebra, since long before 1898; in particular, naval strategist Alfred Thayer Mahan tied control of the islands to the future Central American canal.[8] The navy began bombing practice in Culebra in 1901 and field maneuvers in Vieques as early as the 1920s. In March 1938 President Franklin Roosevelt and Admiral William Leahy observed military exercises near Vieques; soon after, Leahy wrote the first draft of a bill allowing the navy to acquire land for new bases and training areas, which was passed by Congress as Public Law 528. The following year, Leahy was named governor of Puerto Rico and he began planning his new bases.[9]

In March 1941 Congress approved Public Law 13, a sweeping bill allowing the military to expropriate land for ninety-one bases throughout the United States and its territories, including Puerto Rico. The bill set aside $35 million to buy properties in Vieques, which were to be condemned and sold to the U.S. Department of Defense; Public Law 247 (passed in August) allowed the navy to take immediate possession.

Washington's plan to build a giant base to shelter the British fleet plunged Vieques into World War II even before the United States was officially at war. Between 1941 and 1943, the navy took over 21,013 of the island's 33,119 acres. At this time, the navy expropriated the entire western portion of the island—where most of the rural settlements were located—as well as the arid and sparsely settled eastern section and 2,500 acres in the center of the island.

The two largest landowners were fairly well compensated, but dozens of small property owners were offered only a small check for what the navy determined was the value of their property and were given a few days to leave. Even worse, the vast majority—who had use rights but no title—received less than twenty-four-hours' notice, were offered twenty-five dollars, and were warned they would be bulldozed along with their homes if they didn't move fast enough. Some people were told that the navy would return the lands after the war, while others were threatened with jail if they resisted. The displaced were offered lots in the lands taken by the navy in the island's center, on condition that they signed a contract recognizing they could be ordered to vacate "navy property" with a month's notice. These lands were generally rough brushlands without any services or buildings; several women gave birth in the fields because there was no time to build shelters for them.[10]

In time people did build homes in the parcels; however, despite promises, they did not receive title to those lands after the war. Over the years, invasions by squatters helped force the navy to transfer these central lands to the local government. Even today, however, most Viequenses still lack title to their property or the means to buy those or other lands, due in part to land speculation.[11]

Organized opposition to the navy was at first blunted by fear of political persecution, strong support for the Allied war effort, and the many jobs created to build the giant base. The latter included jobs constructing a giant pier that was planned to stretch all the way to Puerto Rico. Other projects flattened and removed land and vegetation to make way for hundreds of underground bunkers and weapons storage facilities, operated rock and sand quarries for building materials, and built military roads and bridges—even through sensitive mangroves and wetlands—to accommodate tanks throughout the western end. The jobs paid better than sugar cane and even attracted workers from Puerto Rico. But by 1943 it became clear that the British navy would not need the shelter, and work on the giant base was abandoned. Not surprisingly, the first major antinavy protest took place in 1943, because Viequenses would soon be left without either land or jobs.[12] In fact, never again would the navy be a primary source of employment in Vieques.

Opposition was also tempered by the expectation that after the war the lands would be returned. In 1945 the navy leased thousands of acres to the Puerto Rican government, which began a series of agricultural projects that rehabilitated some lands and created more than six hundred jobs by the end of 1946.[13] Then in 1947 the navy dropped another bombshell: it announced that it would retake the lands it had leased, as well as expropriate more than 4,000 additional acres. Many of Puerto Rico's government officials expressed disapproval, a local group called Sons of Vieques organized protests, and some landowners took the navy to court. Nonetheless, the navy ended up with 26,000 of Vieques's 33,119 acres—over 76 percent of the island—leaving civilians squeezed in the middle, imprisoned in a reservation.

The eastern half of Vieques became the U.S. Marines' Camp García, which often housed thousands of troops. The section of the island designated as the Eastern Maneuver Area formed part of the Atlantic fleet's favorite bombing, training, and weapons testing facility. It was also used for joint maneuvers with forces maintained by NATO and the Organization of American States, and was even rented out to other countries and weapons manufacturers. In 1948 the navy held its first large-scale war games in Vieques, in which sixty ships, 350 planes, and fifty thousand troops from all branches of the U.S. military participated. The exercise consisted of an invading force (the U.S. troops, called "Blues") conquering the island, which was defended by the Puerto Rico National Guard, called "Blacks."[14] The western lands housed the Naval Ammunitions Supply Depot, which was used to store all kinds of weapons and explosives.

Open burning and detonation of munitions and other toxic substances has been a common practice, even without the required permits.[15] Nonconventional (biological, chemical, and nuclear) weapons practice over the years has included documented use of radioactive materials. For example, in 1966 a nuclear bomb was lost between Puerto Rico and Vieques and was retrieved with trained dolphins; additionally, shells hardened with depleted uranium have been fired, in violation of military protocols forbidding its use for practice. And one navy ship contaminated in the atomic bomb tests in the Marshall Islands was later used for target practice in Vieques and is currently lying just off the southeast coast. Chemical weapons such as napalm and Agent Orange have also been used.[16]

Numerous times, the navy proposed to remove the entire civilian population from Vieques. One plan in 1947 would have removed the entire population to St. Croix, where thousands of Viequenses had already settled, and another suggested sending them to Alaska. Another proposal, in 1961, which called for removing even the dead from the cemetery, was known locally as "Plan Dracula." Each time, popular resistance in Vieques, plus the Puerto Rican government's fears of possible political repercussions in Puerto Rico, defeated the plans.[17]

Tensions rose over the years when military personnel—often thousands of Marines let loose in the civilian sector—engaged in sexual assaults on women and children and drunken brawls with local men. A number of Viequenses were killed in such altercations, as well as in accidents with explosives, for which no military personnel ever faced criminal charges.[18] Official military dealings with the local government were also infused with open racism and colonial contempt. Local resistance grew to such an extent that sailors and Marines were often met with scores of bottles and stones; finally, in the early 1980s the military stopped allowing off-duty personnel to enter the civilian sector.

For years the navy opposed attempts to strongly develop the tourism and manufacturing industries, preferring instead to limit traffic in and around Vieques.[19] Thousands were forced to migrate in search of work, so that the population steadily declined to between seven thousand and eight thousand; it has only recently grown to ninety-three hundred. Another intense round of antinavy activism in the 1970s forced the navy out of Culebra but not out of Vieques. In 1979 several key community leaders from Vieques and Puerto Rico were given federal prison terms for holding a religious service in the restricted area. One of these, Angel Rodríguez Cristobal, was murdered in prison.[20] After the loss of Culebra as a bombing range, the navy intensified its use of Vieques for bombing, land maneuvers, and weapons testing. Interestingly, U.S. Marines were no longer stationed in large numbers in Camp García once destructive practices were intensified; at the same time that toxic contamination grew exponentially, many patrolling and security duties were contracted out to a firm hiring Viequenses.[21]

In 1980 a study conducted by the U.S. House Armed Services Committee, then chaired by Congressman Ron Dellums (D-CA), concluded that the navy should end its use of Vieques.[22] At the same time, the Puerto Rican government filed a lawsuit and conducted studies documenting the adverse environmental effects of military occupation; but in 1983 the government dropped its lawsuit and signed a memorandum of understanding with the navy. In return for continued occupation of and training on Vieques, the navy promised to improve community relations, promote economic development, and protect ecologically sensitive land. Almost twenty years later, even the navy acknowledged that it had failed to honor these commitments. But when Vieques became news in 1999, the military resumed making the same promises.

At the end of the twentieth century, Vieques was an island occupied by a people fighting against extinction. Between 1983 and 1998, the navy dropped 17,783 tons of bombs on the island.[23] The Live Impact Area—900 acres at the eastern end of the island where ships and planes practice bombing—contains more craters per square foot than the moon.[24] Parts of the rock substrata are damaged, and much of the soil has been blown away. Navy-contracted experts have minimized the importance of indigenous sites, and many of these sites have been destroyed. Instead of demonstrating concern about the destruction, the navy produced a document, published in 2001, claiming that, since the bombing had already destroyed so many cultural resources, there probably wasn't much left, so continued bombing would have no significant negative impact![25] Around the bombing zone, key plants and animals in the local food chain show dangerous amounts of heavy metals, particularly components of weapons and targets such as arsenic, barium, cadmium, chromium, cobalt, copper, cyanide, lead, nickel, tin, vanadium, and zinc.[26]

The prevailing easterly trade winds carry contaminated dust—including radioactive material—from the impact area directly into the civilian zone, where the same contaminants show up in excessive amounts in vegetation and residents. Civilian water supplies have also shown traces of military explosives since at least the late 1970s. Moreover, during bombing exercises the radiation levels in the civilian area more than doubled.[27] Cancer and diseases of the heart, kidney, reproductive organs, and skin, among others, which are linked to the kinds of heavy metals used in military explosives, have shown dramatic increases since the 1970s and now occur at higher rates in Vieques than on the big island.[28] If the higher-than-average mortality rate in Vieques cannot be explained by significant differences in age distribution or lifestyle—both of which compare favorably with other rural municipalities—then environmental contamination must be considered. And since so little polluting economic activity occurs in Vieques, the most obvious source of contamination is the navy.

Because the giant Roosevelt Roads Navy Base blocks the shortest sea route to Puerto Rico, people and goods traveling to Vieques must enter via Fajardo, which is seventeen miles and more than an hour away; the detour adds eleven miles to an otherwise short trip. The local clinic is so badly underfunded that most medical needs, including prenatal care and childbirth assistance, are met by traveling to the big island. Not surprisingly, Vieques experiences higher rates of low birth weight and infant mortality than does the rest of Puerto Rico.

The local fishing industry has suffered from damage to marine habitats, which for years have evidenced degradation related to bombing and other military activities.[29] The many days when navy maneuvers severely limited fishing (more than half the year during the 1990s) also hurt the industry.

Tourism is constrained by a lack of space, services, and infrastructure. And the tourism industry that does exist is dominated by a growing settler community of between one and two thousand white North Americans and Europeans, who have driven up real estate prices, have built walled villas and rental condos, and dream of separating Vieques and Culebra from Puerto Rico in order to create the "Spanish Virgin Islands."[30] Young people in Vieques have few alternatives to leaving; some take jobs elsewhere that will allow them to retire early, in the hopes of returning with a pension, but others never come back. One reason for this is that they can't afford the real estate prices on the scarce civilian land, which are driven upward by speculation. Properties are often advertised only within the settler population. More than one Viequense has described his or her own community as an "endangered species" and referred to the ongoing colonization as the "Hawaii-zation" of Vieques.

Since the 1940s, local resistance has been shaped during periods of organized activity, such as a broad-based campaign that prevented further military expropriations in the 1960s and the fishermen-led disruptions of navy exercises during the 1970s. Such periods of open resistance frequently were followed by political buyouts or repression and a less active interlude. Moreover, the municipal assembly has passed resolutions during each decade since the 1950s calling for the navy to leave and return the land to the people. In the early 1990s, Vieques activists formed the Committee for the Rescue and Development of Vieques and continued protesting navy activities in Vieques.

One particularly controversial issue was the destruction of a twenty-five-acre mahogany forest in the western lands to make way for Raytheon Corporation's Realizable Over the Horizon Radar.[31] But the Committee for the Rescue and Development of Vieques did more than just protest. It also offered "la protesta con la propuesta" (the protest with the proposal). Members began to develop proposals for the island's biggest ecological, economic, and social challenges. They testified in 1996 before the U.S. Congress in favor of a bill that would return the western lands to Vieques's control. They proposed an integrated plan for those lands, including some urban growth to ease overcrowding, resumption of agriculture and ranching, and conservation of sensitive and historic sites, along with promotion of fishing and small-scale tourism. They also called for the creation of a community land trust to manage the returned lands and a "community extension program" to fund research, education, and training. Unfortunately, Congress shelved the western lands bill, and the land use plan received little attention. Then, on April 19, 1999, two training bombs killed a civilian navy employee named David Sanes, igniting a major antinavy movement that captured world attention.

Activism since 1999 has included rallies in Puerto Rico, such as the February 2000 march by 150,000 people in San Juan. Other rallies have occurred wherever Puerto Ricans live, including the major protests in New York in 2000 and at the Democratic Convention in Los Angeles that same year. Fund-raising efforts have featured concerts, plays, and films, fueled by a Vieques-inspired cultural explosion. There have also been ongoing funding commitments from labor unions and other organizations. Regular efforts to educate and lobby Congress included a visit by three hundred Viequenses to Washington, D.C., in March 2001, during which some Congress members expressed surprise that Vieques was inhabited.

But by far, the most powerful activism has been militant, nonviolent civil disobedience. Two days after David Sanes was killed, the Puerto Rican environmental activist Alberto de Jesús (known as Tito Kayak) decided to stay on the bombing range to prevent more navy bombing exercises. Hundreds, then thousands, of Puerto Ricans and others followed his example. Within a year, fourteen protest camps had been established, representing diverse groups, such as teachers, fishermen, evangelical churches, and the Puerto Rican Independence Party. By May 4, 2000—when the U.S. government sent in federal marshals, the FBI, and the military—the protesters had built a schoolhouse, a church, and a solar electricity system and had participated in one of the longest sit-ins in history.

After that date, over sixteen hundred Viequenses were arrested for continuing to enter the bombing range—particularly whenever the navy sent its battle groups for bombing practice—and hundreds served prison sentences of up to one year for the misdemeanor offense of trespassing. While well-known arrestees such as the Reverend Al Sharpton, Jacqueline Jackson, and Robert Kennedy Jr. helped bring attention and influence to the Vieques struggle, it was the willingness of ordinary people from all segments of Puerto Rican society to risk their lives that formed the bedrock of the movement.

Protesters also repeatedly tore down the eight-mile-long fence dividing the civilian and military sectors, and this took an economic and psychological toll on the military. In one year the navy spent $11 million on fencing; it was also acknowledged that fence-cutting hurt the morale of military personnel. Moreover, the Vieques struggle linked up with the growing international network against U.S. militarism, engaging in reciprocal visits and coordinated activities with activists from Korea, Okinawa, Hawaii, San Francisco's Bayview-Hunter's Point, and elsewhere.[32]

THE FUTURE?

No one can doubt the difficulty inherent in challenging the world's most powerful military. But a perhaps even greater challenge is that of anticipating what will happen to Vieques after the navy leaves and preparing for it. Before considering the competing proposals for reclaiming the land, it is important to understand what happened on January 31, 2000, when President Bill Clinton and Puerto Rico's Governor Pedro Rosselló agreed to remove the protest camps from the bombing range and resume navy training under conditions meant to appear to resolve the crisis. Clinton issued not a presidential order but only directives, which could be changed by Congress. The directives contained several key points: First, bombing would resume for up to ninety days per year with "inert" (nonexplosive) bombs. Second, Viequenses would vote—on a date set by the navy—between only two options: either navy bombings could continue only until May 2003, in exchange for $40 million, or permanent live fire would resume, in exchange for an additional $50 million. The most popular option, the immediate and permanent end to navy training, was not included. Third, Puerto Rico would police the area near the bases and agree not to file lawsuits. Fourth, the western lands would be cleaned up and—except for the highest points, which house military radar and radio complexes—would be given to Puerto Rico by December 31, 2000.

The navy officially accepted the directives. But its allies in Congress vowed to change them, since the directives did not guarantee the use of Vieques forever. Meanwhile, in Puerto Rico, activists denounced the plan as a fraud. Not surprisingly, in October 2000 an amendment was added to the Federal Defense Authorization Act for the fiscal year 2001 that changed the directives: the navy would not leave the western lands until May 2001, at least six months after the elections in the United States and Puerto Rico. Instead of giving all the land in question back to Puerto Rico for the benefit of Vieques, as the directives stated, most of it would be split between the municipal government of Vieques and the U.S. Department of the Interior. The land transfer was carried out in a hurried meeting in Washington, D.C., on April 30, 2001. The mayor of Vieques was not present because, along with hundreds of others, he was in the bombing range impeding navy exercises at the time.

Fourteen of the seventeen toxic sites that the navy identified within the western lands were located in the portion given to the municipality; those areas, therefore, were to remain under navy control until a cleanup was completed. Significantly, although the Comprehensive Environmental Response, Compensation, and Liability Act, commonly known as the Superfund, requires the cleanup of former military lands, transfer to another federal agency is not considered a change in title. Thus, a cleanup would not be required while the land was under the Interior Department's control. The navy also would restrict the use of more than 600 acres, which were near the radar and radio complex, turned over to Vieques and the Interior Department. And it demanded rights-of-way on civilian roads and in ports. Worst of all: the bill declared that if Vieques voted to remove the navy, the eastern lands would be transferred completely to the Interior Department. In this case the lands would not be cleaned, but would simply be closed to the public and declared a "wilderness reserve."[33] If carried out as written, this act would punish Viequenses for opposing the navy, once again by squeezing them, on their reservation, between contaminated land and restricted federal "conservation" land.

Another proposal on Capitol Hill suggested detaching Vieques from Puerto Rico. Reportedly, a navy employee in Vieques was told that over $200 million dollars could be appropriated for this new entity, in exchange for supporting the navy's continued use of the island. This person was the public face of alleged local support for continued navy use of Vieques. And the navy hadn't given up its dream of getting all of Vieques. For example, in March 2001, one navy ally in Congress told a woman from Vieques that it would be cheaper to move the people off the island than to clean it up![34] And the first draft of the Puerto Rico Planning Board's 2000 land use plan included a "civilian-free Vieques" as one of its alternatives.

Considering Puerto Rico's colonial political status, San Juan is obviously vulnerable to pressure from Washington. Nearly every governor has attempted to end the bombing of Vieques, only to end up making a deal. The pro-statehood government, which was in power from 1992 until the end of 2000, allowed its planning board to work with the navy on the land use plan. According to one observer, the lands not destined for "conservation" would be "cut up like a birthday cake" and put in the hands of business interests already at work on Vieques. These business interests planned, among other things, to open a Texas-owned, walled luxury resort on the north shore that would charge its guests thousands of dollars per night, offering amenities such as an illegally privatized beach. Another proposed large tourist development, one with a golf course on the south shore, also threatened to use up scarce water supplies.[35]

In August 2000, the planning board held a required public hearing in Vieques on the first draft of its land use plan. Public access to the documents was extremely limited. Among its features were plans to build three new factories tied to the military; a plan to build a large new port for cruise ships and commercial traffic near the proposed new resort, which would be far from town; a plan to let the navy run the local clinic; and a plan to attract ten thousand new settlers to Vieques, mainly from military families.[36]

Only one copy of the draft land use plan was placed in Vieques, in the town hall. The hours of access were limited, and reviewers were not allowed to photocopy any part. The only other copy was in the planning board's offices in San Juan. Despite the obstacles, thirty-five members of Vieques community groups and supporting technical experts on planning, health, and environmental issues reviewed the draft and signed up to speak at the hearings. The hearings played to a packed house and lasted over six hours. While speaker after speaker denounced the plan in detail, hundreds of Viequenses held a spirited protest outside. Finally, at midnight, the mayor rejected the plan and ordered a new one based on the navy leaving Vieques.

The second draft, reviewed in November 2000, chose a "navy-free Vieques" as the preferred option, but it too contained serious problems. First, it assumed that agriculture, fishing, and nonmilitary factories were not viable and that Vieques would have to depend almost entirely on foreign tourism. Second, all three land areas—the two military properties and the civilian sector in between—were treated as separate entities instead of as one island. Third, it ignored the need to shorten traveling time between Vieques and the big island by allowing travel between the closest points.

Most troubling was the lack of attention to land tenure.[37] How could native Viequenses stay, when prices were being driven up by outside interests? The planning board members hurriedly approved the land use plan before the New Year, when the new governor would likely replace them. The approved plan did not contain any of the proposals that activists had worked on for years. In January, the new mayor of Vieques, Dámaso Serrano, announced that he would work to revise the plan in order to incorporate some of the proposals.

In 1999 a large group of San Juan–based professionals responded to a call from Vieques activists for ongoing technical assistance. This group, the Technical and Professional Support Group, includes planners, attorneys, health professionals, ecologists, economists, and other individuals with the expertise needed to assist the Viequenses in creating their own development and conservation plans. These people worked on a completely voluntary basis for over three years to flesh out the details of a community-directed, ecologically and socially sustainable land use and development plan. The group began by holding dozens of meetings and workshops in Vieques in order to learn what the people themselves saw as their most pressing problems and possible solutions.

Volume 1 of their work, completed during the summer of 2000, presented a detailed picture of current economic, social, and environmental challenges, including analyses and suggestions given in dozens of community workshops. During the winter of 2001–2002 they worked on a community land trust proposal, and volume 2 detailed specific strategies for responsible and integrated development, some of which received attention from the local government.[38]

Governor Sila María Calderón, while publicly supporting an immediate and permanent cessation of military activities in Vieques, in practice used the police to make entering the navy-occupied lands extremely difficult (though not impossible). She did, however, authorize a referendum in Vieques on July 29, 2001, which, in addition to the two options outlined in the presidential directives, offered a third choice, known as option 2: the immediate and permanent end to military activities, and the cleanup and return of all lands to the people of Vieques.

The navy poured thousands of dollars into getting people to vote for option 3: permanent live bombing, plus $50 million. The navy campaign included posters linking the Vieques activism to Fidel Castro and offered money, jobs, appliances, and project grants, apparently without success. Of the 80 percent of registered voters who cast their votes, 70 percent voted for the navy to leave. Meanwhile, public pressure from solidarity groups in the United States concentrated on lobbying Congress to demilitarize Vieques as part of defense appropriations legislation. Then came September 11.

The Vieques activists, in a gesture of solidarity with the victims in New York and Washington, D.C., called off their preparations for civil disobedience against the navy maneuvers planned for late September 2001. While some observers interpreted the gesture as a collapse of the struggle to get the navy out, the next six months demonstrated that nothing could be further from the truth. In early January 2002, less than a month after he completed a four-month prison sentence for civil disobedience, Mayor Serrano helped create an umbrella working group that included all Vieques organizations, in order to better coordinate efforts for demilitarization, decontamination, and return of all lands. Civil disobedience training continued, fund-raising picked up again after a brief lull, and key organizations resumed their support for Vieques. In particular, the New York groups hosted a major gathering of activists from Vieques, from elsewhere in Puerto Rico, and from throughout the United States during April 2002, aiming to redouble efforts and more fully coordinate the campaign.

The navy's claims of the uniqueness of training maneuvers in Vieques were increasingly contradicted by actual practice, which demonstrated that maneuvers there were, in fact, either obsolete or duplicated in other, less risky locations. The navy's resistance to leaving appears to have more to do with fears of a possible domino effect on other bases if it appeared to bow to community pressure. There is also the expensive cleanup bill to consider, after the base's closure. Nonetheless, in 2002 the navy fired nearly all its civilian employees from Vieques, actually stated that one battle group did not need to train in Vieques in January 2002—before going off to actual war—and admitted that it was tired of dealing with protesters.

Under considerable pressure from congressional supporters, the navy did send a battle group to bomb Vieques during April 2002. Despite increased security, protesters once again managed to reach the bombing range and disrupt the exercises. While sentences for civil disobedience had become more severe, it appeared that enough people and resources could be mobilized to keep challenging the navy's continued use of

Vieques. Some activists began to shift their focus to the more contentious—and potentially more divisive—problems of cleanup and control of the lands. Whether they can successfully apply the experiences of the demilitarization phase to the rest of the struggle remains to be seen.

In May 2003, after sixty-two years of using Vieques as a bombing range, the navy finally left the tiny island. However, it also left behind a legacy of broken promises, thousands of unexploded bombs, poisoned marine life, and toxins that threaten the health of Viequenses.[39] The site has been transferred to the Interior Department—which has promised to administer it as a limited-access wildlife refuge. Hundreds of activists previously jailed for trespassing to block the bombing are currently preparing for their next battle: reclaiming 15,000 acres of land in eastern Vieques transferred to the Interior Department.

Beyond the promised base cleanup, Vieques residents have certain economic concerns. Many would like to see sustainable development practiced on their island. Years of bombing snuffed out much of the local agriculture and fishing industry, leaving pollution and poverty. Over 74 percent of residents here live below the U.S. poverty line, compared with 48 percent on mainland Puerto Rico. Some Viequenses see tourism as bringing needed growth. Others fear that the navy's departure will open the doors to developers who will build Miami-style hotels along the island's palm-lined, white-sand beaches—and displace current residents.[40]

In sum, the Vieques struggle is not only against the navy: it is also against the separation of communities from the environment that sustains them, which they must protect—and they should have the means to do so. The struggle is also against the separation of people from their homelands and communities, which benefits a rich and powerful elite and is unsustainable as well. Endangered species include not only plants and animals but also human communities. Accordingly, the Vieques struggle is for connection and for supporting the local foundations of global sustainability. It argues that economic activity should first benefit the local community, both human and natural. Seen this way, the tourist industry should be a means to an end, not an end in itself. Since diversity is the foundation of sustainability, promoting diverse economic sectors—agriculture, fishing, light industry, communications, education, and tourism, each of which supports the others—would be more likely to benefit Vieques in the long term.

Every Viequense who wants to make a life in Vieques should be able to find work, own property, raise a family, and contribute to the ecological and social well-being of the island. This includes people who were forced to leave the island but who long to return. Some safeguards must be put in place to allow them a chance, so as not to permit colonialist market forces to give outsiders and speculators an unfair advantage.

Finally, the Vieques struggle is important to more than just Puerto Rico. For example, the struggle challenges gentrification, arguing that people of color should have the right and the means to remain in their communities—even after conditions improve! "La protesta con la propuesta" supports indigenous survival and those who care not only about short-term profit but also long-term effects. It is pro-people and pro-environment, affirming connection, cooperation, community, and justice. "El grito de Vieques"—the cry of Vieques—is a call for self-determination. This is the heart and soul of global sustainability.

ORONTO DOUGLAS, DIMIEARI VON KEMEDI,
IKE OKONTA, AND MICHAEL J. WATTS

12

Alienation and Militancy in the Niger Delta
Petroleum, Politics, and Democracy in Nigeria

In the wake of the September 11 attack and the war in Iraq, Nigeria's geopolitical significance to the United States has come into sharper relief. In March and April 2003, militancy across the Niger Delta radically disrupted oil extraction in this major oil-producing nation. News of these actions, following conflict-ridden national elections, has reinforced the notion that Nigeria and the new West African "gulf states" in general are matters of U.S. national security.

The Center for Strategic and International Studies weighed in on these events in the May 2003 edition of its publication *CSIS Africa Notes*. Since the center is one of the most influential Washington think tanks, its analysis matters in the formation of U.S. foreign policy. The brief article "Alienation and Militancy in Nigeria's Niger Delta," by Esther Cesarz, J. Stephen Morrison, and Jennifer Cooke, commands attention, and it merits a serious response.[1]

As the authors state, the recent oil crisis highlights "more profound national challenges" now facing the reelected President Olusegun Obasanjo and his government. In their view, the recent conflicts in the Niger Delta mark a watershed, distinguished in particular by the prospects of "an upward spiral of violence." The new levels of weaponry and criminal activity on the part of a "frustrated and angry youth" suggest "new ambitions and capacities" among the Ijaw—the largest tribe in the Niger Delta—who have taken on the characteristics of an armed militia. The authors see the specter of Colombia now haunting Nigeria. U.S. companies, they believe, will become targets of terrorist activity, and Nigeria's national stability and cohesion will be threatened.[2]

We believe this account is wrongheaded on a number of accounts. It misdiagnoses the nature of the political crisis in the Niger Delta, fails to understand the political dynamics of the Ijaw and minority politics in general, and makes unsubstantiated comparisons with the likes of Aceh province in northern Sumatra (which, like most of Indonesia, is overwhelmingly Muslim, and which has a long history of resistance to outside powers) and Colombia. Astonishingly, it also ignores the role of some key actors, the oil companies foremost among them. And it downplays a number of fundamental political problems that must be faced.

The article does mention several key issues in passing, including federalism, resource allocation, and minority rights. But it gives these issues short shrift while inflating the threat of a new terrorist menace. In doing so, it potentially helps to set the stage for an excessive military response or even a new round of ethnic cleansing. An adequate response to Nigeria's problems requires a serious analysis of the country's historical and political context.[3]

THE NIGER DELTA AND U.S. NATIONAL SECURITY

A year before the events of September 11, 2001, the U.S. Department of State, in its annual encyclopedia of global terrorism, identified the Niger Delta—the geographical heart of oil production in Nigeria—as a breeding ground for militant and "impoverished ethnic groups" involved in numerous terrorist acts (abduction, hostage taking, kidnapping, and extrajudicial killings).[4] A CIA report published in 2000 warned that "environmental stresses" in the oil-rich southern delta could deepen "political tensions" at a time when Nigeria—currently the world's sixth-largest producer of petroleum—was supplying almost 14 percent of U.S. petroleum needs.[5] Throughout the last decade or so, Nigeria has supplied an average of 8–10 percent of U.S. oil imports. During the next decade, as its deepwater fields are exploited (and as new reserves are discovered), Nigeria's annual production could exceed that of Venezuela or Kuwait. Nigeria had, of course, become an archetypal oil nation by the 1970s. Oil revenues currently provide 80 percent of government income, 95 percent of export receipts, and 90 percent of foreign exchange earnings.

AFRICAN OIL AND U.S. NATIONAL SECURITY

The geopolitical significance of Nigerian oil to the United States, particularly against the global backdrop of rising prices, tight markets, and political instability in the Persian Gulf, Indonesia, and parts of Latin America, is widely understood. Even before the September 11 attacks, the Petroleum Finance Company, testifying in Congress before the International Relations Subcommittee on Africa, reported on the strategic and growing security significance of West African oil. In the view of the Petroleum Finance Company, West Africa's high-quality reserves and low-cost output, coupled with massive new deepwater discoveries, required serious attention and substantial foreign investment.

In the wake of the al-Qaeda attacks and the Gulf War, Nigeria and West African producers emerged as "the new Gulf oil states."[6] In January 2002 the Institute for Advanced Strategic and Political Studies provided a forum for the Bush administration to declare that African oil is "a priority for U.S. national security."[7] Since 2002, the ugly footprint of Africa's black gold in Gabon, São Tomé, Angola, and Equatorial Guinea has rarely been off the front pages. And the discovery of oil has been accompanied by the specter of terror: the "nightmare," as the *New York Times* noted, of "sympathizers of Osama bin Laden sink[ing] three oil tankers in the Straits of Hormuz."[8]

OIL CORRUPTION HIGH; LIVING STANDARDS LOW

The mythos of oil wealth has been central to the history of modern industrial capitalism. But in Nigeria, as elsewhere, the discovery of oil, and the current annual oil revenues of $40 billion, has ushered in a miserable, undisciplined, decrepit, and corrupt form of petro-capitalism. After a half century of oil production, almost $300 billion in oil revenues has flowed directly into the federal exchequer (and perhaps $50 billion of these revenues promptly flowed out, only to disappear overseas). Yet Nigerian per capita income stands at $290 per year. For the majority of Nigerians, living standards are no better now than at the start of the country's independence in 1960. A repugnant culture of excessive venality and profiteering among the political class—the U.S. Department of State has an entire website devoted to fraud cases—has won for Nigeria the dubious honor of first place in Transparency International's ranking of most corrupt states.

Paradoxically, the oil-producing states within federated Nigeria have benefited the least from oil wealth. Devastated by the ecological costs of oil spillage and the highest gas-flaring rates in the world, the Niger Delta is a political tinderbox. The militancy of a generation of restive youth, the deep political frustrations among oil-producing communities, and preelectoral thuggery all prosper in the rich soil of political marginalization. Massive election rigging across the Niger Delta in the April 2003 elections simply confirmed the worst for the millions of Nigerians who have suffered from decades of neglect. The great Polish journalist Ryszard Kapuscinski noted in his meditation on oil-rich Iran that "oil creates the illusion of a completely changed life, life without work, life for free. . . . The concept of oil expresses perfectly the eternal human dream of wealth achieved through lucky accident. . . . In this sense oil is a fairy tale and, like every fairy tale, a bit of a lie."[9] It is this lie that currently confronts West African oil producers and the Niger Delta in particular.

OIL VIOLENCE

Since March 12, 2003, mounting communal violence has resulted in the deaths of at least fifty local residents and the leveling of eight communities in and around the petroleum complex in Warri, Nigeria. Seven oil company employees have been killed as well, prompting all the major oil companies to withdraw staff, close down operations, and reduce output by over 750,000 barrels per day (almost half the national output). President Obasanjo dispatched large troop deployments to the oil-producing creeks and marshlands. Ijaw militants, incensed over illegal oil bunkering (in which the security forces were implicated) and indiscriminate military action, threatened to detonate eleven captured oil installations.

Nobody seriously expects that the deeper problems within the oil sector will go away. Strikes on the offshore oil platforms—a long-festering sore that is rarely mentioned in the media—were, however, quickly resolved. Relatively new to delta politics, however, was a series of assassinations, most notably that of Marshall Harry, chieftain of the All Nigeria Peoples Party, a senior member of the main opposition party and a leading campaigner for greater resource allocation to the oil-producing Niger Delta, who was killed in March 2003. Fallout from the Harry assassination became a source of tension in his native oil-producing state of Rivers. Supporters of the main opposition party, the All Nigeria Peoples Party, and another opposition grouping of activists and politicians, the Rivers Democratic Movement, linked the ruling party to the assassination.

The Niger Delta stands at the crossroads of contemporary Nigerian politics. Despite the 13 percent growth of oil revenues in the delta states, the region remains desperately poor. The deepening material and political grievances that have resulted place the Niger Delta at the confluence of four pressing national issues in the wake of the April 2003 elections: (1) the efforts to control resources, led by a number of delta states, which in effect means expanded local access to oil revenues, (2) the struggle for the self-determination of minority people and the clamor for a sovereign national conference to rewrite the federal Constitution, (3) a crisis of rule in the region, as a number of state and local governments have been rendered helpless by militant youth movements, growing insecurity, and intracommunity, interethnic, and state violence, and (4) the emergence of what is called the South-South Alliance linking Nigeria's hitherto excluded oil-producing states, which acts as a bulwark against the ethnic majorities.

A THRESHOLD CROSSED?

The article by the Center for Strategic and International Studies, mentioned earlier, suggests that the current crisis in the Niger Delta represents a threshold increase in violence that threatens Nigeria's national government. This contention must be placed in the larger context of recent history, especially since the end of military rule. Obasanjo's presidential victory in 1999, in the wake of the darkest period of military dictatorship in Nigeria's forty-year, postindependence history, held much promise. An internationally recognized statesman and diplomat imprisoned during the brutal rule of his predecessor, Sani Abacha, Obasanjo inherited a massively corrupt state apparatus, an economy in shambles, and a federation crippled by long-standing ethnic enmity.

Entrusted with reforming a corrupt, undisciplined military, the largest military in Africa, and committed to deepening the process of democratization, Obasanjo was confronted by militant ethnic groups within months of his inauguration. These groups spoke the language of self-determination, local autonomy, and resource control (meaning a greater share of federally allocated oil revenues). In an incident widely condemned by the human rights community, members of one of these groups slaughtered some two thousand persons at Odi, in the state of Bayelsa, after federal troops were dispatched in response to clashes between local militants and the police. Obasanjo has consistently refused to apologize for the murders, and there has been no full inquiry. In 2002, the military was involved in yet another massacre, this time in Nigeria's Middle Belt—which, like the northern region, is largely Muslim—in the states of Benue and Taraba, where it intervened in the most serious communal conflict since the clashes that preceded the outbreak of the Biafran civil war in 1967. Thus, under President Obasanjo's watch, over ten thousand people have perished in ethnic violence, and he has completely failed to address the human rights violations committed by the notoriously corrupt Nigerian security forces.

In Nigeria several glaring deficits compromise the institutions of democratic rule. There is a broad consensus that the 1999 Constitution is deeply flawed. Crafted by the departing soldiers, the Constitution provides no opportunity for ordinary Nigerians to debate what they consider to be the central conundrum of the national crisis: the terms of association in a multiethnic polity. Ethnic militias arose and communal vigilante politics flourished during the Abacha years (1993–1998), when Nigerians experienced the most severe political repression and economic hardship in the country's history. The O'odua Peoples Congress, for example, was established in the Yoruba-speaking Southwest in 1994, largely to protest the annulment of the 1993 elections, in which Moshood Abiola, a Yoruba Muslim, seemingly won the presidency. Led by disenchanted and impoverished youth, the O'odua Peoples Congress claimed that a "northern cabal" in the army had denied Abiola victory, and the organization aggressively pressed for Yoruba political autonomy. Two vigilante groups, the Bakassi Boys and the Movement for the Actualization of the Sovereign State of Biafra, emerged in the Igbo-speaking Southeast two years later. The latter vigilante group claimed that the Nigerian state and its functionaries had systematically oppressed the Igbo people since the end of the civil war. This movement sought to secure self-determination by resuscitating the Republic of Biafra, whose bid to secede from the federation was crushed by Nigerian troops in 1970.

Then the Arewa Peoples Congress emerged in the North in 1999 as a reaction to the killing of northern factions in Lagos and other Yoruba cities and towns by cadres of the O'odua Peoples Congress and as a foil to the new Obasanjo government, which many Northerners viewed as a Yoruba regime. The Arewa Peoples Congress claimed that the harassment of Northerners in the Southwest was part of a Yoruba plan to secede and establish an O'odua republic. It further alleged that President Obasanjo was sympathetic to the goals of the O'odua Peoples Congress, and that the North would go to war if necessary to prevent national dismemberment. They and other ethnic forces, acting largely as party thugs, enforcers, and champions of local interests, have transformed political life.

The 2003 crisis in Warri, where three thousand Nigerian troops were deployed supposedly to restore law and order, cannot be grasped without an understanding of these powerful ethnic tensions and political deficits. The power of militant Ijaw youth has been exaggerated to justify the size of the military response. Reports from refugees fleeing the creeks indicate that the military is engaged in scorched-earth violence designed, like the Odi massacre, to teach the Ijaws a lesson. There have been conflicting accounts of the immediate cause of the violence. One account links it to a disagreement between elements of the Nigerian military and an oil baron over the proceeds of illegal oil bunkering. Central to the Warri crisis, however, is poverty amid unimaginable oil wealth. The oil-producing communities do seek to control "their oil." But this legitimate claim is refracted through the lens of ethnic difference, as Urhobo, Ijaw, and Itsekiri people struggle over the delineation of electoral wards (as a precondition for claiming state oil revenues) and overlapping claims on oil-rich land. Warring factions and the army have thus been responsible for many deaths and the destruction of scores of communities.

It would be naïve to deny the growing violence in the Niger Delta and the extent to which democratization has deepened the politics of ethnic spoils central to postcolonial Nigeria. But it is far too apocalyptic to assume that Nigeria is about to tumble over some historical precipice.

BIGGER AMBITIONS, BETTER CAPACITIES?

Even as Ijaw leaders have worked to address pressing problems in their immediate locality—the Niger Delta—their focus has always been national. In 1958, on the eve of formal independence, the British set up the Willink Commission to inquire into the fears of Nigeria's ethnic minority groups. The Ijaw leaders called for a more inclusive federal state in which they would enjoy the fruits and obligations of full citizenship. Thus they portrayed themselves as both the audience and the site of struggle. Issues such as flaws in the electoral process, resentment of Nigeria's national army, and inequities in the allocation of oil receipts have engaged Ijaw leaders since the late 1950s. At that time, the politics of the eastern region were dominated by a single political party, the National Council of Nigerian Citizens.

This party not only had centralizing ambitions but also excluded significant ethnic minorities, including the Ijaw, from the regional government, which was the source and distributor of patronage and strategic resources. Indeed, questions concerning Nigeria's fundamentally flawed political process, whether concerning military rule or electoral politics, have topped the agenda in the Niger Delta ever since oil became a significant player in the country's political economy. These grievances now appear to be new because the terrain of struggle has, since May 1999, shifted from a vicious military dictatorship that sought to stifle all legitimate dissent by clamping down on civil society to an elected civilian government still dominated by a single political party. The latter does, however, offer some room for mobilized communities and interest groups, including Ijaw leaders and militants, to press their demands on the state.

There is no reliable evidence to support the claim that Ijaw militants have displayed new lethal capacities and a willingness to use them. The events of March 2003 in the Warri area were merely an escalation of a long-standing grievance over the delineation of electoral wards, which Ijaw leaders consider deliberately skewed in favor of the Itsekiri. Clashes between Ijaw and Itsekiri militants have been ongoing since the late 1990s as a result of this perceived injustice. The explosion of violence on the eve of the April 2003 elections was fundamentally the handiwork of rival local politicos who were desperate for success in the polls and were mobilizing all available resources, including festering grievances like the electoral ward issue, to achieve their objectives.

The parochial objectives of self-serving politicians inflame the wider strategic goals of Ijaw leaders for self-determination and of militias alike when funds are disbursed to the militias. Yet, there is nothing to suggest that these developments differ from previous political agitation in the area. Machine guns, satellite phones, and speedboats are standard items in the arsenal of military troops deployed by the Nigerian state to pacify the oil-producing communities. The Royal Dutch/Shell Group and the other oil companies also supply weapons, through a variety of sophisticated fronts, to security operatives and mercenaries (including local youth) that they retain in the Niger Delta. The Nigerian state and the oil companies have thus colluded to contain the legitimate demands of the Ijaw by militarizing the Niger Delta. The glut of arms in the delta warrants urgent concern, but one must first appreciate the problem's origins and dynamic links to the state and corporations.

The attention that media reports have drawn to a "weaponized" Ijaw and to vengeful and bloodthirsty militants is a classic case of giving the dog a bad name in order to hang it. The claim that Ijaw militants are now deliberately targeting and killing oil workers is precarious. Some oil workers were caught in the crossfire as Ijaw and Itsekiri insurgents battled for supremacy in Warri in March 2003. Significantly, however, the deceased were not killed in the oil fields but in the Warri urban area itself. Though kidnapping of oil workers for ransom is a favored tactic of the militants, abuse and killing are rare.

Working at isolated flow stations in the dense delta swamps, the poorly guarded oil company personnel are vulnerable and would be easy targets for these militias, were it a policy to target and kill them. But there have been no independent and credible media reports of mass killings of these oil workers in the Niger Delta. History suggests that by portraying a fully armed and dangerous Ijaw militia as being out for blood, the rumors and insinuations—such as those by oil corporations who have taken out full-page advertisements in the Nigerian dailies to suggest a descent into terrorism—set the stage for yet another cycle of ethnic cleansing reminiscent of the Odi massacre.

OIL COMPANIES GETTING A PASS

Strikingly, current discussions of the security problems in the Niger Delta (including the brief by the Center for Strategic and International Studies) omit the role of Shell and other powerful corporate international actors in deepening and sustaining the crisis. Several independent human rights organizations, most notably Human Rights Watch, have linked the oil company to the spate of killings, rapes, and intercommunal feuds that have crippled social and economic life in the Niger Delta since 1993. These human rights groups have also detailed the company's links to powerful and corrupt Nigerian state officials. Moreover, environmental groups have documented the company's unrelenting attack on the ecosystem on which the local communities rely for sustenance.

The fact that a case against the ChevronTexaco Corporation was heard in the U.S. District Court in San Francisco in 2003 speaks powerfully to these issues of corporate practice.[10] Indeed, detailed local community studies in Nembe, Peremabiri, and Ke/Bille have documented the need for new forms of corporate accountability.[11] Yet, not a single industrialized country consuming Shell's oil has called for sanctions to be imposed on the oil companies operating in the Niger Delta. Any serious attempt to address the problem of alienation and militancy in Nigeria must focus globally, not just on the Niger Delta.

A NEW COLOMBIA?

Amid the political corruption, the deepening crisis of governance, and the escalating violence related to resource control, does it make sense, as the brief by the Center for Strategic and International Studies suggests, to draw a parallel between a "better-positioned Ijaw" and the revolutionary violence associated with the Colombian Revolutionary Armed Forces and the National Liberation Army in Colombia? There are parallels between the two countries regarding the political economy of extraction. Colombia has emerged since the mid-1980s as a significant oil producer (oil revenues now account for 35 percent of legal exports) and a significant supplier to the United States. In Colombia, conflicts between indigenous communities—notably the U'wa—and the state and multinational oil companies are legion. And in that nation, the links between the military, corporate security, and resource extraction—what can best be understood as a militarized oil complex—are structurally analogous to those in Nigeria. But both Colombia and Nigeria have to be grasped regionally (Colombia within the Andean oil region, and Nigeria within the West African petroleum zone).

It is one thing to say that the Ijaw and the U'wa have "raised the stakes" and can "embarrass the government," as has been reported in news accounts, but it is quite another matter to see "Delta ethnic militants" as Maoist insurgents or terrorists. First, the Colombian situation is a long-standing civil war compounded by both narcotics traffic and oil. Colombian political violence is legendary, and it long predates the emergence of oil as a strategic national resource. Second, the role of the armed forces in Colombia has been fundamentally shaped by the drug economy and by the massive military assistance provided by the United States. During the 1990s Colombia became a major recipient of U.S. foreign military aid, and in July 2000 Washington's "Plan Colombia" committed $1.3 billion toward an antinarcotics, counterinsurgency strategy.

The role of the military in Nigeria (and its relation to the oil industry in particular) is obviously key, but there is (thus far) no parallel to the external militarization found in Colombia. President Bill Clinton did commit funds to "reprofessionalizing" the Nigerian army in 1999, which paid for, among other things, equipping and training seven battalions at a cost of over $1 billion. During the Bush imperium, the presence of two hundred Special Forces soldiers stationed in Nigeria, including at on-site training grounds in some of the most sensitive areas of the Muslim North, has generated enormous suspicion and now vocal opposition.

Not unexpectedly, a number of powerful Nigerian constituencies see the beleaguered and corrupt Obasanjo regime as simply another miserable U.S. oil colony. However, this is in no way comparable to the Colombian case, where the United States directly financed a war.

Third, the extreme violence of the Colombian case stems from the fact that Washington, in conjunction with the Colombian military, has provided direct protection for oil installations; for example, the Bush administration spent $98 million in February 2002 to protect the Cano Limon pipeline. This protection is only part of a combination of armed insurgents, right-wing paramilitaries, and so-called legal mercenaries (known as contractors) who operate symbiotically with the likes of the Occidental Petroleum Corporation and Ecopetrol. Although certain elements of this mix are present in the Nigerian situation, there is a qualitative difference between their roles in the two countries.

And finally, to see in the variety of Ijaw (or other ethnic) movements the seeds of leftist revolution is preposterous. Disenfranchised youth groups have acted in violent ways, especially in conflicted oil-producing communities like Nembe and Peremabiri, and the presence of a secondary arms market has transformed the nature of the violence itself. But to suggest that Ijaw ethnic militancy is secessionist, either as a leftist insurgency or as a provocation portending massive civil war, is misguided. These Ijaw activists, like the Ogoni political movement (Movement for the Survival of the Ogoni People) and the Chicoco movement—a leading environmental pressure group representing various activist groups in southern Nigeria—are actively engaged in debates about access to and control over resources within the federation. They seek to modify the Nigerian Constitution, and they wrangle over what it means to be a full citizen. The fact that massive poverty, disenfranchisement, and a long, dark history of military violence should produce forms of politics that are neither civil nor democratic should surprise no one. But to see in the seeds of Ijaw mobilization a new terror is a radical misreading of the current political moment in the Niger Delta.

THE WAY OUT

The strategic significance of Nigeria is incontestable. One of every five Africans is a Nigerian. Nigeria is also the world's seventh-largest exporter of petroleum and a key player in African regional security, most recently in Sierra Leone. And Nigeria is home to a vast Muslim community. Since the oil boom of the 1970s, political power has shifted from the conservative Sufi brotherhoods to well-organized modern Islamist groups like the Yan Izala, founded in 1978. Shari'a law, of a dogmatic and literalist sort, has been adopted and implemented in twelve of the populous northern states, amid considerable political acrimony and international censure.

At least 350 people were killed in four days of rioting in northern Nigeria that was triggered by protests against U.S. military action in Afghanistan. There were particularly bloody clashes between Muslims and Christians in Kano, Kaduna, and Jos. The debacle at the September 2002 Miss World Pageant, in which religious controversy and political violence resulted in the competition being moved from Abuja to London, signaled the extent to which religion has entered the political arena.

The Obasanjo government, torn between championing a united Nigeria and accommodating powerful pro-federal and ethnic autonomy sentiments among key constituencies, has been unable to articulate a coherent policy to contain the conflict raging in the Niger Delta. The advent of electoral politics has even bolstered various mouthpieces for popular grievances, including the ethnic militias, since the central government has dismally failed to tackle pressing economic and social problems.

Ethnic militias, intercommunal violence, and the resurgent cries for a sovereign national conference, true federalism, and resource control all point to the gulf between state and society. Above all there is a profound sense that democracy in Nigeria cannot accommodate the clamor for regional and local autonomy or any new political entitlements. Nigerians remain, despite the democratic dispensation, subjects rather than citizens. Any way out must, in our view, address the citizenship question at a number of levels.

OIL IS KEY

The first issue to be addressed is how the pursuit of oil wealth underlies persistent national policy failures in Nigeria. Since 1970, the country's political, economic, and policy elites have established an authoritarian power structure enabling them to centralize control of strategic resources, including the country's substantial oil deposits. In the process, they have not only banished the majority of ordinary Nigerians from the policy-making process, but they have also pursued shortsighted and self-serving social and economic strategies. The result has been material scarcity, deepening frustration, and social unrest in the Niger Delta and elsewhere.

The government should focus on achieving a just and sustainable political order, giving due weight to the fears, needs, and aspirations of the various social and interest groups in the country. There is a growing consensus that a completely unitary system of government is not suited to a socially diverse country like Nigeria. We recommend, instead, a federal democracy, one that turns on a measured dose of fiscal autonomy for the federating units, not unlike the provisions of the country's independence Constitution. This would help diversify Nigeria's revenue base by enhancing domestic taxation, as non-oil-producing areas are forced to find alternative ways to boost the treasury.

An economically diversified polity would tend to introduce into the policy-making process non-oil players whose interests would serve as a check on the political elites and their cronies, curbing the powerful drive toward political authoritarianism. Political federalism would spawn new social forces throughout Nigeria that could serve as a countervailing force as they press their own demands on the state. Democracy would be enhanced as these actors with diverse social and economic bases competed on a level playing field. No one group would be powerful enough to dominate the state and use its organs to pursue its narrow interests. The need for the institutionalization of a disinterested and efficient public service, corruption-free public agencies, due process, and the rule of law would be more compelling. Those running for office would have to be willing to tackle the structural causes of endemic violence and mass poverty in a political economy in which oil currently contaminates virtually everything. In the absence of robust democratic institutions and a meaningful sense of citizenship, another oil boom—secured perhaps with the heavy artillery of American empire—will only further tear Nigeria apart.

NIGERIA'S SOCIAL CONTRACT

The second issue involves Nigeria's social contract. In order for a federal democracy to be meaningful to ordinary Nigerians, and in order to address their social and economic needs, a new compact between state and society must be worked out. The civic, political, and social rights of the people must be clearly spelled out and made legally enforceable. A socially and economically empowered body politic would eagerly participate in public affairs, and such broad and active participation by an enlightened citizenry is the secret of good government policy.

More than forty years ago, the Willink Commission noted that the

Niger Delta was "poor, backward and neglected."[12] In the wake of several insurrections, including a devastating civil war and nine military coups, all linked to the scramble for the oil resources of the Niger Delta, the people are no better off than they were in 1958. To the people of the Niger Delta, who over the years have clamored for a space in the Nigerian sun, resources are not limited to oil and gas, despite the corporate and governmental scramble for control over those riches. To the indigenous people, resources mean primarily land for agriculture, waters for fishing, forests for harvesting, and air for breathing, as well as other physical and spiritual biota.

"Resource control" is the term used to describe decision-making power over a people's sources of livelihood. In the case of the Niger Delta, these sources of survival have been taken away violently, undemocratically, and unjustly. The term denotes the need to regain ownership, control, use, and management of resources primarily for the benefit of the people on whose land the resources originate, and secondarily for the good governance and development of the entire country. The refusal of successive Nigerian governments to protect the land and people of the Niger Delta from the hazards of hydrocarbon extraction—such as oil spillages and seepages, human rights violations, and poverty—seems to have convinced the people that the oil-military-governmental troika is not good for them or the country. Ironically, the Willink Commission's report—a colonial-period document that remains ignored even as Nigeria's communities clamor for true federalism—could give local authorities significant leverage in holding government and corporations accountable for malfeasances that affect present and future survival.

The solution to the resource conflict in the Niger Delta does not lie with the government alone. The government is an interested party. Avowedly entrenched in resource extraction and revenue politics, the present Nigerian government, like others before it, sees no solution other than military pacification and legalism. However, the problem is political and stems from Olusegun Obasanjo's first appearance as the head of a military junta that seized control of land in Nigeria between 1976 and 1979.

That military junta granted multinational oil companies access to the Niger Delta and helped bury true federalism in multiethnic, multireligious Nigeria. In modern-day Nigeria, issues of environmental security, resource control and management, corporate liability for environmental damage and human rights violations, and livelihood erosion are in danger of being buried beneath the global search for "international networks of criminality and violence." The grave danger, then, at this moment in history, is that such a misreading of the politics of the Niger Delta and of the struggle for environmental and social justice will stigmatize Africa's major oil-producing region as simply another site in which terrorism must be eradicated by any means possible.

NEED FOR MEDIATION

The third festering issue is the need for effective mediation at the community level to address the variety of intra- and intercommunity violence. Mediation, de-escalation, and intercession are crucial to addressing the Warri crisis and other community conflicts in the Niger Delta. To be effective, an effort in this direction must be facilitated by a party with no vested interest. Because the oil companies and the federal government are the most important factors driving interethnic and intercommunity conflicts, these entities must also be willing to submit to a mediation process. Obtaining their good-faith participation in the process and in efforts to restore federalism and resource control will be more useful than asking the federal government "to take swift and meaningful steps to enhance the region's security."[13] Focusing only on the region's security may play into the hands of hawks within the Nigerian federal government and military who seek to continue the rape, looting, mass destruction, and genocide that they started in Umuchem, Ogoni, Kaima, Yenagoa, Odi, and numerous other communities.

IMPACT OF INTERNATIONAL PLAYERS

The fourth and final issue to be addressed is the impact of international players. Even though the current situation in the Niger Delta does not resemble circumstances in Colombia, there is no reason to believe that it never could. A militarization of the West African oil region under the aegis of an American empire intent on rooting out terrorism, as outlined in Washington's September 2002 National Security Strategy, would contribute directly to a "Colombianization" of the Niger Delta. Unless there is serious pressure from both the United States and European governments to ensure accountability and responsibility by the oil companies— many of whom are now anxious to get out of the business of community development in Nigeria—the sense of historical grievance across the Niger Delta will continue to fester.

The annals of oil extraction are an uninterrupted chronicle of naked aggression, exploitation, and the violent mores of the corporate frontier. The nation of Iraq was born from this vile trinity. The current spectacle of oil men parading through the corridors of the White House, the rise of militant Islam across the Q'uran belt, and the carnage on the road to Baghdad, all bear the continuing, dreadful dialectics of blood and oil. Nigeria suffers all the hallmarks of such petro-violence. Breaking with this bloody history will require a major political commitment on both sides of the Atlantic.

DAVID A. MCDONALD

13

Environmental Racism and Neoliberal Disorder in South Africa

n June of 2000 an oil spill off the coast of Cape Town threatened a wide range of marine life, prompting environmental organizations in South Africa and around the world to put in place a wildlife rescue plan. Newspaper advertisements in nations as far away as Canada requested donations to help in the effort. Hundreds of thousands of dollars were raised, several hundred volunteers assisted, and twenty-three thousand marine birds were cleaned and removed from the spill zone within a few short weeks.

Meanwhile, a few miles inland, far from the normally pristine beaches and mountains of Cape Town's Atlantic Coast, hundreds of thousands of poor, black Capetonians were living in the most squalid environmental conditions imaginable: dirty, treeless streets; backed-up sewage pipes; piles of uncollected refuse; and pools of stagnant water. That particular June was relatively dry—though normally June was the rainiest and coldest time of the year in Cape Town—but tuberculosis, diarrhea, and other easily preventable diseases continued to ravage these low-income communities.

No hordes of eco-volunteers came here to wipe away the stains of poverty. No advertisements in the *New York Times* urgently pressed readers to help with this environmental disaster. It was just another day in the life of the poor and black in postapartheid South Africa. But why, a decade after the end of apartheid, should this environmental contradiction still exist? What is being done to address this contradiction, and how likely is it that South Africa will have a truly environmentally just future?

Race and racism have long determined who gets access to environmental resources and safe and healthy working and living environments in South Africa, and they continue to shape environmental thought and practice in the country today. Although denied by many environmental organizations, by apartheid-era bureaucrats, and by private capital, environmental racism is still very much alive and well in postapartheid South Africa.

But as important as racism is, it is neoliberalism and deepening class divides that pose the biggest threats to environmental sustainability and environmental justice for low-income South Africans. Policies of fiscal restraint, cost recovery, privatization, and liberalization threaten to entrench the economic disparities of the apartheid era and to drive an even deeper wedge between the "haves" and the "have-nots" of the country. The fact that many environmentally damaging neoliberal policy decisions are now being designed and imposed by a new black elite merely highlights the increasingly class-based nature of environmental politics in the country.

In the end, however, it is impossible to separate the two issues. As the scholarly work on environmental racism in the United States has forcefully argued, racism cannot be reduced to some aberrant and temporary deviation from theoretically established class interests.[1] Race and class are inextricably intertwined in the struggle for environmental justice in South Africa.

My objective here is to affirm the theoretical and practical importance of *both* analytical categories in South Africa and to discuss their relationship to one another. This is motivated in part by what appears to be an emerging polarization of environmental justice debates in the country—one camp that focuses almost entirely on narrow definitions of environmental racism, and another camp that relegates race to the past, superseded by the class-based environmental injustices of capitalism. (In taking this tack, I have left out some important features of the environmental justice debates in South Africa in this chapter, most notably those related to gender.)[2]

THE EMERGENCE OF AN ENVIRONMENTAL JUSTICE MOVEMENT IN SOUTH AFRICA

Until the early 1990s, the environment was not on the agenda of most antiapartheid organizations in South Africa. The history of environmental politics was such that black South Africans felt alienated from the environmental movement. At best, the environment was regarded as a white, suburban issue of little relevance to the antiapartheid struggle. At worst, environmental policy was seen as an explicit tool of racial oppression.

Under colonial and apartheid governments, thousands of black South Africans were forcibly removed from their ancestral lands to make way for game parks, and billions of dollars were spent preserving wildlife and protecting wildflowers while people in townships and "homelands" lived without adequate food and shelter.[3] Whites-only policies in national parks meant that black South Africans could not enjoy the country's rich natural heritage, and draconian poaching laws kept the rural poor from desperately needed resources.[4] In short, flora and fauna were often considered more important than the majority of the country's population. With the easing of apartheid legislation in the late 1980s and the unbanning of antiapartheid political parties and activists in the early 1990s, all of this was to change. The liberalization of South African politics created discursive and institutional space for rethinking environmental issues, and a vibrant debate on the meaning, causes, and effects of environmental decay began in earnest.

Perhaps the most fundamental of these developments was the simplest: a broadening of the definition of ecology. Once "the environment" was redefined to include the working and living space of black South Africans, it quickly became apparent that environmental initiatives were akin to other postapartheid, democratic objectives. A wide range of trade unions, nongovernmental organizations, civic associations, and academics quickly adopted the new environmental discourse and, within a few short years, began to challenge the environmental practices and policies of the past.[5]

Central to this new discourse was the concept of environmental justice—a language that found its first concrete expression at a conference organized by Earthlife Africa in 1992 titled "What Does It Mean to Be Green?"[6] The conference brought together leading South African environmentalists and academics with their counterparts from around the world in an attempt to map out a future for the environmental justice movement in South Africa. One of the outcomes of the conference was the creation of the Environmental Justice Networking Forum (EJNF), a nationwide umbrella organization designed to coordinate the activities of environmental activists and organizations interested in social and environmental justice. The network rapidly expanded to include 150 member organizations by 1995 and over 500 member organizations by 2000.

With the election of Nelson Mandela's African National Congress (ANC) in 1994, the environmental justice movement had an ally in government as well. Noting that "poverty and environmental degradation have been closely linked" in South Africa, the ANC made it clear that social, economic, and political relations were also part of the environmental equation and that environmental inequalities and injustices would be addressed as an integral part of the party's postapartheid reconstruction and development mandate.[7] Indeed, the new South African Constitution, finalized in 1996, includes a Bill of Rights that grants all South Africans the right to an "environment that is not harmful to their health and well-being" and the right to "ecologically sustainable development" (section 24).

At its core, environmental justice is about incorporating environmental issues into the broader intellectual and institutional framework of human rights and democratic accountability.[8] The term necessarily encompasses the widest possible definition of what is considered "environmental" and is unmistakably anthropocentric in its orientation—placing people, rather than flora and fauna, at the center of a complex web of social, economic, political, and environmental relationships. Most important, it concerns itself primarily with the environmental *in*justices of these relationships and the ways and means of rectifying these wrongs and avoiding them in the future. Siting a toxic waste site next to a poor, black community simply because it is poor and black, for example, is an environmental injustice that violates basic human rights and democratic accountability and demands remediation and prevention.

At this most basic level of definition, it is easy to see why the environmental justice movement in South Africa has attracted a significant following. Forcibly removing people from their ancestral land to make way for a game park with or without consultation or compensation is wrong by most moral standards. Spending millions of dollars on municipal services for one group of people and not providing the most basic of necessities to others is simply undemocratic. Environmental inequities of this sort are so manifestly unjust that it makes intuitive sense to speak of an environmental justice movement to address them.

The following definition of environmental justice provided in the quarterly newsletter of the South African Environmental Justice Networking Forum captures these basic philosophical tenets and exemplifies the focus on human and democratic rights that are so central to environmental justice movements and literature worldwide:

Environmental justice is about social transformation directed towards meeting basic human needs and enhancing our quality of life—economic quality, health care, housing, human rights, environmental protection, and democracy. In linking environmental and social justice issues the environmental justice approach seeks to challenge the abuse of power which results in poor people having to suffer the effects of environmental damage caused by the greed of others. This includes workers and communities exposed to dangerous chemical pollution, and rural communities without firewood, grazing [land] and water. In recognizing that environmental damage has the greatest impact upon poor people, EJNF seeks to ensure the right of those most affected to participate at all levels of environmental decision-making.[9]

Beyond these core principles, however, there is much that fragments the environmental justice movement. One reason for this is that the movement lacks a coherent theoretical framework. There are wide differences of opinion, for example, on the relative importance of race, class, and gender, and there are major splits on the potential for reform in a market economy. Even the efficacy of judicial procedure (that is, whether the courts are an effective means for addressing and preventing environmental injustices) is a matter of debate.

This diversity of opinion is not surprising. As the vast survey literature on environmental theory and its application makes clear, there are simply too many underlying methodological and ideological differences in environmental thought to allow for any neat conceptualization of environmental justice.[10] Ecofeminism, ecosocialism, deep ecology, ecological economics, and social ecology are all concerned to some extent about environmental justice, insofar as they pay attention to how environmental resources and their by-products are distributed (within and across generations) and the inequitable power relations that lead to environmental injustices.

Even the World Bank can claim to be concerned about environmental justice (although it does not use the term), given its emphasis on poverty alleviation and the improvement of basic infrastructure like sewage and sanitation—particularly for women and children.[11] In other words, the environmental justice literature, defined here by its concern with environmental inequalities and democratic accountability, is far from homogenous and in fact contains deep ideological splits on foundational questions.

This lack of coherency is not necessarily a problem. On the contrary, this diversity lends itself to a wide range of social circumstances and ideological positions, drawing people and organizations into an ecological movement that they may not have otherwise connected to. This has certainly been the case in South Africa, where trade unions, civic organizations, democratic activists, and environmentalists of many stripes have joined a loosely aligned environmental justice movement. Membership in the EJNF has included such diverse interests as the Transport and General Workers Union, the Trust for Christian Outreach, the Wilderness Leadership School, and the Help End Marijuana Prohibition in South Africa Society. Together these organizations have contributed to the building of an important new movement in the country and have placed the central concerns of environmental equity and democratic accountability firmly on the South African environmental policy agenda.

But the ideological tensions are not far from the surface. An environmental justice movement as diverse as this in its political orientation and demographic composition is bound to have deep splits. Moreover, with the end of formal apartheid has come a whole new set of highly contentious environmental questions: What are the implications of signing the Kyoto Accord? Are market-based land reforms appropriate? Should wealthy households be allowed to consume vast amounts of water simply because they can afford to do so? Should municipal services be privatized?

The national government's adoption of a fiscally conservative approach to reconstruction and development through the Growth, Employment, and Redistribution program in 1996 has divided the country's democratic movement, and these divisions are becoming apparent in the environmental justice movement as well. Funding and organizational constraints are a factor here, with historically white, suburban-based environmental groups accounting for the lion's share of financial resources and organizational capacity, while most township-based environmental groups struggle to make ends meet, often breaking up after a few years of effort.

ENVIRONMENTAL RACISM: BUSINESS AS USUAL?

What role, then, does racism play in the environmental arena in South Africa? It depends in part on one's definition of racism. This is not the place for an extended discussion of a contentious and complex topic, but laying out some conceptual parameters will be helpful, not only in analyzing environmental racism, but also in discussing, as I do below, neoliberalism and the environmental impacts of this class-oriented agenda.

I adopted Laura Pulido's definition of (white) racism here as "those practices and ideologies, carried out by structures, institutions and individuals, that reproduce racial inequality and systematically undermine the well-being of racially subordinated populations."[12] She goes on to note that racism must be seen at different levels—the personal, the group, the national, and so on: "An individual act of racism is just that, an act carried out at the level of the individual. Nonetheless, that individual is informed by regional and/or national racial discourses, and his/her act informs and reproduces racial discourses at higher scales."[13]

Pulido also highlights the issue of intent. Popular notions of racism rest on the concept of purposeful, individual, and malicious behavior. Pulido insists we look beyond overt and institutionalized racism to what she refers to as "white privilege," the ideologies and practices that reproduce whites' privileged status. In this scenario, "whites do not necessarily *intend* to hurt people of color, but because they are unaware of their white skin privilege, and because they accrue social and economic benefits by maintaining the status quo, they inevitably do. . . . It is this ability to sever intent from outcome that allows whites to acknowledge that racism exists, yet seldom identify themselves as racists."[14]

This definition of racism helps us to bridge the ideological and material gap between race and class. We can see racism not only as a psychologically and individually constructed phenomenon but also as part of a larger societal process shaped and reinforced, at least in part, by the material and class interests of those who have the most to gain from its continuance: that is, the white bourgeoisie. This definition does not resolve the underlying tension of whether one factor—race or class— dominates in the final instance, but it is at least dialectical in nature and underscores the multiple ways in which racism evolves and manifests itself.

One place that environmental racism is evident in South Africa is in the environmental movement itself. In the same way that some of the largest and most prestigious environmental groups in the United States have been accused of being dominated by white, middle-class suburbanites with little interest in, or understanding of, the environmental issues faced by low-income communities and people of color, some of the mainstream environmental groups in South Africa have been blamed for not taking environmental degradation in the townships and former homelands seriously.[15] The opening anecdote in this chapter about the oil spill in Cape Town is but one concrete example of this kind of racism.

This is not to suggest that *all* suburban-based environmental organizations in South Africa are racist. Many have a strong track record of working on environmental issues that affect the working and living environments of the poor, and many work with individuals and organizations based in the townships (for example, Earthlife Africa and the Environmental Monitoring Group). There have been few reports of blatant acts of racism by mainstream environmental organizations. Racism in these groups tends to manifest itself in more subtle ways, such as the use of paternalistic language about the need to "educate" black South Africans about the environment, or the need to protect wildlife reserves from the "population explosion" taking place in the rural (read black) areas surrounding national parks.

The problem is also one of logistics, itself a legacy of apartheid. The offices of most mainstream environmental organizations are located in suburban areas that have the infrastructure and amenities required to run an office and provide a safe working venue for staff and equipment, and that are located close to relevant organizations. Environmental groups in the townships, by contrast, are often run out of makeshift buildings with no water, electricity, or phones and are not safe to work in after dark.

This geographical bias makes it difficult for township-based environmentalists with low (or no) incomes to pay for transportation to work or attend meetings in the suburbs. Even if transportation fees can be paid, most public transport finishes shortly after the end of the workday, making it impossible to come to evening meetings without prior transportation arrangements. Moreover, discussions are generally in English and often are based on voluminous amounts of technical and academic literature, barring many black South Africans from participating effectively.

Some environmental groups have made an effort to address these problems, but environmental organizational dynamics tend to replicate the geographic and socioeconomic disparities of apartheid rather than addressing them as an integral part of an environmental justice agenda. Donor agencies are partly to blame, as they largely pay lip service to notions of grassroots capacity-building but continue to funnel the bulk of their funding to mainstream environmental groups.

The bigger challenge, however, lies outside the environmental movement. Historically, apartheid-era bureaucrats were the very face of South African racism, designing and enforcing some of the worst examples of environmental injustice imaginable. The intentional citing of environmentally noxious facilities near black communities, for example, affected millions of black South Africans. Under apartheid, black residential areas were always situated downwind from, downhill from, and otherwise in

close proximity to toxic waste dumps, sewage plants, coal-fired genera-
tors, industrial areas, highways, and so on. White residential areas, on
the other hand, were located in the most attractive and environmentally
safe areas of a town or city, buffered by parks, rivers, commercial areas,
and open spaces.

Have these bureaucrats changed? Most of the country's civil service
remains white, a legacy of the 1990s negotiations, during which the
ANC guaranteed white bureaucrats their jobs for a period of time in an
effort to avoid bureaucratic sabotage during the transition to democracy
and to divert the potential for more serious armed conflict. Many of the
top bureaucratic positions have since been filled by black (mostly ANC-
aligned) managers, but this layer is thin. This is due in part to an
apartheid education system that trained very few skilled black personnel,
as well as to the fact that this relatively small pool of black skilled workers has been snatched up by the private sector at salaries several times
what the public sector can pay.

The day-to-day operation of the country, therefore, is still very much
in the hands of the civil servants who made decisions about water, roads,
housing, health care, and education during apartheid. It is difficult to say
whether these bureaucrats' attitudes have changed. Certainly there are
few who would publicly identify themselves as racist, and all racially
biased legislation has been removed from the books, making it illegal to
advocate or practice any form of race-based planning.

And yet, signs of bureaucratic environmental racism abound. In my
own interviews with municipal managers over the past ten years, I have
heard such comments as "Teaching an African about the environment is
like trying to teach a baboon" and "There's no point in cleaning up the
townships. . . . They like to live that way."[16] More recent surveys with
managers show a growing trend toward neoliberalism as the dominant
ideological framework with senior personnel, but racism continues to
permeate the civil service.[17]

The ongoing disparities in municipal services in white and black areas
offer a more concrete illustration of bureaucratic racism. Although much
of this can be blamed on policies of fiscal restraint, cost recovery, and privatization (more on this below in the discussion of neoliberalism) part of
the blame must fall on municipal bureaucrats themselves, the people who
make the daily decisions about resource allocation. Detailed case study
research, as well as anecdotal evidence from throughout the country, has
shown that white residential areas continue to receive a disproportionate
share of municipal resources, almost a decade after the end of apartheid.

In Johannesburg and Cape Town, for example, five, ten, and even a hundred times as much is spent per capita in providing water and waste management services in white suburbs as in adjacent black townships.[18] Is this bureaucratic incompetence or simply racist behavior, intentional or otherwise, that "reproduces inequality and systematically undermines the well-being of racially subordinated populations" in order to protect white privilege?[19] My sense is the latter.

To make matters worse, the infrastructural facilities that have created these environmental injustices in the townships are large, fixed assets, long-term in nature and expensive to replace: sewage treatment plants, toxic disposal sites, and so on. Langa, the oldest black township in Cape Town, sits downwind from both a sewage treatment plant and a coal-fired electricity-generating plant, both emitting unpleasant and, at times, noxious fumes. Even with a highly committed, progressive civil service, it will take decades to relocate or decommission all the offending facilities (if they are ever moved). As a result, the legacies of apartheid's built environment mean that racist bureaucratic behaviors of the past will be part of the environmental landscape for many years to come.

But municipal bureaucrats are not the only ones who can be accused of environmental racism in South Africa. Private companies—large mining and chemical companies in particular—have been responsible for some of the most environmentally racist practices. As Thabo Madihlaba explains in his review of the country's mining industry, companies continue to operate with virtual impunity next to poor, black communities, generating toxic leachates and dust, unsightly slag heaps, and dangerous slime dams.[20]

In another case, Bobby Peek has documented the effect of industry on air quality in a valley in South Durban, where close to a quarter of a million low-income black people breathe some of the most intensely polluted air in the world. Five petrol refineries, a massive pulp and paper plant, and an airport are among the contributing sources. Although minor improvements have been made to air quality since the end of apartheid, and media attention has drawn high-profile political figures to the area in an attempt to improve the situation—Nelson Mandela included—fuel leaks, gas flares, and toxic ash continue to plague the community, giving it the highest recorded levels of asthma in the world.[21]

And then there is the case of Thor Chemical.[22] For close to a decade, starting in the mid-1980s, a local subsidiary of the British multinational was importing toxic waste to "recycle." But instead of safely treating the material, the company simply deposited more than ten thousand barrels of mercury, a sludge pond containing an additional 2,561 tons (2,500 metric tons) of toxic waste, and piles of hazardous incinerator ash on the company's property in rural KwaZulu-Natal. It was only in 1990, when a high level of mercury was detected in a river less than fifteen miles from the plant that the alarm bell was sounded. At this time, the mercury level found in the river was a thousand times higher than World Health Organization regulations permit for safe drinking water. Numerous employees of the plant itself also became sick, and several died of mercury poisoning. Greenpeace called it the worst "abuse of an economically dependent, under-educated workforce" it had ever seen.[23] Plans to clean up the mess were not put in motion until 2004.[24]

Do corporations like these behave this way near white communities in South Africa? In short, no. The overwhelming majority—indeed, virtually all—corporate environmental injustices of this sort are perpetrated against black communities. The spatial legacies of apartheid—in which the worst polluting facilities and environmentally degrading industrial operations were situated near blacks—are one reason for this, with industrial pollution inevitably affecting those located closest to it, but one cannot avoid the conclusion that racism remains a key factor. What else could explain the fact that large corporations in South Africa contribute millions of dollars annually to the protection of flora and fauna, and advertise themselves as environmentally responsible businesses, while at the same time contributing to some of the worst environmental health and safety conditions in the world for their black neighbors and employees?

Yet, environmental racism is one of the easier environmental justice issues to deal with in South Africa. As noted earlier, there is a new Constitution in place that grants all South Africans the right to a safe and healthy working and living environment, and there is a plethora of new, and explicitly antiracist, environmental legislation in place.[25] In one celebrated case, a shack dweller near Cape Town won a Supreme Court ruling that forced the Western Cape Provincial Government to provide adequate shelter and basic services to all residents of her shack settlement on the grounds that their "health and well-being" were adversely affected by the state's lack of investment in basic infrastructure (water, sanitation, and so on).[26] Court cases of this nature have not been common—no more than a handful have been tried since the new Constitution came into effect in 1996—but South Africa's array of environmental legislation should mean that environmental injustices committed on the basis of race are at least on the wane.

NEOLIBERALISM: THE NEW ENVIRONMENTAL CHALLENGE

Neoliberalism, by contrast, is proving to be a much more intractable environmental foe. Defined here as policies of fiscal restraint, market liberalization, full cost recovery, privatization, and rapid economic growth (as opposed to a stronger reliance on the redistribution of existing wealth and assets), neoliberalism has become the new dominant ideology in South Africa and informs virtually every aspect of national and local government policy.[27]

Neoliberalism was not the expected outcome of the antiapartheid struggle, however. In their decades-long fight against the apartheid state, the ANC and other liberation organizations focused as much on the role of capital and capitalism in the oppression of black South Africans as they did on racism. "Racial capitalism" was the term used to describe policies of racial subjugation designed to create large pools of cheap, unemployed black labor in the rural hinterlands while at the same time protecting white working-class wages in the city.[28]

Socialist policy formed the basis of much of the antiapartheid movement's political platform, as witnessed by the following quote from the ANC's famous Freedom Charter of 1955, under the heading "The People Shall Share in the Country's Wealth!":

> The national wealth of our country, the heritage of South Africans, shall be restored to the people; The mineral wealth beneath the soil, the Banks and monopoly industry shall be transferred to the ownership of the people as a whole; All other industry and trade shall be controlled to assist the well-being of the people.

For many years this socialist rhetoric was of little concern to big capital. The ANC and other democratic organizations had been banned and contained since the early 1960s. But as the structural contradictions of the apartheid economy became more apparent in the 1970s and 1980s—not enough black consumers able to buy goods, a saturated white consumer market, and international restrictions on trade and investment—big capital started to look for ways to end the apartheid system in order to resuscitate a flagging economy.

In other words, white South Africans did not experience a moral awakening that brought about a change in their attitudes to apartheid; rather, capital and key allies in the apartheid state made a concerted and sophisticated attempt to deal with a crisis of overaccumulation and to preserve capitalism. This push for a postapartheid market solution began in the 1970s and gained real momentum only in the late 1980s, as the economic crisis deepened. The fall of the Soviet Union in the mid-1990s contributed to this market momentum. Under these conditions, the postapartheid neoliberal dispensation of South Africa was forged.

Current President Thabo Mbeki has been the driving force behind much of this ideological shift, but Nelson Mandela set the tone soon after being released from prison in 1990. As *Business Day* noted in 1993:

> We can look with some hope to the evolution in economic thinking in the ANC since the occasion nearly three years ago when Nelson Mandela stepped out of prison and promptly reaffirmed his belief in the nationalisation of the heights of the economy. By contrast . . . Mandela has since gone out of his way to assure a large group of foreign and local journalists that the ANC is now as business-friendly as any potential foreign investor could reasonably ask. He indicated further that ANC economic thinking was now being influenced as much by Finance Minister Derek Keys and by organised business as anyone else.

In Mandela's own words, "[The ANC is] determined to . . . establish the political and social climate which is necessary to ensure business confidence and create the possibility for all investors to make long-term commitments."[29]

This ideological shift culminated in the release of the Growth, Employment, and Redistribution macroeconomic framework in 1996. The ANC compiled and released this program to the public without first consulting its labor and civil-society allies. The program exemplifies the ANC's swing to the right in fiscal and monetary terms and downplays much of the interventionist and redistributive Keynesianism that was to be found as late as 1994 in the program's predecessor, the Reconstruction and Development Program (RDP), upon which the ANC based its election campaign in that year. In practical terms, the Growth, Employment, and Redistribution program has led to the loss of between 500,000 and 1 million jobs; put downward pressure on wages, job security, and health and safety benefits; limited spending on badly needed infrastructure; and led to the privatization and corporatization of a wide range of nationally and municipally owned state services. These losses have hit low-income, black South Africans the hardest, making it difficult for millions of people to afford the most basic essentials of life.[30]

The implications of this neoliberalism for environmental justice are severe and far-reaching. I focus here on four issues: underspending on essential infrastructure, the privatization of municipal services such as water and electricity, market-driven land reforms and housing policies, and the implications of economic growth (versus redistribution) as the engine of change in South Africa.

FISCAL RESTRAINT

Perhaps the single biggest environmental justice challenge in South Africa is the inadequate amount of money being spent on basic infrastructure and services such as water, sanitation, and electricity. Although millions of dollars have been spent on these services since 1994, and millions more people have access to services that were unavailable to them under apartheid, there are still millions without any form of these essential services. Instead, they are expected to use degraded and environmentally unsound services, such as bucket toilets, pit latrines, and overflowing garbage skips.

To be fair, decades worth of underinvestment in services cannot be redressed overnight. There are also dozens of other important problems contending for limited resources: land reform, illiteracy, HIV and AIDS, and so on. It is also true that the South African government has proved itself to be more committed, more focused, and more democratic in its service delivery agenda than most other postcolonial regimes in Africa. A comparison of the dismal track record of other regimes on the continent concerning infrastructure development and illegal transfers to private Swiss bank accounts attests to this. Yet we cannot forget that the South African government has also committed itself to spending more than $4 billion on new military equipment (despite having no apparent enemy) and has provided massive tax cuts to middle- and upper-income households over the past several years. In the 2002 fiscal budget alone, $1.4 billion was allotted for these tax cuts. These figures compare to a mere $.2 billion in infrastructure grants that the national government allotted to local governments in 2001–2002.[31]

More monies have been promised for basic services. For example, the central government has committed itself to providing access to "basic supplies" of water and electricity to all remaining households by 2008 and 2012, respectively.[32] But the bulk of the remaining water and electricity connections will be in difficult-to-access rural areas, where capital and operating costs per unit are significantly higher than in urban areas, due to lower population densities and longer distances from the sources of water and electricity. Because these service extensions will take longer to complete, they will be significantly more costly to install and could result in substantially higher per-unit costs for consumers if direct cost recovery principles are applied.

Following from this last point, cost-recovery policies too have had a negative effect on service delivery for the poor. "Cost recovery" refers to the practice of charging consumers the full cost of delivering a service, as opposed to subsidizing that cost, as was done under apartheid (at least for those South Africans who were provided services).[33] As a result of this policy, an estimated 5 to 10 million South Africans have experienced water or electricity cutoffs since 1994, simply because they were unable to pay their service bills. As many as 2 million people have been evicted from their homes because they couldn't pay their water or electric bills.[34]

There is some subsidization of services taking place, but (white) suburban neighborhoods, industrial areas, and commercial farms continue to receive the cheapest and most heavily subsidized services in the country. Black residents in the former homelands, meanwhile, pay twice as much on average for electricity as suburban residents and as much as twelve times more than industry (which enjoys the lowest industrial electricity rates in the world).[35]

In 2001, the ANC introduced what it described as free lifeline services for water and electricity in an attempt to deal with this affordability crisis. But there have been massive problems in implementing these policies. Critics have castigated the government for not providing sufficient lifeline supplies. The "lifeline" amounts to only 6.6 gallons of water per person per day and 50 kilowatt-hours of electricity per month—only enough water for about two flushes of a toilet per day, and enough electricity to run one or two lightbulbs. As it is, low-income households spend on average between 25 percent and 40 percent of their monthly household incomes on water, electricity, refuse collection, and sanitation services.[36] Unsurprisingly, then, cost-recovery policies have begun to undermine many of the otherwise impressive infrastructural gains made since the end of apartheid.

As a result, millions of families continue to live without access to adequate basic services in environmentally unsafe conditions. Cutting down trees for fuelwood has led to further deforestation, erosion, and siltation. Paraffin used in place of electricity for cooking and lighting has resulted in hundreds of accidental poisonings of children and thousands of shack fires. The piles of refuse that remain uncollected have acted as disease vectors and dangerous playgrounds for young children. Ponds and streams used as toilets and for washing have served as sources for waterborne disease. The most tragic example of the latter in recent years was the cholera outbreak that began in KwaZulu-Natal in mid-2000. Policies of cost recovery had forced hundreds of thousands of people to use stagnant ponds and streams because it became too expensive to use piped water. Within months there was a massive cholera outbreak, resulting in over 150,000 cases of illness and 250 deaths.[37] Neoliberalism is largely to blame for this.

The most recent development on this front has been the introduction of prepaid meters. Users must purchase their water or electricity in advance and then, using a "smart card," load the units into their household meters. Critics have argued that this practice has led people to purchase only as much water and electricity as they can pay for, rather than the amount they actually need to lead healthy and environmentally secure lives. Moreover, prepaid water and electricity services are generally more expensive than credit-metered services and can be burdensome to obtain, since purchasers must buy credit at stores (sometimes located far from township households). And they can run out at inconvenient times. Currently, there is even an effort to take the issue of prepaid meters to the Constitutional Court of South Africa in an effort to render the meters illegal, as has happened in the United Kingdom.[38]

A number of social organizations have taken up the introduction of prepaid meters and water cutoffs as a matter of political protest, among them the Anti-Privatization Forum in Johannesburg, the Concerned Citizens Forum in Durban, and the Anti-Eviction Campaign in Cape Town. These groups have generated considerable media and academic interest in their cause.

PRIVATIZATION

Closely related to policies of fiscal restraint are those of privatization, including private-public partnerships and private-sector management contracts. In the belief that the private sector will save them money, municipalities across South Africa have been privatizing, outsourcing, and otherwise commercializing basic municipal services at an alarming rate.[39] These local decisions are being driven, in turn, by national legislation that provides the institutional, financial, and ideological framework for privatization.[40] South Africa's participation in the World Trade Organization and, in particular, the General Agreement on Trades and Services, has further boosted privatization. Potentially, the World Trade Organization could force South African towns and cities to open their doors to large multinational service providers like Vivendi Water Systems and Waste Management International—many of which have a considerable foothold in the South African market already.

Elsewhere, I have described in detail what privatizing core municipal services can mean for environmental justice,[41] but I will highlight several key points here. The first addresses redlining—the practice of refusing services to low-income neighborhoods because the private-sector company providing them does not want to serve people who might not be able to pay. As a result, municipalities often find themselves stuck with servicing an inefficient patchwork of low-income neighborhoods, further reinforcing the ideological argument that public-sector service providers are inefficient and uninterested in providing quality services.

Privatization can also lead to significant job losses—particularly losses of full-time, union jobs. This has not been a major problem in South Africa yet, where most private-sector initiatives have retained existing municipal workers, but it could be a major concern in the future, as service privatizations in other countries have demonstrated. The workforce providing water in the city of Buenos Aires, for example, was cut in half after the water service was privatized in the 1990s.[42]

There are also concerns about health and safety for workers who retain their jobs under a private company. Safety equipment and training are often the first casualties of profit maximization, worsening the hazardous conditions in which many public-sector workers in South Africa already find themselves. Hazardous jobs of this sort include collecting "night soil" in informal settlements (the euphemistic term for the contents of the buckets that the poor must use in lieu of toilets), picking dead animals off the street, cleaning sewer mains, and fixing electricity towers. All these jobs can be extremely dangerous, unpleasant, and unhealthy, and they require a major commitment on the part of the employer to address safety concerns.

Municipal workers in South Africa constantly complain about the lack of proper health and safety equipment and poor labor-management relations.[43] There are signs that these conditions will deteriorate further under profit-oriented ownership. The death of a worker in early 2002 at the corporatized water service provider in Johannesburg, for example, is being blamed on safety cutbacks by the private company, a subsidiary of Suez-Lyonnaise des Eaux.[44] The working environment of laborers is often ignored in the environmental literature, and yet it is here, on the front lines of environmental management, that some of the most environmentally unjust conditions exist.

A related concern is the use of community organizations and individuals to do work previously done by government workers. In the name of community participation, low-income residents—generally women who are the poorest of the poor—now contribute to the cleanup and maintenance of their own neighborhoods. With little or no training, and little or no equipment and safety gear, citizens are expected to handle potentially toxic waste, disease-infested water, sewage, and so on. Significantly, white South Africans are not expected to expose themselves to these environmental hazards, as indicated by this quote from a young man in the province of KwaZulu-Natal:

> The RDP [Reconstruction and Development Programme established by the ANC in 1994] is ridiculing our mothers. Our mothers are made to dig trenches. It is called employment. Whereby you walk right around this South Africa and you never find a white woman digging a trench. The dignity of our mothers is taken because they have to dig trenches, while they have to feed their babies, cook for their loved ones.[45]

Private-sector service providers are notorious for cutting corners at the expense of the environment to save money: recorded violations of environmental regulations by private firms are now legendary. Toxic spills, illegal dumping, and other bylaw infringements cost governments enormous amounts of money to rectify and, at the same time, place the health and safety of the public and workers at risk. One example occurred in 1999, when Enviroserv, a private waste company, illegally dumped eight truckfuls of dangerous medical waste in the city of Bloemfontein. The waste consisted of syringes, blood products, body parts, and other medical waste. In this case the drivers were caught and the firm bore the costs of cleanup, but the municipal dump where the waste was left was frequented by scavengers. The medical waste not only put the scavengers at risk of infection but also could have resulted in waterborne diseases being spread to the community.[46]

Concerns about waste dumping are heightened by the legacy of corporate racism in South Africa. When private companies dump their waste or otherwise conduct their dirtiest operations near black communities, their potential of being reported—let alone taken to court—is significantly lower than if the same operations were conducted near white neighborhoods. Not all private service-delivery firms violate environmental laws, but the international record of private-sector environmental management is not encouraging. The pressure to cut costs to stay in business is often too great for even the most virtuous of owners or managers.[47]

LAND REFORM AND HOUSING

Two other policy issues that relate to environmental justice are land reform and housing. Under apartheid, the Group Areas Act gave most of the land in South Africa to whites (approximately 87 percent of all land was owned by less than 15 percent of the country's population). Much of this land was taken by the state from its original African occupants, who were forcibly moved to remote and ethnically divided homelands. These homelands were generally poor for agriculture and badly over-crowded; farming them led to erosion, displacement (the land became so badly eroded that it was unfarmable, and then people had to abandon it), poverty, and landlessness for the majority of the population.

Accordingly, the ANC promised massive land reform as part of its postapartheid agenda, pledging in the RDP to reallocate 30 percent of all agricultural land within its first five years in office. More than a decade after the ANC took power, however, these issues remain largely unresolved. Over "13 million people, the majority of them poverty-stricken, remain crowded into the homelands, where rights to land are often unclear or contested and where the system of land administration is in disarray."[48]

High-profile land occupations in neighboring Zimbabwe beginning in 2000 reignited the land debate in South Africa. By mid-2001, however, only 68,878 formal land restitution claims (that is, claims for the return of land that had been forcibly taken away) had been lodged with the Department of Land Affairs. Only 17.9 percent of these claims have been settled and about 746,000 acres of land restored to its former owners—a small fraction of the millions of hectares in question, belonging to a small fraction of the estimated 3.5 million people displaced under apartheid. Land *redistribution* has been even slower. Less than 1 percent of commercial agricultural land has been earmarked for this purpose.

The reasons for this slow pace are complex, but they are shaped in large part by a neoliberal policy framework. Decisions on land redistribution have been left largely to the market: current landowners have been allowed to determine if they want to sell, how much land they are willing to sell, and the price. Meanwhile, the small national budget set aside for land reform—less than one-quarter of 1 percent of government spending—was cut by 23 percent in 2001. At these budgetary levels, argues Edward Lahiff, it will take 150 years to complete the land reform process.[49]

These market-driven reforms have left project design and implementation in the hands of private consultants. Moreover, the reforms are aimed at creating a class of full-time black commercial farmers and do not acknowledge the importance of part-time agricultural activities for low-income rural and urban households. "Given the extreme conditions of racial segregation and poverty in South Africa," concludes Lahiff, "it is simply unrealistic to imagine that [land] transformation can be achieved on the basis of piecemeal reform via the free market."[50]

The land situation in urban areas is not much better. Market-based housing policies have made it virtually impossible to build low-income housing near city centers. Receiving a maximum housing subsidy of approximately $2,800, low-income families are barely able to pay the costs of a one-room house, let alone buy an attractive parcel of land near urban amenities. New homes in more convenient and attractive areas are ten to twenty times this price. A new suburban home in Cape Town begins at $25,000 and may cost $200,000 or more. As a result, the overwhelming majority of new, low-income housing developments in urban areas of the country remain on the periphery of towns and cities, near noxious industrial areas, highways, and airports. These developments are reinforcing, not improving, the environmental injustices of the past.

The quality of housing is also a concern. Although over a million new homes have been built for low-income families since 1994, critics say these houses are little more than matchboxes. A typical "RDP house" (so named after the Reconstruction and Development Program) measures little more than 107 square feet and has one room and a bath. Some have infrastructure for water, electricity, and sewage, but many have only yard taps and pit latrines. Moreover, construction quality has been generally quite poor. Many of the new homes have fallen apart after a few years.

The market-friendly policies of the ANC bear a lot of the responsibility for the urban housing failure.[51] Much of the new-home development has been left to large conglomerates with little experience building low-income housing. These firms continue to use hazardous building products (asbestos board is still used in the western Cape), have little vested interest in ensuring customer satisfaction or in contributing to social cohesion through architectural design, and do virtually nothing to incorporate environment-friendly products such as solar power panels and low-flush toilets into the homes they build. Private banks have been equally problematic. They have redlined low-income areas, denying home loans to the people in them, despite repeated pleas from the state to behave in a socially responsible manner and help boost the economy. Amendments to housing legislation in 2004 were intended to create a more secure lending environment, to encourage private banks to lend money for homes.

HOW MUCH IS ENOUGH?

In the end, though, it is not only *under*consumption that threatens the environmental integrity of South Africa: equally important are the longer-term effects of neoliberalism on the *over*consumption of resources and its effect on distribution and sustainability. Middle- and upper-income South African households are among the most wasteful users of resources in the world. Per capita consumption of water, electricity, and other basic resources in historically white suburbs here is as high or higher than in any country in the world. For example, according to estimates, middle-class South Africans are responsible for up to 2 percent of global greenhouse gas emissions worldwide despite constituting an imperceptible fraction of the world's population.[52] Similar resource abuses relate to water and refuse collection. It has been estimated that as much as 40 percent of water used for domestic consumption in the city of Cape Town goes to watering suburban gardens.[53] Landfills reflect a similar situation: the bulk of commercial and domestic waste originates in white residential areas. Wealthy South Africans simply consume (and discard) too much.

This issue of "how much is enough" is, of course, an age-old question for environmentalists. My purpose here is to highlight how the problems of consumption relate to neoliberalism and to point out how neoliberalism removes much of the political and moral leverage necessary to deal with overconsumption.

Privatization is based on a demand-led approach to service delivery, where customers can buy as much as they can afford. Private companies have no incentive to limit the amount of resources consumed or wastes produced, since they profit from increased levels of both. Nor do they have any incentive to redirect resources in a more equitable manner, since there is no money to be made from doing so. The ANC can ask, as did Jay Naidoo, the former minister who headed the Reconstruction and Development Program, in the mid-1990s, whether it is right to be watering gardens in white suburbs while homes in the townships have no water at all.[54] But under a privatized system, there is no institutional or moral authority for resource allocation.

Privatization effectively depoliticizes societal decisions about resource consumption and distribution and leaves these choices to the rationale of the market. The state—through a regulatory agency or legislation—can attempt to control consumption and distribution by means of progressive block tariffs and required minimums for services, but power asymmetries between the regulator and the private companies often make regulatory interventions ineffective. This is not to suggest that a centralized planning office be developed to monitor and make decisions about every aspect of consumption in South Africa. Such a move would be neither feasible nor desirable in a democratic society. But allowing consumption patterns to be determined by little more than price mechanisms is equally problematic.

The state and other nonmarket institutions, such as unions, civic organizations, and environmental groups, must have a voice in determining how much per capita consumption of a particular service is acceptable in a resource-scarce or damaged environment. If only limited supplies of key resources are available, and if access to these limited resources is badly skewed, as is the case in South Africa, then good moral and environmental reasons exist for placing the resource in public hands.

Challenging the notion of growth is, of course, anathema to neoliberal thought, and it is one reason that the question of overconsumption receives so little theoretical attention in the neoliberal environmental literature. Growth in consumption (and therefore waste) by the middle class is deemed absolutely necessary to the creation of a stronger economy in order to lift the poor out of poverty and environmental degradation. Growth is not a major environmental concern for neoliberal policy makers, because it is assumed that society will always find new ways of alleviating its worst environmental side effects, either through clean technologies, better cost-benefit valuations, stronger laws, or market incentives.

PROSPECTS AND PROGRESS

In the end, some important gains have been made on the environmental front in South Africa, but there have also been spectacular failures. On the positive side, the new Constitution offers one of the most impressive legal foundations in the world for environmental policy development, and the state has made a formal commitment to addressing past environmental racism. Moreover, a highly politicized and dynamic environmental justice movement on the ground—ideological and organizational divisions aside—is keeping environmental justice issues on the national agenda.

Important, concrete gains, such as the closure of Thor Chemical's plant, indicate a potential for further improvements in the daily lives of black South Africans. Although the state itself has failed to introduce sufficient change, the environmental movement in South Africa has changed dramatically since the end of apartheid, much of it for the better.

Nevertheless, environmental racism continues, and environmental inequalities run deep. Both threaten to undermine the gains. Neoliberal reforms in particular threaten to entrench and legitimize the environmental inequities of the past under the banner of "liberal democracy."

One difficulty in tackling these neoliberal threats is that neoliberalism is a relatively abstract set of ideas, which makes it a difficult enemy—particularly when it is driven by a party that enjoys the support of two-thirds of the country's electorate and that has the backing of an irreproachable figure such as Nelson Mandela. Apartheid was an easier political target. Apartheid and its associated injustices were clearly wrong to most minds, and it was easy to directly attribute these injustices to apartheid's racism. As a result, there was strong support internally and externally for antiapartheid organizations and a relatively coherent antiapartheid civil society movement.

One of the key challenges for the environmental justice movement in South Africa today, therefore, is to demonstrate the links between degraded living and working environments and neoliberalism. Some of this work has already begun. Organizations such as the Anti-Privatization Forum and the Anti-Eviction Campaign have responded to neoliberal housing and service-delivery policies, and there has been some concrete collaboration between these groups and environmental justice organizations. But much work remains in order to make clear the link between environmental degradation and the broader socioeconomic questions of poverty and market-driven reforms.

A second challenge for the movement is to make obvious the link between environmental racism and neoliberalism. Earlier, I outlined how these two phenomena might be explained theoretically—that is, as a conception of racism that incorporates institutional factors and the underlying material interests of a privileged group. Environmental racism can be described as the "grease" that allows neoliberalism to inflict environmental damage on low-income, black South Africans. Neoliberalism is driven foremost by the cold calculations of marginal efficiency and competitiveness, but its emergence in South Africa has an undeniable racial dimension. How else can a municipality get away with providing world-class, publicly owned services to white suburban areas and only third-rate, privatized services to neighboring black townships? How else could well-to-do white suburbs receive heavily subsidized services while low-income black townships are expected to either pay the full costs of what they receive or go without? The most orthodox of neoliberal policies in South Africa are maintained, and most aggressively enforced, in black residential areas.

Of course, no smooth dialectical relationship exists between race and class interests. There are now many wealthy and middle-class blacks living in South African suburbs, and most of the politicians and bureaucrats now enforcing neoliberal policies of privatization and cost recovery are black. In the long run, neoliberalism is largely color-blind. Profit potential—not racial bias—drives its logic.

Nevertheless, there are still good reasons to acknowledge and fight environmental racism in South Africa. Even if class interests and market pressures eventually do manage to break down ethnically and racially determined notions of identification in South Africa, environmental racism nonetheless will be with us for many years to come. As John Maynard Keynes noted in his work on theoretical constructs, in the long run, all of us will die, and we can only deal with the real world in which we live today.

The challenge to the environmental justice movement in South Africa is therefore a complex one. No single point of focus is going to remove the contradictions and inequities of postapartheid environmental reforms. Removing them will require a multifaceted effort, one engaged simultaneously in issues of race *and* class, not to mention gender, to bring the country a more environmentally just and sustainable future.

ROBERT D. BULLARD, GLENN S. JOHNSON,
AND ANGEL O. TORRES

14

Addressing Global Poverty, Pollution, and Human Rights

A round the world, people want jobs and economic development. The question is, at what cost to their health and to their environment are jobs and economic development to be provided? The world is not a just place, and it is becoming more unequal. More than 1.2 billion people still live on less than one U.S. dollar a day. A fifth of the world's population living in its richest countries controls 86 percent of its the world's gross domestic product, and the poorest fifth just 1 percent— and the gap between these two groups continues to widen.[1] The politics of pollution have been profitable for some, but have impoverished entire nations and robbed their citizens of their health, wealth, and economic livelihood. This concluding chapter examines some of the changes that have occurred over the past decade as the environmental justice movement has become a global movement.

In 1992, only a handful of environmental justice activists from the United States attended the Earth Summit in Rio de Janeiro. A decade later, their numbers had swelled: hundreds of delegates attended the World Summit on Sustainable Development, also known as the Rio + 10 Earth Summit, held in 2002 in Johannesburg, South Africa. Because the summit was dominated by transnational corporations, it presented some extreme challenges to politically and economically disenfranchised individuals, groups, organizations, communities, regions, and nations. (Environmental justice principles that we developed in 1991 at the First National People of Color Environmental Leadership Summit were infused into the sustainable development dialogue.) In 2001, hundreds of environmental justice leaders had staked out a similar position at the World Conference against Racism in Durban, South Africa. For these activists, environmental justice and eradication of racism were essential ingredients in achieving sustainable development.[2]

POVERTY, POLLUTION, AND GLOBALIZATION

Increased globalization of the world's economy has placed special strains on ecosystems, particularly those inhabited by poor communities and those contained in poor nations that are populated largely by people of color and indigenous peoples. This is especially true in the case of industries extracting resources such as oil, timber, and minerals.[3] The antiglobalization movement is anchored in the age-old quest for social justice, human rights, and democracy.

Globalization is not a product of evolution, nor is it inevitable. It was created by individuals whose goal was to propagate corporate economic values globally.[4] Globalization makes it easier for transnational corporations and capital to operate in areas with the least environmental regulations, best tax incentives, and cheapest labor, thereby permitting the highest profits. We are all connected through globalization. An environmental impact in one region or country has the potential to affect the entire world and all life in it.

Globalization is encouraged and buttressed by elites in the developed and the developing countries; by multilateral and regional economic institutions, such as the World Bank and the International Monetary Fund, among others; by multilateral and regional free trade and investment agreements, such as the North American Free Trade Agreement; by transnational corporations; by large investment and banking institutions; by national export promotion agencies; as well as by corporate affinity groups, such as the World Economic Forum and the U.S. Council for International Business.[5]

In 1970 there were seven thousand transnational companies. By 2000 there were well over fifty thousand. Over the past five decades, the world economy has grown fivefold. Over this same period, world trade grew by a factor of fourteen and is now valued at $16 trillion a year.[6] However, the world is becoming more unequal. International policy experts Robin

Broad and John Cavanagh describe what is happening economically between North and South as "global economic apartheid." They write:

> Despite the perception of an easing of the debt crisis, the overall Third World debt stock swelled by around $100 billion each year during the 1990s (reaching $2.4 trillion in 2001). Southern debt service (which reached $331 billion in 2000) still exceeds new lending, and the net outflow remains particularly crushing in Africa. Thus, although on one level the North-South gap is becoming more pronounced for most Third World countries, on another these global chains blur distinctions. These processes create another geographical North-South divide: the roughly one-third of humanity who make up a "global North" of beneficiaries in every country, and the two-thirds of humanity from the slums of New York to the *favelas* of Rio who are not hooked into the new global menu of producing, consuming, and borrowing opportunities in the "global South."[7]

Despite improvements in environmental protection over the past several decades, nearly 3 billion people, almost half the world's population, live in unhealthy environments on less than $2 a day. The percentage of extremely poor people in the world fell only slightly during the 1990s—from 29 to 23 percent—because of growing human numbers.[8]

Poverty and pollution are intricately linked. Poor people are disproportionately exposed to hazards in their environment. They are made sick by the lack of clean water and air and by inadequate food, shelter, energy, and health care.[9] Poverty affects health because it determines the amount of resources poor people have and defines the amount of environmental risk they will be exposed to in their immediate environment.[10]

It is the "poorest of the poor"—the one-fifth of the world's population living on less than $1 a day and unable to secure adequate food, water, sanitation, shelter, energy, and health care—who are most vulnerable to environmental threats.[11] Most governments in the poorest parts of the world spend around $10 per person per year on health care.[12] Over 25 percent of all preventable illnesses in the world are directly caused by environmental factors.[13] Almost one-third of the global burden of disease falls on the most vulnerable population: children under five years of age who constitute no more than 12 percent of the world's population.

Three environmental problems (contaminated drinking water, untreated human excrement, and air pollution) account for 7.7 million deaths annually, or 15 percent of the global death toll of 52 million. Twenty percent of children in the poorest regions of the world will not live to see their fifth birthday, mainly because of environment-related diseases—that is, malaria, acute respiratory infections, or diarrhea—all of which are largely preventable. Such diseases cause 11 million childhood deaths a year worldwide.[14]

WATER POVERTY AND INADEQUATE SANITATION

Water is required by all life-forms. Water covers most of the earth's crust. However, only 2.53 percent is freshwater; the remainder is salt water. The world's shrinking, clean freshwater reserves are threatened by failed water management policies, which have permitted large dams, overprivatization of freshwater markets, contamination of water by synthetic chemicals, pressures from human settlement patterns (urbanization), contamination by household garbage, and inadequate sanitation.

The United Nations paints a dire picture of the world's limited reserves of clean drinking water.[15] Released in 2003 after more than two years in the making, the *UN World Water Development Report: Water for People, Water for Life* states that "of all the social and natural resource crises we humans face, the water crisis is the one that lies at the heart of our survival and that of our planet Earth."[16] The UN predicts that, by 2050, as many as 7 billion people in sixty countries could face water scarcity. Climate change will account for about 20 percent of the increase in global water scarcity.

The UN has a goal of reducing by one-half the proportion of people who lack reliable access to clean water (access to at least five gallons per person per day from a source within two-thirds of a mile [one kilometer] of the person's home) by 2015. An estimated one-sixth of the world's population (1.1 billion people) remains without access to a clean water supply, and 2.4 billion to adequate sanitation.[17] The 1990s saw the number of people with improved water supplies increase from 4.1 to 4.9 billion. At the current rate of investment, safe drinking water will not be provided to all of the population in Asia before 2025, in Latin America and the Caribbean before 2040, and in Africa before 2050.[18]

Dirty water is the world's deadliest pollutant. Lack of clean water and adequate water-sanitation conditions contributes each year to approximately 2 billion diarrhea infections and 4 million deaths, mostly among infants and young children in developing countries. In the United States, inadequate sanitation accounts for 940,000 diarrhea infections and about 900 deaths each year.[19]

The Intermediate Technology Development Group and Greenpeace, in their report *Sustainable Energy for Poverty Reduction,* outline an action plan for addressing energy poverty in the developing world. Their plan includes "implement[ing] strategies which allow access to clean energy for the world's two billion poorest people in ten years; greatly expand[ing] global renewable energy markets, particularly in the North to create economies of scale; and stimulat[ing] clean and renewable markets in developing countries to increase energy options available for sustainable development."[20]

AIR POLLUTION

Air pollutants adversely affect the health of 4 to 5 billion people world-wide. Globally, over 2.7 million annual deaths can be attributed to air pollution.[21] Two-thirds of the air-pollution-related deaths occur in rural areas, where people burn biomass fuels. Over 3.5 billion people, mostly in rural areas, are exposed to a high level of air pollutants in their homes. Over 2.4 billion people use wood, charcoal, or dung as their principal source of energy for cooking and heating.[22] An estimated 2.5 million people, mostly women and children, die from exposure to cooking smoke inside their homes.[23]

ACCESS TO CLEAN, SUSTAINABLE ENERGY

Poverty cannot be eradicated without addressing energy problems in the developing world. More than 1.6 billion people—more than one-quarter of the world's population—today do not have access to sufficient energy to meet their basic needs.[24] The richest nations, with about a fifth of the world's population, consume some 60 percent of the commercially produced energy. Global mergers have produced a handful of oil conglomerates. The five largest—ExxonMobil, ChevronTexaco, ConocoPhillips, BP, and Shell—control 15 percent of the global oil production, 50 percent of the domestic oil production, 48.8 percent of the domestic refinery capacity, and 61 percent of the retail market.

Energy policies must also address the gender issues concerning rural and urban women in developing countries. Ensuring that the energy supply is sufficient to assist women in their socioeconomic aspirations is key to alleviating poverty and essential to viable, sustainable development.[25]

Resource wars in developing countries, especially transboundary disputes over oil, have brought wealth to a few and hardship and misery to many marginalized families. Corrupt governments and the environmental damage that accompanies oil extraction have given rise to protest movements, which are then countered with violent repression. For example, in a BBC telecast, the Shell Oil Company admitted that its oil activities in Nigeria inadvertently fed conflict, poverty, and corruption.[26] In the oil-rich regions of Africa, the Middle East, Southeast Asia, South America, and North America, poor peoples are caught in the middle of oil conflicts that exacerbate both poverty and pollution.

Clean and affordable energy is central to reducing poverty and improving the health of the most vulnerable populations in the developing world—those who lack access to sufficient energy to meet their basic needs. Bringing clean, sustainable energy to the homes of these 1.6 billion people would cost an estimated $9 billion for ten years, compared to the $250–$300 billion spent subsidizing fossil fuels and nuclear power. Upward of $15 trillion will be invested in new long-term energy facilities over the next decade.[27] Renewables are expected to play an increasingly important role in the world's energy plan, especially for the rural poor without basic energy services.[28]

CHILDHOOD LEAD POISONING

In most large cities in the developing world, the percentage of children affected by lead poisoning is staggering. Motor vehicles account for up to 90 percent of all airborne lead contamination in those urban areas where leaded gasoline is still widely used. Although lead from air pollution causes relatively few deaths, it causes a great deal of disability, particularly among children. According to the Global Lead Network, forty-seven countries had completed phaseouts of leaded gasoline by January 2002.[29] However, many other countries and regions still use gasoline with a high lead content, including eastern Europe, the Middle East, and Africa. Researchers estimate that an increase of ten micrograms of lead per deciliter of blood causes a 2.6-point decrease in IQ level.[30] At higher levels, the effect may be greater.

Lead affects almost every organ and system in the body—including the kidneys and the reproductive system. Studies supported by the National Institute of Environmental Health Sciences and reported in 1996 suggest that a young person's lead burden is not only linked to lower IQ and lower high school graduation rates but to increased delinquency. An estimated 16 percent of juvenile delinquency in the United States is attributable to high lead exposure.[31]

GLOBAL DUMPING GROUNDS

The Third World has become a global dumping ground for hazardous wastes, risky technologies, and economic exploitation. Hazardous waste generation and international movement of hazardous waste still pose some important health, environmental, legal, and ethical dilemmas. The "unwritten" policy of targeting Third World nations for waste trade received international media attention in 1991. Lawrence Summers, who was then chief economist of the World Bank, touched off an international firestorm when his confidential memorandum on waste trade was leaked. Summers wrote, "'Dirty' Industries: Just between you and me, shouldn't the World Bank be encouraging MORE migration of the dirty industries to the LDCs [less developed countries]?"[32]

Between 1989 and 1994, an estimated 2,878 tons of hazardous waste were exported from countries that belonged to the Organization for Economic Cooperation and Development to countries that did not.[33] In a response to the growing exportation of hazardous wastes across their borders, the Organization of African Unity and the G-77 nations (the largest coalition of developing countries in the United Nations) mobilized to pass two important international agreements.[34] On January 30, 1991, the Pan-African Conference on Environment and Sustainable Development in Bamako, Mali, adopted the Bamako Convention on the Ban of the Import into Africa and the Control of Transboundary Movement of Hazardous Wastes within Africa, or the Bamako Convention.[35]

The G-77 nations were instrumental in amending the Basel Convention on the Control of Transboundary Movements of Hazardous Wastes and Their Disposal (the Basel Convention) to include Decision II/12, which banned the export of all hazardous wastes from countries in the Organization for Economic Cooperation and Development to non-OECD countries—despite opposition by the United States. In September 1995, the third Conference of Parties to the Basel Convention approved an amendment that would ban the export of hazardous waste from highly industrialized countries (specifically Lichtenstein and the countries belonging to the Organization for Economic Cooperation and Development) to all other countries.[36] While the Bamako and Basel conventions may have made certain dumping formally illegal, in practice they have not prevented the transboundary movement of hazardous waste to developing countries. Loopholes still allow hazardous waste to enter countries that do not have the infrastructure to handle the wastes. For example, Joshua Karliner reports that "products such as pesticides and other chemicals banned or severely restricted by the United States, Western Europe and Japan because of their acute toxicity, environmental persistence or carcinogenic qualities are still regularly sent to the Third World."[37]

An estimated 40 percent of deaths around the world can now be attributed to various environmental factors, especially organic and chemical pollutants. Approximately eighty thousand different chemicals are now in commercial use, of which nearly 6 trillion pounds are produced annually in the United States.[38] More than 80 percent of these chemicals have never been screened to determine whether they cause cancer, much less tested to see if they harm the nervous, immune, endocrine, or reproductive systems.[39]

Nearly 3.3 million pounds of pesticide products were exported from the United States between 1997 and 2000.[40] The bulk of these products were shipped directly or indirectly to the developing world. Pesticide poisoning continues to be a severe environmental and health problem in developing countries. An estimated 25 million poor farmers and farmworkers suffer from pesticide poisoning each year; hundreds of thousands die.[41]

Of the eighty thousand different pesticides and other chemicals in use today, 10 percent are recognized as carcinogens.[42] Cancer-related deaths in the United States increased from 331,000 in 1970 to 521,000 in 1992.[43] In the year 2003, an estimated 1,334,100 new cases of cancer were diagnosed in the United States, and approximately 556,500 people died from the disease.[44] Each year, the estimated percentage of all cancer deaths caused by occupational exposures varies from 4 percent to over 20 percent; the estimate varies due to the lack of data on the carcinogenic potential of most industrial chemicals and the absence of effective public health surveillance systems for occupational disease.[45]

It is no coincidence that the world's deadliest industrial accident occurred in the Third World. The Bhopal tragedy is fresh in the minds of millions of people who live next to chemical plants. On December 2, 1984, a poisonous gas leak at the Union Carbide Corporation's plant in Bhopal, India, killed thousands of people. The methyl isocyanate gas leak killed 4,000 people within hours, but the death toll over the years exceeded 14,000 as those sickened by the gas later died.

The Dow Chemical Company purchased Union Carbide in February 2001. People are still suffering as a result of the 1984 gas leak, and survivors want the company to provide long-term medical care for the 150,000 with chronic health problems related to the accident. The matter is still being negotiated.[46] In the United States, the only place where methyl isocyanate was manufactured was at a Union Carbide plant in the predominately African American town of Institute, West Virginia.[47] In 1985, a gas leak from this Union Carbide plant sent 135 residents to the hospital.

Even after two decades, the victims of the Bhopal disaster fight on. Two Indian women activists, Rashida Bee and Champa Devi Shukla, have continued to fight for justice. Despite their poverty and poor health due to toxic gas exposure, they have emerged as leaders in the international fight to hold Dow Chemical accountable. They organized the first global hunger strike to draw international attention to Dow's deadly legacy and traveled the world to protest at Dow shareholder meetings. In 2004, on the twentieth anniversary of the disaster, the women became plaintiffs in a class action suit demanding a cleanup of the noxious factory site and damages to cover medical monitoring and costs incurred from years of soil and water contamination. For their work, Bee and Shukla were awarded the 2004 Goldman Environmental Prize.[48]

Transboundary shipment of hazardous wastes, toxic products, and risky technologies to poor communities in developing countries of the South have a lot in common with the systematic destruction of indigenous peoples' land and sacred sites, and the poisoning of African Americans in Louisiana's Lower Mississippi River petrochemical corridor known as Cancer Alley, and the poisoning of Mexicans in the border towns, *colonias*, and industrial plants (maquiladoras) along the U.S.-Mexico border. All have their roots in economic exploitation, racial oppression, devaluation of human life and the natural environment, and corporate greed.[49]

DUMPING ON THE U.S.-MEXICO BORDER

Over the past three decades, the two-thousand-mile border between the United States and Mexico has become a "virtual cesspool and breeding ground for infectious disease."[50] The conditions surrounding the thirty-one hundred maquiladoras—the assembly plants operated by American, Japanese, and other foreign countries—located along this border may contribute a considerable amount to the waste trade. The industrial plants use cheap Mexican labor to assemble products made of imported components and raw materials and then ship finished products back to their parent companies in the United States or other countries.[51] The products of maquiladoras account for 49 percent of Mexico's exports.[52]

The plants provide Mexicans in border cities with jobs, but at low wages and with little job security; workers endure high exposure to toxic chemicals and substandard working conditions.[53] The San Diego–based Environmental Health Coalition reports:

> The "globalization" of the marketplace puts worker health and environmental protection on the auction block in all countries. In the San Diego/ Tijuana region this has resulted in a burgeoning maquiladora industry— foreign-owned companies operating with special tariff reductions in Mexico. Baja California has the largest number of maquiladoras in Mexico, and the industrial pollution from these maquiladoras damages the public's health on both sides of the border.[54]

Over 1 million workers are employed in the maquiladoras.[55] Most of the workers barely earn enough to sustain themselves and their families. The federal minimum wage rate in Mexico is a mere $3.40 per day, compared to $5.15 an hour in the United States. Nearly two-thirds of the maquiladora workers are young women. Child labor (by persons under sixteen years of age) is not uncommon.

All along the Lower Rio Grande Valley, maquiladoras dump their toxic wastes into the river, from which 95 percent of the region's residents get their drinking water.[56] The North American Free Trade Agreement has enabled the creation of such "pollution havens."[57] The Mexican environmental regulatory agency is understaffed and ill equipped to adequately enforce its laws. Many of the Mexican border towns have become cities with skyscrapers and freeways. More important, the "brown pallor of these southwestern skies has become a major health hazard."[58]

MILITARY TOXICS THREAT

War and military activities are big players in environmental degradation. The U.S. military operates facilities in some eight hundred overseas locations, ranging from radio relay sites to major airbases. The U.S. Department of Defense has created deadly toxic waste sites and nuclear weapons garbage in domestic military bases and other locations around the world. The military is in the business of destruction—and too often its installations create, and leave behind, a legacy of unexploded ordinances, toxic and radioactive wastes, and health-threatening contamination. For example, in November 1992, the last of the U.S. troops were pulled out of Clark Air Base and Subic Naval Base in the Philippines, leaving behind a "horror story." A report by the U.S. General Accounting Office confirmed that the sites were left contaminated by polychlorinated biphenyls, lead, and other hazardous substances buried in a landfill; by fuel that had leaked into soil and groundwater; and by other toxic materials left in hot spots at the bases.[59] The closed military bases encompass well over 250 square miles.

In 1999, a report based on a two-year study of seven areas in the former Clark Air Base, conducted through the collaborative efforts of the Philippine environmental organization People's Task Force for Bases Cleanup and Canada's International Institute of Concern for Public Health, revealed ongoing health problems in the surrounding population that were related to toxic contamination at Clark.[60] The U.S. government still takes no responsibility for cleanup of its former military bases in the Philippines or the adverse effects on the health of nearby residents. Communities surrounding the Clark and Subic bases have for many years suffered from mysterious deaths and health complaints, including cancer, nervous system disorders, and reproductive problems. The fate of children who fell ill, allegedly because of contamination caused by toxic waste from base operations, remains uncertain.[61]

The U.S. military created a nightmare for Marshall Islands residents too. The Republic of the Marshall Islands includes thirty-four low-lying atolls and single islands in the Pacific Ocean that are located about twenty-one hundred miles southwest of Honolulu. Between June 1946 and August 1958, the United States detonated sixty-seven atmospheric nuclear devices in the Marshall Islands. The total yield of these tests was 108 megatons, the equivalent of more than seven thousand Hiroshima bombs. Portions of two atolls—Bikini and Enewetak—were actually vaporized, and portions of adjoining atolls were heavily damaged and contaminated with radiation.[62] The first of the nuclear tests, "Baker," left half a million tons of radioactive mud in the Bikini atoll lagoon. The 1954 "Bravo" blast left fallout over a fifty-thousand-square-mile area and bored a one-mile circular hole in the Bikini reef. In preparation for the tests, residents of the atolls were uprooted, relocated, and exiled from their homeland, never to be fully compensated for their losses.

Ironically, most of the nuclear tests were conducted during the period that the United States had administrative responsibility over the Marshall Islands in its role as a trustee for the United Nations Trust Territory of the Pacific Islands. Under the trust agreement, the United States had "full powers of administration, legislation and jurisdiction" and was obligated to promote the political, economic, social, and educational advancement of the islands' inhabitants, to protect their health, and to protect them "against the loss of their lands and resources."[63] (Similarly, Native Americans have over a century's worth of broken treaties with and abuses by the U.S. government, which holds Native Americans' lands in trust.) For decades, Marshall Island residents have waged a campaign for reparations from the U.S. government. Getting reparations for nuclear victims has been an uphill battle—even when they win favorable court rulings.

The United States and the Republic of the Marshall Islands created the Compact of Free Association in 1986, which restored to the Marshall Islands its sovereignty in domestic and foreign affairs in return for giving the United States defense rights in the islands. (The United States is responsible for the country's defense and national security, since the country has no external security force.) On March 5, 2001, the Marshall Islands Nuclear Claims Tribunal, which had been created by the compact, awarded the claimants in a class action lawsuit—every resident of the Marshall Islands—a total of $563,315,500 (which included $278,000 for loss of value, $251,000 for restoration costs, and $33,814,500 for suffering and hardship), a figure that represents the final amount after past compensation by the U.S. government had been deducted.[64] Although the tribunal gave the nuclear victims a favorable ruling on reparations, the United States did not pay the claims as directed.

In June 2002, the Republic of the Marshall Islands hired Richard Thornburgh to conduct an independent assessment of the information used by the Marshall Islands Nuclear Claims Tribunal to adjudicate the compensation claims of island residents in the class action suit. Thornburgh has been counsel to the Washington, D.C., law firm Kirkpatrick and Lockhart and attorney general under Presidents Ronald Reagan and George H. W. Bush. He also served as governor of Pennsylvania. The Thornburgh report was completed in January 2003. Thornburgh and his colleagues concluded that the "personal injury and property damage awards rendered thus far by the Nuclear Claims Tribunal were the result of reasonable, fair and orderly processes that are entitled to respect. Given that those processes have resulted in awards that greatly exceed the Trust Fund's remaining corpus, it is our view that the $150 million initially provided by the U.S. government for the Trust Fund has proven to be manifestly inadequate to fairly compensate the inhabitants of the Marshall Islands for the damages they suffered as a result of the U.S. nuclear testing program that took place in their homeland between 1948 and 1958."[65]

Thousands of claims are still pending. The U.S. government has paid out $191 million since the 1970s. It is offering no further compensation to the victims and no guarantees that the abandoned Bikini atoll is free of radioactivity and safe for Bikinians to return to.[66] On March 17, 2004, the U.S. House of Representatives unanimously adopted a resolution hailing the half century "strategic partnership" with these Pacific island people, a partnership in which the latter lost their home islands to U.S. nuclear bomb tests, and from which they fear Washington may soon walk away. In early 2005, the Bush administration rejected a petition from the Marshall Island government for additional compensation.[67]

The U.S. military has also spoiled pristine lands in Alaska. Alaska has been of strategic importance to the United States since World War II because of its location and remoteness. During the cold war, the country situated more than seven hundred defense installations in the Alaskan landscape. These military installations, both active and abandoned ones, are polluting the land, groundwater, wetlands, streams, and air with extensive fuel spills, pesticides, solvents, polychlorinated biphenyls, dioxins, munitions, and radioactive materials. Many of these military installations are in close proximity to the villages of Alaskan Native Americans and to traditional hunting and fishing areas. Toxic fish pose special health threats to native peoples and others who customarily eat greater quantities of fish than the average consumer eats. Military toxics threaten the entire way of life of Alaska's Native Americans.[68] Those who live near decommissioned military bases have nearly ten times as many toxic chemicals in their blood as average Americans. Alaska Community Action on Toxics, a grassroots environmental group, pressed the government to remove the toxics hot spots left by the military. The U.S. Army Corps of Engineers agreed to spend $58 million dollars over eighteen years to clean up a former Northeast Cape military base, which had served as an important military sounding post near the Siberian Sea during the cold war.[69]

Artic natives in particular are exposed to high levels of polychlorinated biphenyls because global atmospheric distribution patterns deposit them in the north. Polychlorinated biphenyls and other persistent bioaccumulative and toxic pollutants pose a special threat to native subsistence fishers and wildlife consumers. These pollutants travel long distances to regions where they have never been used or produced. They persist in the environment, bioaccumulate through the food web, and have adverse effects on human health and the environment.[70] More important, these pollutants readily transfer through the air, water, and land and cross geographical and generational boundaries.

CLIMATE JUSTICE

Global climate change looms as a major environmental justice issue of the twenty-first century. Mounting scientific evidence documents the degree to which human activities have altered the chemical composition of the atmosphere through the buildup of greenhouse gases—primarily carbon dioxide, methane, and nitrous oxide. As we search for ways to rectify global climate change, we desperately need the input of the populations most likely to be negatively affected: people of color and other poor people in the North and in the developing countries of the South.[71]

Around the world, a movement for climate justice has begun to emerge. Climate justice links human rights and ecological sustainability.[72] In 2000, a Climate Justice Summit held in The Hague, Netherlands—during the meeting of the United Nations Framework Convention on Climate Change, Conference of Parties—attracted several hundred participants representing small island nations, indigenous peoples, people of color, and poor people, who are most affected by climate change. The activists shared their common experiences and decided to take collective action. They agreed that waiting for governments to respond might be deadly for communities of color and the planet.

Changing climates are expected to raise sea levels, alter precipitation and other weather patterns, threaten human health, and harm fish and many types of ecosystems.[73] The adverse effects will fall disproportionately on the poor, including people of color in the United States who are concentrated in urban centers in the South, coastal regions, and areas with substandard air quality.[74] A study of the fifteen largest American cities found that climate change would increase heat-related deaths by at least 90 percent.[75] People of color are twice as likely to die in a heat wave, since disproportionately they are poor, lack air conditioning, and are concentrated in the hottest regions of the country—the South and Southwest.

A 2004 study sponsored by the Congressional Black Caucus Foundation (CBCF) concluded that, unless appropriate actions are taken to mitigate the effects of climate change or to adapt to them, "climate change will worsen existing equity issues within the United States."[76] The report was completed by the Oakland-based environmental group Redefining Progress. The CBCF chairman, Congressman William Jefferson (D-LA), summed up the problem: "We are long past the point where global warming is considered a myth. We are seeing its effects all around us, especially in my hometown of New Orleans, Louisiana, which is expected to experience an increased incidence of flooding that could potentially destabilize its economy and endanger its populace. The CBCF–Redefining Progress report gives us good direction on how to best accomplish the goal of reducing carbon emissions for the future benefit of African Americans and all U.S. citizens."[77]

The United States represents only 4 percent of the world's population but produces 25 percent of the world's carbon dioxide.[78] People of color are concentrated in cities that failed the EPA's ambient air quality standards. Climate change is expected to increase the number of floods, droughts, and fires worldwide. To make matters worse, low-income people typically lack insurance; when they lose their possessions in storms and floods, poverty makes replacement difficult. Only 25 percent of renters have renters insurance.

Climate change will reduce discretionary spending because prices will rise across the board. Poor families will have to spend even more on food and electricity, which already represent a large proportion of their budgets. Indigenous people are losing traditional medicinal plants to the warming climate, and subsistence households are suffering from the loss of species that are unable to adapt.

Climate justice advocates are calling for solutions to ward off global climate warming that do not fall hardest on low-income communities, communities of color, or workers employed by fossil fuel industries.[79] Not surprisingly, resistance to the Kyoto Protocol—the plan for reining in climate-altering activities—has come largely from the fossil fuel lobby, which represents companies that extract, process, or sell fossil fuels; generate electricity using coal, oil, or gas; or make automobiles.

In the final analysis, the impetus for climate justice will not likely come from within government. It is a sure bet that it will not come from the polluting industries. The Environmental Justice and Climate Change Initiative, staffed by the Oakland-based environmental organization Redefining Progress, is bringing a broad cross-section of grassroots groups, academics, educators, policy analysts, and faith-based leaders to the table to discuss climate issues.

The goal of the initiative is to educate the peoples of North America about global climate issues and to prompt them to create and implement just climate policies. The primary focus of the climate justice movement is to change the policies and practices in the United States that have helped create global climate change, but the movement has an international focus as well. The Environmental Justice and Climate Change Initiative supports energy efficiency, renewable energy, and conservation policies and seeks equitable measures to protect and assist the communities most affected by climate change.[80]

THE WAY FORWARD

The environmental justice movement emerged in response to environmental inequities, threats to public health, unequal protection, differential enforcement, disparate treatment of the poor and people of color, and human rights violations. Poverty and environmental degradation are intricately linked and take a heavy toll on billions of people in developing and industrialized countries. Thus, any search for environmental justice and sustainable development must address the root causes of both poverty and pollution and seek solutions to this double threat.

There is little or no correlation between the proximity of industrial plants and employment opportunities for nearby residents. Corporate-state collusion has turned rich oil and mineral fields into toxic wastelands near millions of indigenous peoples around the world. Having military installations, oil wells and refineries, mining and other extraction industries, and industrial facilities as neighbors has been a curse rather than a blessing for many poor communities in the industrial countries of the North and for poor communities in the developing countries of the South, a curse that has relegated many to poverty and poisoned homelands.

As part of a movement for environmental and economic justice, grassroots groups in the United States and around the world are advocating equal environmental protection, vigorous enforcement of human rights, and a reduction of the growing gap between rich and poor nations. As a first step, many activists seek cancellation of the illegitimate debts of Third World nations. It is time for governments not only to guarantee civil and political rights but also to guarantee economic, social, and cultural rights. A significant reduction of inequities—among nations, within nations, between racial and ethnic groups, between social classes, and between men and women—would go a long way toward creating just, healthy, and sustainable societies for all.

Government tax breaks and corporate welfare for the rich have allowed poor communities and poor nations to become the dumping grounds for polluting industries. Industry and government, including the military, have often exploited the economic vulnerability of poor communities, poor states, poor nations, and poor regions for their unsound, risky, and environmentally unsustainable operations. Environmental justice leaders are demanding an end to economic blackmail. Victims of environmental racism are calling for reparations for the harm inflicted on their persons, communities, and environments.

Leaders of the environmental justice movement are also demanding improved health systems that recognize and take precautions to prevent the negative health consequences and other effects of environmentally destructive projects. The poor who bear the burden of unsustainable development are also urging the use and development of technologies and processes that avoid pollution and environmental hazards. Poor people have a right to clean air, clean water, and safe jobs at livable wages.

The National Black Environmental Justice Network developed the following list of objectives to assist nations, local governments, and civil society in ensuring that sustainable development benefits all people, and that environmental racism is eradicated.

1. Recognize the unique and profound environmental challenges faced by people of color and individuals living in rural and urban areas;

2. Develop economic, health, and social indicators to assess and monitor the quality of life for people of color impacted by environmentally destructive or unsustainable development;

3. Improve health systems, education, housing, utilities, drinking water and environmental protection and promote equal opportunities in employment for people of color impacted by unsustainable development;

4. Ensure the right of all people to meaningful participation in decision-making on environmental and health issues and guarantee fair access to judicial and administrative proceedings and remedies for environmental grievances;

5. Implement a just transition to clean, affordable and sustainable modes of production and pollution prevention;

6. Develop, apply, and transfer to all States information and technologies that can reduce and eliminate environmental health hazards and enable the thorough remediation of contaminated sites;

7. Urge United Nations agencies, international and regional financial mechanisms, and donor countries to reform their loan and

grant-making practices to support sustainable development and refrain from the exploitation of developing countries and people who have been historically disenfranchised;

8. Ensure that all governmental policies and practices adhere to the principles of the Rio Declaration on Environment and Development, in particular Principles 15 and 16 that mandate the precautionary approach and the polluter bearing the cost of pollution;

9. Develop and implement programs of sustainable development with the involvement of those affected by environmental racism and other non-State actors in order to redress and improve health, environmental, and economic conditions;

10. Establish programs to protect people from environmental racism caused by military, governmental, and industrial activities; and

11. Reform economic development policies with mechanisms for prioritizing health, social, cultural, and religious/spiritual values.[81]

The environmental justice movement has begun to build a global network of grassroots groups, community-based organizations, university-based resource centers, researchers, scientists, educators, lawyers, and youth groups. Better communication and funding is still needed in every area. Resources are especially scarce for environmental justice groups in developing countries.

Government, industries, and financial institutions must go beyond the elegant rhetoric of commitment to sustainable development. Around the world, people of color are suffering from contaminated environments, substandard housing, and impoverished conditions in close proximity to hazardous and unsustainable development. Such development has been, and is being, promoted by governments and created, in many cases, by a network of investment and lending institutions and industrial corporations. While such conditions may appear irreparable, there must be a concerted effort by governments and civil society to eliminate these fundamental human rights abuses. The communities that suffer from environmental racism must be respected participants in the planning and implementation of sustainable development activities and in the remediation of harms that have resulted from unsustainable development.

Finally, the success of sustainable development will be measured by the conditions existing in communities inhabited by people of color in the United States and around the world, where some of the most destructive industries and other activities are located. For this reason, it is critical that international agreements and acts of cooperation focus on the issue of racial discrimination in environmental protection and development.

Principles of Environmental Justice

PREAMBLE

We the people of color, gathered together at this multinational People of Color Environmental Leadership Summit, to begin to build a national and international movement of all peoples of color to fight the destruction and taking of our lands and communities, do hereby re-establish our spiritual interdependence to the sacredness of our Mother Earth; to respect and celebrate each of our cultures, languages and beliefs about the natural world and our roles in healing ourselves; to insure environmental justice; to promote economic alternatives which would contribute to the development of environmentally safe livelihoods; and, to secure our political, economic and cultural liberation that has been denied for over 500 years of colonization and oppression, resulting in the poisoning of our communities and land and the genocide of our peoples, do affirm and adopt these Principles of Environmental Justice:

1. *Environmental justice* affirms the sacredness of Mother Earth, ecological unity and the interdependence of all species, and the right to be free from ecological destruction.

2. *Environmental justice* demands that public policy be based on mutual respect and justice for all peoples, free from any form of discrimination or bias.

3. *Environmental justice* mandates the right to ethical, balanced and responsible uses of land and renewable resources in the interest of a sustainable planet for humans and other living things.

4. *Environmental justice* calls for universal protection from nuclear testing, extraction, production and disposal of toxic/hazardous wastes and poisons and nuclear testing that threaten the fundamental right to clean air, land, water, and food.

5. *Environmental justice* affirms the fundamental right to political, economic, cultural and environmental self-determination of all peoples.

6. *Environmental justice* demands the cessation of the production of all toxins, hazardous wastes, and radioactive materials, and that all past and current producers be held strictly accountable to the people for detoxification and the containment at the point of production.

7. *Environmental justice* demands the right to participate as equal partners at every level of decision-making including needs assessment, planning, implementation, enforcement and evaluation.

8. *Environmental justice* affirms the right of all workers to a safe and healthy work environment, without being forced to choose between an unsafe livelihood and unemployment. It also affirms the right of those who work at home to be free from environmental hazards.

9. *Environmental justice* protects the right of victims of environmental injustice to receive full compensation and reparations for damages as well as quality health care.

10. *Environmental justice* considers governmental acts of environmental injustice a violation of international law, the Universal Declaration on Human Rights, and the United Nations Convention on Genocide.

11. *Environmental justice* must recognize a special legal and natural relationship of Native Peoples to the U.S. government through treaties, agreements, compacts, and covenants affirming sovereignty and self-determination.

12. *Environmental justice* affirms the need for urban and rural eco-logical policies to clean up and rebuild our cities and rural areas in balance with nature, honoring the cultural integrity of all our communities, and providing fair access for all to the full range of resources.

13. *Environmental justice* calls for the strict enforcement of principles of informed consent, and a halt to the testing of experimental reproductive and medical procedures and vaccinations on people of color.

14. *Environmental justice* opposes the destructive operations of multi-national corporations.

15. *Environmental justice* opposes military occupation, repression and exploitation of lands, peoples and cultures, and other life-forms.

16. *Environmental justice* calls for the education of present and future generations which emphasizes social and environmental issues, based on our experience and an appreciation of our diverse cultural perspectives.

17. *Environmental justice* requires that we, as individuals, make personal and consumer choices to consume as little of Mother Earth's resources and to produce as little waste as possible; and make the conscious decision to challenge and reprioritize our lifestyles to insure the health of the natural world for present and future generations.

Adopted today, October 27, 1991, in Washington, D.C.

Nongovernmental Organization Language on Environmental Racism

Final Draft, August 31, 2001 11:00 A.M.
World Conference against Racism, Durban, South Africa

PREAMBLE

Recognizing environmental racism as a human rights violation is a form of discrimination caused by government and private sector policy, practice, action or inaction which intentionally or unintentionally, disproportionately targets and harms the environment, health, biodiversity, local economy, quality of life and security of communities, workers, groups, and individuals based on race, class, color, gender, caste, ethnicity and/or national origin.

DECLARATION

We condemn the abuse of all forms of power, greed, and exclusion of victims of environmental racism from decision-making, unequal enforcement, non-existent or ineffective environmental laws and regulations, manipulation of media and language barriers to perpetuate and conceal the environmental harms to human health, displacement of people, depletion of natural resources, and the degradation of biodiversity, all of which are manifestations of environmental racism targeting Indigenous Peoples, Africans and African descendants, Asians and Asian descendants, Middle Eastern Peoples, Pacific Islanders, Latinos, Caribbean Peoples, and other social groups most vulnerable to practices of unsustainable development and militarization, especially children, women, the elderly, displaced, [and] immuno-suppressed, as well as low and no income people.

PROGRAM OF ACTION

To promote sustainable development, governments must develop, improve, and apply economic, health, and social indicators to assess the quality of life for people impacted by environmental racism, implement a just transition to clean, affordable and sustainable modes of production, and pollution prevention, develop, apply, and transfer to all States information and technologies that can reduce and eliminate environmental health hazards and enable the thorough remediation of contaminated sites, ensure medical services to persons suffering from toxic exposure, develop laws which prohibit transboundary, especially from industrialized to non-industrialized countries, and intra-border deposition of toxics and polluting technologies, which degrade the environment and harm human health, urge UN agencies, international and regional financial mechanisms, and donor countries to reform their loan and grant-making practices and provide the resources that enable all States to develop, improve, and implement the laws, policies, and practices as called for by this program of action.

Governments must establish, comply with, and enforce international conventions, treaties, declarations, national laws, and policies that ensure the fundamental rights of all people to clean air, land, water, food and safe and decent housing. Such legal instruments and policies must provide protection for urban and rural communities, workers, especially agricultural laborers, from environmental hazards that disproportionately impact people who have historically been subjected to discrimination based on race, class, color, gender, caste, ethnicity and/or national origin, ensure the right of all people to meaningful participation in decision-making on environmental and health issues, including culturally and linguistically appropriate outreach and education as well as guarantee fair access to judicial and administrative proceedings and remedies for environmental racism, and establish legally binding instruments and mechanisms to hold States and corporations accountable to international and domestic laws protecting human rights.

Governments must ensure that all governmental policies and practices adhere to the principles of the precautionary approach and polluter pays as provided in the Rio Declaration on Environment and Development. Develop and implement programs of sustainable development with the involvement of those affected by environmental racism and other non-State actors in order to redress and improve health, environmental, and economic conditions. Establish programs to protect people from environmental racism caused by military, governmental, and industrial activities. Such programs must include protection from dangerous health threats, remediation of environmental degradation caused by the military, governments, and industry, as well as the disposal of toxic stockpiles that meet 100% efficiency. Reform economic development policies with mechanisms for prioritizing health, social, cultural, and religious/spiritual values.

As full partners in the eradication of environmental racism and quest for sustainable development, the NGO Forum calls upon NGOs to: foster meaningful national and international participation in public and private decision-making affecting local communities and their environments; study the effects of environmental racism on our communities; identify and publicize the effects of environmental racism on workers and communities; educate civil society on the impacts of environmental racism; advocate for public and private sector policies and laws that protect natural resources, eliminate contamination affecting communities, and restore contaminated environments; provide victims of environmental racism with legal advisory assistance to access justice and attain fair compensation; and develop regional environmental justice networks to share information, strategies, lessons learned, engage in mutual solidarity actions, and monitor the compliance and enforcement of the obligations of industry, governments, and intergovernmental agencies to make possible equitable and sustainable development.

The NGO Forum calls on governments, intergovernmental agencies, UN agencies and other financial mechanisms, and philanthropic organizations to provide the financing and technical assistance necessary to enable NGOs to carry out this action plan.

Notes

INTRODUCTION

1. Robert D. Bullard, "Environmental Justice Flowering: The Environmental Justice Movement Comes of Age," *Amicus Journal* 16 (Spring 1994): 32–37.

2. National Black Environmental Justice Network, *Combating Environmental Racism with Sustainable Development in the U.S. and around the World — the Time Is Now* (Washington, DC: National Black Environmental Justice Network, March 2002), p. 15. This report was presented to the World Summit on Sustainable Development in 2002.

3. World Health Organization, "About WHO," n.d., www.who.int/aboutwho/en/definition.html (accessed December 1, 2002).

4. People of color in the United States include African Americans, Native Americans, Latino Americans, and Asian and Pacific Islander Americans.

5. The seventeen Principles of Environmental Justice were adopted on October 27, 1991, at the First National People of Color Environmental Leadership Summit, held in Washington, DC.

6. *Environmental Equity: Reducing Risks for All Communities* (1992) can be found at www.epa.gov/comp_risk/history7/equity/contents.htm (accessed December 1, 2002).

7. William J. Clinton, Presidential Memorandum accompanying Executive Order no. 12898, February 11, 1994. See www.environmentaldefense.org/documents/2824_ExecOrder12898.pdf.

8. U.S. Environmental Protection Agency, *Guidance for Incorporating Environmental Justice in EPA's NEPA Compliance Analysis* (Washington, DC: U.S.

EPA, 1998); see also Robert Bullard and Glenn Johnson, "Environmental and Economic Justice: Implications for Public Policy," *Journal of Public Management and Social Policy* 4, no. 4 (1998): 137–48.

9. K. Olden, "The Complex Interaction of Poverty, Pollution, Health Status," *Scientist* 12, no. 2 (February 1998): 7. This article can be found at the Web site of the National Institute of Environmental Health Sciences, Division of Extramural Research and Training, Health Disparities Research, www.niehs.nih.gov/dert/programs/translat/hd/ko-art.htm (accessed December 1, 2002).

10. R. D. Bullard and B. H. Wright, "Environmental Justice for All: Community Perspectives on Health and Research Needs," *Toxicology and Industrial Health* 9, no. 5 (1993): 821–41.

11. Institute of Medicine, *Toward Environmental Justice: Research, Education, and Health Policy Needs* (Washington, DC: National Academy of Sciences, 1999), chap. 1.

12. See "Study: Public Housing Is Too Often Located near Toxic Sites," *Dallas Morning News,* October 3, 2000. See the news report on this study at CNN.com, www.cnn.com/2000/NATURE/10/03/toxicneighbors.ap (accessed December 1, 2002).

13. See R. D. Bullard, Glenn S. Johnson, and A. O. Torres, "Sprawl Atlanta," September 19, 2000, Environmental Justice Resource Center, www.ejrc.cau.edu/raceequitysmartgrowth.htm (accessed December 1, 2002).

14. See Center for Health, Environment, and Justice, *Poisoned Schools: Invisible Threats, Visible Action,* March 2001, Blue Ridge Environmental Defense League, www.bredl.org/press/2001/poisoned_schools.htm (accessed December 10, 2002).

15. C. Lazaroff, "Pesticide Exposure Threatens Children at School," *Environmental News Service,* January 5, 2000.

16. See "Chemical Assault on African American Community: Community Group Wins $42.8 Million Settlement. The People vs. Monsanto: An Interview with Cassandra Roberts," November 27, 2001, Environmental Justice Resource Center, www.ejrc.cau.edu/cassandraroberts.html (accessed December 1, 2002).

17. Robert D. Bullard, "Race and Environmental Justice in the United States," *Yale Journal of International Law* 18 (Winter 1993): 319–35; Robert D. Bullard, "The Threat of Environmental Racism," *Natural Resources and Environment* 7 (Winter 1993): 23–26, 55–56.

18. See United Nations, "Fiftieth Anniversary of the Universal Declaration of Human Rights, 1948–1998," December 10, 1948, www.un.org/Overview/rights.html (accessed September 21, 2004).

19. Martin Wagner, "Trading Human Rights for Corporate: Global Trade Policy Weakens Protections for Health, the Environment," *Race, Poverty, and the Environment* 11, no. 1 (Summer 2004): 26.

20. Aaron Sach, *Eco-Justice: Linking Human Rights and the Environment* (Washington, DC: Worldwatch Institute, 1995).

21. Barbara Rose Johnston, *Life and Death Matters: Human Rights and the Environment at the End of the Millennium* (Walnut Creek, CA: AltaMira Press, 1997).

22. Julian Agyeman, Robert D. Bullard, and Bob Evans, eds., *Just Sustain-*

abilities: Development in an Unequal World (London: Earthscan; Cambridge: MIT Press, 2003).

23. See Robert D. Bullard, *Dumping in Dixie: Race, Class, and Environmental Quality* (Boulder: Westview Press, 2000), pp. 130–32.

24. U.S. Nuclear Regulatory Commission, Atomic Safety Licensing Board, *Final Initial Decision — Louisiana Energy Services,* Docket no. 70-3070-ML, May 1, 1997.

25. Tony Allen-Mills, "Louisiana Blacks Win Nuclear War," *London Sunday Times,* May 11, 1997.

26. U.S. Nuclear Regulatory Commission, Atomic Safety Licensing Board, *Final Decision,* April 3, 1998, Docket no. 70-3070-ML (May 1, 1997).

27. See R. D. Bullard, "Prefiled Testimony of Dr. Robert D. Bullard Regarding Citizens against Nuclear Trash's Contention J-9," Docket no. 70-3070, February 24, 1995, U.S. Nuclear Regulatory Commission, Office of Public Affairs, Washington, DC. The full testimony can be viewed at the Web site of the Environmental Justice Resource Center, Clark Atlanta University, www.ejrc.cau .edu/bulltestles.html.

28. Associated Press, "Black Farmers Unite to Press Bias Suit," *Atlanta Journal-Constitution,* September 22, 2004, p. B3.

29. "Anniston PCB Cases Settle for $700M," *Birmingham Business Journal,* August 20, 2003, p. 1, www.bizjournals.com/birmingham/stories/2003/08/18/ daily24.html (accessed August 20, 2003).

30. See Goldman Environmental Prize, "Margie Eugene-Richard: Growing Up in Cancer Alley," press release, April 19, 2004, www.goldmanprize.org/ recipients/recipientProfile.cfm?recipientID=131 (accessed October 5, 2004).

31. U.S. Environmental Protection Agency, Office of Inspector General, *EPA Needs to Consistently Implement the Intent of the Executive Order on Environmental Justice* (Washington, DC: U.S. EPA, March 1, 2004).

CHAPTER 1. ENVIRONMENTAL JUSTICE IN THE TWENTY-FIRST CENTURY

1. Robert D. Bullard, *Dumping in Dixie: Race, Class, and Environmental Quality,* 3rd ed. (Boulder, CO: Westview Press, 2000).

2. Robert D. Bullard, *Invisible Houston: The Black Experience in Boom and Bust* (College Station: Texas A & M University Press, 1987).

3. U.S. General Accounting Office, *Siting of Hazardous Waste Landfills and Their Correlation with Racial and Economic Status of Surrounding Communities* (Washington, DC: Government Printing Office, 1983).

4. United Church of Christ Commission for Racial Justice, *Toxic Wastes and Race in the United States* (New York: United Church of Christ, 1987).

5. Bullard, *Dumping in Dixie,* chap. 1.

6. See Dana Alston, "Transforming a Movement: People of Color Unite at Summit against Environmental Racism," *Sojourner* 21 (1992): 30–31.

7. William K. Reilly, "Environmental Equity: EPA's Position," *EPA Journal* 18 (March–April 1992): 18–19.

8. See R. D. Bullard and B. H. Wright, "The Politics of Pollution: Implications for the Black Community," *Phylon* 47 (March 1986): 71–78.

9. Julian Agyeman, Robert D. Bullard, and Bob Evans, *Just Sustainabilities: Development in an Unequal World* (London: Earthscan; Cambridge: MIT Press, 2003).

10. For more information on the Environmental Justice Program at the University of Michigan, which is housed in the School of Natural Resources and Environment, see the Web site at http://sitemaker.umich.edu/snre-ej-program/.

11. Angelo Pinto, speaking at the Second National People of Color Environmental Leadership Summit, Washington, DC, October 25, 2002.

12. Robert D. Bullard, "Race and Environmental Justice in the United States," *Yale Journal of International Law* 18 (Winter 1993): 319–35; Robert D. Bullard, "The Threat of Environmental Racism," *Natural Resources and Environment* 7 (Winter 1993): 23–26, 55–56.

13. Louis Sullivan, "Remarks at the First Annual Conference on Childhood Lead Poisoning," in *Preventing Child Lead Poisoning: Final Report,* ed. Alliance to End Childhood Lead Poisoning (Washington, DC: Alliance to End Childhood Lead Poisoning, October 1991), p. A-2.

14. See *Matthews and People United for a Better Oakland v. Coye,* United States District Court, N. D. California. No. C 90 3620 EFL, 1991.

15. Bill Lann Lee, "Environmental Litigation on Behalf of Poor, Minority Children, Matthews v. Coye: A Case Study" (paper presented at the Annual Meeting of the American Association for the Advancement of Science, Chicago, February 9, 1992).

16. Children's Environmental Health Network, "Hot Topics: Childhood Lead Poisoning," 2003, www.nicholas.duke.edu/cehi/health/lead.htm (accessed March 3, 2005).

17. B. P. Lamphear, "Environmental Lead Exposure and Children's Intelligence at Blood Lead Concentration below 10 mg/dl" (paper presented at the American Psychiatric Association Presidential Plenary Session, Pediatric Academy Society Meeting, Baltimore, MD, April 30, 2001).

18. Centers for Disease Control and Prevention, *Second National Report on Human Exposure to Environmental Chemicals* (Atlanta: CDC, January 31, 2003), www.cdc.gov/exposurereport/ (accessed January 31, 2003).

19. Environmental Justice and Health Union, "Environmental Exposure and Racial Disparities," August 2003, www.ejhu.org/eerdexecsum.htm (accessed August 2003).

20. Hugh McDiarmid Jr. and Dan Shine, "State Slow to Act on Lead Paint Threat," *Detroit Free Press,* January 24, 2003.

21. Alliance for Healthy Homes, "Government Lawsuits against the Lead Industry," July 2004, www.afhh.org/aa/aa_legal_remedies_lawsuits.htm (accessed July 2004).

22. Saundra Torry, "Lead Paint: The Next Big Legal Target," *Washington Post,* Thursday, June 10, 1999, p. A1.

23. Carolyn Raffensperger and Joel Tickner, *Protecting Public Health and the Environment: Implementing the Precautionary Principle* (Washington, DC: Island Press, 1999).

24. Ruth Rosen, "Better Safe Than Sorry: SF Precautionary Principle Ordinance," *San Francisco Chronicle,* June 19, 2003.

25. Robert D. Bullard, "Unequal Environmental Protection: Incorporating Environmental Justice in Decision Making," in *Worst Things First? The Debate over Risk-Based National Environmental Priorities,* ed. Adam M. Finkel and Dominic Golding, Washington, DC: Resources for the Future, 1994), pp. 237–66.

26. Ibid.

27. Paul Mohai and Bunyan Bryant, "Race, Poverty, and the Environment," *EPA Journal* 18 (March–April 1992): 1–8; R. D. Bullard, "In Our Backyards," *EPA Journal* 18 (March–April 1993): 11–12; D. R. Wernette and L. A. Nieves, "Breathing Polluted Air," *EPA Journal* 18 (March–April 1992): 16–17; Patrick C. West, "Health Concerns for Fish-Eating Tribes?" *EPA Journal* 18 (March–April 1992): 15–16.

28. Marianne Lavelle and Marcia Coyle, "Unequal Protection," *National Law Journal* (September 21, 1992): S1–S2.

29. Luke W. Cole and Sheila R. Foster, *From the Ground Up: Environmental Racism and the Rise of the Environmental Justice Movement* (New York: New York University Press, 2001); Laura Westra, Bill E. Lawson, and Peter S. Wenz, *Faces of Environmental Racism: Confronting Issues of Global Justice,* 2nd ed. (Lanham, MD: Rowan and Littlefield, 2001).

30. See Robert D. Bullard, ed., *Confronting Environmental Racism: Voices from the Grassroots* (Boston: South End, 1993); Robert D. Bullard, "The Threat of Environmental Racism," *Natural Resources and Environment* 7 (Winter 1993): 23–26; Bunyan Bryant and Paul Mohai, eds., *Race and the Incidence of Environmental Hazards* (Boulder, CO: Westview Press, 1992); Regina Austin and Michael Schill, "Black, Brown, Poor, and Poisoned: Minority Grassroots Environmentalism and the Quest for Eco-Justice," *Kansas Journal of Law and Public Policy* 1 (1991): 69–82; Kelly C. Colquette and Elizabeth A. Henry Robertson, "Environmental Racism: The Causes, Consequences, and Commendations," *Tulane Environmental Law Journal* 5 (1991): 153–207; Rachel D. Godsil, "Remedying Environmental Racism," *Michigan Law Review* 90 (1991): 394–427.

31. Devon Peña, *The Terror of the Machine: Technology, Work, Gender, and Ecology on the U.S.-Mexico Border* (Austin: University of Texas Press, 1997); Davis Naguib Pellow, *Garbage Wars: The Struggle for Environmental Justice in Chicago* (Cambridge: MIT Press, 2002); Ike Okonta and Oronto Douglas, *Where Vultures Feast: Shell, Human Rights, and Oil* (New York: Verso, 2003); Mario Murillo, *Island of Resistance: Vieques, Puerto Rico, and U.S. Policy* (New York: Seven Stories Press, 2001).

32. See Robert D. Bullard, *Unequal Protection: Environmental Justice and Communities of Color* (San Francisco: Sierra Club Books, 1994).

33. Charles M. Haar and Jerold S. Kayden, eds., *Zoning and the American Dream: Promises Still to Keep* (Chicago: American Planning Association, 1999).

34. National Academy of Public Administration, *Addressing Community Concerns: How Environmental Justice Relates to Land Use Planning and Zoning* (Washington, DC: NAPA, July 2003), p. 50.

35. Juliana Maantay, "Zoning Law, Health, and Environmental Justice: What's the Connection?" *Journal of Law, Medicine, and Ethics* 30, no. 4 (Winter 2002): 572.

36. Yale Rabin, "Expulsive Zoning: The Inequitable Legacy of Euclid," in *Zoning and the American Dream: Promises Still to Keep*, ed. Charles M. Haar and Jerold S. Kayden (Chicago: American Planning Association, 1999), pp. 106–8.

37. Ibid., p. 25.

38. See Manuel Pastor Jr., Jim Sadd, and John Hipp, "Which Came First? Toxic Facilities, Minority Move-In, and Environmental Justice," *Journal of Urban Affairs* 23, no. 1 (2001): 3; see also Daniel R. Faber and Eric J. Krieg, *Unequal Exposure to Ecological Hazards: Environmental Justice in the Commonwealth of Massachusetts* (Boston: Northeastern University, 2001).

39. Joe R. Feagin, *Racist America: Roots, Current Realities, and Future Reparations* (New York: Routledge, 2001).

40. Laura M. Padilla, "But You're a Dirty Mexican: Internalized Oppression, Latinos, and Law," *Texas Hispanic Journal of Law and Policy* 7 (Fall 2001): 61–113.

41. See National League of Cities, *Promoting Racial Justice: A Workbook for Cities* (Washington, DC: National League of Cities, 2002), www.nlc.org/nlc_org/ site/files/reports/cprj.pdf (accessed July 1, 2004).

42. See R. D. Bullard and Joe R. Feagin, "Racism and the City," in *Urban Life in Transition*, ed. M. Gottdiener and C. V. Pickvance (Newbury Park, CA: Sage), pp. 55–76; Robert D. Bullard, "Dismantling Environmental Racism in the USA," *Local Environment* 4 (1999): 5–19.

43. See W. J. Kruvant, "People, Energy, and Pollution," in *The American Energy Consumer*, ed. D. K. Newman and Dawn Day (Cambridge, MA: Ballinger, 1975), pp. 125–67; Robert D. Bullard, "Solid Waste Sites and the Black Houston Community," *Sociological Inquiry* 53 (Spring 1983): 273–88; United Church of Christ Commission for Racial Justice, *Toxic Wastes and Race in the United States;* Dick Russell, "Environmental Racism," *Amicus Journal* 11 (Spring 1989): 22–32; Eric Mann, *L.A.'s Lethal Air: New Strategies for Policy, Organizing, and Action* (Los Angeles: Labor/Community Strategy Center, 1991); D. R. Wernette and L. A. Nieves, "Breathing Polluted Air: Minorities Are Disproportionately Exposed," *EPA Journal* 18 (March–April 1992): 16–17; Bryant and Mohai, *Race and the Incidence of Environmental Hazards;* Benjamin Goldman and Laura J. Fitton, *Toxic Wastes and Race Revisited* (Washington, DC: Center for Policy Alternatives, NAACP, and United Church of Christ), 1994.

44. On consumption of contaminated fish, see Patrick C. West, J. Mark Fly, and Robert Marans, "Minority Anglers and Toxic Fish Consumption: Evidence from a State-Wide Survey in Michigan," in *Race and the Incidence of Environmental Hazards*, ed. Bunyan Bryant and Paul Mohai (Boulder, CO: Westview Press, 1992), pp. 100–13. On the siting of municipal landfills and incinerators, see Robert D. Bullard, "Solid Waste Sites and the Black Houston Community," *Sociological Inquiry* 53 (Spring 1983): 273–88; Robert D. Bullard, *Invisible Houston: The Black Experience in Boom and Bust* (College Station: Texas A & M University Press, 1987), chap. 6; Robert D. Bullard, "Environmental Racism and Land Use," *Land Use Forum: A Journal of Law, Policy, and Practice* 2 (Spring 1993): 6–11. On toxic waste dumps, see United Church of Christ Commission for Racial Justice, *Toxic Wastes and Race;* Paul Mohai and Bunyan Bryant, "Environmental Racism: Reviewing the Evidence," in *Race and the*

Incidence of Environmental Hazards, ed. Bryant and Mohai (Boulder, CO: Westview Press, 1992); Paul Stretesky and Michael J. Hogan, "Environmental Justice: An Analysis of Superfund Sites in Florida," *Social Problems* 45 (May 1998): 268–87. On toxic schools, see Center for Health and Environmental Justice, *Poisoned Schools: Invisible Threats, Visible Actions* (Falls Church, VA: Child Proofing Our Communities—Poisoned School Campaign, Center for Health, Environment and Justice, March 2001), www.childproofing.org/mapindex.html (accessed March 2001). On toxic housing, see "Study: Public Housing Is Too Often Located Near Toxic Sites," *Dallas Morning News,* October 3, 2000, www.cnn.com/2000/NATURE/10/03/toxicneighbors.ap (accessed October 3, 2000). On toxic air releases, see J. Sadd and M. Pastor, "Every Breath You Take . . . : The Demographics of Toxic Air Releases in Southern California," *Economic Development Quarterly* 13 (1999): 107–23.

45. Dee R. Wernette and Leslie A. Nieves, "Breathing Polluted Air: Minorities Are Disproportionately Exposed," *EPA Journal* 18 (March–April 1992): 16–17.

46. American Lung Association, "Fact Sheet: Children and Air Pollution," September 2000, www.lungusa.org/air/children_factsheet99.html (accessed December 1, 2002).

47. R. McConnell, K. Berhane, F. Gilliland, S. J. London, T. Islam, W. J. Gauderman, E. Avol, H. G., Margolis, and J. M. Peters, "Asthma in Exercising Children Exposed to Ozone: A Cohort Study," *Lancet* 359 (2002): 386–91.

48. U.S. Environmental Protection Agency, Office of Air Quality Planning and Standards, *Review of National Ambient Air Quality Standards for Ozone: Assessment of Scientific and Technical Information,* OAQPS Staff Paper, EPA-452/R-96-007 (Research Triangle Park, NC: Office of Air Quality Planning and Standards, June 1996); H. Ozkaynk, J. D. Spengler, M. O'Neil, J. Xue, H. Zhou, K. Gilbert, and S. Ramstrom. "Ambient Ozone Exposure and Emergency Hospital Admissions and Emergency Room Visits for Respiratory Problems in Thirteen U.S. Cities," in *Breathless: Air Pollution and Hospital Admissions/Emergency Room Visits in 13 Cities,* ed. American Lung Association (Washington, DC: American Lung Association, 1996); American Lung Association, *Out of Breath: Populations-at-Risk to Alternative Ozone Levels* (Washington, DC: American Lung Association, 1995).

49. U.S. Environmental Protection Agency, National Center for Environmental Assessment, "Health Assessment Document for Diesel Exhaust," EPA/600/8-90/057E (Washington, DC: September 2002); Health Effects Institute, *Diesel Exhaust: A Critical Analysis of Emissions, Exposure, and Health Effects* (Cambridge, MA: Health Effects Institute, 1995).

50. State and Territorial Air Pollution Program Administrators and the Association of Local Air Pollution Control Officials, *Cancer Risk from Diesel Particulate: National and Metropolitan Area Estimates for the United States* (Washington, DC: State and Territorial Air Pollution Program Administrators and the Association of Local Air Pollution Control Officials, March 2000).

51. Prakash, S. "Breathe at Your Own Risk: Dirty Diesels, Environmental Health, and Justice" (paper commissioned for the Second National People of Color Environmental Leadership Summit, Washington, DC, October 23, 2002).

52. P. L. Kinney, M. Aggarwal, M. E. Northridge, N. A. H. Janssen, and

P. Shepard, "Airborne Concentrations of PM 2.5 and Diesel Exhaust Particles on Harlem Sidewalks: A Community-Based Pilot Study," *Environmental Health Perspectives* 108, no. 3 (March 2000): 213–8.

53. P. van Vliet, M. Knape, J. de Hartog, N. Janssen, H. Harssema, and B. Brunekreef, "Motor Vehicle Exhaust and Chronic Respiratory Symptoms in Children Living near Freeways," *Environmental Research* 74, no. 2 (1997): 122–32.

54. A. E. Pribitkin, "The Need for Revision of Ozone Standards: Why Has the EPA Failed to Respond?" *Temple Environmental Law and Technology Journal* 13 (1994): 104.

55. President's Task Force on Environmental Health Risks and Safety Risks to Children, "Asthma and the Environment: A Strategy to Protect Children" (Washington, DC: President's Task Force on Environmental Health Risks and Safety Risks to Children, 2000), www.epa.gov/children/whatwe/fin.pdf (accessed December 10, 2002).

56. D. Bollier, *How Smart Growth Can Stop Sprawl: A Briefing Guide for Funders* (Washington, DC: Essential Books, 1998).

57. Centers for Disease Control and Prevention, "Asthma Prevalence, Health Care Use and Mortality, 2000–2001," www.cdc.gov/nchs/products/pubs/pubd/hestats/asthma/asthma.htm (accessed September 19, 2004).

58. U.S. Commission on Civil Rights, *Not in My Backyard: Executive Order 12898 and Title VI as Tools for Achieving Environmental Justice* (Washington, DC: U.S. Commission on Civil Rights, 2003), p. 27.

59. U.S. Environmental Protection Agency, Office of Inspector General, *EPA Needs to Consistently Implement the Intent of the Executive Order on Environmental Justice,* Report no. 2004-P-00007 (Washington, DC: Office of Inspector General, March 1, 2004).

60. U.S. Commission on Civil Rights, *Not in My Backyard*, p. 75.

61. Ibid., p. 40.

62. Julie H. Hurwitz and E. Quita Sullivan, "Using Civil Rights Laws to Challenge Environmental Racism: From *Bean* to *Guardians* to *Chester* to *Sandoval*," *Journal of Law and Society* 2 (Winter 2001): 55–57.

63. Marty Hair, "Plant Turns Infested Ash Trees into Electric Power," *Detroit Free Press,* December 16, 2002.

64. Wade Rawlins, "Dump's Days Fade," *News and Observer,* November 11, 2003, p. 1, www.ncwarn.org/media/Related%20News%20Articles/art-11-11-03DumpsDaysFade.htm (accessed December 1, 2004).

65. Thomas C. Ricketts and David L. Pope, "Demography and Health Care in Eastern North Carolina," *North Carolina Medical Journal* 62 (January 2002): S20–25.

66. Mike McLaughlin, "Center Says Eastern North Carolina Lags the State on Infrastructure, Human Needs," North Carolina Center for Public Policy news release, n.d., www.nccppr.org/easternnc2.html (accessed September 8, 2004).

67. Ricketts and Pope, "Demography and Health Care in Eastern North Carolina," p. 21.

68. U.S. Environmental Protection Agency, Office of Inspector General, *EPA*

Needs to Consistently Implement the Intent of the Executive Order on Environmental Justice.

69. Ibid., p. 1.

CHAPTER 2. NEIGHBORHOODS "ZONED" FOR GARBAGE

1. Much of the analysis presented in this chapter is based on firsthand accounts I gleaned from personal interviews, written court testimony, and reports prepared over the past two decades. In particular, I collected information while serving as an expert witness on the lawsuit *Bean v. Southwestern Waste Management Corp.,* and as a researcher on the case while employed as an untenured assistant professor at Texas Southern University.

2. Henry Allen Bullock, *Pathways to the Houston Negro Market* (Ann Arbor, MI: J. N. Edwards, 1957), pp. 60–61.

3. Robert D. Bullard, *Invisible Houston: The Black Experience in Boom and Bust* (College Station: Texas A & M University Press, 1987), pp. 14–31.

4. Ibid.

5. Ibid., pp. 60–75.

6. Ruth Rosen, "Who Gets Polluted: The Movement for Environmental Justice," *Dissent* (Spring 1994): 223–30; R. D. Bullard, "Environmental Justice: It's More Than Waste Facility Siting," *Social Science Quarterly* 77 (September 1996): 493–99.

7. Diane Takvorian, "Toxics and Neighborhoods Don't Mix," *Land Use Forum: A Journal of Law, Policy, and Practice* 2 (Winter 1993): 28–31; R. D. Bullard, "Examining the Evidence of Environmental Racism," *Land Use Forum: A Journal of Law, Policy, and Practice* 2 (Winter 1993): 6–11.

8. See Robert D. Bullard, "Endangered Environs: The Price of Unplanned Growth in Boomtown Houston," *California Sociologist* 7 (Summer 1984): 84–102; Richard Babcock, "Houston Unzoned, Unfettered, and Mostly Unrepentant," *Planning* 48 (1982): 21–23; Joe R. Feagin, "The Global Context of Metropolitan Growth: Houston and the Oil Industry," *American Journal of Sociology* 90 (May 1985): 1204–30.

9. Robert D. Bullard, "Solid Waste Sites and the Black Houston Community," *Sociological Inquiry* 53 (Spring 1983): 273–88.

10. "Council Awards Garbage Transfer Station Contract," *Houston Chronicle,* March 3, 1983.

11. Mike Snyder, "Neglected Neighborhoods: Hasty Annexations Left a Legacy of Blighted Neighborhoods," *Houston Chronicle,* November 19, 2002.

12. Kristen Mack, "Acres Homes as Impoverished Today as It Was 10 Years Ago," *Houston Chronicle,* November 19, 2002.

13. Robert D. Bullard, J. Eugene Grigby II, and Charles Lee, *Residential Apartheid: The American Legacy* (Los Angeles: UCLA Center for African American Studies Publication, 1984).

14. National Advisory Commission on Civil Disorders, *Report of the National Advisory Commission on Civil Disorders* (New York: E. P. Dutton, 1968), pp. 40–41.

15. Lori Rodriguez, "Dump Plan Would Hurt Area, Residents Tell Court," *Houston Chronicle*, November 16, 1979.

16. Patricia Reaux, quoted in ibid.

17. For a more detailed account of this dispute, see Bullard, *Invisible Houston*, chap. 6; *Houston Chronicle*, November 8, 11, 15, 22, 1979, December 15, 22, 1979, June 19, 1980; *Houston Post*, December 15, 1981.

18. Lori Rodriguez, "School Superintendent Testifies: Racial Reason Claimed in Dump Site Selection," *Houston Chronicle*, November 22, 1979.

19. Ibid.

20. "Judge Denies Request to Halt Dump Opening," *Houston Chronicle*, December 22, 1979.

21. Ibid.

22. Robert D. Bullard, eyewitness account of court hearing, Houston, Texas, 1984. Judge Singleton continued to refer to blacks as "nigras" even after it was pointed out that the term was seen as derogatory toward blacks.

23. Raul Reyes, "Council Resolution Condemns Sanitary Landfill Site," *Houston Chronicle*, June 19, 1980, p. 11.

24. Jim Barlow, "Sen. Ogg Explains His Role in Landfill Permit Controversy," *Houston Chronicle*, April 23, 1982, p. 6.

25. Memorandum, "Statement of Charges," from Ed Shannon to Image Transition, Houston, Texas, September 30, 1980; memorandum from Charles A. Moore of Image Transition to James B. Mattley, Regional Vice President, Southwest Region, Browning Ferris Industries, October 20, 1980.

26. Memorandum, "Re List of Northside Residents/Browning-Ferris Situation," from Ed Shannon to Dr. Charles Moore, Image Transition, Houston, Texas, October 8, 1980.

CHAPTER 3. WOMEN WARRIORS OF COLOR ON THE FRONT LINE

1. See the Environmental Justice Resource Center's Web site for a listing of heroes and "sheroes" in the environmental justice movement, www.ejrc.cau.edu/ (accessed April 19, 2004).

2. See Robert D. Bullard, "Crowning Women of Color: The Real Story behind the EJ Summit II," December 31, 2002, Environmental Justice Resource Center, www.ejrc.cau.edu/.

3. See "Crowning Women: Honoring Women in the Environmental Justice Movement," November 12, 2002, Environmental Justice Resource Center, www .ejrc.cau.edu/SummCrowning01.html (accessed September 7, 2004).

4. For a comprehensive profile of "voices from the grassroots," see Robert D. Bullard, *People of Color Environmental Groups Directory*, 2000 (Flint, MI: C. S. Mott Foundation, 2000).

5. Dana Alston, *We Speak for Ourselves: Social Justice, Race, and Environment* (Washington, DC: Panos Institute, 1990).

6. Michael Satchel, "A Black and Green Issue Moves People," *U.S. News and World Report Online*, April 21, 1997, http://faculty.maxwell.syr.edu/spencer/images/21just.htm (accessed October 5, 2004).

7. "Superfund Homes Set for Demolition," *Pensacola News Journal*,

November 30, 2003, p. 1, www.pensacolanewsjournal.com/news/113003/Local/ ST009.shtml# (accessed September 7, 2004).

8. Charles Lee, *From Plantations to Plants: Report of the Emergency National Commission on Environmental and Economic justice in St. James Parish, Louisiana* (Cleveland: United Church of Christ Commission for Racial Justice, September 15, 1998).

9. U.S. Environmental Protection Agency, *Toxic Release Inventory 2002* (Washington, DC: U.S. EPA, 2004), www.epa.gov/triexplorer/geography.htm.

10. Gail Small, paraphrased from Bob Strickland and Ray King, "A Breath of Fresh Air: Surrounded by a Massive Industrial Buildup, the Northern Cheyenne Tribe Defends Its Homeland," *High Country News* 35, no. 1 (January 20, 2003): 7, www.hcn.org/servlets/hcn.PrintableArticle?article_id =13658 (accessed September 7, 2004).

11. The Sweet Valley–Cobb Town neighborhood in Anniston typified the chemical assault on poor communities. The neighborhood was largely a low-income, black community that had been poisoned by Solutia, a spin-off of the giant Monsanto Company, which manufactures chemicals. Community residents fought back. The Sweet Valley–Cobb Town residents organized themselves into a task force and filed a class action lawsuit against Monsanto for contaminating their community with polychlorinated biphenyls (PCBs). Monsanto manufactured PCBs from 1927 through 1972 for use as insulation in electrical equipment, including transformers. The EPA banned PCB production in the late 1970s amid questions of health risks.

12. In April 2001, a group of fifteen hundred Sweet Valley–Cobb Town plaintiffs reached a $42.8-million out-of-court settlement with Monsanto in the federal District Court of the Northern District of Alabama. There is little doubt that the community was determined to get justice in their fight against Monsanto.

13. The groundbreaking work of Cassandra Roberts and her neighbors set the stage for the 2003 settlement, in which the Monsanto Company, Solutia, and the Pharmacia Corporation agreed to pay $700 million to twenty thousand Anniston plaintiffs damaged by PCB contamination. "Anniston PCB Cases Settle for $700M," *Birmingham Business Journal,* August 20, 2003, www.bizjournals.com/ birmingham/stories/2003/08/18/daily24.html (accessed September 7, 2004).

14. Goldman Environmental Prize, "Margie Eugene-Richard: Growing Up in Cancer Alley," press release, April 19, 2004, www.goldmanprize.org/recipients/ recipientProfile.cfm?recipientID=131 (accessed October 5, 2004).

15. Ibid.

16. This passage draws on the oral testimony given by Margie Richard at the United Nations Human Rights Commission in Geneva, Switzerland, June 2000.

17. Celene Krauss, "Women of Color on the Front Line," in *Unequal Protection: Environmental Justice and Communities of Color,* ed. Robert D. Bullard (San Francisco: Sierra Club Books, 1996).

CHAPTER 4. LIVING AND DYING IN LOUISIANA'S "CANCER ALLEY"

1. Robert D. Bullard, *In Search of the New South: The Black Urban Experience in the 1970's and 1980's* (Tuscaloosa: University of Alabama Press, 1991), chap. 1.

2. Donald Schueler, "Southern Exposure," *Sierra* 77 (November–December, 1992): 45.

3. Robert D. Bullard, *Dumping in Dixie: Race, Class, and Environmental Quality* (Boulder, CO: Westview, 2000), chap. 1.

4. Ibid.

5. Schueler, "Southern Exposure," p. 46.

6. Ibid., pp. 46–47.

7. "Ex-La. Chief Guilty in Casino Case: Edwin Edwards and His Son Are Convicted of Racketeering and Conspiracy Related to the Awarding of Licenses," *St. Petersburg Times,* May 10, 2000, www.sptimes.com/News/051000/news_pf/Worldandnation/Ex_La_chief_guilty_in.shtml (accessed October 10, 2004).

8. U.S. Bureau of the Census, *Income, Poverty, and Health Insurance Coverage in the United States, 2003,* Census Report P60-226 (Washington, DC: U.S. Government Printing Office, August 2004).

9. See Thomas Esterbrook, "Clean Production in Louisiana" (paper produced for the Conference on Clean and Just Production, Xavier University, New Orleans, September 23–25, 2004).

10. Nikki D. Thanos, "Economic Development, Corporate Accountability, and the Environment: Comparative Case Studies from Costa Rica and Louisiana" (B.A. thesis, Tulane University, New Orleans, May 9, 2000), www.tulane.edu/~eaffairs/thanos.html (accessed June 2000).

11. Louisiana Department of Economic Development, "Louisiana Overview: Petroleum Refining," November 2000, www.lded.state.la.us/overview/ (accessed March 15, 2005.

12. Thanos, "Economic Development, Corporate Accountability, and the Environment."

13. Ibid., p. 19.

14. James O' Byrne and Mark Schleifstein, "Dumping Ground: State a Final Stop for Nation's Toxic Waste," *New Orleans Times-Picayune,* March 26, 1991.

15. Z. Nauth and the Louisiana Coalition for Tax Justice, *The Great Louisiana Tax Giveaway* (Baton Rouge: Louisiana Coalition, 1990).

16. Thanos, "Economic Development, Corporate Accountability, and the Environment," p. 21.

17. Louisiana Association of Business, "About LABI," www.labi.org/custompage.cfm?pageid=2 (accessed March 15, 2005).

18. Donald L. Barlett and James B. Steele, with reporting by Laura Karmatz and Aisha Labi, "Special Report: Corporate Welfare," *Time* 152 (November 9, 1998): 9.

19. Paul H. Templet, Defending the Public Domain: Pollution, Subsidies, and Poverty, Political Economy Research Institute Working Paper no. DPE-01-03 (Amherst: University of Massachusetts, Political Economy Research Institute, 2001), p. 6, www.umass.edu/peri/pdfs/WP12.pdf (accessed March 15, 2005).

20. Ernie Niemi and Paul Templet, *Building Common Ground: Business, Labor, and the Environment in Louisiana* (New Orleans: Loyola University Center for Environmental Communications, 2001), p. 34.

21. Alan Sayre, "Jobs Are Primary Concern in Louisiana," Associated Press, April 17, 2004.

22. Chris Kromm, Keith Ernst, and Jaffer Battica, *Gold and Green Report, 2000* (Durham, NC: Institute for Southern Studies, 2000), www.southernstudies .org/goldgreen2000.html.

23. U.S. Public Interest Research Group Education Fund, *Irresponsible Care: The Failure of the Chemical Industry to Protect the Public from Chemical Accidents,* April 2004, p. 20, www.pirg.org/ (accessed April 2004).

24. Jeremiah Baumann and U.S. Public Interest Research Group Education Fund, *Protecting Our Hometowns: Preventing Chemical Terrorism in America,* March 7, 2002, p. 18, www.pirg.org/ (accessed March 7, 2002).

25. For an in-depth discussion of the connection between pollution, subsidies, and poverty, see Templet, *Defending the Public Domain,* pp. 6, 13.

26. Paul H. Templet, "Energy Price Disparity and Public Welfare," *Ecological Economics* 36 (2000): 443–60.

27. U.S. Environmental Protection Agency, *Toxic Release Inventory,* 2002, www.epa.gov/triexplorer/geography.htm; Right to Know Network, *Toxic Release Inventory,* 2002 database, www.rtknet.org/tri/ (accessed March 15, 2005).

28. U.S. Environmental Protection Agency, "Toxic Release Inventory State Fact Sheets," 1997, www.epa.gov/tri/tridata/tri97/fact/index.htm.

29. See Beverly H. Wright, D. Sarpong, and A. Babafemi, *The Socioeconomic Impact of Air Toxics on Disproportionately Exposed Communities* (New Orleans: Deep South Center for Environmental Justice, Xavier University, 2001).

30. J. M. Blers, "Shell Norco Toxic Neighbors," *New Orleans Times-Picayune,* June 21, 1999.

31. Environmental Defense Fund, *Pollution Prevention Performance Rankings among Oil Refinery Facilities* (New York: EDF, 1999).

32. Goldman Environmental Prize, "Margie Eugene Richard: Growing Up in Cancer Alley," press release, April 19, 2004, www.goldmanprize.org/recipients/ recipientProfile.cfm?recipientID=131 (accessed October 5, 2004).

33. See Steve Lerner, *Diamond: A Struggle for Environmental Justice in Louisiana's Chemical Corridor* (Cambridge: MIT Press, 2004).

34. M. Swerczek, "Shell Offers Buyout for All of Diamond," *New Orleans Times-Picayune,* June 11, 2002.

35. For an in-depth analysis of the history and events surrounding the relocation struggle in Norco's Diamond Community, see Lerner, *Diamond.*

36. Alicia Lyttle, "Agricultural Street Landfill Environmental Justice Case Study," University of Michigan School of Natural Resource and Environment, December 2000, www.umich.edu/~snre492/Jones/agstreet.htm (accessed October 6, 2004).

37. Beverly H. Wright, Pat Bryant, and Robert D. Bullard, "Coping with Poisons in Cancer Alley," in *Unequal Protection: Environmental Justice and Communities of Color,* ed. Robert D. Bullard (San Francisco: Sierra Club Books, 1996), pp. 110–29.

CHAPTER 5. ENVIRONMENTAL INEQUITY IN METROPOLITAN LOS ANGELES

1. See David E. Camacho, ed., *Environmental Injustices, Political Struggles: Race, Class, and the Environment* (Durham, NC: Duke University Press, 1998).

2. U.S. General Accounting Office, *Siting Hazardous Waste Landfills and Their Correlation with Racial and Economic Status of Surrounding Communities* (Gaithersburg, MD: U.S. General Accounting Office, 1983).

3. United Church of Christ, *A National Report on the Racial and Socio-Economic Characteristics of Communities with Hazardous Waste Sites* (New York: United Church of Christ Commission for Racial Justice, 1987).

4. See Douglas Anderton, Andy Anderson, et al., "Environmental Equity: The Demographics of Dumping," *Demography* 31, no. 2 (1994): 229–48; Douglas Anderton, Andy Anderson, et al., "Hazardous Waste Facilities: Environmental Equity Issues in Metropolitan Areas," *Evaluation Review* 18 (1994): 123–40; William Bowen, *Environmental Justice through Research-Based Decision Making* (New York: Garland, 2001); Christopher Foreman Jr., *The Promise and Peril of Environmental Justice* (Washington, DC: Brookings Institution Press, 1998).

5. Robert Bullard, "Solid Waste Sites and the Black Community," *Sociological Inquiry* 53 (1983): 273–88; United Church of Christ, *A National Report on the Racial and Socio-Economic Characteristics of Communities with Hazardous Waste Sites;* Dee Wernett and Leslie Nieves, *Minorities and Air Quality Non-Attainment Areas: A Preliminary Geo-Demographics Analysis* (Baltimore, MD: U.S. Department of Energy, 1991); Bunyan Bryant and Paul Mohai, "Environmental Racism: Reviewing the Evidence" (paper presented at the University of Michigan Law Symposium on Race, Poverty, and the Environment, Ann Arbor, January 1–20, 1992); Bunyan Bryant and Paul Mohai, eds., *Race and the Incidence of Environmental Hazards* (Boulder, CO: Westview Press, 1992), 163–76; Mariane Lavelle and Marcia Coyle, "Unequal Protection," *National Law Journal* (September 21, 1992): S2; Rae Zimmerman, "Social Equity and Environmental Risk," *Risk Analysis* 13, no. 6 (1993): 649–66; William Bowen, Mark Salling, et al., "Toward Environmental Justice: Spatial Equity in Ohio and Cleveland," *Annals of the Association of American Geographers* 85, no. 4 (1995): 641–63; Theodore S. Glickman and Robert Hersh, *Evaluating Environmental Equity: The Impacts of Industrial Hazards on Selected Social Groups in Allegheny County, Pennsylvania* (Washington, DC: Resources for the Future, 1995); Michael Kraft and Denise Scheberle, "Environmental Justice and the Allocation of Risk: The Case of Lead and Public Health," *Policy Studies Journal* 23, no. 1 (1995): 113–22; Phillip Pollock and M. Elliot Vittas, "Who Bears the Burden of Environmental Pollution? Race, Ethnicity, and Environmental Equity in Florida," *Social Science Quarterly* 76, no. 2 (1995): 294–310; Laura Pulido, "A Critical Review of the Methodology of Environmental Racism Research," *Antipode* 28, no. 2 (1996): 142–59; J. Tom Boer, Manuel Pastor, et al., "Is There Environmental Racism? The Demographics of Hazardous Waste in Los Angeles County," *Social Science Quarterly* 78, no. 4 (1997): 793–810; James Sadd, Manuel Pastor, et al., " 'Every Breath You Take . . . ': The Demographics of Toxic Air Releases in Southern California," *Economic Development Quarterly* 13, no. 2 (1999): 107–23; Rachel Morello-Frosch, Manuel Pastor, et al., "Environmental Justice and Southern California's 'Riskscape': The Distribution of Air Toxics Exposures and Health Risks among Diverse Communities," *Urban Affairs Review* 36, no. 4 (2001): 551–78.

6. Vicki Been, "Analyzing Evidence of Environmental Justice," *Journal of Land Use and Environmental Law* 11 (Fall 1995): 1–37; Andrew Szasz and Michael Meuser, "Environmental Inequalities: Literature Review and Proposals for New Directions in Research and Theory," *Current Sociology* 45, no. 3 (1997): 99–120.

7. Been, "Analyzing Evidence of Environmental Justice"; James Hamilton, "Testing for Environmental Racism: Prejudice, Profits, and Political Power?" *Journal of Policy Analysis and Management* 14, no. 1 (1995): 107–32.

8. Anderton, Anderson, et al., "Environmental Equity"; Anderton, Anderson, et al., "Hazardous Waste Facilities."

9. On the exclusion of certain areas from analysis, see Been, "Analyzing Evidence of Environmental Justice"; Robert Bullard, "Environmental Justice: It's More Than Waste Facility Siting," *Social Science Quarterly* 77, no. 3 (1996): 493–99. Some have argued that these studies were biased because they were funded by a grant from the largest waste management firm in the United States.

10. James P. Lester, David W. Allen, and Kelly M. Hill, *Environmental Injustice in the United States: Myths and Realities* (Boulder, CO: Westview Press, 2000).

11. Sadd, Pastor, et al., "Every Breath You Take . . ."

12. Bowen, Salling, et al., "Toward Environmental Justice"; Glickman and Hersh, "Evaluating Environmental Equity"; Tracy Yandle and Dudley Burton, "Reexamining Environmental Justice: A Statistical Analysis of Historical Hazardous Waste Landfill Siting Patterns in Metropolitan Texas," *Social Science Quarterly* 77 (1996): 477–92; Brett Badem and Don Coursey, *The Locality of Waste Sites within the City of Chicago: A Demographic, Social, and Economic Analysis* (Chicago: Irving B. Harris Graduate School of Public Policy Studies, University of Chicago, 1997); Evan J. Rinquist, "Equity and the Distribution of Environmental Risk: The Case of TRI Facilities," *Social Science Quarterly* 78, no. 4 (1997): 811–29.

13. Robert T. Fetter, "The Demographics of Pollution: Evidence from the EPA's Relative Risk-Based Environmental Indicators Model" (Master's thesis, Department of Resource Economics, University of Massachusetts, Amherst, 2002), p. 104.

14. On early watershed studies of environmental inequality, see Bullard, "Solid Waste Sites and the Black Community"; U.S. General Accounting Office, *Siting Hazardous Waste Landfills and Their Correlation with Racial and Economic Status of Surrounding Communities;* United Church of Christ, *A National Report on the Racial and Socio-Economic Characteristics of Communities with Hazardous Waste Sites;* Bryant and Mohai, "Environmental Racism: Reviewing the Evidence."

15. Boer, Pastor, et al., "Is There Environmental Racism?"

16. Our regression results remained consistent even when the percentages of African American and Latino residents were entered as separate variables in the regression (results not shown in the table). On land use specifically, see the argument by Laura Pulido, "Rethinking Environmental Racism: White Privilege and Urban Development in Southern California," *Annals of the Association of American Geographers* 90, no. 1 (2000).

17. Sadd, Pastor, et al., "Every Breath You Take . . ."

18. The 33/50 Program was designed to lower the emission of seventeen high-priority chemicals, most of them carcinogens. The agency's goal was a 33 percent reduction in releases and transfers of these chemicals by 1992 and a 50 percent reduction by 1995 (compared to 1988, which was the starting point, or baseline year).

19. Morello-Frosch, Pastor, et al., "Environmental Justice and Southern California's 'Riskscape.'"

20. CBE was particularly interested in having us collect local epidemiological data. On the paucity of such data, see Institute of Medicine, *Toward Environmental Justice: Research, Education, and Health Policy Needs* (Washington, DC: Committee on Environmental Justice, Health Sciences Policy Program, Health Sciences Section, Institute of Medicine, 1999).

21. U.S. Environmental Protection Agency, Interim Guidance for Investigative Title VI Complaints Challenging Permits (Washington, DC: U.S. EPA, February 1998). After a robust stakeholder-involvement process, the EPA published two draft Title VI guidance documents in the Federal Register on June 27, 2000, for public comment. The first document was the *Draft Title VI Guidance for EPA Assistance Recipients Administering Environmental Permitting Programs* ("Draft Recipient Guidance"). This document was written at the request of the states and was intended to offer suggestions to assist state and local recipients in developing approaches and activities to address potential Title VI concerns. During the comment period, the Office of Civil Rights conducted seven public listening sessions throughout the United States. The second document was the *Draft Revised Guidance for Investigating Title VI Administrative Complaints Challenging Permits* ("Draft Revised Investigation Guidance"). It describes a framework through which the Office of Civil Rights can process complaints that allege discrimination in environmental permitting. Public comments were accepted for this document through August 28, 2000.

22. On the Cumulative Exposure Project's modeling analysis, see Jane Caldwell, Tracey Woodruff, et al., "Application of Health Information to Hazardous Air Pollutants Modeled in EPA's Cumulative Exposure Project," *Toxicology and Industrial Health* 14, no. 3 (1998): 429–54; Tracey Woodruff, Daniel Axelrad, et al., "Public Health Implications of 1990 Air Toxics Concentrations across the United States," *Environmental Health Perspectives* 106, no. 5 (1998): 245–51; Arlene Rosenbaum, Daniel A. Axelrad, et al., "National Estimates of Outdoor Air Toxics Concentrations," *Journal of the Air and Waste Management Association* 49 (1999): 1138–52; Rachel Morello-Frosch, Tracey Woodruff, et al., "Air Toxics and Health Risks in California: The Public Health Implications of Outdoor Concentrations," *Risk Analysis* 20, no. 2 (2000): 273–91.

23. In 1990, Congress established a goal for the Clean Air Act: to reduce the lifetime cancer risk, so that only one person per million will develop cancer from major sources of hazardous air pollutants. The act required that, over time, EPA regulations for major sources would "provide an ample margin of safety to protect public health." Clean Air Act, sec. 112(f)(2).

24. Background concentrations are attributable to long-range transport, resuspension of historical emissions, and natural sources derived from measurements taken at clean air locations remote from known emissions sources.

25. Manuel Pastor, James Sadd, et al., "Which Came First? Toxic Facilities, Minority Move-In, and Environmental Justice," *Journal of Urban Affairs* 23, no. 1 (2001): 1–23.

26. Eric Mann, *A New Vision for Urban Transportation: The Bus Riders Union Makes History at the Intersection of Mass Transit, Civil Rights, and the Environment* (Los Angeles: Labor/Community Strategy Center, 1996); Manuel Pastor, "Common Ground at Ground Zero? The New Economy and the New Organizing in Los Angeles," *Antipode* 33, no. 2 (2001): 260–89.

27. See Jesus Sanchez, "L.A.'s Cornfield Row: How Activists Prevailed," *Los Angeles Times,* April 17, 2001.

28. Rachel A. Morello-Frosch, "Environmental Justice and California's 'Riskscape': The Distribution of Air Toxics and Associated Cancer and Non-Cancer Health Risks among Diverse Communities" (Ph.D. diss., University of California, Berkeley, 1998); James Boyce, Andrew Klemer, et al., "Power Distribution, the Environment, and Public Health: A State-Level Analysis," *Ecological Economics* 29 (1999): 127–40.

CHAPTER 6. TOXIC RACISM ON A NEW JERSEY WATERFRONT

1. The author acknowledges the residents of Camden for their brave and persistent struggle against environmental racism and injustice, especially the founders and officers of South Camden Citizens in Action: Bonnie Sanders, Phyllis Holmes, Barbara Pfeiffer, Pauline Woods, and Rose Townsend. The author also thanks her cocounsel in the litigation on behalf of the South Camden Citizens in Action described in this chapter—Michael Churchill and Jerome Balter of the Public Interest Law Center of Philadelphia and Luke Cole of the Center on Race, Poverty, and the Environment, San Francisco—for their many and extensive contributions to the legal and advocacy work in Camden.

2. Only 7.1 percent of Camden residents are non-Hispanic whites; in contrast, in Camden County almost 70 percent of residents are non-Hispanic whites. See U.S. Census Bureau, *Demographic Profile: Camden, New Jersey,* 2000, http:// censtats.census.gov/data/NJ/1603410000.pdf.

3. See Center for Health Statistics, New Jersey Department of Health and Senior Services, "New Jersey Health Statistics, 1998," Table M43: "Infant and Fetal Mortality in Selected Municipalities" (last updated March 18, 2002), www.state.nj.us/health/chs/stats98/m43.htm (accessed November 18, 2003).

4. The EPA considers 1 in 10,000 to 1 in 1,000,000 an acceptable cancer risk. The elevated risk found here, of 1.8 in 100, grossly exceeds this standard.

5. U.S. Environmental Protection Agency, "NPL Site Narrative for Martin Aaron, Inc., Camden, New Jersey," *Federal Register,* July 22, 1999, p. 1, www.epa.gov/superfund/sites/npl/nar1559.htm (accessed March 25, 2005).

6. As of November 6, 2003, there were 1,242 sites on the EPA's National Priorities List awaiting cleanup. At one time, the EPA cleaned up over eighty sites per year. Under the Bush administration the number dropped to forty, and the pace will be even slower in the future unless more funding is appropriated.

7. New Jersey Department of Environmental Protection, *2000 Air Quality*

Report (Trenton: New Jersey Department of Environmental Protection, Bureau of Air Monitoring, January 2002), www.state.nj.us/dep/airmon/njooaqrp.pdf (accessed November 18, 2003).

8. Ibid. Camden is ranked as being in "severe non-attainment" for ozone pollution. Ozone pollution, like particulates, causes and aggravates respiratory ailments.

9. New Jersey Department of Environmental Protection, "Camden Community Joins DEP 'Bucket Brigade' to Fight Air Pollution," New Jersey Department of Environmental Protection news release, January 16, 2004, www .state.nj.us/dep/newsrel/releases/04_0002.htm (accessed October 6, 2004).

10. Ibid., p. 2.

11. Pamela Dalton, "Odor, Annoyance, and Health Symptoms in a Residential Community Exposed to Industrial Odors," (manuscript in author's possession, November 1997). Dalton is an environmental psychologist at the Monell Chemical Senses Center.

12. "From the Lab to Real Life," *Monell Connection Newsletter* (Spring 1998): 5, www.monell.org/Newsletters/Monell_Spring98.pdf (accessed November 18, 2003).

13. See U.S. Census Bureau, *American FactFinder, Census 2000:* "Quick Tables and Geographic Comparison Tables for New Jersey and Camden County," 2000, http://factfinder.census.gov/; U.S. Census Bureau, *QuickFacts,* 2000, http://quickfacts.census.gov/ (accessed November 18, 2003).

14. The lawsuit was brought on behalf of the SCCIA by Jerome Balter of the Public Interest Law Center of Philadelphia.

15. Olga Pomar, "Fighting for Air," *National Housing Institute Shelterforce Online* 126 (November–December 2002), www.nhi.org/online/issues/126/ camdenair.html (accessed November 18, 2003).

16. PM-10 is particulate matter sized 10 microns or smaller.

17. PM-2.5 is particulate matter sized 2.5 microns or smaller.

18. See Yale Rabin, "Expulsive Zoning: The Inequitable Legacy of Euclid," in *Zoning and the American Dream: Promises Still to Keep,* ed. Charles Harr and Jerold Kayden (Washington, DC: American Planning Association Press, 1989).

19. Clean Air Act, 42 U.S.C. secs. 7401 et seq. (2001); *N.J. Admin. Code* tit. 7, ch. 27 (2001).

20. The EPA has established health-based standards for six "criteria" pollutants: carbon monoxide, lead, ozone, nitrogen dioxide, sulfur dioxide, and particulates (PM-10). 40 CFR Pt. 50 (2001).

21. In 1997, after having studied extensive scientific research, the EPA issued a new, more stringent PM-2.5 standard. The standard was immediately challenged by industry groups, and although the U.S. Supreme Court upheld its validity, it has not yet been put in effect. *American Trucking Assn. v. EPA,* 175 F.3d 1027 (D.C. Cir. 1999), *modified on reh'g,* 195 F.3d 4 (D.C. Cir. 1999), *aff'd in part, rev'd in part sub nom. Whitman v. American Trucking Assn,* 531 U.S. 457 (2001).

22. New Jersey law allows a company to construct, but not to operate, a facility once the application is deemed administratively complete but before the Department of Environmental Protection issues a "permit to construct." *N.J.*

Stat. Ann. sec. 26:2C-9.2(j) (West 2001); *N.J. Admin. Code* tit. 7, sec. 27–8.24 (2001). Because the developer may not hold the department liable for any losses if the department ultimately denies the permit, construction under these terms is a "risk" for the business.

23. Title VI of the Civil Rights Act of 1964, 42 U.S.C. sec. 2000d et seq.; EPA Title VI regulations, 40 C.F.R. Part 7. Title VI prohibits discrimination by recipients of federal funding. The U.S. Supreme Court has ruled that the statute prohibits only intentional discrimination. Federal agencies, however, have enacted regulations to enforce Title VI that also prohibit unintentional discriminatory conduct—specifically, they prohibit agencies from applying seemingly race-neutral policies in a way that results in discriminatory effects. The SCCIA sought to enforce the EPA's regulations that protect communities from such "disparate impacts."

24. 42 U.S.C. sec. 3601 *et seq.*

25. *South Camden Citizens in Action v. NJ DEP,* 145 F. Supp. 2d 446 (D. NJ 2001).

26. Ibid., pp. 497–505.

27. *Alexander v. Sandoval,* 532 U.S. 275 (2001).

28. *South Camden Citizens in Action v. NJ DEP,* 145 F. Supp. 2d 446 (D. NJ 2001).

29. The value of the decision as a precedent is reflected in the number of amicus curiae briefs submitted on appeal for both sides. Major civil rights groups, including the NAACP, Puerto Rican Legal Defense Fund, and ACLU, and major environmental organizations, such as the Natural Resources Defense Council, Environmental Defense (formerly the Environmental Defense Fund), and the Sierra Club, supported the SCCIA, while industry groups, including the Chamber of Commerce, National Association of Manufacturers, and Washington Legal Fund, filed briefs on behalf of the appellants. A total of thirteen amicus briefs, signed by forty-nine different organizations and individuals, were filed.

30. *South Camden Citizens in Action v. NJ DEP,* 274 F.3d 771 (3d Cir. 2001).

31. See National Academy on Public Administration, *Models for Change: Efforts by Four States to Address Environmental Justice* (Washington, DC: National Academy on Public Administration for the U.S. Environmental Protection Agency, June, 2002).

32. Most communities affected by environmental injustice do not have free legal and technical help available to address environmental justice problems. More resources must be directed toward ensuring that groups can access lawyers and environmental experts to enable them to protect their rights in the courts. However, even when a group such as the SCCIA can find lawyers and wants to resort to a legal process, it may find that the needed legal tools are missing.

33. *Gonzaga University v. Doe,* 536 U.S., 70 USLW 4577, 122 S.Ct. 2268, is a Supreme Court decision that limits the ability of private citizens to enforce federal laws through section 1983.

34. Possible legislative remedies on the federal, state, and local levels could include amendments to the Civil Rights Act, such as a legislative "fix" to *Sandoval;* more protective environmental regulations that consider the existing health conditions of a community or the cumulative and synergistic effects of

pollutants; new permitting requirements that require greater community involvement and reflect civil rights concerns; and even zoning-type regulations like those enacted in Chester, Pennsylvania, which generally prohibit siting waste disposal facilities in residential areas.

CHAPTER 7. ANATOMY OF THE URBAN PARKS MOVEMENT

1. The work on urban parks by the Center for Law in the Public Interest is made possible in part by the generous support of the Ford, Resources Legacy Fund, David and Lucile Packard, and Surdna Foundations. Information on the center can be found at www.clipi.org/.

2. Declaration of the Rights of the Child, Proclaimed by General Assembly resolution 1386 (XIV) of 20 November 1959, Principle 7; United Nations' Convention on the Rights of the Child, General Assembly resolution 44/25 of 20 November 1989, Article 31.

3. Robert García et al., "Healthy Children, Healthy Communities: Schools, Parks, Recreation, and Sustainable Regional Planning," *Fordham Urban Law Journal* 31 (2004): 1267-90.

4. Eloisa Gonzalez, M.D., M.P.H., L.A. County Department of Public Health, testimony before the Los Angeles Unified School District Citizens' School Bond Oversight Committee, January 21, 2004. See also Jennifer Radcliffe, "Going to War against Epidemic of Childhood Obesity," *Daily News*, January 27, 2004, p. 1; "The Schools Go Flabby," *Los Angeles Times*, May 22, 2004, p. B18.

5. U.S. Department of Health and Human Services, www.surgeongeneral.gov/topics/obesity/calltoaction/fact_glance.htm (accessed March 25, 2005).

6. California Department of Education, "State Schools Chief O'Connell Announces California Kids' 2002 Physical Fitness Results," press release, January 28, 2003.

7. Ibid.

8. Cara Mia DiMassa, "Campus Crowding Can Make P.E. a Challenge," *Los Angeles Times*, November 19, 2003, p. B2.

9. California Center for Public Health Advocacy, *An Epidemic: Overweight and Unfit Children in California Assembly Districts*, December 2002, www.publichealthadvocacy.org/policy_briefs/study_documents/Full_Report.pdf.

10. Ibid., p. 18.

11. Gold Coast Collaborative, "A Health Crisis in Paradise," September 2003, www.sbcphd.org/documents/nutrition/PolicyBrief8-1-03.pdf (accessed March 18, 2005).

12. Richard J. Jackson and Chris Kochtitzky, *Creating a Healthy Environment: The Impact of the Built Environment on Public Health*, Sprawl Watch Clearinghouse Monograph Series, Public Health/Land Use Monograph, www.sprawlwatch.org/health.pdf (accessed March 18, 2005).

13. Allison L. Diamant, Susan H. Babey, E. Richard Brown, and Neetu Chawla, *Diabetes in California: Findings from the 2001 California Health Interview Survey* 54 (Los Angeles: UCLA Center for Health Policy Research, April 2003).

14. Russell R. Pate et al., "Sports Participation and Health-Related Behaviors

among U.S. Youth," *Archives of Pediatrics and Adolescent Medicine* (September 2000).

15. Anastasia Loukaitou-Sideris and Orit Stieglitz, "Children in Los Angeles Parks: A Study of Equity, Quality, and Children's Satisfaction with Neighborhood Parks," *Town Planning Review* 73, no. 4 (2002): 1–6.

16. See Peter Harnak, *Inside City Parks* (Washington, DC: Urban Land Institute, 2000).

17. See Steve Lerner and William Poole, *The Economic Benefits of Parks and Open Space* (Washington, DC: Trust for Public Land, 1999), pp. 12, 13, 17, 20, 26.

18. Letter from Frederick Law Olmsted to the Board of Commissioners of Central Park, May 31, 1858, quoted in Witold Rybczynski, *A Clearing in the Distance* (New York: Simon and Schuster, 1999), p. 177.

19. Anastasia Loukaitou-Sideris, "Urban Form and Social Context: Cultural Differentiation in the Uses of Urban Parks," *Journal of Planning and Education Research* 14 (1995): 89–102.

20. Juan Gonzalez, *Harvest of Empire: A History of Latinos in America* (New York: Viking, 2000): 142, 145.

21. *Brown v. Board of Education,* 347 U.S. 483 (1954).

22. Professor Lakoff identifies from a cognitive perspective six types of progressives with shared values: (1) socioeconomic: all issues are a matter of money and class, (2) identity politics: our group deserves its share now, (3) environmentalists: we must have respect for the earth for a healthy future, (4) civil libertarians: freedoms are threatened and have to be protected, (5) spiritual progressives: religion and spirituality nurture us and are central to a fulfilling life, and (6) antiauthoritarians: we have to fight the illegitimate use of authority. See George Lakoff, *Don't Think of an Elephant! Know Your Values and Frame the Debate* (White River Junction, VT: Chelsea Green, 2004); George Lakoff, *Moral Politics: How Liberals and Conservatives Think* (Chicago: University of Chicago Press, 2002).

23. Los Angeles Almanac, "City of Los Angeles Population by Community and Race, 2000 Census," www.losangelesalmanac.com/topics/Population/po24la.htm (accessed March 18, 2005).

24. Los Angeles Almanac, "Parks of the City of Los Angeles," www.losangelesalmanac.com/topics/Parks/pa12.htm (accessed 2004).

25. The center's report *Green Access Guide to Parks and Schools*—which uses geographic information systems mapping and 2000 census data—will be available at www.clipi.org/ (forthcoming, 2005).

26. Robert García et al., *The Cornfield and the Flow of History: People, Place, and Culture* (Los Angeles: Center for Law in the Public Interest, 2004), available at www.clipi.org/; Josh Sides, *L.A. City Limits: African American Los Angeles from the Great Depression to the Present* (Berkeley: University of California Press, 2003), pp. 95–130; Mike Davis, *City of Quartz* (New York: Vintage Books, 1990), pp. 160–64; Mike Davis, *Ecology of Fear* (New York: Metropolitan Books, 1998), pp. 59–91; California Department of Parks and Recreation, *Five Views: An Ethnic Sites Survey for California* (Sacramento, 1988), 68–69, available at www.clipi.org/.

27. Sides, *L.A. City Limits,* p. 21.

28. Ibid.

29. Shirley Leung, "Riordan Seeks More Funds for Urban Core," *Wall Street Journal*, April 28, 1999.

30. Jocelyn Stewart, "Officials Resort to Creativity to Meet Need for Parks," *Los Angeles Times*, June 15, 1998.

31. Jennifer Wolch, John P. Wilson, and Jed Fehrenbach, *Parks and Park Funding in Los Angeles: An Equity Mapping Analysis* (Los Angeles: University of Southern California, May 2002), www.usc.edu/dept/geography/ESPE/documents/publications_parks.pdf.

32. Mark Baldasare, *Public Policy Institute of California Statewide Survey: Special Survey on Californians and the Environment* (San Francisco: PPIC, June 2002), p. vi.

33. Stewart, "Officials Resort to Creativity to Meet Need for Parks"; Stewart analyzes the number of acres of parks in city council districts based on 1990 census data.

34. Community Conservancy International, memorandum (based on 1990 census data), in the authors' possession.

35. "How Propositions 40 and 45 Fared among Voters," *Los Angeles Times*, March 7, 2002 (statewide exit poll).

36. Chapter coauthor Robert García served on the executive committee for the Yes on Prop 40 campaign.

37. Olmsted Brothers and Bartholomew and Associates, *Parks, Playgrounds, and Beaches for the Los Angeles Region* 1 ("the Olmsted Report") (1930), reprinted in Greg Hise and William Deverell, *Eden by Design* (Berkeley: University of California Press, 2000). The report recognized the need to incorporate the Angeles National Forest, the San Gabriel and San Bernardino mountains, and other outlying areas, including Catalina Island, to serve the recreation and open space needs of Los Angeles County. Olmsted Report, pp. 85–88, 92, 93. The Center for Law in the Public Interest has a digital edition of the Olmsted vision available at www.clipi.org/.

38. Olmsted Report, pp. 17, 37–43, 100–102, 138.

39. See Hise and Deverell, *Eden by Design,* pp. 7–56; Davis, *Ecology of Fear,* pp. 59–91. In contrast, in 2003, Seattle, Washington, and Portland, Oregon, celebrated the centennial of the implementation of their own Olmsted plans. See www.ci.seattle.wa.us/friendsofolmstedparks/home.htm/; web.pdx.edu/~poracskj/OlmstedConf_JP.html (accessed March 18, 2005).

40. Juan Crespí, *A Description of Distant Roads,* revised journals, entry for August 2, 1769, quoted in Blake Gumprecht, *The Los Angeles River: Its Life, Death, and Possible Rebirth* (1999), p. 38. See also the map of agricultural lands of Los Angeles in 1849, p. 59.

41. The population of California is 32 percent Latino, 10 percent Asian, 47 percent non-Hispanic white, and 6 percent African American. The population of Los Angeles County is 45 percent Latino, 12 percent Asian, 31 percent non-Hispanic white, and 10 percent African American. Source: Greeninfo Network using 2000 census data (in the authors' possession).

42. Ibid.

43. Jesus Sanchez, "L.A.'s Cornfield Row: How Activists Prevailed," *Los Angeles Times*, April 17, 2001, p. A1.

44. Ibid.

45. Ibid.

46. García et al., *The Cornfield and the Flow of History*.

47. Gumprecht, *The Los Angeles River*, pp. 44–63; Dolores Hayden, *The Power of Place: Urban Landscapes as Public History* (Cambridge: MIT Press, 1997), pp. 210–25.

48. William Deverell, *Whitewashed Adobe: The Rise of Los Angeles and the Remaking of Its Mexican Past* (Berkeley: University of California Press, 2004), p. 93. See generally George Hargreaves, ed., *LA River Studio Book* (Cambridge: Harvard University Graduate School of Design, Department of Landscape Architecture, 2002); Richard Sommer and Mary Margaret Jones, eds., *Supernatural Urbanism* (Cambridge: Harvard Design School, 2003); *Cornfield of Dreams: A Resource Guide of Facts, Issues, and Principles* (Los Angeles: UCLA School of Public Policy and Social Research, 2000).

49. Sanchez, "L.A.'s Cornfield Row," p. A1.

50. Ibid.

51. Ibid.

52. Letter from Office of the Secretary, U.S. Department of Housing and Urban Development, to Los Angeles Deputy Mayor Rocky Delgadillo, Re: City of Los Angeles—Section 108 Application—Cornfields B-99-MC-06-0523, September 25, 2000 (in the authors' possession).

53. Sanchez, "L.A.'s Cornfield Row," p. A1.

54. Matea Gold, "State Plans Two Parks by L.A. River," *Los Angeles Times*, December 22, 2001.

55. Marilu Meza, "Anuncian Compra de Terrenos para Parques," *La Opinion*, December 22, 2002.

56. *Cornfield of Dreams*; Bill Donahue, "Year of the Park," *Land and People Magazine* (Trust for Public Land), (Fall 2001), www.tpl.org/tier3_cd.cfm?content _item_id=5304&folder_id=1545 (accessed March 18, 2005).

57. Miguel Bustillo, "State, Youth Advocates Clash over Best Use of Parks," *Los Angeles Times,* December 22, 2002.

58. Robert García et al., *Dreams of Fields* (Los Angeles: Center for Law in the Public Interest, 2002), www.clipi.org/.

59. Chapter coauthor Robert García is a member of the Cornfield Advisory Committee. The report *A Unified Vision for Cornfield State Park,* April 2003, is available online at www.parks.ca.gov/pages/21491/files/recommendationsreport .pdf (accessed April 2003).

60. James Ricci, "A Park with No Name (Yet) but Plenty of History," *Los Angeles Times Magazine*, July 15, 2001. The *Los Angeles Times* has repeatedly editorialized in support of the parks in the Cornfield, Taylor Yard, and the Baldwin Hills. The BBC produced a documentary on the struggle for the parks in the Cornfield and Taylor Yard, called "Who Killed the L.A. River?" (in authors' possession).

61. A parkscape is composed of linked parks with distinguishing characteris-

tics and features, and is especially considered to be a product of modifying or shaping processes and agents; a bird's-eye view, plan, sketch, or map of same. This definition is based on *Oxford English Dictionary*, 2nd ed., s.v. "landscape."

62. Hayden, *The Power of Place*, pp. 9–10.

63. See Robert García and Thomas A. Rubin, "Crossroad Blues: The MTA Consent Decree and Just Transportation," in *Running on Empty: Transport, Social Exclusion, and Environmental Justice*, ed. Karen Lucas (Portland, OR: Policy Press, 2004), pp. 221–56; Ron Frescas et al., *Public Transportation to the Local National Forests* (Los Angeles: Center for Law in the Public Interest, 2004), available at www.clipi.org/.

64. See Robert García et al., *Diversifying Access to and Support for the Forests* (Los Angeles: Center for Law in the Public Interest, 2004). See also James K. Boyce and Barry G. Shelley, eds., *Natural Assets: Democratizing Environmental Ownership* (Washington, DC: Island Press, 2003), pp. 207–60. The Center for Law in the Public Interest is also combating efforts by wealthy, gated communities to cut off public access to natural lands near the Angeles National Forest and in the Santa Monica Mountains Conservancy.

65. U.S. Forest Service, *Draft Land Management Plan*, Part 1: *Southern California National Forests Vision* (Washington, DC, 2004), vision 3.

66. U.S. Forest Service, *Revised Land and Resources Management Plans for Angeles, Cleveland, Los Padres, and San Bernardino National Forests, CA* (Washington, DC, 2004), p. 3–269.

67. Ibid., p. 3–267.

68. Greeninfo Network using 2000 census data (in authors' possession).

69. Los Angeles Department of City Planning, *West Adams-Baldwin Hills-Leimert Socio-Economic Analysis* (Berkeley: University of California Press, 1971), quoted in Sides, *L.A. City Limits*, p. 191.

70. Sides, *L.A. City Limits*, pp. 190–91.

71. Comments by the Center for Law in the Public Interest are available on the Web at www.clipi.org/.

72. Greeninfo Network using 2000 census data (in authors' possession).

73. Comments by the Center for Law in the Public Interest are available on the Web at www.clipi.org/.

74. See Robert García, *Equal Access to California's Beaches, Second National People of Color Environmental Leadership Summit — Summit II Resource Paper Series*, 2002, Environmental Justice Resource Center, www.ejrc.cau.edu/summit2/Beach.pdf/; Robert García et al., *Free the Beach!* (Los Angeles: Center for Law in the Public Interest, 2004), www.clipi.org/; *Brenden P. Leydon v. Town of Greenwich*, 257 Conn. 318 (Ct. 2001).

75. Chapter coauthor Robert García chairs the Los Angeles Unified School District Citizens' School Bond Oversight Committee.

76. The considerations for placement of elementary schools "are practically the identical considerations that should control the placing of recreation centers for children of elementary school age. And the considerations controlling locations of high schools and junior high schools are substantially those that might control the placing of recreation facilities for adults. This practical identity of policy strongly counsels associating school playgrounds, as far as practicable,

with other local recreation grounds in combined neighborhood units." Olmsted Report, p. 47.

77. *Alexander v. Sandoval*, 532 U.S. 275 (2001).

78. Brookings Institution, *Racial Change in the Nation's Largest Cities: Evidence from the 2000 Census* (Washington, DC: Center on Urban and Metropolitan Policy, April 2001).

79. Robert García et al., "We Shall Be Moved: Community Activism as a Tool for Reversing the Rollback," in *Awakening from the Dream: Pursuing Civil Rights in a Conservative Era*, ed. Denise C. Morgan et al. (Durham: Carolina Academic Press, forthcoming 2005).

CHAPTER 8. RESOURCE WARS AGAINST NATIVE PEOPLES

1. This article is a revised, updated, and abridged version of chapters from *Resource Rebels: Native Challenges to Mining and Oil Corporations* (Boston: South End Press, 2001).

2. Roger Moody, "South Counts the Cost of North's Bonanza," *Panoscope* 35 (April 1993): 11.

3. Robert K. Hitchcock and Tara M. Twedt, "Physical and Cultural Genocide of Various Indigenous Peoples," in *Genocide in the Twentieth Century: Critical Essays and Eyewitness Accounts,* ed. Samuel Totten, William S. Parsons, and Israel W. Charny (New York: Garland Publishing, 1995), p. 486.

4. John H. Bodley, *Victims of Progress,* 3rd ed. (Mountain View, CA: Mayfield, 1990), p. 7.

5. Helen Fein, "Scenarios of Genocide: Models of Genocide and Critical Responses," in *Toward an Understanding and Prevention of Genocide,* ed. Israel W. Charny (Boulder: Westview Press, 1984), p. 8.

6. Project Underground, *Blood of Our Mother: The U'wa People, Occidental Petroleum and the Colombian Oil Industry* (Berkeley, CA: Project Underground, 1998), p. 10.

7. Barbara Rose Johnston, *Who Pays the Price? The Sociocultural Context of Environmental Crisis* (Washington, DC: Island Press, 1994), p. 10.

8. Al Gedicks, *The New Resource Wars: Native and Environmental Struggles against Multinational Corporations* (Boston: South End Press, 1993), p. 61.

9. Gary Gardner and Payal Sampat, "Forging a Sustainable Materials Economy," in *State of the World, 1999: A Worldwatch Institute Report on Progress toward a Sustainable Society,* ed. Linda Starke (New York: W. W. Norton, 1999), p. 46.

10. Roger Moody, "Mining the World: The Global Reach of Rio Tinto Zinc," *Ecologist* 26 (March–April 1996): 46.

11. Ibid.

12. Geoff Nettleton, "Philippines: The New Mining Code," *Higher Values: The Minewatch Bulletin* (London) 7 (January 1996): p. 4.

13. Geoff Nettleton, "Constitution Undermined by Mining Code," *Higher Values: The Minewatch Bulletin* (London) 9 (March 1996): 18.

14. Survival International, *Mountains of Gold: The Mining Threat to Tribal Peoples in the Philippines* (London: Survival International, 1996), p. 3.

15. Robin Broad and John Cavanagh, *Plundering Paradise: The Struggle for the Environment in the Philippines* (Berkeley: University of California Press, 1993), p. 30.

16. Survival International, *Mountains of Gold*, p. 2.

17. R. K. Tartlet, "The Cordillera People's Alliance: Mining and Indigenous Rights in the Luzon Highlands," *Cultural Survival Quarterly* 25: 1 (Spring 2001): 17.

18. Roger Moody, "Terror and Resistance, as Philippines goes 'Code Red' " *Higher Values: The Minewatch Bulletin* (London) 11 (February 1997): 26.

19. Tartlet, "The Cordillera People's Alliance," p. 17.

20. Russel Barsh, *The World's Indigenous Peoples*, Investment Philosophy Social Screens Social Funds White Paper (Lethbridge, Alberta, Canada: Department of Native American Studies, University of Lethbridge, 1999), p. 5.

21. Renee Ross, "Philippines: Mining Accident Prompts Criminal Charges," *Clementine* (Mineral Policy Center, Washington, DC) (Winter 1996–97): 12.

22. Antonio Tujan Jr., "Corporate Imperialism in the Philippines," in *Moving Mountains: Communities Confront Mining and Globalisation*, ed. Geoff Evans, James Goodman, and Nina Lansbury (Sydney: Oxford Press, 2001), p. 154.

23. Ibid., p. 153.

24. Ibid., p. 155.

25. Tartlet, "The Cordillera People's Alliance," p. 17.

26. Tujan, "Corporate Imperialism in the Philippines," p. 157.

27. Nettleton, "Constitution Undermined by Mining Code," pp. 18–19.

28. In January 2004 the Philippine Supreme Court declared that the government does not have the power to grant contracts allowing foreign mining companies to own and manage mining concessions. The Philippine government said it would appeal the Supreme Court decision. *Engineering and Mining Journal* 205, no. 2 (February 2004): 17.

29. Project Underground, "Philippine Province Bans Mining for Twenty-Five Years," *Drillbits and Tailings* (Berkeley, CA) 7, no. 2 (February 28, 2002), www.moles.org/ProjectUnderground/drillbits/7_02/1.html.

30. Project Underground, "A Disaster Looms for Communities in Marinduque, Philippines," *Drillbits and Tailings* (Berkeley, CA) 7, no. 4 (April–May 2002), www.moles.org/ProjectUnderground/drillbits/7_04/3.html.

31. Tartlet, "The Cordillera People's Alliance," p. 17.

32. Rainforest Action Network and Project Underground, *Drilling to the Ends of the Earth* (Berkeley, CA: Rainforest Action Network and Project Underground, 1998), pp. 3–4.

33. Michael Ross, *Extractive Sectors and the Poor: An Oxfam America Report* (Washington, DC, 2001), www.oxfamamerica.org/newsandpublications/press_releases/archive2001/pdfs/eireport.pdf.

34. Michael Renner, "Breaking the Link between Resources and Repression," in *State of the World 2002: A Worldwatch Institute Report on Progress toward a Sustainable Society*, ed. Christopher Flavin, Hilary French, and Gary Gardner (New York: W. W. Norton, 2002), p. 149.

35. Michael Ross, "The Political Economy of the Resource Curse," *World Politics* 51 (January 1999).

36. Jeff Wollock, "Eclipse over Colombia: Events and Consequences of the Murder of Ingrid Washinawatok and Her Companions," *Native Americas: Akwe:kon's Journal of Indigenous Issues* (Ithaca, NY) 16, no. 2 (1999): 31.

37. Amazon Watch, *Report on Civil Conflict and Indigenous Peoples in Colombia* (Washington, DC: Amazon Watch, March 2002), p. 2.

38. Organizacion Nacional Indigena de Colombia, *Desecrated Land: Large Projects and Their Impact on Indigenous Territories and the Environment in Colombia* (London: National Indigenous Organization of Colombia and Survival, 1996), p. 295.

39. Human Rights Watch, *War without Quarter: Colombia and International Humanitarian Law* (New York: Human Rights Watch, 1998), p. 44, www.hrw.org/reports98/colombia/.

40. Coletta Youngers, "U.S. Entanglements in Colombia Continue," *NACLA Report on the Americas* 31 (March–April 1998): 34.

41. Clifford Krauss, "An Aimless War in Colombia Creates a Nation of Victims," *New York Times,* September 10, 2000.

42. Camille T. Taiara, "Dying for Oil: U'wa Leader Roberto Perez Speaks about Indigenous Resistance to the Colombian Oil Rush," *Bay Guardian* (San Francisco), February 7, 2001.

43. "Al Gore and Big Oil Genocide," *Earth Island Journal* 15, no. 2 (Summer 2000): 23.

44. U'wa Nation, "Oxy Invades U'wa Territory," press release, January 20, 2000.

45. Rainforest Action Network and Project Underground, *Drilling to the Ends of the Earth,* p. 1.

46. Steven Dudley and Mario Murillo, "Oil in a Time of War," *NACLA Report on the Americas* 31, no. 5 (March–April 1998): 45.

47. Rainforest Action Network and Project Underground, *Drilling to the Ends of the Earth,* p. 4.

48. U'wa Nation, "Oxy Invades U'wa Territory."

49. Rainforest Action Network and Project Underground, *Drilling to the Ends of the Earth,* p. 5.

50. Mario A. Murillo, "Under Fire from All Directions: Colombia's Indian Communities," *Native Americas: Akwe:kon's Journal of Indigenous Issues* (Ithaca, NY) 16, no. 2 (1999): 46.

51. Ibid.

52. Jesus Avirama and Rayda Marquez, "The Indigenous Movement in Colombia," in *Indigenous Peoples and Democracy in Latin America,* ed. Donna Lee Van Cott (New York: St. Martin's Press, 1996), p. 85.

53. Rainforest Action Network and Project Underground, *Drilling to the Ends of the Earth,* p. 24.

54. James Zackrison and Eileen Bradley, *Colombian Sovereignty under Siege,* Strategic Forum no. 112 (Washington, DC: National Defense University, Institute for National Strategic Studies, 1997), p. 1.

55. Dudley and Murillo, "Oil in a Time of War," p. 44.

56. Ibid., p. 42.

57. Human Rights Watch, *Colombia's Killer Networks: The Military-*

Paramilitary Partnership and the United States (New York: Human Rights Watch, 1996), p. 3.

58. Amazon Watch, *Report on Civil Conflict and Indigenous Peoples in Colombia*, p. 9.

59. Rainforest Action Network, "Call for V.P. to Take Action for U'wa People," press release (October 2000), www.ran.org/newsitem.php?id=105+area=oil/.

60. Amazon Watch, *Report on Civil Conflict and Indigenous Peoples in Colombia*, p. 9.

61. Peter Waldman, "A Rain Forest Tribe Brings Its Eco-Battle to Corporate America," *Wall Street Journal,* June 7, 1999.

62. Rainforest Action Network, "Grassroots Pressure Forces Fidelity Investments to Dump 60% of Their Oxy Stock!" San Francisco, CA: U'wa Emergency Updates, 2000, www.1worldcommunication.org/colombia.html#Grassroots%20Pressure.

63. "Potential Oil Industry Flashpoint Centers on Oxy's Colombian Rainforest Wildcat," *Oil and Gas Journal* 97 (November 29, 1999): 18.

64. Alexei Barrionuevo and Thaddeus Herrick, "Wages of Terror: For Oil Companies, Defense Abroad Is the Order of the Day," *Wall Street Journal,* February 7, 2002.

65. "Big Oil's Dirty Secrets," *The Economist* 367, no. 8323 (May 10, 2003): 54.

66. "Protecting the Pipeline: The U.S. Military Mission Expands," *Colombia Monitor* (Washington Office on Latin America) (May 2003): 1.

67. Gabrielle Banks, "Colombian Tribe Topples Mighty Oil Giant," *News from Indian Country: The Independent Native Journal* (Hayward, WI) (May 2002): 9A.

68. U'wa Nation, press release, October 25, 2002.

69. ABC Colombia Group (London), info brief, March 10, 2003, p. 1.

70. Midwest Treaty Network, "Multicultural Alliance Stymies Wisconsin Mining," *Earth First! Journal* 19, no. 4 (March–April 1999).

71. The Stockbridge-Munsee are a blend of the remnants of the Mohican Nation and the Lenni-Lenape (Delaware) Nation. See the Wisconsin Cartographers' Guild, *Wisconsin's Past and Present: A Historical Atlas* (Madison: University of Wisconsin Press, 1998), p. 6.

72. Frances Van Zile, interview by author, June 18, 1994.

73. Mike Flaherty, "State Sues over Indian Water Law," *Wisconsin State Journal,* January 30, 1996.

74. Lee Bergquist, "Decision Puts Water Quality in Tribe's Hands," *Milwaukee Journal Sentinel,* June 4, 2002, p. 1A.

75. Rennard Strickland, Stephen J. Herzberg, and Steven R. Owens, "Keeping Our Word: Indian Treaty Rights and Public Responsibilities" (manuscript, University of Wisconsin, Madison School of Law, 1990), p. 24. This report was presented to the U.S. Senate Committee on Indian Affairs.

76. Witness for Nonviolence is a support group organized by the Midwest Treaty Network to prevent, deflect, and document the violence against Ojibwe spearfishers. The network is a Madison-based native and non-native alliance that

has been working since 1989 for treaty rights, sovereignty, cultural respect, and environmental protection.

77. Midwest Treaty Network and Cathy Debevec, *Wisconsin Treaties: What's the Problem?* (Madison, WI: Midwest Treaty Network, 1991), p. 1.

78. In 1982, Exxon Minerals' chief lobbyist James Klauser told the Wisconsin Manufacturers and Commerce Association the state could host up to ten major metal mines by the year 2000. See Ron Seely, "Mining Has Strong Potential in Wisconsin," *Wisconsin State Journal*, January 31, 1982.

79. Will Fantle, "In Making Deal, Laws Were Broken," *Isthmus Newsweekly* (Madison, WI) (December 3, 1999).

80. Ron Seely, "Firm, Town, Trade Barbs," *Wisconsin State Journal*, June 18, 1999.

81. Robert Imrie, "Court Upholds 1996 Mine Agreement," *Wisconsin State Journal*, January 30, 2002. The town's Web site was www.nashvillewiundersiege .com/.

82. Ron Seely, "No Special Rules for Mining Law," *Wisconsin State Journal*, October 10, 1998.

83. Nikki Kallio, "New Mine Owners Face Opposition," *Wausau Daily Herald* (Wausau, WI), October 18, 2000.

84. Mole Lake has set up a Wolf River Protection Fund to help pay for its half of the purchase. See www.wolfriverprotectionfund.org/.

85. Julie Deardorff, "Firm May Abandon Battle to Mine Ore," *Chicago Tribune*, September 18, 2002.

86. Amy Rinard and Meg Jones, "Tribe's Purchase Ends Crandon Mine Tussle," *Milwaukee Journal Sentinel*, October 29, 2003.

87. "Troubled Times; Brighter Future," *North American Mining* 2, no. 4 (August–September 1998): 3.

88. Bob Webster, "Barbarians at the Gates of Cyberspace," *Mining Voice* 4, no. 1 (January–February 1998): 38–43.

89. Tracey Khanna, *Mining Environmental Management* 8, no. 3 (May 2000): 19.

CHAPTER 9. TIERRA Y VIDA: CHICANO ENVIRONMENTAL JUSTICE STRUGGLES

1. On the role of activists in the National Environmental Justice Advisory Council, see C. H. Foreman Jr., *The Promise and Peril of Environmental Justice* (Washington, DC: Brookings Institution Press, 1998), pp. 34–63.

2. An acequia is a "traditional gravity-driven irrigation ditch used in arid lands and the organization of a community of farmers who receive their water from the ditch." "So What's an Acequia Anyway?" http://southwest.fws.gov/ refuges/newmex/lasvegas/acequia.htm (accessed October 2003).

3. C. Marentes, "Food Production under Globalization and Neoliberalism: The Plight of the Workers of the Land" (paper presented at the 1997 Agricultural Missions Annual Meeting, Study Session on Economic Globalization, El Paso, TX, May 2, 1997; www.farmworkers.org/foodsys.html (accessed March 21, 2003).

4. E. Leon, *The Health Condition of Migrant Farmworkers,* Occasional Paper

no. 71 (East Lansing: Julian Samora Research Institute, Michigan State University, August 2000); www.jsri.msu.edu/RandS/research/ops/oc71abs.html (accessed August 2000).

5. F. J. Frommer, "Immigrant and Hispanic Workers Describe Unsafe Working Conditions," *San Francisco Chronicle,* February 27, 2002); www.sfgate .com/cgi-bin/article/cgi?file=/news/article/2002/02/27/national1836ESTo833 .DTL (accessed March 21, 2003).

6. Farm Labor Organizing Committee, *Farm Workers and Farm Labor Conditions,* www.iupui.edu/~floc/fws.htm (accessed January 1, 2000). Also see J. Kay, "California's Endangered Communities of Color," in *Unequal Protection: Environmental Justice and Communities of Color,* ed. R. D. Bullard (San Francisco: Sierra Club Books, 1994), pp. 155–88. Kay notes that, of the 175 chemicals used to formulate pesticides, only 41 have been fully tested to determine their correlation with cancers, birth defects, nerve damage, or other chronic diseases. Nationwide, the EPA currently lists 65 pesticides used on food crops as possible, probable, or known carcinogens (p. 173).

7. M. Reeves, K. Schafer, K. Hallward, and A. Katten, *Fields of Poison: California Farmworkers and Pesticides* (San Francisco: Californians for Pesticide Reform, Pesticide Action Network; Sacramento: California Rural Legal Assistance Foundation; Watsonville: United Farm Workers of America, 1997); www.igc.org/panna/resources/documents/fields.pdf (accessed March 21, 2003).

8. Ibid., p. 30.

9. Ibid.

10. S. Greenhouse, "As U.S. Economy Booms, Housing for Migrant Workers Worsens," *New York Times,* Sunday, March 31, 1998.

11. M. Teitel and K. A. Wilson, *Genetically Engineered Food: Changing the Nature of Nature* (Rochester, VT: Park Street Press, 1999).

12. D. G. Peña, "Latinos and Biotechnology: Environmental and Health Risks of Emergent Technologies," in *Rural Latino Communities: Comparative Regional Perspectives,* ed. Refugio Rochin et al. (Philadelphia: University of Pennsylvania Press, forthcoming).

13. The Farm Worker Network has nine affiliates, including Comité de Apoyo a los Trabajadores Agrícolas (based in New Jersey), Centro Independiente de Trabajadores Agrícolas (New York), Confederación Nacional Campesina (Dominican Republic), Farm Labor Organizing Committee (Ohio), Farm Worker Association of Florida (Florida), Organización de Trabajadores Agrícolas de California (California), Union Sín Fronteras (California), Union de Trabajadores Agrícolas Fronterizos (Texas), and Washington Farmworkers Union (Washington).

14. From the Web site of the Farm Worker Network for Economic and Environmental Justice, www.farmworkers.org/fwspage.html (accessed March 4, 2005).

15. R. Rochin, "The Conversion of Chicano Farm Workers into Owner-Operators of Cooperative Farms, 1970–1985," *Rural Sociology* 51 (1988): 97–115.

16. There were 16,184 farms operated by Latinas and Latinos in 1982, 17,476 in 1987, 20,956 in 1993, and more than 23,000 in 1997. At this rate, there will be more than 50,000 Latina- or Latino-operated farms by 2022. Also see R. Rochin, "Hispanic Americans in the Rural Economy: Conditions, Issues,

and Probable Future Adjustments," in *National Rural Studies Committee: A Proceedings*, ed. E. Castle (Corvalis, OR: Western Rural Development Center, 1992); U.S. Department of Agriculture, *Census of Agriculture: State and County Summaries* (Washington, DC: U.S. Government Printing Office, 1997), www .usda.gov/ (accessed March 4, 2005). Also see USDA, "How Many Minority Farmers Are There, and What Are Their Characteristics?" www.ers.usda.gov/ briefing/farmstructure/Questions/minority.htm (accessed March 4, 2005).

17. Robert Gottlieb, *Forcing the Spring: The Transformation of the American Environmental Movement* (San Francisco: Sierra Club Books, 1993), pp. 235–44; 270–306.

18. A. de la Torre and A. Estrada, *Mexican Americans and Health: Sana! Sana!* (Tucson: University of Arizona Press, 2001), pp. 18–19.

19. R. Morales and P. M. Ong, "The Illusion of Progress: Latinos in Los Angeles," in *Latinos in a Changing U.S. Economy*, ed. R. Morales and F. Bonilla (Newbury Park: Sage, 1993), pp. 28–54; D. G. Peña, *The Terror of the Machine: Technology, Work, Gender, and Ecology on the U.S.-Mexico Border* (Austin: CMAS Books, University of Texas Press, 1997).

20. On the GTE-Lenkurt struggle, see S. Fox, *Toxic Work: Women Workers at GTE-Lenkurt* (Philadelphia: Temple University Press, 1991); P. Almeida, "The Network for Environmental and Economic Justice in the Southwest: An Interview with Richard Moore," in *The Struggle for Ecological Democracy: Environmental Justice Movements in the United States*, ed. D. Faber (New York: Guilford, 1998), p. 172. The deaths of the former GTE-Lenkurt workers is reported in SouthWest Organizing Project, ed., *Intel Inside New Mexico: A Case Study of Environmental and Economic Injustice* (Albuquerque: SWOP, 1995); an additional seventy-five have cancer and seventy-five are totally disabled (p. 23).

21. R. Kazis and R. Grossman, *Fear at Work: Job Blackmail, Labor, and the Environment* (Philadelphia: New Society Publishers, 1991); D. Rosner and G. Markowitz, eds., *Dying for Work* (Bloomington: University of Indiana Press, 1987); C. Levenstein and J. Wooding, "Dying for a Living: Workers, Production, and the Environment," in *The Struggle for Ecological Democracy: Environmental Justice Movements in the United States*, ed. D. Faber (New York: Guilford, 1998), pp. 60–80.

22. For discussion of the impact of the North American Free Trade Agreement on labor and environmental standards, see P. M. Johnson and A. Beaulieu, *The Environment and NAFTA: Understanding and Implementing the New Continental Law* (Washington, DC: Island Press, 1998); R. Nader and L. Wallach, "GATT, NAFTA, and the Subversion of the Democratic Process," in *The Case against the Global Economy*, ed. J. Mander and E. Goldsmith (San Francisco: Sierra Club Books, 1996), pp. 92–107.

23. E. Martínez, *De Colores Means All of Us* (Boston: South End Press, 1998), p. 82.

24. Ibid.

25. L. W. Cole and S. R. Foster, *From the Ground Up: Environmental Racism and the Rise of the Environmental Justice Movement* (New York: New York University Press, 2001), p. 164; also see Martínez, *De Colores Means All of Us*, pp. 112–15.

26. See, generally, D. G. Peña, ed., *Chicano Culture, Ecology, Politics: Subversive Kin* (Tucson: University of Arizona Press, 1998).

27. U.S. General Accounting Office, *Treaty of Guadalupe Hidalgo: Definition and List of Community Land Grants in New Mexico*, Exposure Draft GAO-01-330 (January 2001), www.gao.gov/new.items/d01330.pdf (accessed March 4, 2005).

28. C. Wilmsen, "The Vallecitos Federal Sustained Yield Unit: A Case Study of Forest Management and Rural Poverty in Northern New Mexico" (paper presented at the session "Economy and Ecology in United States Regions" at the annual meetings of the Association of American Geographers, San Francisco, CA, March 29, 1994), p. 5.

29. S. Forrest, "The Vallecitos Federal Sustained Yield Unit: The (All Too) Human Dimension of Forest Management in Northern New Mexico," in *Forests under Fire: A Century of Ecosystem Management in the Southwest*, ed. C. J. Huggard and A. R. Gómez (Tucson: University of Arizona Press, 2001); Wilmsen, "The Vallecitos Federal Sustained Yield Unit."

30. See C. Wilmsen, "Fighting for the Forest" (Ph.D. diss., Geography, University of Wisconsin, 1997), pp. 57, 67–69.

31. Vallecitos Sustained Yield Unit Association, as quoted in Wilmsen, "The Vallecitos Sustained Yield Unit," p. 14, parentheses added.

32. L. Torres, as quoted in Wilmsen, "The Vallecitos Sustained Yield Unit," p. 16.

33. In April 1993, the U.S. Fish and Wildlife Service listed the Mexican spotted owl as endangered, as required by the Endangered Species Act. However, it seems clear that the owl had already been extirpated from its historical range in much of northern New Mexico, including the Vallecitos Unit. This sensitive indicator species had probably been driven out during the period when the largest cuts were taking place in the Vallecitos Unit, during the heyday of timber sales by the Duke City Lumber Company, in the 1970s and 1980s. In an interview, Ike de Vargas once observed that the environmentalists "were nowhere when we were trying to save the old growth Ponderosa in the 1970s and 80s." It was tragic that the latecomers would now block a local culture from finally asserting "historic use rights that predate the establishment of the Vallecitos Unit by at least a hundred years." I. de Vargas, personal communication to the author, Ojo Caliente, New Mexico, May 1997. In the Field Notes and Journals Collection of the Rio Grande Bioregions Project, Department of Anthropology, University of Washington, Seattle.

34. The "Inhabited Wilderness" pledge appeared in New Mexico daily newspapers in 1998.

35. On the Ganados del Valle conflict, see D. G. Peña, "The 'Brown' and the 'Green': Chicanos and Environmental Politics in the Upper Rio Grande," *Capitalism, Nature, Socialism* 3 (1992): 79–103; L. Pulido, *Environmentalism and Economic Justice: Two Chicano Struggles in the Southwest* (Tucson: University of Arizona Press, 1996); L. Pulido, "Ecological Legitimacy and Cultural Essentialism: Hispano Grazing in the Southwest," in *The Struggle for Ecological Democracy: Environmental Justice Movements in the United States,* ed. D. Faber (New York: Guilford, 1998), pp. 293–311; D. G. Peña and M. Mondragon-

Valdéz, "The 'Brown' and the 'Green' Revisited: Chicanos and Environmental Politics in the Upper Rio Grande," in *The Struggle for Ecological Democracy: Environmental Justice Movements in the United States*, ed. D. Faber (New York: Guilford, 1998), pp. 312-48.

36. Peña and Mondragon-Valdéz, "The 'Brown' and the 'Green' Revisited," p. 323.

37. Pulido, "Ecological Legitimacy and Cultural Essentialism," p. 296.

38. Ibid.; Peña and Mondragon-Valdéz, "The 'Brown' and the 'Green' Revisited."

39. S. Rodríguez, "Land, Water, and Ethnic Identity in Taos," in *Land, Water, and Culture: New Perspectives on Hispanic Land Grants*, ed. C. L. Briggs and J. R. Van Ness (Albuquerque: University of New Mexico Press, 1987), pp. 314-403; S. Rodríguez, "Art, Tourism, and Race Relations in Taos," in *Discovered Country: Tourism and Survival in the American West*, ed. S. Norris (Albuquerque: Stone Ladder Press, 1994), pp. 143-60.

40. D. G. Peña, "Los Animalitos: Culture, Ecology, and the Politics of Place in the Upper Rio Grande," in *Chicano Culture, Ecology, Politics: Subversive Kin*, ed. D. G. Peña (Tucson: University of Arizona Press, 1998), pp. 25 57.

41. D. G. Peña and R. O. Martínez, *Upper Rio Grande Hispano Farms: A Cultural and Environmental History of Land Ethics in Transition, 1598-1998: Final Report to the National Endowment for the Humanities*, Grant # RO 22707-94 (Seattle: Rio Grande Bioregions Project, Department of Anthropology, University of Washington, January 2000).

42. J. Gallegos, "Sangre de Tierra: Six Generations in the Life of an Acequia Farming Family" (manuscript, 2002); Peña and Martínez, *Upper Rio Grande Hispano Farms*.

43. For a history and legal analysis of *Rael v. Taylor*, see R. D. García and T. Howland, "Determining the Legitimacy of Spanish Land Grants in Colorado: Conflicting Values, Legal Pluralism, and Demystification of the Sangre de Cristo/Rael Case," *Chicano-Latino Law Review* 16 (1995): 39-68.

44. D. G. Peña, "Identity and Place in Communities of Resistance," in *Just Sustainabilities: Environmental Justice in an Unequal World*, ed. J. Ageyman, R. D. Bullard, and B. Evans (London: Earthscan Publications; Cambridge: MIT Press, 2002).

45. J. Brooke, "In a Colorado Valley: Hispanic Farmers Battle a Timber Baron," *New York Times*, March 24, 1997.

46. R. M. Figueroa, "Other Faces: Latinos and Environmental Justice," in *Faces of Environmental Racism: Confronting Issues of Global Justice*, ed. L. Westra and B. E. Lawson (London: Rowman and Littlefield, 2001), pp. 167-86.

47. Peña, "Identity and Place in Communities of Resistance."

48. D. G. Peña, "Cultural Landscapes and Biodiversity: The Ethnoecology of an Upper Rio Grande Watershed Commons," in *Ethnoecology: Situated Knowledge, Located Lives*, ed. V. Nazarea (Tucson: University of Arizona Press, 1998).

49. D. G. Peña and J. Gallegos, "Nature and Chicanos in Southern Colorado," in *Confronting Environmental Racism: Voices from the Grassroots*, ed. R. D. Bullard (Boston: South End Press, 1993), pp. 141-60; D. G. Peña, "An

Orchard, a Gold Mine, and an Eleventh Commandment," in *Chicano Culture, Ecology, Politics: Subversive Kin,* ed. D. G. Peña (Tucson: University of Arizona Press, 1998), pp. 249–78.

50. D. G. Peña, R. Martínez, and L. McFarland, "Rural Chicana/o Communities and the Environment: An Attitudinal Survey of Residents of Costilla County," *Perspectives in Mexican American Studies* 4 (1993): 45–74.

51. D. G. Peña and J. Gallegos, "Local Knowledge and Collaborative Environmental Action Research," in *Building Community: Social Science in Action,* ed. P. Nyden et al. (Thousand Oaks: Pine Forge Press, 1997), pp. 85–91.

52. The proposal for a Costilla County land use plan and watershed protection zone were first outlined in R. Curry, M. Soulé, D. G. Peña, and M. McGowan, *Montana Best Management Practices: A Critique and Sustainable Alternatives: Report submitted to the Costilla County Land Use Planning Commission* (San Luis, CO: La Sierra Foundation and Costilla County Conservancy District, October 1997).

53. J. A. Rivera, *Acequia Culture: Water, Land, and Community in the Southwest* (Albuquerque: University of New Mexico Press, 1999); G. Hicks and D. G. Peña, "Acequias and the Evolution of Colorado Water Law: Common Property Resources in the Age of Water Privatization," (manuscript, research grant report, Center for Labor Studies, University of Washington, December 2001). Available from the author.

54. Peña and Martínez, *Upper Rio Grande Hispano Farms.*

55. Hicks and Peña, "Acequias and the Evolution of Colorado Water Law."

56. Ibid.; also see Peña, "A Gold Mine, an Orchard, and an Eleventh Commandment," pp. 249–65; Rivera, *Acequia Culture.*

57. Peña, "Cultural Landscapes and Biodiversity"; Peña and Martínez, *Upper Rio Grande Hispano Farms.*

58. Hicks and Peña, "Acequias and the Evolution of Colorado Water Law."

59. See M. Davis, *Magical Urbanism: Latinos Reinvent the U.S. Big City* (London: Verso, 2001).

60. Ibid.; reviewed by Frontlist Books at www.frontlist.com/detail/ 185984328X/ (accessed March 4, 2005).

61. Davis, *Magical Urbanism,* pp. 3–6.

62. Jeanne Gauna, interview by Rebeca Rivera, March 2001, in the audio collection of the Rio Grande Bioregions Project, Department of Anthropology, University of Washington, Seattle.

63. The concept of sacrifice zones was first proposed by the Nixon administration in the late 1960s and applied to Native American reservations on which the nation's principal source of uranium lay. Obtaining that uranium was considered a matter of national security. On the Native American reservations, principally the Navajo, normal environmental and occupational health and safety regulations were to be sacrificed in the interests of national security. For further discussion, see W. Churchill and W. LaDuke, "Native America: The Political Economy of Radioactive Colonialism," *Insurgent Sociologist* 13 (1986): 51–78; A. Gedicks, *The New Resource Wars: Native American Environmental Struggles against Multinational Corporations* (Boston: South End Press, 1993).

64. On Kettleman City, see Cole and Foster, *From the Ground Up;* also see

R. Austin and M. Schill, "Black, Brown, Red, and Poisoned," and J. Kay, "California's Endangered Communities of Color," in *Unequal Protection: Environmental Justice and Communities of Color,* ed. R. D. Bullard (San Francisco: Sierra Club Books, 1994).

65. On the struggle in South Tucson, see R. Augustine, "Tucsonians Fight for a Clean Environment," in *People of Color Environmental Groups,* ed. R. D. Bullard (Atlanta: Environmental Justice Resource Center, 2000), pp. 32–33; J. N. Clarke and A. K. Gerlak, "Environmental Racism in Southern Arizona: The Reality beneath the Rhetoric," in *Environmental Injustices, Political Struggles: Race, Class, and the Environment,* ed. D. A. Camacho (Durham, NC: Duke University Press, 1998), pp. 82–100.

66. Clarke and Gerlak, "Environmental Racism in Southern Arizona," p. 84.

67. The journalist Jane Kay wrote the series for the local daily newspaper, the *Arizona Daily Star*; the series was published between 1981 and 1985.

68. Clarke and Gerlak, "Environmental Racism in Southern Arizona," pp. 87–88.

69. For more on Madres del Este de Los Angeles, see M. Pardo, *Mexican American Women Activists: Identity and Resistance in Two Los Angeles Communities* (Philadelphia: Temple University Press, 1999); M. Pardo, "Gendered Citizenship: Mexican American Women and Grassroots Activism in East Los Angeles, 1986–1992," in *Chicano Politics and Society in the Late Twentieth Century,* ed. D. Montejano (Austin: University of Texas Press, 1999), pp. 58–81; G. Gutiérrez, "Mothers of East Los Angeles Strike Back," in *Unequal Protection: Environmental Justice and Communities of Color,* ed. R. D. Bullard (San Francisco: Sierra Club Books, 1994), pp. 220–33.

70. Pardo, "Gendered Citizenship," pp. 74–75.

71. SouthWest Organizing Project, ed., *Intel Inside New Mexico.*

72. Ibid., p. 56.

73. S. Chunn, "Intel Boss Urges End to Red Tape," *Albuquerque Journal,* as posted at Campaign for Responsible Technology, List Serve Letter 1 (December 1997), www.svtc.org/listserv/letter1.htm (accessed March 4, 2005).

74. The mission statement is from the Labor/Community Strategy Center's Web site, www.thestrategycenter.org/.

75. E. Mann and the Labor/Community WATCHDOG Organizing Committee, *LA's Lethal Air: New Strategies for Policy, Organizing, and Action* (Los Angeles: Labor/Community Strategy Center Books, 1991).

76. Ibid., pp. 65–72.

77. R. Pinderhughes, "Poverty Reduction, Environmental Protection, Environmental Justice: The Urban Agriculture Connection," in *Natural Assets: Democratizing Environmental Ownership,* ed. J. K. Boyce and B. Shelly (Washington, DC: Island Press, 2003), p. 299.

78. Ibid., p. 6.

79. Ibid., p. 12.

80. Ibid.

81. This is based on the author's personal observations during recent visits to Los Angeles. One Zapotec family was maintaining three separate milpas in a South Central Los Angeles neighborhood. It was planted with native land race

varieties of maize, bean, calabacita, avocado, lime, chile, and numerous aromatic or medicinal herbs. Many of the seeds for family heirloom crops such as these are brought to the United States from Oaxaca as part of immigrants' biological baggage or "contraband."

82. M. Pepin, *Texas Colonias: An Environmental Justice Case Study,* November 5, 1998, http://itc.ollusa.edu/faculty/pepim/philosophy/cur/colonias .htm#OLE_what/ (accessed March 4, 2005).

83. Ibid.

84. Texas Water Development Board, *Water and Wastewater Needs of Texas Colonias* (Austin: TWDB, 1992); also see Pepin, *Texas Colonias.*

85. T. Barry and B. Sims, *The Challenge of Cross-Border Environmentalism: The U.S.-Mexico Case* (Albuquerque, NM: Resource Center Press; and Bisbee, AZ: Border Ecology Project, 1994), pp. 35–36.

86. Ibid., p. 31; also see C. R. Bath, J. M. Tanski, and R. E. Villarreal, "The Failure to Provide Basic Services to the Colonias of El Paso County: A Case of Environmental Racism?" in *Environmental Injustices, Political Struggles: Race, Class, and the Environment,* ed. D. A. Camacho (Durham, NC: Duke University Press, 1998), pp. 125–37.

87. For more on the Sociedad Cooperativa de Seleccionadores de Materiales, see Peña, *The Terror of the Machine,* pp. 213–43.

88. Bath, Tanski, and Villarreal, "The Failure to Provide Basic Services to the Colonias of El Paso County," p. 132.

89. Ibid.; also see Pepin, *Texas Colonias.*

CHAPTER 10. ENVIRONMENTAL REPARATIONS

1. For examples of these viewpoints, see George Perkins Marsh, *The Earth as Modified by Human Action* (New York: Scribner, Armstrong, 1877); and Roderick Nash, *Wilderness and the American Mind* (New Haven: Yale University Press, 1982).

2. Phillip Shabecoff states, "Unfortunately, it is true that the leadership of national environmental groups is largely white, male, and well educated, with incomes above the national average." See *A Fierce Green Fire: The American Environmental Movement* (New York: Hill and Wang, 1993), pp. 281. In 1991, the Wilderness Society had no people of color on its board, and minorities occupied only four of the eighty professional positions. At the Sierra Club, one out of fifteen directors was a member of a minority, and at the Audubon Society only two out of thirty-three directors were members of minorities. Peter Steinhart, "What Can We Do about Environmental Racism?" *Audubon Magazine* (May 1991): 18–20. See also Dorceta Taylor, "Can the Environmental Movement Attract and Maintain the Support of Minorities?" in *Race and the Incidence of Environmental Hazards,* ed. Bunyan Bryant and Paul Mohai (Boulder, CO: Westview Press, 1992).

3. Matthew Daly, "Environmental Justice and Sustainability in the City," *Journal of Environmental Law and Litigation* 17, no. 1 (Spring 2002): 97–144 (proceedings of the First Annual Freedom Colloquium, Jackson State University, Jackson, MS, April 7, 2000); Robert W. Collin and Robin Morris Collin, "Urban Environmentalism and Race," in *Urban Planning and the African American*

Community: In the Shadows, ed. June Manning Thomas and Marsha Ritzdorf (Thousand Oaks, CA: Sage Publications, 1997), pp. 220–38. Also, Robert Gottlieb, *Forcing the Spring: The Transformation of the American Environmental Movement* (Washington, DC: Island Press, 1993).

4. Robert Emmet Jones and Lewis F. Carter, "Concern for the Environment among Black Americans: An Assessment of Common Assumptions," 75 *Social Science Quarterly* (1994): 560, 579.

5. Thomas Jefferson, letter to Benjamin Rush, in *The Works of Thomas Jefferson,* ed. P. Ford (New York: G. P. Putnam's, 1905), 146–47.

6. Thomas Jefferson, *Notes on the State of Virginia, 1785* (Williamsburg, VA: Institute of Early American History and Culture; Chapel Hill, NC: University of North Carolina Press, 1955), p. 158.

7. William E. B. DuBois, *The Souls of Black Folk* (New York: Gramercy Books, 1903).

8. Elizabeth Howe and Sue Hendler, *Teaching Ethics: An Introduction to American and Canadian Ethics* (Chicago: American Planning Association, 1995), videorecording.

9. Robert W. Collin and Robin Morris Collin, "The Role of Communities in Environmental Decisions: Communities Speaking for Themselves," *Journal of Environmental Law and Litigation* 13 (1998): 37–89.

10. James Allen, Hilton Als, John Lewis, and Leon Litwack, *Without Sanctuary: Lynching Photography in America* (Santa Fe, NM: Twin Palms, 2000); Donald A. Grinde and Bruce E. Johansen, *Ecocide of Native America: Environmental Destruction of Indian Lands and Peoples* (Santa Fe, NM: Clear Light, 1995).

11. Wendy E. Wagner, "The Science Charade in Toxic Risk Regulation" *Columbia Law Review* 95 (1995): 1613, 1614.

12. The Precautionary Principle requires that, when a proposed action poses a threat to human health or the environment, reasonable protective measures must be taken even if there is no scientific certainty of harm. Tim O'Riordan and James Cameron, eds., *Interpreting the Precautionary Principle* (London: Earthscan Publications, 1994).

13. Robert Riddell, *Sustainable Urban Planning: Tipping the Balance* (Malden, MA: Blackwell, 2003).

14. Randall Robinson, *The Debt: What America Owes to Blacks* (New York: Dutton, 2000); Roy L. Brooks, ed., *When Sorry Isn't Enough: The Controversy over Apologies and Reparations for Human Injustice* (New York: New York University Press, 1999).

15. This reuse would depend on the owner of the site but would require the approval of the environmental review board. This board would be modeled on the architectural review board used in historic preservation.

16. Derrick Bell, *And We Are Not Saved: The Elusive Quest for Racial Justice* (New York: Basic Books, 1987), pp. 123–39.

17. Nicole Itano, "Former Colonies Calling For Reparations," *Christian Science Monitor,* September 5, 2001. The United States withdrew from this conference when the African delegates called upon the United States to make restitution for the slave trade.

18. The concept of average reciprocity of value explains why historic preservation land use requirements are not considered illegal takings of private property. The application of any particular historic preservation law may be expensive for the owner but, on the average, the property of everyone in the district gains value.

19. Luke W. Cole and Sheila R. Foster, *From the Ground Up: Environmental Racism and the Rise of the Environmental Justice Movement* (New York: New York University Press, 2001).

CHAPTER 11. VIEQUES: THE LAND, THE PEOPLE, THE STRUGGLE, THE FUTURE

1. Information for this article was obtained from cited documents, interviews, and personal observation.

2. Juan A. Bonnet Benítez, *Vieques en la historia de Puerto Rico* (San Juan, P.R.: F. Ortiz Nieves, 1977); U.S. Department of Agriculture, *Soil Map of Puerto Rico* (Washington, DC, 1936).

3. Luís A. Chanlatte Baik, *Arqueología de Vieques* (Río Piedras, P.R.: University of Puerto Rico, 1983); Miguel Rodríguez, "La Marina y el patrimonio arqueológico de Vieques," testimony presented to the Special Commission on Vieques, June 15, 1999.

4. Eugenio Fernández Méndez, *Las encomiendas y esclavitud de los Indios de Puerto Rico, 1508–1550* (Río Piedras, P.R.: University of Puerto Rico, Río Piedras, 1984); Bonnet Benítez, *Vieques en la historia de Puerto Rico*, pp. 12, 20–21, 28.

5. Bonnet Benítez, *Vieques en la historia de Puerto Rico*, pp. 28–32.

6. César Ayala, "From Sugar Plantations to Military Bases: The U.S. Navy's Expropriations in Vieques, Puerto Rico, 1940–45," *CENTRO Journal* 13, no. 1 (Spring 2001): 22–41.

7. Bonnet Benítez, *Vieques en la historia de Puerto Rico*, pp. 108–111; Robert Rabin, *Historia de Vieques: Cinco Siglos de Lucha de un Pueblo Puertorriqueño*, 1999, Archivo Histórico de Vieques, P.R.

8. Déborah Berman Santana, "Puerto Rico's Operation Bootstrap: Colonialist Roots of a Persistent Model for 'Third World' Development," *Revista Geográfica*, no. 124 (1998): 87–116.

9. Arturo Meléndez López, *La batalla de Vieques* (Mexico City: COPEC, 1982).

10. Cruz Cordero Ventura, *Vieques: Sesenta Años de bombardeos en tiempos de paz* (San Juan, P.R.: Metropolitana, 2001).

11. Juan Giusti, *Informe histórico preliminar Asociación Pro-Títulos de Monte Santo et al. vs. Estado Libre Asociado et al.*, Civil Núm. KPE 96-0729 (907), Tribunal de Primera Instancia, Sección Superior de San Juan, 1999.

12. Ayala, "From Sugar Plantations to Military Bases," p. 36.

13. Meléndez, *La batalla de Vieques*, pp. 52–53, Bonnet Benítez, *Vieques en la historia de Puerto Rico*, pp. 121–26.

14. Meléndez, *La batalla de Vieques*, pp. 78–79.

15. John Lindsay-Poland and Déborah Berman Santana, *Environmental Impacts of Navy Training*, Vieques Issue Briefs, no. 1 (San Francisco: Fellowship of Reconciliation Taskforce on Latin America, 2001).

16. Irene Garzón Fernánswz, "Despierta alerta un buque hundido: Piden se investigue su radiactividad," *Primera Hora* (May 24, 2002); Juan Giusti-Cordero, "One-Stop Shopping for Navy Facts: A Response to the Navy's Vieques Website," www.viequeslibre.addr.com/articles/articles.htm (accessed on August 17, 2000).

17. Irwin W. Silverman, "Vieques Island, Puerto Rico," Memorandum from the Acting Director of the U.S. Department of the Interior to U.S. Navy Undersecretary Chapman, dated August 8, 1947, www.vieques-island.com/board/navy/mcmostcroix.html; Luís Muñoz Marín, letter sent by Puerto Rico's governor to U.S. President John F. Kennedy, dated December 28, 1961, in Arthur M. Schlesinger, *A Thousand Days* (New York: Houghton-Mifflin, 1963), p. 772; Meléndez, *La batalla de Vieques,* pp. 131–32.

18. Cordero Ventura, *Vieques;* Iván Ramos Soler, "Vieques: Bombs Have Killed Many Civilians," posted at the Vieques Libre Web site, www.viequeslibre .addr.com/articles/articles.htm (accessed August 12, 2001).

19. Meléndez, *La batalla de Vieques,* pp. 129–31.

20. Ibid., pp. 164–68.

21. Radamés Tirado, former mayor of Vieques, testimony before the Special International Tribunal on the Situation of Puerto Rico and the Island Municipality of Vieques, Vieques, P.R., November 19, 2000. A copy of the testimony may be found in the Vieques Historical Archives, "International Tribunal, Vieques November 2000" folder, Vieques, P.R.

22. Congress, House, Panel to Review the Status of Navy Training Activities on the Island of Vieques, of the Committee on Armed Services of the U.S. House of Representatives, 96th Congress, 2nd sess. The panel issued its final report on February 3, 1981.

23. Commander, U.S. Second Fleet, and Commander, U.S. Marine Corps Forces, Atlantic Fleet, *The National Security Need for Vieques: A Study Prepared for the Secretary of the Navy* (Washington, DC, July 15, 1999). By comparison, the Hiroshima and Nagasaki atomic bombs dropped 12,500 and 22,000 tons, respectively.

24. José Seguinot, *Geografía, ecología y derecho de Puerto Rico y el Caribe* (San Juan, P.R.: First Books Publishing of Puerto Rico, 1994), p. 114.

25. U.S. Navy, *Programmatic Environmental Assessment (EA) for Continued Use with Non-Explosive Ordnance of the Vieques Inner Range,* prepared for the Commander in Chief, U.S. Atlantic Fleet in compliance with Section 102(2)(c) of the National Environmental Policy Act of 1969, February 14, 2001, pp. 4:13–14.

26. Arturo Massol Deyá and Elba Díaz de Osbourne, *Ciencia y ecología: Vieques en crisis ambiental* (Adjuntas, P.R.: Publicaciones Casa Pueblo, 2001).

27. Benjamín Torres Gotay, "Doble la radiación ambiental durante las maniobras," *El Nuevo Día,* April 7, 2002.

28. Carmen Ortiz Roque, José Ortiz Roque, and Dulce Albandoz Ortiz, *Exposición a contaminantes y enfermedad en Vieques: Un trabajo en progreso* (San Juan, P.R.: Colegio de Médicos y Cirujanos de Puerto Rico, September 14, 2000).

29. See, for example, James W. Porter, *The Effects of Naval Bombardment on the Coral Reefs of Isla Vieques, Puerto Rico. Part 1: Based on the First Coral Ref.*

Survey Trip to Vieques, study prepared for the Government of Puerto Rico, March 20, 2000; Hilda Díaz Soltero, *Ponencia oficial del Departamento de Recursos Naturales con relación a la certificación del permiso de agua de la Marina en Vieques* (San Juan, P.R.: Puerto Rico Department of Natural Resources, July 20, 1981).

30. Tourist brochures often refer to "Vieques, USA" or "Culebra, USA," in an apparent effort to disassociate these two island municipalities from Puerto Rico. There is also an attempt to fabricate a historic "Spanish Virgin Islands," which in fact never existed. See, for example, Randall Peffer, *Lonely Planet's Travel Guide to Puerto Rico* (New York: Lonely Planet, 1999).

31. Colegio de Médicos y Cirujanos de Puerto Rico, testimony regarding Realizable Over the Horizon Radar in public hearings convened by the Puerto Rico House of Representatives, April 4, 1997. This radar is used for electronic warfare training and for the "drug war," although its record in the latter is poor. It is reportedly capable of influencing weather and setting fires up to a thousand miles away—deep inside Colombia, for example.

32. Robert Rabin, *Two Years and a Referendum* (Vieques, P.R.: Committee for the Rescue and Development of Vieques, April 15, 2001), www.cpeo.org/ lists/military/2001/msg00221.html (accessed March 5, 2005).

33. *Floyd D. Spence National Defense Authorization Act for Fiscal Year 2001,* Public Law 106-398, Cong. 106, 2nd sess. (October 30, 2000). Sections 1503–1508 concern Vieques.

34. The $200-million offer was reported in the *Vieques Times* (March–April 2001). In March 2001, a delegation from Vieques lobbied Congress, and one congressman made the statement about moving people off the island, to one of the delegation, who reported it to me.

35. Personal communication from an environmental planner, San Juan, July 2000.

36. Puerto Rico, Junta de Planificación, *Plan de Ordenación Territorial — Borrador* [draft] (San Juan, P.R., August 2000).

37. Puerto Rico, Junta de Planificación, *Plan final: Plan de Ordenación Territorial* (San Juan, P.R., November 2000).

38. Grúpo de Apoyo Técnico y Profesional, *Guías para el Desarrello sustentable de Vieques* (San Juan, P.R.: Universidad Metropolitana, vol. 1, 2000; vol. 2, 2002).

39. "Navy Leaves Vieques," *Miami Herald,* May 5, 2003, www.miami.com/ mld/miamiherald/news/opinion/5786428.htm (accessed May 6, 2003).

40. Jonathan Geld, "Navy Exit from Vieques Seen as Merely a Start," *Philadelphia Inquirer,* April 14, 2003, www.philly.com/mld/inquirer/news/front/ 5629846.htm (accessed April 20, 2003).

CHAPTER 12. ALIENATION AND MILITANCY IN THE NIGER DELTA

1. Esther Cesarz, J. Stephen Morrison, and Jennifer Cooke, "Alienation and Militancy in Nigeria's Niger Delta" *CSIS Africa Notes,* no. 16 (May 2003), www .csis.org/africa/ANotes/.

2. Ibid., p. 4.

3. This chapter was first published in *Foreign Policy In Focus (FPIF)*, a joint project of the Interhemispheric Resource Center (IRC, online at www.irc-online .org/) and the Institute for Policy Studies (IPS, online at www.ips-dc.org/), July 2003.

4. "Africa Overview: Patterns of Global Terrorism," April 30, 2001, U.S. Department of State, www.state.gov/s/ct/rls/pgtrpt/2000 (accessed March 5, 2005).

5. Central Intelligence Agency, *Nigeria: Environmental Stressors and Their Impacts over the Next Decade* (Washington, DC: DCI Environmental Center, 2000), www.cia.gov/emeu/cabs/nigeria.html.

6. Jean-Christophe Servant, *Le Monde Diplomatique*, January 13, 2003.

7. Available at the Institute for Advanced Strategic and Political Studies, www.iasps.org/ (accessed March 5, 2005).

8. Neela Banerjee, "Fears, Again, of Oil Supplies at Risk," *New York Times*, October 1, 2001, business sec. 3, p. 1.

9. R. Kapuscinski, *Shah of Shahs* (New York: Harcourt, 1982), p. 34.

10. The case against ChevronTexaco concerns a collaboration between the company's security forces and Nigerian security forces that resulted in the serious injury and deaths of local residents. At the time of this writing, the case was in the discovery stage.

11. V. Kemedi, *Oil on Troubled Waters,* Environmental Politics Working Papers (Berkeley, CA: Institute of International Studies, University of California, Berkeley, 2002), http://globetrotter.berkeley.edu/ (accessed March 5, 2005).

12. The British imperial government appointed a minorities commission in 1957 to look into the fears by minorities in the northern, eastern, and western regions of Nigeria. Sir Henry Willink headed the commission and released the report that bears his name, the Willink Commission, in 1958. *Nigeria: Report of the Commission Appointed to Inquire in the Fear of Minorities and the Means of Allaying Them* (the Willink Commission) (London: HHSO, 1958).

13. Ibid.

CHAPTER 13. ENVIRONMENTAL RACISM AND NEOLIBERAL DISORDER IN SOUTH AFRICA

1. See, for example, M. Omi and H. Winant, *Racial Formation in the United States from the 1960s to the 1990s* (New York: Routledge, 1994); L. Pulido, "Rethinking Environmental Racism: White Privilege and Urban Development in Southern California," *Annals of the Association of American Geographers*, 90, no. 1 (2000): 12–40; R. Holifield, "Defining Environmental Justice and Environmental Racism," *Urban Geography*, no. 22 (2001): 78–90; D. T. Goldberg, *The Racial State* (Oxford: Blackwell Publishers, 2002). I am grateful to Audrey Kobayashi for her assistance in helping me think through some of the issues of racism that I raise in this chapter.

2. On this point see B. Dodson, "Searching for a Common Agenda: Ecofeminism and Environmental Justice," in *Environmental Justice in South Africa*, ed. D. A. McDonald (Athens, OH: Ohio University Press; Cape Town: University of Cape Town Press, 2002).

3. "Township" refers to urban areas of formal and informal housing that were designated as "blacks only" during the apartheid era. "Homeland" refers to

rural areas designated as "blacks only" under apartheid, some of which were declared independent states by the apartheid regime but were not recognized by the international community.

4. W. Beinart and P. Coates, *Environment and History: The Taming of Nature in the USA and South Africa* (London: Routledge, 1995); J. Carruthers, *The Kruger National Park: A Social and Political History* (Scottsville: University of Natal Press, 1995; E. Koch, "Nature Has the Power to Heal Old Wounds: War, Peace, and Changing Patterns of Conservation in Southern Africa," in *South Africa in Southern Africa: Reconfiguring the Region,* ed. D. Simon (Cape Town: David Philip, 1998); J. Cock and D. Fig, "From Colonial to Community-Based Conservation: Environmental Justice and the Transformation of National Parks (1994–1998)," in *Environmental Justice in South Africa,* ed. D. A. McDonald (Athens, OH: Ohio University Press; Cape Town: University of Cape Town Press, 2002); F. Khan, "The Roots of Environmental Racism and the Rise of Environmental Justice in the 1990s," in *Environmental Justice in South Africa,* ed. D. A. McDonald (Athens, OH: Ohio University Press; Cape Town: University of Cape Town Press, 2002); M. Draper and G. Mare, "Going In: The Garden of England's Gaming Zookeeper and Zululand," *Journal of Southern African Studies* 29, no. 2 (2003): 551–69.

5. Jacklyn Cock and Eddie Koch, eds., *Going Green: People, Politics, and the Environment in South Africa* (Cape Town: Oxford University Press, 1991); M. Ramphele, ed., *Restoring the Land: Environment and Change in Post-Apartheid South Africa* (London: Panos Institute, 1991).

6. D. Hallowes, ed., *Hidden Faces: Environment, Development, Justice: South Africa and the Global Context* (Scottsville: Earthlife Africa, 1993).

7. African National Congress, *The Reconstruction and Development Programme* (Johannesburg: Umyanyano Publications, 1994), p. 38.

8. P. S. Wenz, *Environmental Justice* (Albany: State University of New York Press, 1988); D. E. Taylor, "Blacks and the Environment: Toward an Explanation of the Concern and Action Gap between Blacks and Whites," *Environment and Behavior* 21 (1989): 175–205; R. D. Bullard. *Dumping in Dixie: Race, Class, and Environmental Quality* (Boulder, CO: Westview Press, 1990); S. Capek, "The 'Environmental Justice' Frame: A Conceptual Discussion and an Application," *Social Problems* 40 (1993): 5–24; B. Bryant, *Environmental Justice: Issues, Policies, and Solutions* (Washington, DC: Island Press, 1995); S. Cutter, "Race, Class, and Environmental Justice," *Progress in Human Geography* 19 (1996): 111–22; D. Harvey, *Justice, Nature, and the Geography of Difference* (Oxford: Blackwell Publishers, 1996); M. Heiman, "Race, Waste, and Class: New Perspectives on Environmental Justice," *Antipode* 28 (1996): 111–21; A. Dobson, *Justice and the Environment: Conceptions of Environmental Sustainability and Theories of Distributive Justice* (New York: Oxford University Press, 1998); D. Schlosberg, *Environmental Justice and the New Pluralism: The Challenge of Difference for Environmentalism* (Oxford: Oxford University Press, 1999); W. M. Bowen and K. E. Haynes, "The Debate over Environmental Justice," *Social Science Quarterly* 81 (2000).

9. "Environmental Justice Networking Forum," *Environmental Justice Networker* (Autumn 1997): 1.

10. D. Pepper, *The Roots of Modern Environmentalism* (London: Routledge, 1984); C. Merchant, ed., *Ecology: Key Concepts in Critical Theory* (Humanities Press: New Jersey, 1994); M. Redclift and T. Benton, eds., *Social Theory and the Global Environment* (London: Routledge, 1994); D. Goldblatt, *Social Theory and the Environment* (Cambridge, U.K.: Polity Press, 1996); A. De-Shalit, *The Environment: Between Theory and Practice* (Oxford: Oxford University Press, 2000); P. Macnaghten and J. Urry, eds., *Bodies of Nature* (London: SAGE Publications, 2001; R. E. Dunlap, ed., *Sociological Theory and the Environment: Classical Foundations, Contemporary Insights* (Lanham, MD: Rowman and Littlefield, 2002); D. Simon, *Dilemmas of Development and the Environment in a Globalising World* (Egham: Bedford College, University of London, 2001).

11. World Bank, *World Development Report, 1992: Development and the Environment* (New York: Oxford University Press, 1992); World Bank, *World Development Report, 1994: Development and the Environment* (New York: Oxford University Press, 1994).

12. Pulido, "Rethinking Environmental Racism," p. 15. Pulido builds this definition on Omi and Winant's idea of race as a "concept which signifies and symbolizes social conflicts and interests by referring to different types of human bodies." M. Omi and H. Winant, *Racial Formation in the United States from the 1960s to the 1990s* (New York: Routledge, 1994), p. 55.

13. Pulido, "Rethinking Environmental Racism," p. 15.

14. Ibid. Emphasis in the original.

15. Khan, "The Roots of Environmental Racism and the Rise of Environmental Justice in the 1990s."

16. D. McDonald, "Neither from Above, Nor from Below: Municipal Bureaucrats and Environmental Policy in Cape Town, South Africa," *Canadian Journal of African Studies* 30 (1997): 315-40.

17. On my conversations with managers, see D. McDonald and L. Smith, *Privatizing Cape Town: Service Delivery and Policy Reforms since 1996,* Occasional Papers, no. 7 (Cape Town: Municipal Services Project, 2002). In my work with the Municipal Services Project (www.queensu.ca/msp), I continuously hear from workers and shop stewards in the South Africa Municipal Workers Union about explicitly racist behavior on the part of white and "coloured" managers. For a detailed report on worker-manager relations in the city of Cape Town, see Municipal Services Project, "Survey of Municipal Workers in the Cape Metropolitan Area, Report Submitted to the Unicity Commission (Cape Town)" (mimeograph, May 2000). Also available online at the MSP Web site, www .queensu.ca/msp/pages/Project_Publications/Reports/survey.htm.

18. F. Barchiesi, "Fiscal Discipline and Worker Response: The Restructuring of Johannesburg's Solid Waste Management," in *The Commercialisation of Waste Management in South Africa,* ed. Mskoli Qotole, Mthetho Xali, and Franco Barchiesi, Occasional Papers, no. 3 (Cape Town: Municipal Services Project, 2001), www.queensu.ca/msp/pages/Project_Publications/Series/3.htm; McDonald and Smith, *Privatizing Cape Town: Service Delivery and Policy Reforms since 1996.*

19. Pulido, "Rethinking Environmental Racism," p. 15.

20. T. Madihlaba, "The Fox in the Henhouse: The Environmental Impact of

Mining on Communities," in *Environmental Justice in South Africa,* ed. D. A. McDonald (Athens, OH: Ohio University Press; Cape Town: University of Cape Town Press, 2002).

21. B. Peek, "Doublespeak in Durban: Mondi, Waste Management, and the Struggles of the South Durban Community Environmental Alliance," in *Environmental Justice in South Africa,* ed. D. A. McDonald (Athens, OH: Ohio University Press; Cape Town: University of Cape Town Press, 2002).

22. F. Kockott, *Wasted Lives: Mercury Recycling at Thor Chemicals* (Johannesburg: Earthlife Africa and Greenpeace International, 1994); M. Butler, "Lessons from Thor Chemicals: The Links between Heath, Safety, and Environmental Protection," in *The Bottom Line: Industry and Environment in South Africa,* ed. L. Bethlehem and M. Goldblatt (Cape Town: University of Cape Town Press, 1997).

23. Kockott, *Wasted Lives,* p.1.

24. Sieseko Njobeni, "Cato Ridge Mercury Waste Cleanup Begins at Last," *Business Day* (August 4, 2004).

25. J. Glazewski, "The Rule of Law: Opportunities for Environmental Justice in the New Democratic Legal Order," in *Environmental Justice in South Africa,* ed. D. A. McDonald (Athens, OH: Ohio University Press; Cape Town: University of Cape Town Press, 2002).

26. On this point, see Patrick Laurence, "Watershed Rights Ruling in Favour of the Poor," *Financial Mail* (11 October 2000).

27. M. Murray, *The Revolution Deferred: The Painful Birth of Post-Apartheid South Africa* (London: Verso, 1994); D. O'Meara, *Forty Lost Years: The Apartheid State and the Politics of the National Party, 1948–1994* (Johannesburg: Ravan Press, 1996); H. Marais, *Limits to Change* (Cape Town: University of Cape Town Press; London: Zed Press, 1998); D. McDonald, "Three Steps Forward, Two Steps Back: Ideology and Urban Ecology in the New South Africa," *Review of African Political Economy* 75 (1998); P. Bond, *Elite Transition: From Apartheid to Neoliberalism in South Africa* (Durban: Natal University Press, 2000); P. Bond, *Cities of Gold, Townships of Coal: Essays on South Africa's New Urban Crisis* (Trenton: Africa World Press, 2001); P. Bond, *Unsustainable South Africa: Environment, Development, and Social Protest* (Durban: University of Natal Press, 2002); D. McDonald and J. Pape, *Cost Recovery and the Crisis of Service Delivery in South Africa* (London: Zed Press, 2002); D. McDonald and L. Smith, "Privatizing Cape Town: From Apartheid to Neoliberalism in the Mother City," *Urban Studies* 41, no. 8 (July 2004): 1461–84.

28. J. S. Saul and S. Gelb, *The Crisis in South Africa: Class Defence, Class Revolution* (London: Monthly Review Press, 1981); D. O'Meara, *Volkskapitalisme: Class, Capital, and Ideology in the Development of Afrikaner Nationalism, 1934–48* (Cambridge: Cambridge University Press, 1983).

29. *Business Day* (13 January 1993); *Financial Mail* (7 February 1992). Returning from a conference in Davos, Switzerland, Mandela said, "They changed my views altogether. I came home to say: 'Chaps, we have to choose. We either keep nationalisation and get no investment, or we modify our own attitude and get investment'" (quoted in A. Sampson, *Nelson Mandela: The Authorised Biography* [Johannesburg: Jonathan Ball, 1999], 435). I am indebted to Ian Taylor and Simon Kimani Ndung'u for several such references.

30. For a full discussion, see Marais, *Limits to Change,* chap. 6.

31. Presentation by the minister for provincial and local government, F. S. Mufamadi, Government Communication and Information System, Parliamentary Media Briefing, Cape Town, 12 August 2002.

32. South African Press Association, "Basic Water Provision for All by 2008: Kasrils," press release, February 12 2002; "Electrification Plan 'Will Need Huge Subsidies,'" *Business Day* (March 7, 2002).

33. D. McDonald and J. Pape, eds., *Cost Recovery and the Crisis of Service Delivery in South Africa* (Cape Town: Human Sciences Research Council, 2002).

34. D. McDonald, "The Bell Tolls for Thee: Cost Recovery, Cutoffs, and the Affordability of Municipal Services in South Africa," in *Cost Recovery and the Crisis of Service Delivery in South Africa,* ed. D. McDonald and J. Pape (Cape Town: Human Sciences Research Council, 2002).

35. M. Fiil-Flynn, *The Electricity Crisis in Soweto,* Occasional Papers, no. 4 (Cape Town: Municipal Services Project, 2001).

36. McDonald, "The Bell Tolls for Thee."

37. H. Deedat and E. Cottle, "Cost Recovery and Prepaid Water Meters and the Cholera Outbreak in KwaZulu-Natal," in *Cost Recovery and the Crisis of Service Delivery in South Africa,* ed. D. McDonald and J. Pape (Cape Town: Human Sciences Research Council, 2002).

38. See S. Flynn and D. M. Chirwa, "The Constitutional Implications of Commercializing Water in South Africa," in *The Age of Commodity: Water Privatization in Southern Africa,* ed. D. A. McDonald and G. Ruiters (Earthscan Press: London, 2004); M. Drakeford, "Water Regulation and Pre-payment Meters," *Journal of Law and Society* 25, no. 4 (December 1998): 588–602.

39. I adopt a broad definition of "commercializing" here to include the sale of public assets, public-private partnerships, corporatization, outsourcing, and other forms of "running public services like a private business." For a more detailed discussion, see D. A. McDonald and G. Ruiters, "Theorizing Water Privatization in Southern Africa," in *The Age of Commodity: Water Privatization in Southern Africa,* ed. D. A. McDonald and G. Ruiters (Earthscan Press: London, 2004). See also P. Bond, *Cities of Gold, Townships of Coal: Essays on South Africa's New Urban Crisis* (Trenton, NJ: Africa World Press, 2000); J. Beall, O. Crankshaw, and S. Parnell, *Uniting a Divided City: Governance and Social Exclusion in Johannesburg* (London: Earthscan, 2002); D. McDonald and J. Pape, eds., *Cost Recovery and the Crisis of Service Delivery in South Africa* (Cape Town: Human Sciences Research Council, 2002); McDonald and Smith, "Privatizing Cape Town: From Apartheid to Neoliberalism in the Mother City."

40. The Growth, Employment, and Redistribution framework, the Municipal Infrastructure Investment Unit, and the Municipal Systems Act are but three such initiatives that affect policy choices. For further discussion see McDonald and Smith, "Privatizing Cape Town: From Apartheid to Neoliberalism in the Mother City."

41. On the implications of privatizing core municipal services, see D. McDonald. "Up against a (Crumbling) Wall: The Privatization of Urban Services and Environmental Justice," in *Environmental Justice in South Africa,* ed. D. A. McDonald (Athens, OH: Ohio University Press; Cape Town: University of Cape Town Press, 2002).

42. A. Loftus and D. McDonald, "Of Liquid Dreams: A Political Ecology of Water Privatization in Buenos Aires," *Environment and Urbanization* 12 (2001).

43. D. McDonald, "Black Worker, Brown Burden: Municipal Labourers and the Environment," *South African Labour Bulletin* 18 (1994); Municipal Services Project, "Survey of Municipal Workers in the Cape Metropolitan Area."

44. "Samwu Lashes at Water Company Boss," *Cosatu Weekly* (July 19–26, 2002).

45. Cited in D. Budlender, *The People's Voices: National Speak Out on Poverty Hearings, March to June 1998* (Johannesburg: Commission on Gender Equality, South African Human Rights Commission and South African NGO Coalition, 2002), p. 21.

46. *Johannesburg Mail and Guardian,* September 9, 1999.

47. See the Web site of Public Services International Research Unit at www.psiru.org/ for extensive accounts of environmental and occupational health and safety violations on the part of private-sector service providers around the world.

48. Edward Lahiff, *Land Reform in South Africa: Is It Meeting the Challenge?* Programme for Land and Agrarian Studies, Policy Brief no. 1 (Cape Town: University of Western Cape, 2001): 1.

49. Ibid., p. 4.

50. Ibid., p. 6.

51. Bond, *Cities of Gold, Townships of Coal,* pt. 3.

52. Anton Eberhard and Clive van Horen, *Poverty and Power: Energy and the South African State* (London: Pluto Press, 1995).

53. B. Davies and J. Day, *Vanishing Waters* (Cape Town: University of Cape Town Press, 1998), p. 9.

54. J. Naidoo, "Taking the RDP Forward: Report to Parliament" (mimeograph, 1995), p. 6.

CHAPTER 14. ADDRESSING GLOBAL POVERTY, POLLUTION, AND HUMAN RIGHTS

1. "At a Glance: Globalization, Poverty, Trade, and the Environment," *Our Planet* 13, no. 4 (2003).

2. Robert D. Bullard, "Confronting Environmental Racism in the 21st Century," (paper presented to the United Nations Research Institute for Social Development, Race, and Public Policy Conference, World Conference against Racism, Durban, South Africa, September 3–5, 2001).

3. Al Gedicks, *Resource Rebels: Native Challenges to Mining and Oil Corporations* (Boston: South End Press, 2001); Winona LaDuke, *All Our Relations: Native Struggles for Land Rights and Life* (Boston: South End Press, 1999); Joshua Karliner, *The Corporate Planet: Ecology and Politics in the Age of Globalization* (San Francisco: Sierra Club Books, 1997).

4. International Forum on Globalization, *Alternatives to Economic Globalization: A Better World Is Possible* (San Francisco: Berrett-Koehler Publishers, 2002), p. 18.

5. Carolyn L. Deere, ed., *Globalization and Grantmakers: Why Should We*

Care? (San Francisco: Funders Network on Trade and Globalization, 2001), pp. 112–13.

6. "At a Glance: Globalization, Poverty, Trade, and the Environment," *Our Planet,* no. 13 (2003), p. 18.

7. Robin Broad and John Cavanagh, "Global Economic Apartheid," in *Globalization and Grantmakers: Why Should We Care?* ed. Carolyn L. Deere (San Francisco: Funders Network on Trade and Globalization, 2001), pp. 33–34; Robin Broad and John Cavanagh, "Development: The Market Is Not Enough," *Foreign Policy* 101 (Winter 1995–96).

8. "At a Glance: Globalization, Poverty, Trade, and the Environment," p. 18.

9. Robert D. Bullard and Beverly H. Wright, "Environmental Justice for All: Community Perspectives on Health and Research Needs," *Toxicology and Industrial Health* 9, no. 5 (1993): 821–41.

10. Kenneth Olden, "The Complex Interaction of Poverty, Pollution, Health Status," *Scientist* 12, no. 2 (February 16, 1998): 7; Robert D. Bullard, "It's Not Just Pollution," *Our Planet* 12, no. 2 (2001): 22–24.

11. Human Development Report, *Making New Technologies Work for the Poor* (New York: United Nations, 2000).

12. Nat Quansah, "Pharmacies of Life," *Our Planet* 12, no. 2 (2001): 12.

13. Thorbjorn Jagland, "Everything Connects," *Our Planet* 12, no. 2 (2001): 7.

14. Leslie Roberts, *World Resources, 1998–1999* (London: Oxford University Press, 1998).

15. Rick Weiss, "Threats Posed by Water Scarcity Detailed," *Washington Post,* March 5, 2003.

16. United Nations, World Water Assessment Programme, *UN World Water Development Report: Water for People, Water for Life* (Paris: United Nations Educational, Scientific, and Cultural Organization; Oxford: Berghahn Books, 2003), p. 4.

17. Ibid., p. 11.

18. Geoffrey Lean, "At a Glance: Water and Sanitation," *Our Planet* 14, no. 4 (2004).

19. Geoffrey Lean, "At a Glance: Water and Sanitation," *Our Planet* 12, no. 2 (2001): 16.

20. Intermediate Technology Development Group and Greenpeace, *Sustainable Energy for Poverty Reduction: An Action Plan,* 2002, www.itdg.org/html/advocacy/docs/itdg-greenpeace-study.pdf (accessed March 8, 2005).

21. Davis J. Tenenbaum, "Tackling the Big Three," *Environmental Health Perspective* 106 (May 1998).

22. Intermediate Technology Development Group and Greenpeace, *Sustainable Energy for Poverty Reduction.*

23. Ian Johnson and Kseniya Lvosvsky, "Double Burden," *Our Planet* 12, no. 2 (2001): 19.

24. Intermediate Technology Development Group and Greenpeace, *Sustainable Energy for Poverty Reduction.*

25. Youba Sokona, "New Energy to Assault Poverty," *Our Planet* 14, no. 3 (2003): 25.

26. See Global Policy Forum, "Shell Admits Fuelling Corruption," June 11,

2004, www.globalpolicy.org/security/natres/oil/2004/0611shell.htm (accessed July 3, 2004).

27. Ibid.

28. Corrado Clini, "Power to the People," *Our Planet* 12, no. 3 (2001), www.ourplanet.com/imgversn/123/content.html.

29. Global Lead Network, "Worldwide Phase-Out of Leaded Gasoline," n.d., Global Lead Network Web site, www.globalleadnet.org/policy_leg/policy/leadgas_progress.cfn (accessed March 9, 2005).

30. David C. Bellinger, "Interpreting the Literature on Lead and Child Development: The Neglected Role of the Experimental System," *Neurotoxicology and Teratology* 17 (1995): 201–12; Hebert L. Needleman, Julie Reiss, Michael Tobin, Gretchen Biesecker, and Joel Greenhouse, "Bone Lead Levels and Delinquent Behavior," *Journal of the American Medical Association* 263 (1996): 363–96; Joel Schwartz, "Low-Level Lead Exposure and Children's IQ: A Meta-analysis and Search for a Threshold," *Environmental Research* 65 (1994): 42–55.

31. H. Needleman, J. Reiss, M. Tobin, G. Biesecker, and J. Greenhouse, "Bone Lead Levels and Delinquent Behavior," *Journal of the American Medical Association* 275, no. 5 (1996).

32. Greenpeace, *The Case for a Ban on All Hazardous Waste Shipments from the United States and Other OECD Member States to Non-OECD States,* (Washington, DC: Greenpeace, June 1993), pp. 1–2.

33. Greenpeace, *The Database of Known Hazardous Waste Exports from OECD to Non-OECD Countries, 1989–1994* (Washington, DC: Greenpeace, 1994).

34. Rozelia S. Park, "An Examination of International Environmental Racism through the Lens of Transboundary Movement of Hazardous Wastes," *Indiana University Law School Journal* 5, no. 2 (1999): 659–709, www.law.indiana.edu/glsj/vol5/no2/14/14parks.html.

35. Organization of African Unity, Bamako Convention on the Ban of the Import into Africa and the Control of Transboundary Movement and Management of Hazardous Wastes within Africa, adopted by the Conference of Environment Ministers at Bamako, Mali, opened for signature on January 29, 1991.

36. Mary Tiemann, *Congressional Research Service, Report to Congress, Waste Trade and the Basel Convention: Background and Update,* report prepared for the 106th Congress, December 30, 1998.

37. Karliner, *The Corporate Planet*, p. 152.

38. See Gary Cohen, "Eliminating Toxic Chemical Threats: A New Framework," n.d., Third World Network, www.twnside.org.sg/title/gary-cn.htm (accessed March 9, 2005).

39. Ibid.

40. Al Krebs, "Chemical Poison Exports Abroad Increase in 1997–2000 by 15% from 1992–1996, Including 65 Million pds. of U.S. Banned Poisons," *Agribusiness Examiner,* no. 142 (February 4, 2002).

41. Geoffrey Lean, "At a Glance: Water and Sanitation," *Our Planet* 12, no. 2 (2001): 16.

42. Environmental Pollution and Degradation Causes 40 Percent of Deaths

Worldwide, Cornell Study Finds," *Cornell News*, September 30, 1998, www .news.cornell.edu/releases/Sept98/ecodisease.hrs.html.

43. Ibid.

44. Ahmedin Jemal, Taylor Murray, Alicia Samuels, Asma Ghafoor, Elizabeth Ward, and Michael J. Thun, "Cancer Statistics, 2003," *CA: A Cancer Journal for Clinicians* 53 (2003): 5-26.

45. Occupational and Environmental Working Group–Toronto Cancer Prevention Coalition, *Preventing Occupational and Environmental Cancer: A Strategy for Toronto*, 2001, www.uswa.ca/eng/hs&e/prevcancer.pdf (accessed November 8, 2002).

46. Christopher Snowbeck, "Pain from Poison Gas Leak Still Haunts Them, Bhopal Survivors Say," *Pittsburgh Post-Gazette*, May 26, 2003, www.post-gazette.com/World/20030526bhopal0526p2.asp/ (accessed May 28, 2003).

47. Robert D. Bullard, *Dumping in Dixie: Race, Class, and Environmental Quality* (Boulder, CO: Westview Press, 2000).

48. Goldman Environmental Prize, "Champa Devi Shukla and Rashida Bee: The Bhopal Chemical Disaster: 20 Years Later," April 19, 2004, www.goldmanprize .org/recipients/recipientProfile.cfm?recipientID=136.

49. Robert D. Bullard, *Confronting Environmental Racism: Voices from the Grassroots* (Boston: South End Press, 1993).

50. Public Citizen, *NAFTA's Broken Promises: The Border Betrayed*, 1996, www.citizen.org/pctrade/nafta/reports/enviro96.htm.

51. Elyse Bolterstein, "Environmental Justice Case Study: Maquiladora Workers and Border Issues," n.d., www.umich.edu/~snre492/Jones/maquiladora .htm (accessed October 6, 2003).

52. Federal Reserve Bank of Dallas, "Maquiladora Industry Update," August 2003, www.dallasfed.org/data/data/maq-charts.pdf (accessed March 9, 2005).

53. Environmental Health Coalition, "Border Environmental Justice Campaign," n.d., www.igc.org/ehc/border.html (accessed October 6, 2003).

54. Ibid.

55. Steve Sawicki, "The Maquiladoras: Back Door Pollution," *Norwalk: The Environmental Magazine* 9 (July–August 1998).

56. Beatriz Johnston Hernandez, "Dirty Growth," *New Internationalist* (August 1993).

57. Marisa Jacott, Cyrus Reed, and Mark Winfield, *The Generation and Management of Hazardous Wastes and Transboundary Hazardous Waste Shipment between Mexico, Canada, and the United States, 1990–2000* (Austin: Texas Center for Public Policy, 2002), p. 41. This report was prepared for the Commission for Environmental Cooperation of North America and is available at www.texascenter.org/bordertrade/haznafta/htm (accessed November 1, 2003).

58. Tom Barry and Beth Simms, *The Challenge of Cross Border Environmentalism: The U.S.-Mexico Case* (Albuquerque, NM: Inter-Hemispheric Education Resource Center, 1994), p. 37.

59. David Berteau, principal deputy assistant secretary of defense, stated that Subic is a "horror story" and admitted that the U.S. military "poured tons of toxic chemicals into Subic Bay." U.S. General Accounting Office, *Military Base*

Closures: US Financial Obligations in the Philippines, GAO/NSIAD-92-51 (Washington, DC, January 1992).

60. Rosalie Bertell, *Health for All: A Study of the Health of People Living on or Near to the Former US Clark Air Force Base 1996–1998* (Joint Project of the International Institute of Concern for Public Health [Canada] and People's Task Force for Bases Cleanup [Philippines], 1999).

61. Jose Enrique Soriano, "Childhood of Pain," *In Black and White* 9 (September–October 2003), www.pcij.org/imag/Black&White/toxicwaste.html (accessed December 20, 2003).

62. Dick Thornburgh, Glenn Reichardt, and John Stanley, *The Nuclear Claims Tribunal of the Republic of the Marshall Islands: An Independent Examination and Assessment of Its Decision-Making Processes* (Washington, DC: Kilpatrick and Lockhard, January 2003), p. 5.

63. Ibid., p. 72.

64. See Trusteeship Agreement for the Former Japanese Mandated Islands, 61 Stat. 3301, T.I.A.A. no. 1665 (1947), App. 277, Arts. III, VI.

65. Thornburgh, Reichardt, and Stanley, *The Nuclear Claims Tribunal of the Republic of the Marshall Islands*, pp. 72–73.

66. Charles J. Hanley, "Exiled Bikinians Sing of Promise, but Face Exodus without End," *Associated Press*, April 25, 2004.

67. Bernice Powell Jackson, "Turning Our Backs on the Marshall Islands, Again: No Justice for America's Nuclear Guinea Pigs" *Counterpunch* (March 9, 2005), www.counterpunch.org/jackson03092005.html (accessed March 25, 2005).

68. Pamela K. Miller, "The War against Military Toxics in Alaska," in *People of Color Environmental Groups Directory, 2000,* ed. R. D. Bullard (Flint, MI: Charles Stewart Mott Foundation, 2000).

69. Tom Kizzia, "Toxic PCB Levels Soar above Norm in St. Lawrence Natives: Tests, Old Military Bases Are the Suspected Cause of the Pollution," *Anchorage Daily News*, October 3, 2002, www.adn.com/front/story/1884270p-1998499c.html (accessed October 17, 2002).

70. U.S. Environmental Protection Agency, *Breaking the Cycle: PBT Program Accomplishments, 2001–2002* (Washington, DC: U.S. EPA, 2003).

71. Environmental Justice Climate Change Initiative, press release, New York, January 29, 2002.

72. Environmental Justice Climate Change Initiative, "U.S. Environmental Justice Groups to Release 10 Principles for Just Climate Change Policies on Thursday, August 29," 2002, www.ejcc.org/releases/020828.html (accessed March 9, 2005).

73. U.S. Environmental Protection Agency, "Global Warming: Impacts—Health," July 6, 1999, www.epa.gov/globalwarming/impacts/health/index.html (accessed March 9, 2005).

74. U.S. Bureau of the Census, *American Housing Survey* (Washington, DC: U.S. Government Printing Office, 1999).

75. Laurence S. Kalkstein, "Impact of Global Warming on Human Health: Heat Stress–Related Mortality," in *Global Climate Change: Implications and*

Mitigation, ed. S. K. Majumdar, L. S. Kalkstein, B. Yarnal, E. W. Miller, and L. M. Rosenfeld (Easton: Pennsylvania Academy of Sciences, 1992).

76. Congressional Black Caucus Foundation, *African Americans and Climate Change: An Unequal Burden* (Washington, DC: Congressional Black Caucus Foundation, July 21, 2004), p. 3.

77. Redefining Progress, "Groundbreaking Study of the Impact of Climate Change: Unequal Burden on African Americans," press release, July 21, 2004, p. 1, www.rprogress.org/newmedia/releases/040721_climate.html (accessed March 9, 2005).

78. Herman Daly, *For the Common Good: Redirecting the Economy toward Community, the Environment, and a Sustainable Future* (Boston: Beacon Press, 1994).

79. See Kenny Bruno, Joshua Karliner, and China Brotsky, *Greenhouse Gangsters vs. Climate Justice* (San Francisco: Transnational Resource and Action Center, November, 1999), p. 3.

80. See the Environmental Justice Climate Change initiative Web site at www.ejcc.org/.

81. National Black Environmental Justice Network, *Combating Environmental Racism with Sustainable Development in the U.S. and around the World — the Time Is Now* (Washington, DC: National Black Environmental Justice Network Report for the World Summit on Sustainable Development, March 2002).

Selected Bibliography

Adamson, Joni. *American Indian Literature, Environmental Justice, and Eco-criticism: The Middle Place*. Tucson: University of Arizona Press, 2001.

Adamson, Joni, Mei Mei Evans, and Rachel Stein. *The Environmental Justice Reader: Politics, Poetics, and Pedagogy*. Tucson: University of Arizona Press, 2002.

Agyeman, Julian, Robert D. Bullard, and Bob Evans. *Just Sustainabilities: Development in an Unequal World*. London: Earthscan; Cambridge: MIT Press, 2003.

Barlett, Donald L., and James B. Steele. "Paying a Price for Polluters." *Time* (November 23, 1998): 72–80.

Baxter, Brian. *A Theory of Ecological Justice*. New York: Routledge, 2005.

Bruno, Kenny, Joshua Karliner, and China Brotsky. *Greenhouse Gangsters vs. Climate Justice*. Oakland, CA: CorpWatch, November 1999.

Bryant, Bunyan. *Environmental Justice: Issues, Policies, and Solutions*. Washington, DC: Island Press, 1995.

Bryant, Bunyan, and Paul Mohai. *Race and the Incidence of Environmental Hazards*. Boulder, CO: Westview Press, 1992.

Bullard, Robert D. "Solid Waste Sites and the Black Houston Community." *Sociological Inquiry* 53 (Spring 1983): 273–88.

———. *Invisible Houston: The Black Experience in Boom and Bust*. College Station: Texas A & M University Press, 1987.

———. "Ecological Inequities and the New South: Black Communities under Siege." *Journal of Ethnic Studies* 17 (Winter 1990): 101–15.

————. "Environmental Blackmail in Minority Communities." In *Race and the Incidence of Environmental Hazards,* ed. Bunyan Bryant and Paul Mohai, pp. 82–95. Boulder, CO: Westview Press, 1992.

————. *Confronting Environmental Racism: Voices from the Grassroots.* Boston: South End Press, 1993.

————. *Unequal Protection: Environmental Justice and Communities of Color.* San Francisco: Sierra Club Books, 1996.

————. "Dismantling Environmental Racism in the USA." *Local Environment* 4 (1999): 5–19.

————. *Dumping in Dixie: Race, Class, and Environmental Quality.* 3rd ed. Boulder, CO: Westview Press, 2000.

————. *People of Color Environmental Groups Directory, 2000.* Flint, MI: Charles Stewart Mott Foundation, 2000.

Bullard, Robert D., J. Eugene Grigsby, and Charles Lee. *Residential Apartheid: The American Legacy.* Los Angeles: University of California at Los Angeles Center for African Studies Publication, 1994.

Bullard, Robert D., and Glenn S. Johnson. *Just Transportation: Dismantling Race and Class Barriers.* Gabriola Island, BC: New Society Publishers, 1997.

Bullard, Robert D., Glenn S. Johnson, and Angel O. Torres. *Sprawl City: Race, Politics, and Planning in Atlanta.* Washington, DC: Island Press, 2000.

————. *Highway Robbery: Transportation Racism and New Routes to Equity.* Boston: South End Press, 2004.

Camacho, David. *Environmental Injustices, Political Struggles: Race, Class, and the Environment.* Durham, NC: Duke University Press, 1998.

Checker, Melissa. *Toxic Doughnut: Environmental Racism, Community Activism, and Social Activism.* New York: Routledge, 2004.

Cole, Luke, and Sheila R. Foster. *From the Ground Up: Environmental Racism and the Rise of the Environmental Justice Movement.* New York: New York University Press, 2001.

Collin, Robert W., and Robin Morris Collin. "The Role of Communities in Environmental Decisions: Communities Speaking for Themselves." *Journal of Environmental Law and Litigation* 13 (1998): 37–89.

Commission for Racial Justice. *Toxic Wastes and Race in the United States.* New York: United Church of Christ, 1987.

Cooney, C. M. "Still Searching for Environmental Justice." *Environmental Science and Technology* 33 (May 1999): 200–205.

Council on Environmental Quality. *Environmental Justice: Guidance under the National Environmental Policy Act.* Washington, DC: CEQ, December 10, 1997.

Edelstein, Michael R. *Poisoned Places: Seeking Environmental Justice in a Contaminated World.* Boulder, CO: Westview Press, 2004.

Escobedo, Duwayne. "EPA Gives In, Will Move All at Toxic Site." *Pensacola News Journal,* October 4, 1996, p. A1.

Faber, D. *The Struggle for Ecological Democracy: Environmental Justice Movements in the United States.* New York: Guilford Press, 1998.

Foreman, Christopher H., Jr. *The Promise and Perils of Environmental Justice.* Washington, DC: Brookings Institution, 2000.

Frynas, George Jedrzej. *Transnational Corporations and Human Rights*. New York: Palgrave Macmillan, 2003.

Gedicks, Al. *The New Resource Wars: Native and Environmental Struggles against Multinational Corporations*. Boston: South End Press, 1993.

———. *Resource Rebels: Native Challenges to Mining and Oil Corporations*. Boston: South End Press, 2001.

Gibson, William E. *Eco-Justice: The Unfinished Journey*. Albany: State University of New York Press, 2005.

Gottlieb, Robert. *Environmentalism Unbound: Exploring New Pathways for Change (Urban and Industrial Environments)*. Cambridge: MIT Press, 2001.

Greenpeace. *The Case for a Ban on All Hazardous Waste Shipments from the United States and Other OECD Member States to Non-OECD States*. Washington, DC: Greenpeace, June 1993.

———. *The Database of Known Hazardous Waste Exports from OECD to Non-OECD Countries, 1989–1994*. Washington, DC: Greenpeace, 1994.

Hernandez, Beatriz Johnston. "Dirty Growth." *New Internationalist* 246 (August 1993).

Hoversten, Paul. "EPA Puts Plant on Hold in Racism Case." *USA Today*, Thursday, September 11, 1997, p. A3.

Institute of Medicine. *Toward Environmental Justice: Research, Education, and Health Policy Needs*. Washington, DC: National Academy Press, 1999.

Johnston, Barbara Rose. *Life and Death Matters: Human Rights and the Environment at the End of the Millennium*. Walnut Creek, CA: AltaMira Press, 1997.

Karliner, Joshua. *The Corporate Planet: Ecology and Politics in the Age of Globalization*. San Francisco: Sierra Club Books, 1997.

LaDuke, Winona. *All Our Relations: Native Struggles for Land Rights and Life*. Boston: South End Press, 1999.

Lavelle, Marianne, and Marcia Coyle. "Unequal Protection." *National Law Journal* (September 21, 1992): 1–2.

Lazaroff, Cat. "Environmental Justice Issues Force Cement Plant to Close," 2001, Environmental News Service, ens.lycos.com/ens/apr2001/2001L-04-24-06.html (accessed April 26, 2001).

Lerner, Steve. *Diamond: A Struggle for Environmental Justice in Louisiana's Chemical Corridor*. Cambridge: MIT Press, 2004.

Low, Nicholas, and Brendan Gleeson. *Justice, Society, and Nature: An Exploration of Political Ecology*. New York: Routledge, 1998.

Lucas, Karen. *Running on Empty: Transport, Social Exclusion, and Environmental Justice*. Portland: International Specialized Book Services, 2004.

McDonald, David A. *Environmental Justice in South Africa*. Athens, OH: Ohio University Press, 2002.

Moore, Donald S., Jake Kosek, and Anand Pandian. *Race, Nature, and the Politics of Difference*. Durham, NC: Duke University Press, 2003.

Motavalli, Jim. "Toxic Targets: Polluters That Dump on Communities of Color Are Finally Being Brought to Justice." *E Magazine* (July–August 1998): 28–41.

Novotny, Patrick. *Where We Live, Work, and Play: The Environmental Justice*

Movement and the Struggle for a New Environmentalism. Westport, CT: Praeger, 2001.

Nuclear Regulatory Commission. "Final Initial Decision—Louisiana Energy Services." U.S. Nuclear Regulatory Commission, Atomic Safety, and Licensing Board, Docket No. 70-3070-ML, May 1, 1997.

Park, Rozelia S. "An Examination of International Environmental Racism through the Lens of Transboundary Movement of Hazardous Wastes," 1999, *Indiana University Law School Journal,* www.law.indiana.edu/glsj/vol5/no2/14/14parks.html (accessed March 5, 2005).

Pellow, David Naguib. *Garbage Wars: The Struggle for Environmental Justice in Chicago (Urban and Industrial Environments).* Cambridge: MIT Press, 2002.

Peña, Devon. *The Terror of the Machine: Technology, Work, Gender, and Ecology on the U.S.-Mexico Border.* Austin: University of Texas Press, 1997.

————. *Culture, Ecology, Politics: Subversive Kin.* Tucson: University of Arizona Press, 1998.

Pinderhughes, Raquel. "Who Decides What Constitutes a Pollution Problem?" *Race, Gender, and Class* 5 (1997): 130–52.

Pulido, Laura. *Environmentalism and Economic Justice: Two Chicano Struggles in the Southwest.* Tucson: University of Arizona Press, 1996.

Reaves, Jessica, and Mark Thompson. "Vieques under Fire: Standoff in Puerto Rico," April 27, 2001, TIME.com, www.time.com/time/nation/article/0,8559,107846,00.html (accessed April 28, 2001).

Reuter, Rosemary Radford. *Women Healing Earth: Third World Women on Ecology, Feminism, and Religion.* Maryknoll, NY: Orbis Books, 1996.

Roberts, J. Timmons. *Chronicles from the Environmental Justice Frontline.* New York: Cambridge Press, 2001.

Robinson, Deborah M. "Environmental Racism: Old Wine in a New Bottle," *Echoes* 17 (2000), World Council of Churches, www.wcc-coe.org/wcc/what/jpc/echoes/echoes-17-02.html (accessed December 23, 2001).

Roisman, Florence W. "The Lessons of American Apartheid: The Necessity and Means of Promoting Residential Racial Integration." *Iowa Law Review* (December 1995): 479–525.

Sachs, Aaron. *Eco-Justice: Linking Human Rights and the Environment.* Washington, DC: Worldwatch Institute, 1995.

Santana, Deborah Berman. *Kicking off the Bootstraps: Environment, Development, and Community Power in Puerto Rico.* Tucson: University of Arizona Press, 1996.

Scholsberg, David. *Environmental Justice and the New Pluralism: The Challenges of Difference for Environmentalism.* New York: Oxford University Press, 2002.

"Second Day of Protest Greets Vieques Exercise," April 28, 2001, CNN.com, www.cnn.com/2001/US/04/28/vieques.protests/ (accessed April 29, 2001).

Shrader-Frechette, Kristin. *Environmental Justice: Creating Equality, Reclaiming Democracy.* New York: Oxford University Press, 2002.

Steady, Filomina Chioma. *Women and Children First: Environment, Poverty, and Sustainable Development.* Rochester, VT: Schenkman Books, 1993.

Stretesky, Paul, and Michael J. Hogan. "Environmental Justice: An Analysis of Superfund Sites in Florida." *Social Problems* 45 (May 1998): 268–87.

Templet, Paul H. "The Positive Relationship between Jobs, Environment, and the Economy: An Empirical Analysis and Review." *Spectrum* (Spring 1995): 37–49.

Tiemann, Mary. *Congressional Research Service, Report for Congress, Waste Trade and the Basel Convention: Background and Update.* Report no. 98-638 ENR, Library of Congress, December 30, 1998.

U.S. Environmental Protection Agency. *Environmental Equity: Reducing Risk for All Communities.* Washington, DC: U.S. EPA, 1992.

———. *Escambia Treating Company Interim Action: Addendum to April, 1966, Superfund Proposed Plan Fact Sheet.* Atlanta: U.S. EPA, Region IV, August 1996.

———. *Guidance for Incorporating Environmental Justice in EPA's NEPA Compliance Analysis.* Washington, DC: U.S. EPA, 1998.

———. "Global Warming: Impacts—Health," July 6, 1999, U.S. Environmental Protection Agency, www.epa.gov/globalwarming/impacts/health/index .html (accessed October 19, 1999)

U.S. General Accounting Office. *Siting of Hazardous Waste Landfills and Their Correlation with Racial and Economic Status of Surrounding Communities.* Washington, DC: Government Printing Office, 1983.

Weaver, Jane. *Defending Mother Earth: Native American Perspectives on Environmental Justice.* Maryknoll, NY: Orbis Books, 1996.

Westra, Laura, and Bill E. Lawson. *Faces of Environmental Racism: Confronting Issues of Global Justice.* 2nd ed. Lanham, MD: Rowman and Littlefield, 2001.

Wright, Beverly H. *St. James Parish Field Observations.* New Orleans: Deep South Center for Environmental Justice, Xavier University of Louisiana, 1998.

About the Contributors

ROBERT D. BULLARD is the Ware Distinguished Professor of Sociology and Director of the Environmental Justice Resource Center at Clark Atlanta University. He is the author of eleven books that address sustainable development, environmental racism, urban land use, industrial facility siting, community reinvestment, housing, transportation, and smart growth. His book *Dumping in Dixie: Race, Class, and Environmental Quality* (Westview Press, 2000), is a standard text in the environmental justice field. His most recent books include *Just Sustainabilities: Development in an Unequal World* (Earthscan and MIT Press, 2003) and *Highway Robbery: Transportation Racism and New Routes to Equity* (South End Press, 2004).

ROBERT COLLIN is a senior scholar in residence for the Center for Public Policy at Willamette University in Salem, Oregon. He has written numerous law review and peer reviewed articles, book chapters, and other publications on issues of homelessness, environmental justice, environmental regulation, and sustainability, and he is currently researching and writing a book on environmental justice and sustainability. He is an ex officio member of the Oregon Governor's Environmental Justice Advisory Board, an Environmental Justice representative at the U.S. Environmental Protection Agency, and a federal expert witness on environmental justice for a Pacific Northwest tribe.

ROBIN MORRIS COLLIN is a professor of law at Willamette University in Salem, Oregon. Prior to teaching, she was a staff attorney in the Credit Practices Division of the Bureau of Consumer Protection at the Federal Trade Commission in Washington, D.C. She is a founding and current board member of the Oregon Toxics Alliance and also serves on the Oregon State Bar Affirmative Action Committee. Collin is a member of the National Advisory Council for Environmental Policy and Technology, Standing Committee on Sectors (a federal advisory committee to the U.S. Environmental Protection Agency). She serves on the board of the Red River Shipping Company, the first and only vessel line owned and operated by African Americans.

ORONTO DOUGLAS is Nigeria's leading environmental human rights lawyer. He is deputy director of Environmental Rights Action/Friends of the Earth, Nigeria, and has been a visiting lecturer and speaker at community-organized events, international conferences, and universities all over the world. Douglas was a member of the legal team that represented Ken Saro-Wiwa before he was executed by the Nigerian military junta in November 1995. He received degrees in law from the University of Science and Technology, Port Harcourt, Nigeria, and De Montfort, Leicester, England. His articles and speeches have been published in books, journals, and magazines in Nigeria, Europe, and the United States. He is the coauthor of *Where Vultures Feast: Shell, Human Rights, and Oil in the Niger Delta* (Sierra Club, 2001).

ERICA S. FLORES is a staff attorney with the Center for Law in the Public Interest in Los Angeles. She received her degree in law from the University of California at Berkeley, Boalt Hall, where she earned the Francine Diaz Memorial Award for her steadfast commitment to public interest work and her plans to pursue a career in public interest law after law school.

ROBERT GARCÍA is the director of The City Project at the Center for Law in the Public Interest, a national nonprofit law firm. He has extensive experience in public policy and legal advocacy, mediation, and litigation involving complex civil rights, environmental, and criminal justice matters. García was a key member of the legal team in the historic environmental justice class action *Labor/Community Strategy Center v. Los Angeles County Metropolitan Transportation Authority*, in which the MTA agreed to invest over $2 billion to improve the bus system and lower the bus fare, the largest civil rights settlement ever. He graduated from Stanford University and Stanford Law School, where he served on the board of editors of the *Stanford Law Review*.

AL GEDICKS is a professor of sociology at the University of Wisconsin-LaCrosse and the executive secretary of the Wisconsin Resource Protection Council. In 1977 he founded the Center for Alternative Mining Development Policy to assist Indian Tribes and rural communities in the upper Midwest in resisting ecologically destructive mining projects. He has written extensively on the social, economic, and environmental impacts of mining and energy development and is the author of two books on the subject, *The New Resource Wars: Native Americans against Multinational Corporations* (South End Press, 1993) and, most recently, *Resource Rebels: Native Challenges to Mining and Oil Corporations* (South End Press, 2001) on case studies of globalization from above and below.

GLENN S. JOHNSON is a research associate in the Environmental Justice Resource Center and associate professor in the Department of Sociology and Criminal Justice at Clark Atlanta University. He coordinates several major research activities, including transportation, urban sprawl, smart growth, public involvement, facility siting, and toxics. He has worked on environmental policy issues for nine years and assisted Robert D. Bullard in the research for the book *Dumping in Dixie: Race, Class, and Environmental Quality* (Westview Press, 2000 [3rd ed.]). He is coeditor of the book titled *Just Transportation: Dismantling Race and Class Barriers to Mobility* (New Society Publishers, 1997). He also coedited with Robert D. Bullard and Angel O. Torres, *Sprawl City: Race, Politics, and Planning in Atlanta* (Island Press, 2000) and *Highway Robbery: Transportation Racism and New Routes to Equity* (South End Press, 2004).

DIMIEARI VON KEMEDI is an Environmental Politics Visiting Fellow, taking leave of absence from his work as head of programs of Our Niger Delta, a nongovernmental organization based in Port Harcourt and Yenagoa, in the Niger Delta, Nigeria. On return to Nigeria he will join his colleagues in a grassroots campaign to build peace in the three states of the Niger Delta, and in a meditation project in the coastal area of Bayelsa State.

DAVID A. MCDONALD is the director of the Development Studies Program at Queen's University in Kingston, Ontario, Canada, and Codirector of the Municipal Services Project, a research program examining the impact of policy reforms on the delivery of basic municipal services to the urban and rural poor in southern Africa. He is the editor of *Environmental Justice in South Africa* (Ohio University Press, 2002).

RACHEL MORELLO-FROSCH is an assistant professor at Brown University. An epidemiologist and environmental health scientist, she conducts research on air toxics, comparative risk assessment, and environmental justice, and conflicts over science and risk in environmental policy making. Her recent publications include "Air Toxics and Health Risks in California: The Implications of Outdoor Concentrations," *Risk Analysis* 20, no. 2 (2000): 273–91 (with Tracey Woodruff, Daniel Axelrad, and Jane Caldwell), and "The Politics of Reproductive Hazards in the Workplace: Class, Gender, and the History of Occupational Lead Exposure," *International Journal of Health Services* 27, no. 3 (1997): 501–21.

IKE OKONTA, writer and journalist, was part of the editorial team that founded *Tempo,* the underground newspaper in Lagos, Nigeria, that played a critical role in ousting the dictator General Ibrahim Babangida in 1993. Okonta also worked closely with the late Ken Saro-Wiwa and other activists with the Movement for the Survival of the Ogomi People, and he is on the management committee of Environmental Rights Action/Friends of the Earth, Nigeria. His first collection of short stories, *The Expert Hunter of Rats,* won the Association of Nigerian Authors Prize in 1998. Okonta is presently at St. Peter's College, Oxford, England. He is the coauthor of *Where Vultures Feast: Shell, Human Rights, and Oil in the Niger Delta* (Sierra Club, 2001).

MANUEL PASTOR JR. is a professor of Latin American and Latino Studies and director of the Center for Justice, Tolerance, and Community at the University of California, Santa Cruz. His most recent books are *Up against Sprawl: Public Policy and the Making of Southern California* (University of Minnesota Press, 2004, coauthored with Jennifer Wolch and Peter Dreier), *Searching for the Uncommon Common Ground: New Dimensions on Race in America* (W. W. Norton Press, 2002, coauthored with Angela Glover Blackwell and Stewart Kwoh) and *Regions That Work: How Cities and Suburbs Can Grow Together* (University of Minnesota Press, 2000, coauthored with Peter Dreier, Eugene Grigsby, and Marta Lopez-Garza). His current research interests include environmental equity and changing labor markets in regional economies.

DEVON G. PEÑA is a professor of anthropology and ethnic studies at the University of Washington, where he serves as coordinator of the doctoral program in environmental anthropology. His most recent books include *Mexican Americans and the Environment: Tierra y Vida* (University of Arizona Press, 2003), *Chicano Culture, Ecology, Politics: Subversive Kin* (University of Arizona, 1998), and *The Terror of the Machine: Technology, Work, Gender, and Ecology on the U.S.-Mexico Border* (University of Texas Press, 1997, a *Choice Magazine* Outstanding Academic Book for 1998). He is currently completing work on several forthcoming books including *Voces de la Tierra: Four Hundred Years of Acequia Farming in the Rio Arriba* and *Gaia en Aztlan: Endangered Landscapes and Disappearing People in the Politics of Place*.

OLGA POMAR is an attorney with Camden Regional Legal Services and is lead counsel for South Camden Citizens in Action. She filed a suit on behalf of ten Camden, New Jersey, Waterfront South residents.

JAMES L. SADD is an associate professor of Environmental Science and chair of the Environmental Science and Studies Program at Occidental College in Los Angeles, California. His research includes spatial analysis using geographic information systems and remote sensing tools to evaluate environmental justice questions, historical reconstruction of sedimentation, and pollution histories in marine environments. His recent publications on environmental justice include "Every Breath You Take . . .": The Demographics of Toxic Air Releases in Southern California," *Economic Development Quarterly* 13, no. 2 (1999): 107–23 (with Manuel Pastor, J. Thomas Boer, and Lori Snyder) and "Which Came First? Toxic Facilities, Minority Move-in, and Environmental Justice," *Journal of Urban Affairs* 23, no. 1 (2001): 1–21 (with Manuel Pastor and John Hipp).

DÉBORAH BERMAN SANTANA grew up in Puerto Rico and New York City, and is her family's first high school graduate. She earned her doctorate in geography at the University of California, Berkeley (1993). Her book *Kicking Off the Bootstraps: Environment, Development, and Community Power in Puerto Rico* (University of Arizona Press, 1996) won the *Choice Magazine* Outstanding Academic Book award of 1997. Currently Associate

Professor in the Ethnic Studies Department of Mills College (Oakland, California), she teaches courses that explore the effects of racism and colonialism on economic, political, and environmental issues in Latin America and the Third World, as well as on communities of color in the United States. Recent publications reflect her interest in examining indigenous perspectives on social and human-environment relations, as an alternative to the destructive dominant paradigm. A longtime community activist, she also serves as an advisor on military, environmental, and land use issues to the Committee for the Rescue and Development of Vieques.

PEGGY MORROW SHEPARD is the executive director and cofounder of West Harlem Environmental Action. Founded in 1988, the organization was New York's first environmental justice organization created to improve environmental health and quality of life in communities of color. She is the 2003 recipient of the Heinz Award for the Environment. Shepard is a former Democratic district leader and represented West Harlem from 1985 to April 1993; she served as president of the National Women's Political Caucus-Manhattan from 1993 to 1997. From January 2001 to 2003, she served as the first female chair of the National Environmental Justice Advisory Council to the U.S. Environmental Protection Agency. She is cochair of the Northeast Environmental Justice Network.

DAMU SMITH is the executive director of the National Black Environmental Justice Network. Before joining this network, he was a campaigner with the Greenpeace Toxics Campaign. He served as Executive Director of the Washington Office on Africa during the height of the antiapartheid movement; as Associate Director of the Washington Bureau of the American Friends Service Committee; and as a program consultant for the United Church of Christ Commission for Racial Justice. He helped organize the First People of Color Environmental Leadership Summit in Washington, D.C., in 1991, and coordinated the largest ever gathering of environmental justice activists: the 1992 Southern Community/Labor Conference on Environmental and Economic Justice held in New Orleans.

ANGEL O. TORRES, M.C.P., is a geographic information systems training specialist with the Environmental Justice Resource Center at Clark Atlanta University. He has a master's degree in city planning from Georgia Institute of Technology, with a concentration in geographic information systems. He has expertise in several mapping programs, including Maptitude, TransCad, Landview, Atlas-GIS, ARC-Info, and ArcView. Torres previously worked for the Corporation for Olympic Development of Atlanta and the Atlanta Project, where he was the geographic information systems specialist on several neighborhood and housing redevelopment plans. He coedited with Robert D. Bullard and Glenn S. Johnson *Sprawl City: Race, Politics, and Planning in Atlanta* (Island Press, 2000) and *Highway Robbery: Transportation Racism and New Routes to Equity* (South End Press, 2004).

MAXINE WATERS is considered by many to be one of the most powerful women in American politics today. She has gained a reputation as a fearless and outspoken advocate for women, children, people of color, and poor people. Elected in November 2004 to her eighth term in the House of Representatives with an overwhelming 80 percent of the vote in the 35th District of California, Waters represents a large part of South Central Los Angeles, the Westchester community, and the diverse cities of Gardena, Hawthorne, Inglewood, and Lawndale. She holds a bachelor of arts degree from California State University, Los Angeles. Throughout her twenty-five years of public service, Waters has been on the cutting edge, tackling difficult and often controversial issues. She has combined her strong legislative and public policy acumen and high visibility in Democratic Party activities with an unusual ability to do grassroots organizing.

MICHAEL J. WATTS is the director of the Institute of International Studies and Chancellor's Professor of Geography at the University of California, where he has taught for twenty-five years. Trained in geography and economics at University College, London, he worked in a variety of capacities in West Africa in the early 1970s before returning to conduct his doctoral research at the University of Michigan on the political economy of famine in Nigeria. Virtually all his research over the past thirty years has addressed the relations between capitalist accumulation, the environment, and questions of social and political justice. Watts has conducted field research in India, Vietnam, and California on agriculture, the agro-food system, and industrial agriculture. He has also lectured widely around the world, served as a consultant to the United Nations Development Program, OXFAM, and other development organizations, and serves on the boards of Food First and the Pacific Institute. Over the past decade Watts has been working on an environmental history of the Niger

Delta with a particular focus on the conflicts generated in and around oil in the oilfields of the delta. He has worked closely with Our Niger Delta and Environmental Rights Action in Nigeria and is currently engaged in research with Ike Okonta and Von Kemedi on oil politics and conflicts in the Niger Delta.

BEVERLY WRIGHT is a sociologist and the founding director of the Deep South Center for Environmental Justice at Dillard University in New Orleans. She is a leading scholar, advocate, and activist in the environmental justice arena. She serves on the U.S. Commission of Civil Rights for the state of Louisiana and on the city of New Orleans' Select Committee for the Sewerage and Water Board. She chaired the 2002 Second People of Color Environmental Leadership Summit's executive committee and the Environmental Justice Climate Change Initiative.

Index

Page numbers in italics refer to tables and figures

Rivera, Fidelina, 73
Roberts, Cassandra, 79–82, 317n13
Roberts, Clifford, 70
Roberts, Gloria Weaver, 65, 70, 71, 102
Robinson, Florence, xiii
Robinson, Jackie, 147
Robinson, Judson Jr., 54
Rodríguez, Sylvia, 195
Rodríguez Cristobal, Angel, 228
Roosevelt, Franklin, 225
Roski, Ed Jr., 152–53
Rosselló, Pedro, 232
Royal Dutch/Shell Group, 177, 179, 246
Rule 1402, 112
rural areas, 301; air pollution, 283; colonias, 205–6; South Africa, 347–48n3. *See also* agriculture; farmers

sacred sites: native peoples', 77, 177, 182. *See also* religious communities
sacrifice zones. *See* environmental sacrifice zones.
St. Francis Prayer Center v. Michigan Department of Environmental Quality (Genesee Power Station), 37–38
St. James Citizens for Jobs and the Environment, 10, 65, 70–73, 100–102
St. James Parish, Louisiana, 68–73, 100–102
St. Lawrence Cement Company (SLC), 131–36
Samore/Siriri oil block, 177–81
Sanders, Bonnie, 129, 133
San Diego, Environmental Health Coalition, 122, 285
Sandoval (court decision), 135, 140, 165–66
Sanes, David, 231
Sangre de Cristo land grant, 196
sanitation, 205–6, 259, 268, 271, 281, 282–83. *See also* sewage; waste facilities
San Luis Peoples Ditch v. Battle Mountain Gold, Inc., 198
Savoy, Homoizelle, 49
Scalia, Antonin, 165
SCCIA. *See* South Camden Citizens in Action
schools: environmental hazards by, 4, 36, 57, 70, 73, 99; industrial tax exemption and, 91–92; Los Angeles, 149, 162, 164–65; playgrounds, 149, 164–65, 330–31n76
Schwarzenegger, Arnold, 162–63
science, distrust of, 215
Second National Report on Human Exposure to Environmental Chemicals, 27

segregation. *See* racial segregation
separate but equal, 87, 147, 212
September 11, 2001, 5, 236, 239
Serrano, Dámaso, 236
services, municipal. *See* municipal services
sewage: Camden plant, 127–28, 130, 131, 137–38; South African privatization and, 271; World Bank and, 259. *See also* sanitation
Shari'a law, 250
Sharpton, Reverend Al, 232
Shell, 283; Louisiana, xi–xii, 11, 82–84, 96–98, 106; Nigeria, 246, 247, 284; Royal Dutch/Shell Group, 177, 179, 246
"shelter in place" emergency response, 5
Shepard, Peggy Morrow, xiii, 62, 64, 65
Shintech Corporation, 10, 70–73, 100–102, 106
Shukla, Champa Devi, 287
Sierra Club: Earthjustice Legal Defense Fund, 6, 8, 178; minority membership, 342n2; SCCIA supported by, 325n29
La Sierra Foundation, 198
Silicon Valley, Superfund sites, 203
Simmons, Dee, 71
Sindab, Jean, 24
Singleton, John, 58
Siriri/Samore oil block, 177–81
Siting of Hazardous Waste Landfills and Their Correlation with Racial and Economic Status of Surrounding Communities, 20
slavery: U.S., 87, 88–89, 102–6, 217, 343n17; Vieques, 224
Small, Gail, 75–79
Snyder, Mike, 48
social contract, Nigeria, 251–53
socialism, South Africa, 266
social justice movement, 5–6, 20. *See also* civil rights
Sokaogon Ojibwe Nation, 181–87
Solutia corporation, 11, 317nn11,13
South, U.S., 87–88
South Africa, xvii, 255–78; Anti-Privatization Forum, 270, 277; Concerned Citizens Forum, 270; Constitution, 258, 265, 270; World Conference against Racism, 218, 280, 303–5; World Summit on Sustainable Development (Rio + 10 Earth Summit), 279–80. *See also* apartheid era, South Africa
South Camden Citizens in Action (SCCIA), 129–41, 325nn23,29,32
South Camden Citizens in Action v. NJ DEP, 125, 131, 134–36, 140